Geary Hag

11/21/13

HARRIMAN VS. HILL

HARRIMAN VS. HILL

WALL STREET'S GREAT RAILROAD WAR

LARRY HAEG

University of Minnesota Press
Minneapolis • London

Original maps by Philip Schwartzberg, Meridian Mapping, Minneapolis

Published by the University of Minnesota Press
111 Third Avenue South, Suite 290
Minneapolis, MN 55401–2520
http://www.upress.umn.edu

Library of Congress Cataloging-in-Publication Data

Haeg, Lawrence Peter, 1945–
Harriman vs. Hill : Wall Street's great railroad war / Larry Haeg.
Includes bibliographical references and index.
ISBN 978-0-8166-8364-2 (hc)
ISBN 978-0-8166-8365-9 (pb)
  1. Harriman, Edward Henry, 1848–1909. 2. Hill, James Jerome, 1838–1916. 3. Railroads—United States—History—20th century. 4. Capitalists and financiers—United States—Biography. 5. Stock exchanges—United States—History—20th century. 6. Speculation—United States—History—20th century. I. Title.
HE2752.H34 2013
385'.1097309041—dc23
2013027118

Printed in the United States of America on acid-free paper

The University of Minnesota is an equal-opportunity educator and employer.

20 19 18 17 16 15 14 13   10 9 8 7 6 5 4 3 2 1

For all the talented team members, past and present,
with whom I was privileged to ride the Wells Fargo stagecoach

Did ye not hear it?—No; 'twas but the wind,
Or the car rattling o'er the stony street;
On with the dance! let joy be unconfined;
No sleep till morn, when youth and pleasure meet
To chase the glowing hours with flying feet.
But hark!—that heavy sound breaks in once more,
As if the clouds its echo would repeat;
And nearer, clearer, deadlier than before;
Arm! arm! it is—it is—the cannon's opening roar!

—Lord George Gordon Byron, "The Eve of Waterloo," 1816

In the stock-market, "corner" spells ruin, backward and forward, and spells
it in big black capitals. No one can tell until a corner is over who is beneath
the ruins. Often those buried deepest have had no part in the making of it or
in the operations that brought it about.

—Thomas W. Lawson, 1905

Tell them you're a speculator; that you buy them if you like them
and sell them if you don't like them. It doesn't matter whether you
[don't] have them when you sell them, and buy them later, or
whether you buy them first and sell them later.

—Eugene Meyer Jr., advising Bernard Baruch, 1917

CONTENTS

PREFACE

The seed for this book was planted more than a half-century ago by my father, who had the wisdom to bring American history into our home. He subscribed to *American Heritage*, the hardcover monthly, many of which now are stacked forlornly in used bookstores but are still unsurpassed for their vivid style and broad appeal. He also subscribed to the now largely forgotten Book-of-the-Month Club, every month's selection delivered to the mailbox of our home in a suburb of Minneapolis.

One month came *The Good Years: From 1900 to the First World War*, by the masterful historian Walter Lord, who wrote with such elegant simplicity. One of the book's chapters, "Big Stick, Big Business," recalled the Northern Pacific corner, Harriman versus Hill, and the coming of Teddy Roosevelt, the "trustbuster." The story jumped off the pages at me not just because of Lord's mastery or because it was such a colossal battle but because James J. Hill was from Minnesota. The tracks of a branch of his old St. Paul, Minneapolis & Manitoba Railroad (later the Great Northern) helped create our town, founded by an employee of the Hill predecessor road, and passed only a half mile from our home.

Harriman versus Hill stuck in my mind; so much so that in 2004 I searched for a full-length account of the story. I couldn't find one. So, as the saying goes, to read it I had to write it. The definitive biographies of Edward Henry Harriman, by Maury Klein, and James Jerome Hill, by Albro Martin, were indispensable starting points for understanding the two major protagonists and their time, as were other books by these two giants of American railroad history. I relied on dozens of newspapers and magazines of the period to re-create the key hour-by-hour events of April and May 1901.

The more I read about the Northern Pacific corner the more I realized it really hadn't been forgotten. It simply had been overshadowed by the financial panic of 1907, the crash of 1929, and the Depression. As a result, it comes down to us as an afterthought in generic capsules, tucked into broader histories, with its set-piece episodes (Hill's fictive dash in panic from Seattle to New York, Jacob Schiff at the synagogue, Edward Harriman bedridden in his New York home, J. P. Morgan at Aix-les-Bains). The repetition of these summaries perpetuated exaggerations and inaccuracies, propagated by the Internet, and deprived the story of its drama, detail, and, most important, its meaning for us today.

This is the first attempt to bring it all back to life: a full-length, stand-alone account of this continental struggle; an understanding of the protagonists and what motivated them, what it felt like to live through the market tumult of that time. May 9, 1901, was the stock market equivalent of a bungee-cord jump off the Brooklyn Bridge: perhaps the swiftest, most precipitous decline, then or since, in American stock values, and then the fastest recovery. It remains the most famous corner in the history of the New York Stock Exchange, and the most ironic. It was the last thing Morgan, Hill, Harriman, and Schiff wanted. It also was poetic injustice for the "shorts." They guessed right that Northern Pacific was grossly overpriced. They had realistically gauged its intrinsic value and performed an essential service for free markets. They were dead right. Their timing could not have been worse.

The story as told here is only incidentally about western railroads, Wall Street, government regulations, or New York's Fifth Avenue. It is really about character and the volatile mix of analytics, emotion, and ethics (or lack thereof) that governs how business leaders decide how to raise and invest their company's capital (largely the capital of others entrusted to them), how they choose to compete, how they communicate with their audiences. The tension among these forces certainly clouded many decisions in this story. Morgan, Hill, Harriman, Schiff, and all the supporting players were men of great power, influence, and intellect but they were, after all, only human. They had to decide every day, just like the rest of us, whether to lie or tell the truth, build trust or destroy it, be clear or evasive, be chameleons or men of their word, seek revenge or conciliation, be principled or expedient. As the esteemed corporate attorney John Graver Johnson, who argued for Hill and Morgan before the U.S. Supreme Court, once said: "Important affairs are controlled far more by sentimentalities and personal feeling, than we are willing to admit." Some understanding of the backgrounds, values, and personalities of the principal figures is essential at the opening of our story, as is a brief overview of the dominant influence of railroads on American life at the beginning of the twentieth century. To translate the value of money in this story, a dollar in 1901 had about twenty-six times the purchasing power of a dollar today.

My wife, Mary, has asked me (more than once) if it really makes any difference today whether Harriman–Schiff or Hill–Morgan controlled the Burlington or the Northern Pacific. Maybe in the long run it didn't. What did matter was how they went about it.

Warren Buffett, the head of Berkshire Hathaway and a student of financial history, ultimately became owner of the so-called Hill roads. Several years ago, when his company was beginning to invest in the Hill legacy property, he said he would ask MBA students from prestigious schools about the Northern Pacific corner only to discover "they don't know about it." Now they have no excuse.

DRAMATIS PERSONAE, 1901

ROBERT BACON, 40, junior partner, J. P. Morgan and Company, New York. In charge of the firm during Morgan's trip to England and France, April 3–July 4, 1901.

GEORGE FISHER BAKER, 61, cofounder and president, First National Bank of New York. Hill–Morgan ally.

EDWARD HENRY HARRIMAN, 53, head of the Union Pacific and the Southern Pacific, New York City.

JAMES JEROME HILL, 63, head of the Great Northern; purchaser of the Chicago, Burlington & Quincy; holder of working control with J. P. Morgan of the Northern Pacific, St. Paul.

OTTO HERMANN KAHN, 34, junior partner, Kuhn, Loeb and Company, New York City. Harriman ally.

JAMES ROBERT KEENE, 63, Wall Street's premier manager of speculative stock pools, New York City. Thoroughbred racehorse owner and breeder. Morgan ally.

JOHN STEWART KENNEDY, 71, Scots-born railroad financier, London. Hill–Morgan ally.

DANIEL SCOTT LAMONT, 50, vice president, the Northern Pacific, New York City. Former chief of staff to President Cleveland; former U.S. Secretary of War. Hill–Morgan ally.

JOHN PIERPONT MORGAN, 64, head of J. P. Morgan and Company, New York City. World's most powerful financier.

CHARLES ELLIOT PERKINS, 61, president and later chairman, the Chicago, Burlington & Quincy, Burlington, Iowa. Hill ally.

GEORGE WALBRIDGE PERKINS, 39, junior partner, J. P. Morgan and Company, and vice president, New York Life Insurance Company, New York City.

WILLIAM AVERY ROCKEFELLER, 63, Standard Oil Company, New York City. Harriman–Schiff ally.

THEODORE ROOSEVELT, 42, President of the United States of America, Washington D.C.

JACOB HENRY SCHIFF, 54, head of Kuhn, Loeb & Company, New York City. Second to J. P. Morgan in power and influence in investment banking. Alternately ally of both Harriman and Hill.

DONALD ALEXANDER SMITH (LORD STRATHCONA), 80, Scots–Canadian, Hudson's Bay Company leader, an organizer of the Canadian Pacific Railway, London. Hill ally.

GEORGE STEPHEN (LORD MOUNT STEPHEN), 71, Scots–Canadian, president, Bank of Montreal, London. Helped finance the building of the Canadian Pacific Railway. Cousin of Donald Alexander Smith. Hill ally.

JOHN WILLIAM STERLING, 57, corporate lawyer, chief counsel to James J. Stillman and National City Bank, New York City. Harriman–Schiff ally.

JAMES JEWETT STILLMAN, 51, head of National City Bank of New York (predecessor of today's Citigroup), New York City. Harriman–Schiff ally.

⊸⊸⊸ INTRODUCTION ⊸⊸⊸
A RAILROAD WORLD

In the spring of 1901 the two most powerful men in America's railroads, then the nation's dominant industry, got into a climactic fight for control of two pivotal western railroads, first the Chicago, Burlington & Quincy and then the Northern Pacific. The winner (if there was one) could be known, in the way newspapers spoke in those days, as railroad king of the world. He could control his access through Chicago, which was, in the newly ascendant American economy, the railroad capital of the world. He also could dominate the geography of four of the six major railroads in the western United States. An entire half century of boom and bust in America's western railroads came down to this battle for supremacy.

Behind these two railroad leaders stood the world's most powerful financiers. To oversimplify, it was big steel versus big oil. Arm and arm on one side was James J. Hill of the Great Northern Railway and the Northern Pacific, backed by John Pierpont Morgan, George F. Baker of the First National Bank of New York, and a host of wealthy, influential investors in America and Europe. Against them was Edward H. Harriman of the Union Pacific and the Southern Pacific, with investment banker Jacob H. Schiff of Kuhn, Loeb (second only to Morgan), James J. Stillman of National City Bank of New York, and William A. Rockefeller of Standard Oil. The battle was the first serious challenge to Morgan's global preeminence in private finance. It ended in a deadlock and inadvertently in a corner, or monopoly, of the stock of the Northern Pacific, which rose in sixteen heart-stopping hours of trading from $110 on Monday morning, May 6, to $1,000 just before noon on Thursday, May 9, 1901. All this for the stock of a government-chartered, twice-bankrupt railroad, kicked around the block five years earlier for as little as twenty-five cents a share. The market always seemed spooked by a railroad property that, despite Hill–Morgan's reconstructive surgery, never quite could shake its legacy as the

1

byzantine creation of government central planners. A free market, allowed to work its will, would have let the Northern Pacific be absorbed into a larger, more efficient system years earlier. Inevitably, the market did work its will: seven decades later.

The corner caused the first modern-day panic on the New York Stock Exchange. It was mediated within hours in a truce and settlement by the adversaries themselves, with no government or Exchange involvement. It led to the creation of a holding company that the U.S. Supreme Court narrowly declared unconstitutional, a ruling containing the first of the great opinions, this one on property rights, from the associate justice who came to be known as the "Great Dissenter," Oliver Wendell Holmes. The court's ruling rippled through the rest of the twentieth century and lives with us today as we still debate one of capitalism's most perplexing questions: "How big is too big?"

The ruling gave clarity and strength to the Sherman Anti-Trust Act, defined the "trustbusting" presidency of Teddy Roosevelt (the first of some forty such federal lawsuits in his seven years as president), and energized the so-called progressive movement. It also led to stifling government regulations that crippled America's railroads for seven decades. All the human forces that caused the Northern Pacific corner on the trading floor and in boardrooms, brokerages, and banks still pulse through America today—the desire for freedom of enterprise and creativity; the rowdy capitalist instinct to dream, risk, invest, build, and rebuild; the abhorrence of waste and inefficiency; the temptation to try to get rich quick without working for it; and yet, also, our leavening desire for fairness in open competition that can be achieved only with thoughtful government and industry oversight that emphasizes principles not just more rules.

There had been convulsions that caused stock market panics with regularity long before 1901—the attempt to corner the stock of the Bank of the United States in 1792; Andrew Jackson's attack on the Second Bank of the United States, which caused inflated asset values and bank failures in 1837; the speculation and overbuilt railroads that collapsed the stock market in 1857; the Jay Gould–Jim Fisk attempt to corner the gold market leading to the collapse of railroad stocks in 1869; the Jay Cooke–Northern Pacific bond fiasco that closed the New York Stock Exchange for ten days in 1873; and the depression of 1893 to 1897 caused by a mountain of corporate debt and overbuilt railroads.

The Northern Pacific corner and panic were different from these earlier events in at least four ways. First, they affected, for the first time, almost coast-to-coast and border-to-border a broad number of small retail investors. Flush with cash, these investors bought stocks on margin, thought there was no end to American prosperity, and used their paper profits to "pyramid" their risk (also called "kite-flying") by buying even more stocks on even greater margins. Technology made this possible. You didn't have to be in New York anymore to buy or sell stock. You could do it from Cleveland or Minneapolis–St. Paul or Omaha or Denver (and soon, San Francisco) through the so-called wire houses, the brokerage firms in New York, Boston, or Chicago that leased private wires of copper from A.T. & T. or Western Union, connecting them with customers electromagnetically in brokerage offices across the continent. It no longer took hours or even a day for a "buy" or "sell" order to be sent from Chicago and then executed on the floor of the New York Stock Exchange, it took only four minutes. Unfortunately, speed alone was no more a guarantee of profit then than it is today. The lessons for the losers had to be learned all over again and with much more pain twenty-eight years later, when many investors had forgotten, ignored, or had never heard of the events of 1901.

Second, this was the first such market event in America viewed widely as a "stock gamblers' panic." It was caused in part by the ill-timed bets of short-sellers. Like the "stags" who gambled on railway stocks in what came to be called Stag Alley outside London's Capel Court in the early 1840s, the "shorts" were seen as turning the New York Stock Exchange into a casino with brokers as croupiers. "When a speculator wins he don't stop till he loses," wrote George Horace Lorimer in *Letters from a Self-Made Merchant to His Son*, published a year after the Northern Pacific corner, "and when he loses he can't stop till he wins." Or, maybe not. Perhaps Lorimer and his ilk spoke merely for a certain crabby puritanical crowd that didn't quite get the spirit of America. What was the difference, after all, between a trader taking a risk on a stock and a small business owner taking a risk on a new product or a new store? "Americans are great business men," wrote Edwin Lefevre, wise observer of Wall Street's morals, "because they are great gamblers... They have... keenness of perception, the rapidity of thought, the intrepidity of the young, and the national sense of humor... [They] crack jokes with disaster."

No one really knew where the boundary was between reasoned speculation, where thoughtful risk earned its legitimate reward, and mere dice rolling and bar bets, but they had no patience for the nuance. They felt a line had been crossed. Something was wrong. Two of those who felt this way happened to be the president of the United States and the attorney general.

The incentive to speculate and the market convulsions it could cause were aggravated by the lack of regulatory control. In 1901 there was no Federal Reserve, no Securities and Exchange Commission, no Financial Industry Regulatory Authority, no laws against insider trading, no "fair disclosure" regulations. And, if you won in the market, you kept it all. There was no income tax, no capital gains tax.

Third, the events of 1901 showed many Americans the enormous economic gap between Wall Street traders—who won or lost hundreds, thousands, or millions of dollars in a single day—and the lives of hard-working Americans for whom a dollar could almost be a day's wage. The average construction worker in America in 1901 earned twenty-four cents an hour. The average annual household income was $750. Children contributed to that income in almost one of every four households. Eggs were twenty-two cents a dozen, a pound of bacon sixteen cents. And on Wall Street someone was netting $25,000, thirty-three times the average annual American household income, in less than four minutes on a sale of Northern Pacific common stock, or paying $25,000 to rent five hundred shares of it overnight to meet a short-sale delivery date. The natural laws of capitalist risk–reward were at work in roughly the same measure then as today.

And, fourth, we learn how slow virtually all of the heads of finance and industry of 1901 were to understand, appreciate, and practice the art of communicating the value and benefits of their enterprise to the customers of their businesses and to those who someday could be their customers. Their first instinct was to hide. They thought the good they did would speak for itself but their businesses had grown too large, too complex, too distant to fathom for the homemaker in Omaha, the coal miner in Pennsylvania, the dock worker in Seattle. They thought their only audience was their shareholders. They paid a dear price for their arrogance and ignorance. The two big bankers in this story—George F. Baker (First National) with Hill–Morgan and James Stillman (National City) with Harriman–Schiff—were both distant from ordinary New Yorkers. Neither bank dirtied its hands with retail deposits, perhaps fearing the mob psyche of panicky, small depositors in an era before federal safety nets. Baker was renowned for his fairness and justice, but even his First National posted a sign: "No personal accounts, large or small, wanted." Stillman's bank was too busy helping the U.S government buy the Philippines from Spain or forming Amalgamated Copper Company to be bothered with mattress money.

One could find no better example of the aloofness of the heads of finance of this time than to read the *Wall Street Journal* on Monday, January 28, 1901. Rumors were flying that Morgan and Hill were going after the Rockefellers's Chicago, Milwaukee & St. Paul Railway. Its stock had risen twelve points in the first hour of trading the previous Saturday morning. Reporters staked out the corridors as the principals conferred. They spotted Morgan coming out of a conference and asked him about the rumors. Morgan replied, "This is the most extraordinary thing I ever heard of. Don't you know I never talk to reporters? When I have an announcement to make I will send for you." Times were different then but it is still painful to read those words. Perhaps it was because in 1901 many were suspicious of business leaders who talked too much. It seemed undignified. Better to be suspected a self-promoter than to speak and remove all doubt. "If the affairs of a corporation are in need of effective management," said *Harper's Weekly* in early 1901, "efficiency can rarely be promoted through publicity."

Morgan himself (who never made a speech, never felt he had to) slowly realized his shortcomings in this area, which is one reason he hired the savvy George Walbridge Perkins, master builder of the culture of the New York Life Insurance Company. Only Hill, among the four principals of this story, grasped the importance of communicating with the American worker. He could match Roosevelt as an evangelist for a point of view. He was available, quotable, forceful, and clear in his language, except, of course, when he lost his temper. He was, however, swimming against a tsunami of anger against large companies, which found themselves, in many cases, guilty until proven innocent. Only six days after the Northern Pacific corner and seven months before the formation of its mega-trust progeny, the Northern Securities Company, the *New York Evening Post* asked the question we still ask today: "Who owns this country?"

Railroads didn't "own" America in 1901, but over the previous half century they had revolutionized its commerce and culture in a way that had made them, as Anthony Trollope wrote, "first necessity of life...only hope of wealth...right arm of civilization." Today they are still the heavy lifters of the American economy but they're now largely invisible (unless they happen to be in your backyard), existing on a sort of nostalgic periphery, mostly an intrusion at signal crossings. At the time of this story, however, railroads were America's manifest destiny, prime agent of the Industrial Revolution, first modern business enterprise, first big business, greatest centralizing technology in history, mobilizers of the "greatest era of civilized progress the world had ever known," primary tool for settling the unpopulated West, and creator of global markets for isolated towns.

Railroads represented the largest investment of capital in any enterprise in human history, equaling about one-eighth of the total wealth of the United States. Their annual revenue was about three times that of the federal government. Deemed to be "public functions" because they provided such an indispensable service, they were regarded as state-privileged private entities, and were the largest private landowners in America. They comprised two-thirds of the listings on the New York Stock Exchange; the other third couldn't do without them. A stockbroker's bible was *Poor's Manual of the Railroads of the United States*. They employed more people than any other American enterprise. About one of every ten Americans depended on railroads for a living. In the early 1890s the Pennsylvania Railroad alone employed more people than the U.S. Postal Service. The total value of the "Pennsy's" stock approached the size of the U.S. total gross debt.

In the context of human history the growth of the railroads happened with brutal swiftness. In 1814 George Stephenson lit the boiler on the first steam railway locomotive, pulling eight wagons with thirty tons of coal 450 feet at four miles an hour up a hill in the coal country of Newcastle, England, near ruins of Hadrian's Wall. By the end of the 1820s the first steam-powered locomotive moved down a track in Carbondale, Pennsylvania. By the early 1840s Joseph Dart in Buffalo, New York, built a steam-powered grain elevator. By the 1850s the Pennsylvania Railroad had breached the Alleghenies, connecting Pittsburgh to the east. Erastus Corning of Albany, New York, had merged fourteen small railroads to create the New York Central, which then reached Chicago about the same time as the "Pennsy." The first railroad bridge spanned the Mississippi, connecting Rock Island, Illinois, and Davenport, Iowa. Even then, however, a town merchant would have felt more at home in a fifteenth-century Italian village than in 1901 America.

The collapse of distance created an empire of economic opportunity. One could travel by rail from New York to Minnesota in five or six days, a trip that took six weeks by horse in 1830. In the 1860s, some twenty years after Samuel Morse of New York City sent the first telegraph message, Hiram Sibley of Rochester, New York, combined smaller telegraph companies into a national system called Western Union. Trains now could be dispatched by telegraph, synchronizing railroad operations, increasing efficiency, driving down costs.

In England, Henry Bessemer created steel for rails—stronger, cheaper, and more flexible than iron. America had only 3,000 miles of track in the 1840s. It had ten times that by the end of the 1850s, more than double that by the start of the 1870s, and in the 1880s added an average of 7,000 miles of track each year, still a record. Some of those miles were rickety "blackmail roads," built only to be bought out. In 1887 alone, railroads added 13,000 track miles. It all turned out to be twice as much railroad as the nation then needed. To pay for it the railroads issued four times as many securities as they could pay dividends on.

In 1870 a new law broke the monopoly of wholesale merchants on the eastern seaboard. Inland custom houses, especially in the Midwest, could for the first time collect duties on imported goods shipped "in bond" from East Coast ports. Two years later a railroad bridge spanned the Missouri River, connecting Council Bluffs, Iowa, and Omaha, Nebraska, opening the first unbroken route to the Pacific. A new, spurious word entered the American lexicon: the "transcontinental," more marketing ploy than reality. The Central Pacific and the Union Pacific joined at Promontory, Utah. Collis Huntington's Southern Pacific reached New Orleans and linked with the Atchison, Topeka & Santa Fe in New Mexico. Then came automatic air brakes (applied at the same time through an entire train), automatic couplers, and the refrigerated car.

Railroads created virtually every major American industry: coal, oil, gas, steel, lumber, farm equipment, grain, cotton, textile factories, California citrus. They made a new market not only in grain but in the price of grain called futures contracts, legally binding forecasts of how much grain prices would rise or fall. It wasn't long before speculators in grain futures contracts (able to name virtually any price they wished because the contracts were under civil law) learned how to manipulate the market by forcing others to deliver real physical grain instead of merely settling price differences. Railroads themselves helped popularize the control of the supply of a tradable commodity, called a "corner."

Organizations this big had to have some government oversight. It was because of railroads that the federal government in 1887 created, for better and worse, its first independent regulatory agency, the Interstate Commerce Commission.

Railroads spawned modern finance, investment banking, and perfected a new template of American capitalism, improving underperforming businesses by investing in their future earnings power. They created standards for grading and weighing grain. They concentrated the livestock trade in Chicago.

They created full-service wholesalers, inventory management and "stock-turn," the contractor construction company, the modern banking industry. They brought the goods to local merchants as they needed them so manufacturers could be paid for products immediately on sale rather than waiting six months to a year. Railroad securities created the modern New York Stock Exchange and speculative tools such as puts, calls, margin trading, and the call loan market. Railroads created mail order catalogue companies; Montgomery Ward's catalogue grew from one page in 1872 to twelve hundred in 1900. They helped create department stores by enabling them to sell directly to their final customers, encouraging the growth of advertising agencies and mass marketing. They even were a major advocate for public schools: new legions of railroad clerks needed a solid grounding in reading, writing, and elementary mathematics.

Railroads were the first to show there was only one way to run a business and that was to finance growth with retained earnings. They created the modern American corporation, the modern business executive, full-time salaried managers, management hierarchy, the separation of corporate line and staff. A big, complex business created complex legal exposure. This increased the demand for lawyers and helped expand the legal profession. The railroads organized the army of the Industrial Revolution and its battalions of wage laborers—the division superintendents, the road masters, mechanics, station agents, conductors, locomotive engineers, shop foremen, ticket agents, freight agents, telegraphers, foremen, brakemen, mechanics, engine and car repairmen. Their broad neglect for the health and safety of their workers fueled the growth of labor unions. Railroads were the first American business to create a system for capital accounting, separating operating expense from capital investment. They helped develop cost accounting and the concept of unit cost: the cost to carry one ton one mile. They figured out a process for reasonable rates and ways to end destructive rate cutting and avoid the laying of parallel, duplicate tracks.

They created the "through bill of lading," billing for shipments that moved over long distances and across several railroad lines; these bills became negotiable paper and a regular medium of exchange. They provided right of way for telegraph and telephone lines that shaped the modern postal system. They even controlled ocean shipment; by the end of the nineteenth century they ran almost all U.S. steamship companies. It was no accident that American exports to Japan grew sevenfold from 1896 to 1905: the railroad-steamship system of James J. Hill was largely responsible for the growth.

Railroads standardized everything they touched: track gauges, equipment, accounting, even the clock. The velocity of the railroad and telegraph destroyed local time. On Sunday morning, November 18, 1883, railroad standard time became a reality; three hundred local time zones collapsed to four: Eastern, Central, Mountain, and Pacific. Western Union no longer telegraphed its subscribers in their local time, based on when the sun passed over, say, Mason City, Iowa, but on where Mason City was in national standard time. "Mobility of population," said historian Frederick Jackson Turner ten years later at the World's Columbian Exposition in Chicago, "is death to localism."

All of this—the standardization, the management techniques, the technology, the mobilizing of capital and risk-taking, the trial and error—had produced what government statistician Joseph Nimmo in 1903 called "the best regulated and most efficient transportation system in the world." Two numbers said it all. In 1870 it cost an average of $1.99 to ship one ton one mile on a railroad. In 1901 it cost $0.74.

This is the world—a railroad world—we enter on Wednesday, April 3, 1901, the day that triggers the events of our story, the day Morgan leaves for Europe.

$\rightarrow\!\!\Longrightarrow$ **1** $\Longleftarrow\!\!\leftarrow$

MR. MORGAN AND MR. HILL

Wall and Broad Streets, New York City

It was two minutes before 10 a.m. and the trading floor of the New York Stock Exchange—"magnetic pole of the modern industrial world"—was ready to erupt, again. Chairman McPherson Kennedy, gavel in hand, stepped to the rostrum. He gazed out over a three-story expanse of fourteen thousand square feet, a cathedral of commerce designed to evoke the Italian Renaissance in an arabesque of green, gold, and auburn. Sixty-foot Corinthian columns blossomed up to stained-glass skylights. From the ornate, coffered ceiling hung three huge circular fan shades of translucent glass. A wrought iron railing of golden lattice, with visitor galleries on the north, south, and east balconies, ribboned the trading floor, T shaped and opening onto Broad, New, and Wall Streets.

Patterned across the floor below Kennedy, bathed in diffuse light through a fog of cigar smoke, was a thin forest of black ornamental iron pillars, each bearing the name of a company's stock, most of them major railroads including Union Pacific, New York Central, Lackawanna, Erie, Baltimore & Ohio, Pennsylvania, Northern Pacific, Delaware & Hudson, Rock Island, Louisville & Nashville, Chicago, Milwaukee & St. Paul (the "St. Paul"), Atchison, Topeka & Santa Fe, and Chicago, Burlington & Quincy (the "Burlington"). At the iron pillar for each major stock was a movable blackboard called the "marker," where the last trade was chalked. Rimming the floor at desks, booths, and posts were some five hundred telephones, each with an assigned messenger who wrote the orders he received from his commission house over a dedicated phone then brought the buy or sell order slips to his floor broker. Telegraph operators stood at every post, poised to write every order on a pad and then tap it out to the Exchange's central office for telegraphing to A.T.&T. or Western Union for tickers across the globe.

The Exchange was not yet a for-profit business. It was unincorporated, run like a club. It was limited to eleven hundred members, or seats, which fluctuated in value and were being offered for more than $60,000 in early 1901. Some members had bought their seats on margin, further extending their risk. For the first time, some members were virtually present, living and working in Chicago, Pittsburgh, Cleveland, Minneapolis–St. Paul, or Omaha, linked by private wires to New York where about five hundred Exchange firms transacted its business. Record trading volume had overwhelmed the space. In twenty-one business days trading would cease here and move to temporary quarters at the nearby Produce Exchange for two years until a new, larger headquarters would open.

The clock struck ten. Chairman Kennedy, who joined the Exchange twenty-one years earlier when Edward H. Harriman and James J. Hill were just entering railroading, thwacked his large gavel. What had been a low hum of hundreds of echoed voices exploded in a roar. A raucous knot of traders clustered at the post of the Burlington, yelling and waving. Trading was by gesture and word only, "open outcry." It gave all members on the floor the opportunity to hear in an open market both the price, offered and bid, and the number of shares traded. There was no time for written contracts, "a broker's nod is as binding as his bond," it was said, "and . . . the raising of a finger frequently sets an irrevocable seal on a bargain." It was a fraternity bound together with leavening, mordant wit. Every trader on the floor knew, especially in this wild market, he was just one trade away from disaster. One man said he kept a diagram of the poorhouse, which he placed every night under his pillow.

Burlington opened at 179¾. It rose six points in an hour. Rumors were growing. Were Hill and Morgan pursuing it? Some traders had "shorted" it, selling shares they didn't own by paying interest to rent borrowed shares, betting the price would go down before they had to make delivery the next day, hoping to buy the shares at a reduced price, and to pocket the difference.

Their gain was limited: Burlington stock couldn't go below zero, but their loss could be infinite. With the rise, they had to extend their margin loans to "cover" their equity investment. Messengers stood at each trading post, wrote down each trade and rushed to the telegraph operators who tapped out the prices for quotation companies to stock tickers in brokerage houses across the globe: 100 S T 83———500 N P P R———54 1–4———E 27 5–8 3–4 (one hundred shares of Chicago, Milwaukee & St. Paul sold for $83 a share; five hundred shares of Northern Pacific preferred bought for $54.25 each; Erie shares offered at $27.75, with a $27.62½ bid).

"Specialists" at each trading post bought and sold only that stock, and in a bewildering conflict of interest they traded at the same time for their own account and brokered for customers. Behind the scenes, pools of speculators manipulated prices, giving the appearance of activity in a stock by issuing buy and sell orders for the stock at the same time with different brokerage houses, so-called matched orders. When a stock reached a predetermined "peg" level the pool managers "pulled the peg," took their gains and let the shorts hammer it down, even if some pool members were left in the lurch. Liberal rules seemed to encourage gambling: one need put down only $10 to buy $100 worth of stock. It was, however, very much like buying a house. The margin one provided to buy the stock was like the down payment on a home mortgage.

Some brokers watching the trading thought they saw signs of manipulators attacking the "extended short interest." Louisville & Nashville rose 3 percent. Northern Pacific rose 2 percent. Yelling erupted at the Erie post. There was "enormous purchasing" in the common stock of the Morgan-controlled Erie in lots of 1,000 to 6,000 shares. When Hill–Morgan get the Burlington, the thinking went, they then will have a transcontinental link at Chicago to the Erie all the way to Jersey City.

This sparked buying in other so-called coalers, the coal railroads such as the B&O, the Norfolk & Western, Morgan's Reading, and the Lackawanna. The Delaware & Hudson shot up ten points on rumors the New York Central would buy it and guarantee a dividend. The market became "wild and feverish" during the noon hour. Delaware & Hudson up a stunning 13½, Burlington up 8⅜, Lackawanna up 6½. In the final hour, with momentum from the Burlington, buying surged in the Chicago, Rock Island & Pacific Railway System (the "Rock Island"), stretching 3,800 miles to Omaha, Denver, and Colorado Springs and via Kansas City to Fort Worth.

There were rumors that James and William Moore, the flamboyant brothers from Chicago who had just sold their sheet steel and can companies to Morgan and made millions, now were buying into the Rock Island. There also were rumors of an organized, unlimited pool in Rock Island buying. Strong, Sturgis & Company had bought 30,000 shares of it, perhaps for the Moore brothers or the pool. If the Burlington was worth $200 a share to Hill–Morgan, the thinking went, then certainly the Rock Island, also based in Chicago, was undervalued. It closed at 151, up 12.

Buying in the Burlington and the Rock Island had fueled talk for months that two other Chicago-based roads that dominated the upper Midwest wheat and corn belts could be absorbed into transcontinentals. One was the Rockefeller-controlled Chicago, Milwaukee & St. Paul (the "St. Paul") with 6,400 miles of track. The other was Marvin Hughitt's Chicago & North Western, dominated by the Vanderbilts, with 8,300 miles of track and its alliance with the Union Pacific across Iowa.

News of yet another rally pulsed across the globe almost instantly on ticker machines. In 1901, long before radio, television, and the Internet, Wall Street got its news before the newspapers because it had three news bureaus: Dow, Jones & Company, the New York News Bureau, and J. Arthur News Bureau. The first two had reporters and a telegraph and cable service. The Dow distributed news on yellow carbon-copied slips of paper and the New York News Bureau on white, which messengers delivered to brokers' offices. These slips of news, called "flimsy," began arriving every morning at about nine; by three in the afternoon a broker's office would have received a hundred or two hundred in "unending procession." For $30 a month a broker's office could even get bulletins before the "flimsy" slips came. Prefiguring the battle for headlines every second among Reuters, Bloomberg, and the Wall Street Journal, the bureaus' reporters stood ready at telephones at the headquarters of, say, the Chicago, Milwaukee & St. Paul on 30 Broad Street to relay news of its dividend announcement to their bureaus.

Trading closed "excited and bullish" on strong volume of 1.9 million shares. A rising economic tide was lifting all railroad stocks. Had you bought a basket of a dozen railroad stocks last November 3, 1900, when McKinley was reelected, they would have appreciated thusly through April 3, 1901: Erie, +234 percent; Wabash, +184; Denver & Rio Grande, +127; Texas & Pacific, +123; Atchison, Topeka & Santa Fe common, +96; Missouri Pacific, +91; Northern Pacific common, +74; Delaware & Hudson, +60; Union Pacific, +57; Burlington, +44; Rock Island, +39; the St. Paul, +39. The Burlington attracted much of the attention. For the first four months of 1901 it was front page news (mostly upper fold) for half the editions of the Wall Street Journal.

Hidden in the stampede of this great bull run was the Northern Pacific. Hardly anyone thought it unusual that its common stock, even its preferred stock, should rise in such a market.

White Star Pier, Lower Manhattan

It had rained and howled all night along the entire Eastern Seaboard. Gusts up to forty-eight miles an hour blew through the darkened streets of Manhattan, carved into Long Island's beaches and the shores of the New Jersey coast. The wind had whipped up the inland sea in the channel at Sandy Hook, the front door to the Atlantic, into a dangerous froth for outbound pilots.

The nor'easter kept blowing as noon approached on April 3, 1901. On the White Star pier at the foot of West Tenth Street in lower Manhattan, the elegant liner RMS *Teutonic* seemed oblivious to it all. She departed New York harbor every fourth Wednesday at this time for her eight days across the North Atlantic to Queenstown and Liverpool, and it took more than a nor'easter to stop her. She was one of the grand dames of Bruce Ismay's fleet, 528 feet long—almost two American football fields. She was one of the largest ships afloat, but as graceful and sleek as a yacht with her straight cutter stem and tapered stern. In first class she was all brass and oak, leather and muslin, ivory and stained glass, with a majestic staircase of dark English oak and a polished balustrade. Her library was paneled in pale blue satin, her smoking salon decorated in gilt gold, the enameled walls of her Renaissance dining room tinted in ivory and gold.

The clock ticked to departure at noon. The pulse of ship and pier quickened. The *Teutonic's* engines throbbed awake, her huge bronze propellers foaming the water, smoke pouring from her two towering funnels. One hundred and sixty deck and cabin stewards swarmed the ship, hauling the last steamer trunks up the gangplanks. The ship's whistle bellowed, stewards roamed the decks pounding gongs. All ashore! The four-year depression of the 1890s was receding. The U.S. economy had boomed with unprecedented prosperity in the heady six months since McKinley's reelection. Exports were growing with bumper crops. Manufacturing was booming. Spindletop had come-a-gushin' oil in southeast Texas. Companies were combining in record numbers, squeezing out expense. Reorganized railroads, pulled from bankruptcy, were making money. For the first time the flow of investment across the Atlantic had reversed. America was, as *Harper's Weekly* called it, the "youngest and the greatest industrial and commercial giant the world has ever known." American capital now flowed back into American enterprise, not just European securities. The stock market was on a powerful bull run, setting records for prices and volume far above the fundamental value of the properties. The United States was more self-sustaining than any nation in history, providing more than half the world's cotton, corn, copper, and oil and at least a third of all its steel, iron, silver, and gold. More Americans were flush with cash. Travel to Europe and all that went with it seemed affordable again. The *Teutonic* was at or near capacity, ship and pier jammed with thousands.

Ten minutes before departure, a private horse-drawn carriage, known as a brougham, sped down the opposite side of the pier to its end in a choreographed move to escape the crowd. From the cab into the wind and rain emerged two older women and then a distinguished, heavy-set man more than six feet tall with gray hair, dark mustache, arching black eyebrows, and a bulbous, inflamed strawberry nose. He wore a waterproof trench coat with velvet collar, brown sack suit, an old-fashioned white-wing collar along with a blue cravat with white stripes, and carried a silver-tipped mahogany walking stick. A subtle, extra touch bespoke aristocracy. His black Duke of York hat, silk lined and flat topped, had a buckle in the hat band, made only in Paris. Protected by a clutch of detectives ("who stuck to him as closely as brothers") and plainclothes policemen, the three passengers were met at the entrance to the second cabin by a Mr. Pendleton, superintendent of the dock, who whisked them up the "immigrants gangway" onto the promenade and into Cabin B and their first-class staterooms.

A murmur spread. Morgan is on board. And there he was. Sixty-four-year-old John Pierpont Morgan was the most powerful financier in the world, the man who built giant corporations, who single-handedly as lender of last resort saved the U.S. Treasury in 1895 to back the currency with a private bond issue to buy and deliver three and a half million ounces of gold when the government's supply was down to a day's worth of its reserves. "With the right foot planted in Wall Street, the left in Capel Court," it was written, as if he were the Colossus of Rhodes, "he bestrides the Atlantic." Who knew if it was true, but it certainly sounded so: English investors had insured his life for $20 million. His every step was followed. "When the cable announces that he has bought a new pair of striped trousers at Poole's," said the original *Life* magazine, "all Wall Street cables to Poole for striped trousers."

His hair was a bit grayer than when he steamed for Europe a year ago, but he still had his penetrating "blazing dark eyes" of hazel-yellow that photographer Edward Steichen later said were like "the headlights of an express train bearing down on you." He tossed his traveling bag into his stateroom and strode onto the promenade deck, went well aft and leaned on the rail to view the harbor. His two traveling companions were both recently widowed—his younger sister, Mary Lyman Morgan Burns, and the woman who stood next to him at the rail, Elizabeth Putnam Peabody Rogers, widow of the recently deceased Jacob Crowninshield Rogers, the Boston attorney for J. P. Morgan & Company. Mary and Elizabeth occupied a select circle. Morgan tended to be surprisingly shy and somewhat fumbling around women, but he had a deep need for their companionship, especially since he and his wife of forty years, Fanny, had drifted apart and were married in name only. Other close friends were there to wish him bon voyage, including Episcopal Bishop Henry Codman Potter, pastor to New York's elite Protestant smart set, who didn't mind traveling in Morgan's private railroad car to church conventions.

Reporters found Morgan on the promenade, surrounded by a crowd of friends and the curious, which one reporter estimated fifteen deep. Was he going to England to interest investors in his new United States Steel Corporation, the world's largest in market capital? "To interest investors?" said Mr. Morgan. "I am not going for any such purpose. Investors in England know what to do with their money without coming to you or me or anybody else over here to tell them." The reporters barely had time to scramble off the ship before the gangway ladders lifted, winches raised anchor, the Teutonic's whistle blasted, its lines taken in and slackened. It nudged slowly from the pier, two pilot boats bobbing to guide it down the harbor. The steward's band played "America" and thousands on the pier and on board cheered and waved. Some spotted Morgan and yelled to him a gracious good-bye as he waved both hands in a final adieu. As the Teutonic disappeared into the fog and mist down the river, one could still see Morgan waving.

Despite the grand gestures, he was a tired man. He long ago avoided exercise at the advice of his doctor ("You have formed the habit of living without exercise, giving your energy to your brain. It is too late to change the habit of a lifetime," was the counsel), so he ate what he pleased, loved his port or claret with dinner, and smoked (and chewed) too many cigars. He still had tremendous stamina but he was, after all, only human. Carrying the weight of global finance on his burly shoulders as a sort of de facto Central Bank and exporter of American financial capital, he often exhausted his strength and sank privately into a black hole of depression. He always said he could do a year's work in nine months but not in twelve. So every spring since 1890 he retreated to the mineral baths at Aix-les-Bains at the foot of the Alps in southeast France,

Edward J. Steichen's 1903 portrait of John Pierpont Morgan, the world's most influential financier, de facto Central Banker, builder of trusts, "head-keeper of the railroad morgue," and Hill partner in the Northern Pacific and in pursuing the Burlington. LIBRARY OF CONGRESS, PRINTS AND PHOTOGRAPHS DIVISION [LC-USZ62–108604].

then on to buying art in Paris and London where he could practice what someone later called, perhaps unfairly, his "life of organized self-indulgence."

He needed to recover from the last few months. They were perhaps the most intense of his forty years in finance: buying the Pennsylvania Coal Company and transferring it to the Erie Railroad, buying the Central Railroad of New Jersey through the Reading, and buying control of the Lehigh Valley

Railroad. Then, a month ago to this day, the deal of the new century—pinnacle of his career to date—buying Carnegie Steel for $480 million and combining it with almost a dozen other steel companies. With their mills, furnaces, ovens, mines, barges, steamships, and railroads he had created, but not yet begun to organize, a vertically integrated colossus. He called it United States Steel Corporation. It controlled half the nation's steel-making capacity, making more than two-thirds of America's steel (more than all of Great Britain), the world's first billion dollar company in capital.

U.S. Steel sparked even more combinations in other industries, creating even more wealth. This year was to be the high-water mark in the young nation's first great merger movement. Thirty-four firms merged in 1900, compared to 123 in 1901. There was much unfinished business with U.S. Steel, including how to manage the behemoth and integrate its plants, finance its operations, and resolve the bickering among its senior heads. All that could wait until Morgan returned in three months. His diplomatic lieutenant, Robert Bacon, was heading the company's finance committee, and he could manage the details.

Seeing Morgan on the promenade, portly and graying, a trifle deaf, it took some effort to imagine him in his vigorous youth. His lineage in business traced, as for so many prominent American financiers, to the wholesale clothing business of the early nineteenth century, when the makers and marketers borrowed money from their wholesalers against the account of their unsold merchandise. He was born, as was said, "in the purple." His father, Junius Spencer Morgan, began as a wholesaler of clothing, drifted into finance, and eventually made a huge market selling state bonds in America to build canals and railways. He made a fortune in 1870 by leading a syndicate to refinance France's debt from the Napoleonic wars. His son, John Pierpont, Hartford-born, educated in Boston and Germany, was a math prodigy, an accountant, and a banker trading in government securities and foreign exchange, and in the early 1870s helped refinance the post–Civil War debt of the federal government by partnering with Tony Drexel of Philadelphia. Drexel, head of one of the wealthiest banking houses in America, was connected to English capital through the banking house of Morgan's father and also to the banking house of Levi P. Morton, Junius's former partner and a future vice president of the United States.

Young John Pierpont came of age with the rise of syndicated loans to share risk, first in funding government debt and then funding the debt of the largest corporations, American railroads. His defining moment came with

J. P. Morgan and Company headquarters at "the corner," Wall and Broad streets, New York City: the "magnetic pole of the modern industrial world." LIBRARY OF CONGRESS, PRINTS AND PHOTOGRAPHS DIVISION, DETROIT PUBLISHING COMPANY PHOTOGRAPH COLLECTION [LC-D4–18309].

the Vanderbilts in 1879. Commodore Vanderbilt had died two years earlier and handed down to his oldest son, the tentative William H., 87 percent of the stock of his New York Central Lines. The New York legislature, finding that the railroad was giving lower rates to oil refiners, threatened to raise its taxes. The Legislature might blink, however, if William H. became a minority shareholder by selling a large portion of his stock. Morgan's firm was chosen to handle the delicate liquidation. How does one dump 250,000 shares of New

York Central on the market without depressing the price? Morgan quietly sold most of the shares abroad, many in London to investors who had been burned on American railroad stocks. It was an amazing sales job and the Morgan firm earned a fee of $3 million. Morgan demanded and got a seat on the New York Central board, and he became a proxy for London interests. The New York Central over the years became a Morgan-influenced railroad, and J. P. Morgan & Company became the Vanderbilts' bank.

Morgan, however, didn't pretend to be a railroad man. He was an agent for equity and bondholders whose capital had been squandered by overbuilding, watered stock, fraud, and parallel, inefficient roads. He brought discipline and efficiency to overbuilt railroads by gaining proxies and creating "voting trusts" (the control of competing companies via transfer of stock to one board of trustees) to merge systems and management, protect a railroad from being taken over by speculators, and ensure Morgan's oversight of its finances. By April 1901 he had become a sort of "custodian of the railroad industry," or more cynically, "head-keeper of the railroad morgue." He would buy control of a bankrupt road, install a new board, appoint new (and honest and efficient) management, simplify the corporate structure, refinance debt, reduce fixed charges on bonded debt by converting bonds into preferred stock, force the common stockholders to provide new capital (by exchanging four, five, or six shares of old common for new common and thereby evaporate the water in the stock, known facetiously as an "Irish dividend"), reinvest in the property, reduce branch lines that weren't paying their way, and return the system to profitability.

Morgan had been doing this for seventeen years. He had mediated a truce to avoid overbuilding between the nation's two great trunk lines that linked the East with the Great Lakes and Chicago—the Pennsylvania Railroad and the New York Central—by helping them acquire and reorganize parallel lines. He refinanced the Northern Pacific in 1883 and took charge of its board. He reorganized the Reading Railroad in 1884, the Baltimore & Ohio in 1885, the Chesapeake & Ohio in 1888, then the Erie, the Southern, and in 1896, for the second time, the Northern Pacific. If stockholders balked at an assessment to help reduce the debt of their roads, then under terms of the takeover their stock reverted to Morgan.

He now dominated, through voting trusts or stock ownership, railroads with almost thirty thousand miles of track, one of every six miles of track in the United States, and a quarter of all U.S. railroad earnings. Few questioned his integrity. "I want business done up here," he told his partners, raising his hand high, "not down here," dropping his hand low. Confidence in him was confidence in America. "He was not a brake," wrote historian Frederick Lewis Allen, "he was an engine." He claimed, however, that his power came not from money. Months before his death more than a decade later, when he was testifying before a congressional committee investigating the so-called money trust, the government attorney, Samuel Untermyer, asked him, "Is not commercial credit based primarily on money or property?" "No sir," replied Morgan, "the first thing is character." "Before money or property?" "Before money or property or anything else," Morgan said. "Money cannot buy it . . . Because a man I do not trust could not get money from me on all the bonds in Christendom." Sacred oaths such as this gave Morgan his mythic aura.

On this April 3, 1901, Morgan was the linchpin of negotiations for one more major railroad merger. The target was so profitable, so geographically valuable, so highly prized that the steady rise in its stock the last few months, the thinnest of rumors about its suitor or its sale price, could levitate or drag the entire stock market and its 175 listings. It had become a bellwether for the bulls.

The center of this merger was Chicago, "center hall of America," "Rome of the railroads," where the great trunk lines from the east terminated, where the west began, where geography had bestowed on it a providential location: the divide between the Great Lakes and the upper Mississippi watershed. Chicago had become the "junction of Eastern means and Western opportunity," the world's greatest manufacturing wholesaling entrepôt, twentieth-century equivalent of the ancient star caravan routes. It was the world's largest food distribution center, a huge funnel for the great rolling movement of grain, livestock, coal, and lumber, moving mostly west to east (mostly north to south before railroads) across the United States. It was the largest transportation center closest to the largest, purest iron ore deposits in the world. It had more shipping vessels and shipped more tons than any marine port in the world. It had just surpassed Philadelphia as the nation's second-largest city.

Morgan's man in these negotiations was one of America's great railroad minds, James Jerome Hill, prime builder and head of the Great Northern Railway. He and Morgan also had a large minority interest and thus working control of its parallel line, the Northern Pacific, giving them dominance across the entire northern tier west of Chicago to Seattle and its shipping path to Asia. Neither the Great Northern nor the Northern Pacific, however, had a direct line through Chicago. The Great Northern ended at St. Paul on the

Mississippi with a branch to Duluth on Lake Superior; the Northern Pacific ended at Duluth with a branch to St. Paul. This was what made the Hill–Morgan target, the venerable Chicago, Burlington & Quincy Railroad, so valuable.

As the *Teutonic* steamed out of the harbor, Morgan believed he and Hill almost had the Burlington in their pocket. It was already being called the best-conceived merger of regional railroads in the United States. Perhaps he even heard the joke going around this year: Who made the world? God did. But Morgan, Hill, and Rockefeller reorganized it in 1901. He knew some of Hill's competitors felt threatened by the deal. One even hinted at retaliating but Morgan was used to threats. He breathed in the sea air. There didn't seem to be anyone or anything standing in his way.

Fortress Monroe, Chesapeake Bay

Four hundred miles south of New York City the *Wacouta*, a yacht 248 feet long with a hull of steel, had swayed through the night in the gale of the nor'easter. It was anchored off the wharf at Fortress Monroe, the federal battlement on the southern tip of the Virginia peninsula at the entrance to Chesapeake Bay. The *Wacouta* could accommodate sixteen passengers; on this voyage it held just four. Its owner was the short, stocky James J. Hill, balding and gray bearded. With him were his wife, Mary, and two of their nine children, twenty-two-year-old Ruth and eighteen-year-old Gertrude. Mary and the daughters had boarded the *Wacouta* in Baltimore harbor a week and a half earlier. They had anchored for several days at the Navy Yard on the Potomac for sightseeing in Washington, D.C., where Hill had joined them the evening of Monday, April 1.

The family planned to go ashore the evening of April 2 to dine with Hill's close friend and trusted colleague, the shrewd, influential Daniel S. Lamont of the Northern Pacific, with his wife, Julia, at the palatial Queen Anne–style resort hotel, the Chamberlin. Lamont, balding and inscrutable behind a walrus mustache, was a former New York assemblyman, "silent secretary" to President Grover Cleveland, and former secretary of war—one of the best-connected men in Washington. He had a calculating side and could summon a "chilling politeness," honed by his years in Albany's broth of patronage and bribery. After his government service he made his fortune with William C. Whitney and Oliver H. Payne by consolidating Manhattan's streetcar lines. He had been a confidant of Hill's since Cleveland's first term, and now as chief presence for the Northern Pacific in New York he was so allied with Hill pursuing the Burlington that the *New York Herald* called it the "Hill–Lamont scheme."

Through the portholes of their yacht, which they bought the previous year, the Hills could see the Chamberlin's six stories glowing in the dark at Old Point Comfort. But, as Mary Hill put it in her diary, "Wind has risen to such strength that with heavy rain it is too much of an undertaking." So the Hills spent the evening pampered by a crew of thirty-eight, ensconced in the *Wacouta*'s formal dining room, main saloon, and social hall, paneled in oak and connected by an elegant stairway, amid Tiffany lamps, upholstered divans, mahogany furniture, and ten staterooms.

No one slept well in the storm, but the next morning when the sun flashed through the clouds the *Wacouta*'s Captain Weed lowered a launch and ferried Hill to the wharf where he strode down the dock to the Chamberlin to meet with Lamont. They spent most of their time discussing Hill's negotiations with his longtime friend Charles Elliot Perkins, chairman of the Chicago, Burlington & Quincy. The past two decades, Hill and his associates had built the closely held Great Northern into one of the nation's most efficient, profitable railroad systems. It stretched 5,200 miles through the wheat fields of Minnesota and North Dakota to the coal and copper mines of Montana, then into the forests of the Pacific Northwest to Puget Sound; then via steamship to Asia. The time had arrived, Hill wrote his longtime Canadian investor, Lord Mount Stephen, head of the Bank of Montreal, "when we should make our own territorial combination" for "traffic, terminal cities, terminal facilities, and territorial control, which is now the strongest in the west and will daily grow stronger" without having to divide the "through rate" with a competitor. It was time to buy the Burlington.

Hill already had shown extraordinary vision. He'd found a way, with little public fanfare, to move cotton from the South on the Great Northern to the Puget Sound and via steamship to Japan. Its shipments east to the United States had made the Great Northern a twentieth-century "silk road." Hill did all this by agreeing to "through rates" from New Orleans to Chicago with Stuyvesant Fish of the Illinois Central, the nation's only north–south transcontinental. He had to depend on other alliances, however, to move the goods from Chicago to St. Paul. Only two railroads had the attributes to be Hill's missing link: the Chicago, Milwaukee & St. Paul and the much stronger Burlington. If either fell to a competitor it would threaten Hill's entire western traffic.

Hill was hauling so much lumber east from the Pacific Northwest he was stuck with more and more empty or lightly loaded cars going west. Only by controlling his access in and out of Chicago could he load more freight west to Puget Sound. His Great Northern and the Northern Pacific would be like the beam and handles of a plow. The Burlington could be the "point of the plow." Asia had half the world's population. The shortest, cheapest route from the cotton fields of the southern United States to China was not via Los Angeles or San Francisco but by Puget Sound. To ship west to Asia, Western Europe had to cross two oceans. America had only to cross one. Hill's view was global: his Puget Sound terminus competed not so much against other U.S. railroads but against the Suez Canal, Europe's shortest water route east to Asia. He was building not merely a transcontinental railroad across western America but a global transport system. Railroad freight between Chicago and Puget Sound, however, remained the heart of his business. Ocean transport, for the time being, was a money loser. It was simply, in his words, for "securing loads for westbound cars to the Coast which are wanted there to bring lumber east."

The Chicago-based Burlington, run by old Boston money, was perhaps the nation's most valued, well-run independent railroad system, greatest of the so-called Granger roads. It was known for its consistent earnings power, conservative balance sheet, and aversion to debt—an investor's road, not a banker's road. Its 7,900 miles of track ran northwest from Chicago to St. Paul and Minneapolis, and swept west to the great provision centers beyond the direct reach of the Great Northern and Northern Pacific: southwest to St. Louis (connecting with southern markets and the Gulf), west to Kansas City, St. Joseph, Omaha, Denver, Cheyenne, the Black Hills, and Billings.

Bound together with the Great Northern and Northern Pacific at Chicago, the Burlington could give Hill 17,800 miles of track, control not just of the entire northern tier but his "land bridge" to the east, freeing him from the rate-making tyranny of trunk lines east of Chicago, such as the New York Central and the Pennsylvania, especially for grain and flour to Buffalo.

He could reduce terminal charges even further through his control with Morgan of the Erie Railroad. The Burlington could connect directly with Hill's roads in Nebraska and Montana, carry beef, cotton, iron, steel, and farm machinery west and bring lumber, coal, and copper east on the Great Northern and Northern Pacific. It could put Hill on the doorstep of the southeastern United States, connect the Burlington with the Gulf Coast and carry the South's cotton north and west. It could give him access through St. Louis to

Texas, the Southwest, and to the northern Pacific Coast without having to rely on any competitor. And it could make his roads do all this faster than ever before. For all these reasons Hill believed buying the Burlington even more important than his decision to build west to the coast.

As good as the Burlington was, Hill knew it could be better. Engines on many of its lines could handle many more tons, in some cases five times as much. Many of its grades could be lowered and its curves straightened. A curve, he learned early, cost as much as a hill. In some stretches the Burlington needed new rails and stronger ties. Its passing tracks could be lengthened, its terminals improved. Hill said he thought he could increase the freight volume of the Burlington an astounding 30 percent. He had proven it could be done with the Northern Pacific. Five or six years earlier, the languid Northern Pacific generated only $1.60 per freight mile. By 1901, with Hill's guidance, it was $3 a mile.

Perhaps one could forgive the extravagance of Hill's yacht this late in his career given the wealth he had created for his shareholders the last two decades. He had done more than just make the wealthy more so. He helped transform the nation's economy, bringing new wealth to thousands of communities and customers, dramatically reducing railroad operating costs and his customers' rates, and promoting immigration to populate the northwest. A railroad ignored the law of gravity at its own peril. Thus he built his tracks on the straightest line possible with the lowest grades, fewest curves, least friction, taking advantage of the world's most efficient method of transport—the curving surface contact point of steel wheel to rail is only about the size of a dime.

Hill reinvested surplus profit into more powerful locomotives, into new boxcars, gondolas, flatcars, stronger bridges and roadbeds, stronger steel rail, more efficient transfer yards, terminals, and shops. Do it once and do it right. "There is but one way to have it done," he wrote in 1890, "that is to make the work permanent and good in every respect so that it will not have to be done over again." Hill was among the first to show that railroads were the most efficient, least expensive way to haul heavy loads long distances. For a small load over a short distance, as someone said, only the wheelbarrow was cheaper. For a very small load over a very short distance the cheapest means was a shovel.

Hill's roads transported more and more tons per mile with better equipment at lower cost on stronger track at lower prices than virtually any competitor. When his St. Paul neighbor, Frederick Weyerhaeuser, had sawed through the white pine of the upper Midwest and moved to the Pacific Northwest it was Hill who helped him reduce his freight charges from ninety to forty cents per hundred pounds. Customers who shipped heavier loads over longer distances deserved more favorable pricing than lighter loads over shorter distances. They also expected guaranteed "through" rates over the entire length of the haul, all the more reason a long-distance railroad needed to control its territory and pricing. The goal for expanding, his biographer wrote, should be "to get as much traffic as possible, as far out on your own line as possible, and to keep it on your line for as long a haul as possible." This could be done only if traffic was balanced: cars moving in both directions had to be loaded. An empty car is a thief. Railroading is a high fixed-cost business; about sixty cents of every dollar a railroad spent was not affected by how much traffic it carried. So Hill's mind thrummed with ratios: revenue per ton-mile, loaded freight car miles, traffic units carried per locomotive. Every railroad car, freight or passenger, had to pay for itself, or as Hill put it, "every tub must stand on its bottom."

Hill never knew a coffee break. He often worked seven-day weeks, trudging home from his office up from the banks of the Mississippi many evenings after midnight. One colleague said he could work thirty-six to forty-eight hours straight, eat a big dinner, then go to bed and sleep for sixteen hours, "regardless of demands." But even when he was exhausted, sleep often didn't come easy; he suffered neuralgic headaches, chest colds, a poor diet, and chronic hemorrhoids. Hill disdained pretense and personal ornament, dressing for business in plain sack suits and a dented homburg. When traveling alone in the 1880s as head of his St. Paul, Minneapolis & Manitoba Railway (chrysalis for the Great Northern) he used the same washroom as the "drummers," the traveling salesmen.

Even when Hill's position and wealth dictated he should have a private car it was nothing fancy; rather than give it some grand name he merely had it stenciled "A-1." He normally didn't even use the car east of Chicago. One newspaper called him a "calculating machine" that "never permits an invested nickel to be diverted from its duty of making more nickels." His St. Paul headquarters was unadorned and he wanted the same for his railroad. "Please have all trimmings good and *plain* [underlined twice]," he wrote his engine builders, "such as will not be hard to keep up." He was nothing for ceremony. When his crews drove the final spike on January 6, 1893, in the Cascades near Scenic, Washington, connecting the Great Northern from St. Paul to Seattle,

James J. Hill, railroad genius, builder of the Great Northern and single-largest individual shareholder of the Northern Pacific: "Make the work permanent and good in every respect so that it will not have to be done over again." *PHOTOGRAPH BY PACH BROTHERS. COURTESY OF MINNESOTA HISTORICAL SOCIETY.*

the foreman could barely get the corporal's guard to leave the cooking shack long enough to observe the "ceremony." Hill was home in bed nursing a cold.

He hated deadheads (empty cars) and even half-empty cars. Alternate the thick and thin ends of shingles when you stack them in my cars, he told his workers, so they'll make flat, square packages. He had no patience for deadbeats. "I know you will do it [the work] the best and the fastest way you can," he wrote a manager on the line in the late 1870s. "Do not allow any trifle to stand in the way . . . Have every man do his full duty or clean him out." Once he visited the headquarters of a railroad whose stock he'd just bought in large quantity. Perhaps it was the Baltimore & Ohio, which he helped guide out of bankruptcy and revitalize at the invitation of financier Jacob Schiff in the late 1890s. Hill surveyed one of the railroad's large offices and asked one of the employees, "How many men here?" "About eighty-five," was the response. "Can't you get along with less?" asked Hill. "No," said the employee, "We never could." "Well," said Hill, "I'll get a man who can."

He was naturally engaging, gregarious, a talker holding forth for hours around hot stoves and railroad sidings, testing his thinking wherever he could find willing ears. He liked to debate, persuade, lecture, and harangue, gesturing with the pinky of his right hand. He wore his biases on his sleeve. Middlemen were "economic waste." Lawmakers were akin to a "fly [that] buzzes about a horse." So-called progressives were a bunch of "college tack-head philosophers." There were immutable laws of commerce beyond the power of legislators or bureaucrats to control. In the long run, transportation always adapts to the line of least resistance. Public enterprises cost more than private ones. "Trade will go her own way, even though she must walk in leg irons." "All progress is the development of order. A uniform method is the highest form of order."

Hill's bluntness was double-edged: he went straight to the point but was prone to bullying in negotiations and was a hopeless micromanager. He cut the wages of his lowest-paid employees in 1894 during the depression rather than reduce dividends. He worked his managers to exhaustion, second-guessed their decisions, and was close to incompetent in grooming talent. His profane, volcanic temper erupted in episodes of door kicking, shattering a desk, ripping a telephone from the wall and kicking it to pieces. At age sixty-nine, after ceding the presidency to his son Louis W., he got into a smash-up brawl in the Great Northern's St. Paul offices with fifty-seven-year-old railroad veteran F. H. McGuigan, whom he had hired from the Grand Trunk Railroad of eastern Canada only six months earlier to run the railroad's operating departments. McGuigan quit, accusing Hill of "dictatorial methods."

Hill also could not always be trusted, most notably in the mid-1890s. He promised the Canadian Pacific Railway that if it sold him a small railroad northwest of Lake Superior, which owned one hundred square miles of iron ore land, he would give it perpetual right to use the railroad and guarantee it eastbound traffic from his lines. The Canadian Pacific agreed. The 63,000 acres he gained turned out to be among the half dozen most valuable tracts of iron ore in the world, but he never gave the Canadian Pacific the traffic he promised. No surprise to the Canadian Pacific's respected president, William C. Van Horne, who called Hill a "skunk" and accused him of personal slanders and malicious lying "always administered with an appearance of friendship."

Hunched over his mahogany rolltop desk, Hill was a hawk for detail. As a young commission agent he caught the Michigan Central Railroad passing along an exorbitant charge for transferring goods from dock to railroad cars. Nothing in the books got past him: repairs for a collision, he noticed, should not be charged to the construction account. As a coal distributor he demanded and got more accurate railroad scales when he found actual weights were as much as 3 percent below the billed rate. He relished writing balance sheets in his strong cursive. "I have been up at the front on both lines," he said in the late 1870s as he and his associates prepared to take over the bankrupt railroad that would make them wealthy, "and I find it pays to be where the money is being spent."

Hill claimed the three most valuable contributors to the "happiness of the people" were Christianity, public schools, and the railroads, and he could have added a fourth: family. He and his wife, the former Mary Theresa Mehegan, daughter of Irish immigrants, met, so the story goes, when she waited on tables at the Merchants' Hotel in St. Paul where he boarded. They were married in 1867 and had ten children, perhaps the largest family of any major business leader of his time, though later it grew dysfunctional.

Of the four major principals in this story—Morgan, Hill, Harriman, and Schiff—Hill was the only one who got his hands dirty in the business. Raised on a farm in Eramosa, Ontario, third of four children of Scots-Irish parents, he came up the Mississippi on a steamboat to St. Paul at age seventeen in 1856, carrying just a valise. For five years in Ontario, under the wise and patient Quaker minister William Wetherald, he had learned English grammar, arithmetic, algebra, the theory of land surveying, history, and geography. He then clerked in general stores, learning to write clear, concise business letters, double-entry bookkeeping, and how to measure a customer's character and credit worthiness. One could scarcely notice Hill was blind in his right eye. When he was nine a homemade bow snapped in his hands, propelling the end of the arrow back, destroying his optic nerve. He compensated with a muscular upper body, hulking shoulders, a bull neck, and an even stronger mind.

Hill read widely in history and literature throughout his life. He could quote Shakespeare when it suited him, and in what little leisure time he had he could be found reading Boccaccio, Montaigne, Carlyle, and Rabelais. Over his desk in his private railroad car he kept volumes of Ruskin, William Morris, Longfellow, and Emerson. His longtime banker, George F. Baker of New York, called Hill the best-read man he ever knew. He remembered traveling west with Hill in his private car on the Great Northern with Hill's close friend, Judge Greenleaf Clark of St. Paul. Clark quoted a passage from the Bible and Hill responded by quoting the one that followed. "Clark tried it again and again," said Baker, "and each time Hill capped his quotation." Baker wrote Hill's wife the next day, saying he thought her husband should have been a minister. It was this Lincolnesque intimacy with the Bible and his familiarity with his workers that enabled Hill to speak and write with such clarity. He spoke and wrote so his brakemen could understand.

Hill's first job was as a steamboat agent before the Minnesota territory had a single track of rail, slopping through the muck of the levee, loading and unloading plows, salt, nails, groceries, furniture, yard goods, cooking stoves, wagons, and harnesses. He worked four years on the same levee for wholesale grocers and distributors, including two as a wharf master. He bought oats for his own account and noticed something: it cost more to ship them on a steamboat than the goods cost themselves. As a young wharf master he was said to have chased for miles through muddy streets a runaway horse that had bolted from its wagon. He collected every piece of the wagon and reassembled it.

By the end of the Civil War in 1865 Hill was a freight and passenger agent for a packet company that served a small railroad. He now thoroughly understood shipping up and down the levee and the river. On land leased from a railroad on the levee he built his own warehouse at dock level, 100 feet by 330 feet, where customers' baled hay could be stacked, where millers stored their flour for the winter. The warehouse allowed him to bypass the wagons that charged a dollar for every ton of freight hauled from boat to rail. Five years later he ran a steamboat business on the north-flowing Red River toward Canada, using the profit to start a business for transporting, storing, and selling coal, especially premium-priced fine anthracite from the east used for heating homes. He then bought coal land in Iowa and became a coal expert, using his well-thumbed copy of the 1873 *Coal-Regions of America* by James Macfarlane. In turn, coal led him to its symbiotic cousin, railroads.

The state-chartered St. Paul & Pacific Railroad was a patchwork of 437 miles of track from St. Paul through western and central Minnesota. It attracted measly traffic and defaulted on its bond payments after the financial panic of 1873. Hill began stalking it, Samuel Elliot Morison wrote later, the way a prairie wolf tracks a weak buffalo. On March 13, 1878, with three associates, none of whom had significant fortunes or direct experience running a railroad, Hill gambled all he had. He fully tapped his personal credit and possessions to exchange the IOUs of a new company for the IOUs of the old company, buying the bonds of Dutch investors with a face value of $28 million for $4.4 million. He and his associates also gained 2.6 million in Minnesota state land grant acres (bestowed on the former territory by Congress), worth $7 million, but those could be sold only once. The road had to earn its way thereon. He planned his own towns along the line in Dakota Territory through his own land company to help pay for building his road.

In five years what appeared to be "a rundown, bankrupt railroad out on the edge of nowhere" gradually became a first-class railroad through the bonanza wheat country of Minnesota and the Dakota Territory, a winning bet on an increasing flow of immigrants. By 1883 Hill claimed his railroad carried over one-fifth the U.S. spring wheat crop. By November 1885 his one-fifth share in the St. Paul, Minneapolis & Manitoba Railroad was worth $4.97 million. There was hardly a mile of his track he didn't know intimately. He had slept along its route in freight cars, general stores, and farmhouses, hunted prairie chickens across its prairies, and once in late winter, stripped to his underwear, he crossed a stream up to his waist. When an old friend of his in Fargo claimed a ditch maintained by the Northern Pacific caused flooding on his farm land, Hill wrote to the railroad's vice president, Dan Lamont, and asked him to "fix him up in some way. I know the location well and know he is right." One friend swore Hill could spot a spike in the grass from a train going sixty miles an hour; another that he could identify every single trestle and culvert on his line for a hundred miles out of St. Paul, in the dark. It didn't matter how many data books Hill's managers brought with them on inspection tours with the boss; while they looked up figures Hill would recite them.

Hill could judge a crop. He once asked guests in his car as they sped past wheat fields if they could tell how much a certain field would yield. Someone guessed fifteen bushels an acre. Another twenty-five. "No, you're wrong," he said. "That field is hardly worth cutting. You make the mistake of judging by appearances . . . It is the heads, not the straw, that fill grain bins."

Hill's dramatic push west began in 1886, across the Dakota Territory toward Montana coal, copper, and waterpower on the Missouri River at Great Falls. The next summer his crews laid the longest stretch of track ever built by a railroad in one season from one end of the track: 643 miles between

Minot, North Dakota, and Helena, Montana. On August 8, 1887, his workers laid eight miles of track in one day. By the spring of 1888, his system was no longer a regional carrier but a major railroad. It could carry wheat a thousand miles from western Montana to Duluth and later via his steamships on the Great Lakes to Buffalo, and then return with coal. By early 1889 he made up his mind to build to Puget Sound to control his own destiny on what he called "our own line in the North" toward "the largest supply of standing timber in the world," and on to the Pacific toward Japan and China. Any western road, he predicted, that did not control its own route to the Pacific sooner or later would disappear. "This country," he told the Burlington's John Murray Forbes in the late 1880s, "must go through the fire," meaning that its overbuilt railroads would have to consolidate. He had to thread his way as a latecomer between two other transcontinentals: the Northern Pacific to the south connected six years earlier, and the Canadian Pacific to the north connected four years earlier.

Hill reached the coast in early January 1893, just in time. As he feared it would, the year of the "great divide" had begun. The Philadelphia & Reading Railroad, overbuilt and overborrowed, collapsed in February, the National Cordage Company followed in May. Then the dominos fell, buried in debt and overbuilt ahead of demand: the Erie in July, the Union Pacific and Northern Pacific in October, the Atchison, Topeka & Santa Fe in December. Gambling in railroad stocks was land speculation in disguise. Gold fled to Europe. Some six hundred banks failed, some fifteen thousand businesses went bankrupt. A third of all railroads were broke. From 1894 to 1898, lenders foreclosed on about one of every five miles of track.

From his perch in the storm at the fortressed Great Northern (never defaulting on bond payments, never missing a dividend, only "transcontinental" never to go bankrupt), with its strong cash reserve, solid track and equipment, and efficient lines, Hill viewed the financial wreckage of the Northern Pacific, which ran parallel just south of his road to the coast. He knew this was the time to buy it for pennies on the dollar, merge it with his system, and run it as it should be run. His Great Northern, in many ways, was private enterprise's answer to a government-created, parallel railroad. He might never have created the Great Northern if the Northern Pacific had been conceived, financed, built, and managed right the first time. Hill considered its routes and grades "abominable," and said that, "practically, it would have to be built over." He confided to friends that the Northern Pacific hadn't been run as a railroad for years but as a stock and bond jobber. He knew when the depression lifted there would be a combining of America's western railroads that would define its control for decades. His Great Northern could not afford to be pinned and isolated against the Canadian border.

The Northern Pacific had been cursed from the start. It was conceived not by market entrepreneurs such as Hill who earned their success and labored without direct benefit of federal land grants. It was created by political entrepreneurs, who persuaded the government to subsidize their business or to pass laws to handicap their competitors, in effect charging someone else for their risk. Its early weakness was "the persistent leaning upon the government for help." It could have saved itself a lot of money had it used that time to devise a financial plan to pay its own way. President Lincoln had signed the Northern Pacific into existence forty years earlier, a land grant creature of Congress, requiring it to be built at both ends of the system at the same time, even though it served no urgent national interest and its eastern terminus, Lake Superior, was frozen five months of the year at Duluth. "You can't build a railroad," Cornelius Vanderbilt once said, perhaps speaking of the Northern Pacific, "from nowhere to nowhere." Its federally granted 47 million acres, however, were the largest extended to any American railroad, twice the size of Indiana, holding coal, precious metals, and timber beyond measure. The Northern Pacific became the federal instrument of "manifest destiny" for extricating those resources and turning that "nowhere" into money. For that to happen safely, there would have to be, in railroad euphony, "the permanent pacification of the Indians." It was, furthermore, built too far ahead of settlement, a distance of Paris to Petersburg.

Worse, its managers gave inordinate power to their mobilizer of credit: a reclusive, absentee bond salesman who lived 1,300 miles away in New York City. Jay Cooke had become a national hero by raising a quarter of the Union's funds for war against the Confederacy; he made a fortune on insider war information, and built himself a fifty-three room mansion on two hundred acres near Philadelphia. Unable to attract bank loans, he sold bonds to gullible investors, hyped by his planted newspaper stories and market manipulation. He persevered, inspired by what he called "this great work...in the faith of my Christian duty" to populate the Northwest by "filling in a godly and moral population." In just two years, he sold some $33 million in bonds to some 11,000 investors, making the Northern Pacific the most widely held railroad security.

The early Northern Pacific made so much sense on paper: shortest land route between the coasts of any of the "Pacifics," closest to Chicago, closest to Asia from its terminus, the "northwest passage" of Lewis and Clark that followed the rivers. On land, however, it was, in many respects, an engineering disaster, plagued by shoddy construction and built through the black mush of northern Minnesota's swamps and sinkholes. Some of its feeble track was laid in the winter and sank in the spring thaw. It was an accounting disaster, millions of dollars disappeared from its books. Cooke & Company went under in the panic of 1873 and the Northern Pacific went bankrupt two years later, staying solvent only by trading its land for bonds. It also was the enemy of the Indians: Custer's mission, after all, was to protect its surveys and construction. In the late 1870s Frederick Billings and a group of eastern investors reorganized it and resumed laying track from the east into Dakota Territory and from the west in Washington Territory.

Enter, in 1881, a forty-six-year-old German immigrant, Ferdinand Heinrich Gustav Hilgard, who became the P. T. Barnum of American railroads. Americanized as Henry Villard, he had bounced around Illinois, Wisconsin, Ohio, Indiana, and Colorado in the 1850s and 1860s, writing for German-language newspapers, selling literary encyclopedias, hawking real estate, selling U.S. railroad bonds to German investors. Posing with patrician manners, he befriended the famous, living beyond his means in fine hotels. In 1879, representing European investors and relying heavily on Deutsche Bank of Berlin, he bought the Oregon Steamship and Navigation Company with money borrowed from its assets, perhaps the first leveraged buyout. Villard controlled Portland but the Northern Pacific controlled Seattle and Tacoma, blocking his path to control transport of lumber east and threatening his monopoly of river and rail transport in Oregon.

Villard circulated to fifty-five wealthy friends a confidential prospectus proposing to form an audacious "blind pool," which raised $8 million to acquire a mystery property (to prevent a rise in its stock price). It turned out to be Northern Pacific. To house his properties he created one of America's first holding companies. Fixating on his operatic vision to be the first northern transcontinental, he ignored cost overruns, shifted assets among properties in a shell game, issued worthless bonds, paid out dividends even though expenses exceeded revenue, then built himself a compound of Gilded Age brownstone mansions covering two blocks on New York's Madison Avenue. He also built inefficient, low-volume branch lines and ran "light" trains, sometimes nothing more than a locomotive and one or two cars.

Two years to the day after forming the "blind pool" he became president of the Northern Pacific. He completed its transcontinental route at Cold Creek east of Helena and spent $300,000 on a lavish ceremony to drive the golden spike, using the event as an infomercial to sell more bonds. That day the New York Herald hit newsstands with a report, probably planted by Villard's enemies including "hired plungers," that a "very damaging statement" of the Northern Pacific's affairs was due soon. Between 1880 and 1883 the Northern Pacific's bonded debt ballooned from $3.8 million to $39.5 million. Its fixed charges rose seven and a half fold. Wall Street bears attacked, Villard's stocks tanked, he was ousted as president at year-end, and he vacated his New York mansion after living there only four and a half months. He resurfaced at the end of the decade, when he regained control of the Oregon companies and earned enough proxies to return to the Northern Pacific board. He presided over the Northern Pacific's disastrous attempt to build a line to Chicago from Minneapolis–St. Paul, marking its inevitable slide into the financial panic of 1893 and its second bankruptcy.

Hill was waiting for the Northern Pacific with open arms, but he had to wait four years. He signed an agreement with Deutsche Bank in London in 1895 (the so-called London agreement) to acquire the Northern Pacific on behalf of his Great Northern, guaranteeing Northern Pacific's interest charges up to $6 million a year in return for a majority of the Northern Pacific's capital stock. Hill convinced two of his longtime associates, John Stewart Kennedy and Mount Stephen (George Stephen), to buy significant amounts of its stock. Morgan likewise invested in the Great Northern and headed the syndicate to underwrite the new Northern Pacific securities. As part of this plan, Morgan decreed that every holder of Northern Pacific common stock would be assessed $15 a share. Many refused, so some 300,000 shares reverted to Morgan. He sold them to Hill and Mount Stephen for $4.1 million or $16 a share, which gave Hill and his associates 10 percent of the total shares of the reorganized company, making them its single largest shareholders. With Morgan's presumed control of the reorganized company, this was Hill's lever on the Northern Pacific to force it to avoid wasteful spending that, if unimpeded, could tempt it to cut rates below cost.

The marketplace seemed to have decided there was not enough traffic to support two northern transcontinentals. A law, however, kept the moribund

Northern Pacific on life support. In 1896 the U.S. Supreme Court threw out the "London agreement," citing an 1874 Minnesota statute, like others in more than half the states, prohibiting joint ownership of parallel, competing lines. Morgan and his railroad paramedics then took full control of the reorganized Northern Pacific, creating a voting trust for five years with Deutsche Bank. He installed three of his men on its board including his junior partner, vigilant workaholic and railroad mind Charles Coster, the hyperactive, pale accountant he hired twelve years earlier from a shipping firm. Coster has been called, rightly so, a "rare genius, a sort of financial chemist" who could untangle and make sense of the "interwoven relations of railroad obligations, bonds, underlying bonds, [and] collateral trust mortgages," and offer Morgan clear, sound solutions. His job also was to make sure Hill didn't meddle.

Three days after the U.S. Supreme Court ruling in late March 1896, Hill and Morgan met in London and agreed that the "Great Northern and reorganized Northern Pacific shall form a permanent alliance, defensive and in case of need offensive, with a view of avoiding competition and aggressive policy and of generally protecting the common interests of both companies." Despite the ruling of the U.S. Supreme Court, from this day forward the Northern Pacific became a "second track" of the Great Northern, though they remained separate companies. Both lines agreed to divide all competitive business "upon equitable terms," not to build into each other's territory, and to keep the Northern Pacific's link between Spokane and the Pacific "independent and available on the same terms to all connecting railways." No more rate wars. No more fighting over who got how much business from Anaconda Copper. No more invading each other's turf. It was all a clever legal wink at the Sherman Anti-Trust Act, and the Justice Department said not a word. Morgan wanted to protect his investment and keep it independent of Hill's Great Northern for the time being, but he and Hill both knew if all went as planned Hill eventually would control the Northern Pacific.

Meanwhile, Hill kept badgering. He sent long letters to Edward D. Adams, Morgan's interim head of the Northern Pacific, showing him exactly how it could approach the Great Northern in tons per mile. In the spring of 1897 over a dinner in London, Hill reminded "Mr. Morgan" that he and German investors owned a majority of Northern Pacific's stock, which they bought assuming Hill soon would control it. But then Coster, serving on fifty-nine boards, exhausted from overwork and sleep deprived, ashen and drawn, caught a cold that became pneumonia. He died on March 13, 1900, at his home at 37 East Thirty-Seventh Street in New York at age forty-seven. The following Saturday, Morgan and his junior partner, Robert Bacon, were two of the seven pallbearers who accompanied his casket down the aisle at Grace Church. With his "railroad mind" Coster gone, Morgan's hand was forced. Furthermore, Hill seemed to be running the Northern Pacific as if he owned it. Weeks before Coster's death he helped engineer the sale of 900,000 acres of Northern Pacific timberland west of the Cascades to the Weyerhaeuser syndicate for six dollars an acre, one of the largest land transfers in U.S. history.

On November 12 Morgan cabled Hill: the trustees had voted, a year ahead of schedule, to dissolve Morgan's Northern Pacific voting trust. After two decades of rate wars with a poorly run, government-subsidized transcontinental with all its useless branches paralleling his straight and strong Great Northern, Hill entered the new century as a major influence over the Northern Pacific. He held a large minority of its common stock, with his friend Lamont overseeing it, just as the economy was reviving and traffic and immigration were building. Eastbound Northern Pacific trains, instead of being deadheads, could carry Pacific Northwest lumber over upgraded tracks with heavier steel, lower grades, and fewer curves. He also could use the Northern Pacific to park the surplus earnings of the Great Northern.

On the wharf at Fortress Monroe, James and Mary Hill and their daughters settled in for their last evening together on the *Wacouta*. The next morning, April 4, "Papa" would board a B&O train in Baltimore to New York and then to Boston for another secret meeting with Chairman Charles Elliot Perkins of the Burlington. The deal was almost done. All that remained to settle was the final price and terms of the Great Northern and Northern Pacific joint bonds to be exchanged for Burlington stock. The offer of a joint purchase by both roads was a Morgan masterstroke, presenting them to the market, in effect, as one enterprise. Perkins demanded $200 a share in cash, a 10 percent premium to its opening price this April 3, 1901, which was 55 percent higher than when McKinley was reelected just five months earlier. Hill and Morgan were ready to pay it, but before he left for Europe Morgan told Hill and his banking ally Baker that he could finance the purchase at $200 a share for the Burlington but in 4 percent bonds, not in cash as Perkins and his board demanded. Cash would require an underwriting syndicate on terms less favorable to Morgan than bonds. Thus bonds, mostly, it would be.

1 Park Avenue, New York City

The evening of April 3, 1901, with Morgan out on the north Atlantic and Hill on his yacht in Chesapeake Bay, forty-year-old Bob Bacon was driven in a private carriage three miles uptown from his Wall Street office to his three-story Gothic home covered in vines at one of the city's most prestigious addresses: 1 Park Avenue at Thirty-Third. There to greet him was his elegant wife of eighteen years, Martha, their four children ages ten to sixteen, and three servants.

Even at home it was impossible for him to escape the pressure of work and Morgan's shadow. With his colleague Charles Coster's sudden death a year earlier, Bacon now was being tested as never before: left in charge of the most powerful investment bank in the world, a firm widely known as a "partner killer." He and Charles Steele, a lawyer Morgan had hired to replace Coster (at Coster's funeral, no less), focused intently on the Burlington. They were working with Hill and their lawyers to negotiate the final, delicate terms of an acceptable deal to satisfy its fourteen thousand shareholders spread across the United States and abroad, especially its wealthy, conservative Boston blue bloods.

On paper and by pedigree, Bacon seemed ready for the challenge. Descended from an unbroken line of Puritan ancestors to 1639 in Cornwall, England, he entered Harvard at age sixteen, youngest of a class that included Theodore Roosevelt. Bacon was a scholar, thespian, and president of his class. He was tanned and classically handsome, blessed with a physique reminiscent of a Greek sculpture, and was an outstanding athlete in football (team captain), baseball, boxing, track, and number seven on the rowing crew. Even now, twenty years later, he walked up Wall Street with an athlete's agile grace and poise. He was so duty bound that a few years after leaving Morgan to work at the State Department he chose to take a midnight train back to Washington from Boston to complete unfinished business, and by doing so missed seeing three of his sons compete for Harvard in crew against Yale. After several years with Boston investment bankers, he caught Morgan's eye and joined the firm in 1894. Morgan found him irresistible, taken with his "charm of manner, tact and skill in negotiation."

Hill professed total confidence in Bacon, but perhaps he said so simply for Morgan's benefit. Others had doubts. The authoritarian Morgan had a weakness for hiring suave, pedigreed yes men. Some wondered if Bacon was one of them, a "charming lightweight." Bacon was overwhelmed: the Burlington deal, the new U.S. Steel, the anthracite coal miners' complaints, a possible

Morgan's dutiful lieutenant Robert Bacon, in charge while Morgan was in Europe, was overwhelmed with responsibilities. He almost uncovered the Harriman–Schiff plot and months later suffered a "nervous breakdown." LIBRARY OF CONGRESS, PRINTS AND PHOTOGRAPHS DIVISION, HARRIS AND EWING COLLECTION [LC-DIG-HEC-16169].

north Atlantic steamship merger, all manner of foreign loans. He had no idea that only a block or two away Schiff and Harriman were plotting to buy control of the Northern Pacific, and the Burlington with it, right out from under him. His Harvard degree and charm would count for little in this fight.

Despite all his talent, skill and diplomatic poise, he sometimes appeared to be, remembered one of his Harvard classmates, "careless of details, leaving them to be attended to by other hands with a simple and almost humorous faith that was seldom disappointed." In the run-up to the Northern Pacific corner and panic, it was going to be his fatal flaw.

2

MR. HARRIMAN AND MR. SCHIFF

Mr. Harriman: 120 Broadway, New York City

If you walked this April 3 morning a block west from the House of Morgan on Wall Street, took a right on Broadway, and strode another block and a half north, you would come to Henry Baldwin Hyde's Equitable Life Assurance Society building at 120 Broadway, a stately ten-story office tower of gray Quincy granite in the ornate French second-empire style with mansard roof. Passing under its high arch and ornate, bronze grillwork you would enter a grand arcade a hundred feet long and forty-four feet wide with a barrel-vaulted ceiling of stained glass, lined with rose-colored marble columns and statues on a checkered marble floor. It was perhaps the most elegant interior courtyard in America, patterned after the Galleria Vittorio Emanuele in Milan. Entering one of the passenger elevators with its cushioned, red velvet seats, you might find yourself next to a pale, mousy little man, five feet four, shallow-chested, wearing steel-rim spectacles with thick lenses, with sad, rheumy eyes and a drooping, unkempt mustache. His suit looks a size too large. You could mistake him for the elevator operator—until, that is, you followed him as he ambled bow-legged down the corridor of the fourth floor to his office. There you would discover that he was Edward Henry Harriman, chairman of the Union Pacific, perhaps the most powerful man in the most powerful industry in the United States.

Harriman's railroad network encompassed 20,000 miles of track, more than any other American railroad system, covering virtually the entire western United States. It included, directly and indirectly, the Union Pacific from Council Bluffs to Ogden, Utah, and Portland, Oregon; the Illinois Central from Chicago south to New Orleans and west to Sioux City; the Kansas City & Southern from Kansas City to Port Arthur, Texas, and the Gulf of Mexico;

the Chicago & Alton; the Chicago & Terminal Transfer; and most recently, the Southern Pacific from New Orleans to San Francisco and north to Portland and Ogden. The Southern Pacific alone was the largest transportation company in the world, with 7,200 miles of rail and 16,000 miles of steamship routes. Harriman paged intently through the papers on his desk, scanning, penciling, deep in thought. The Southern Pacific's annual stockholders' meeting was in just a few hours. He and his colleagues, proxies in hand, had made it a formality. The board would expand from twelve to fifteen members including seven from the old Southern Pacific board. Harriman would add himself and seven others for a majority, and he would head the executive committee and run it with his people.

The size and scope of Harriman's system now far exceeded Hill's, and Harriman was being mentioned as Morgan's railroad equal. The past fifteen years he and Morgan had grown to be bitter enemies. They collided for the first time in 1887 when Harriman, an obscure vice president for finance at the Illinois Central, defeated Morgan for control of the board of the Dubuque & Sioux City Railroad. The Illinois Central operated the road under a lease and wanted to buy it outright as a feeder, but the Dubuque's majority stockholders objected and parked their securities with Morgan. Harriman, however, appeared at the Dubuque's annual meeting with a lawyer and argued a legal technicality: Morgan's proxies were signed by his firm personally not as trustees. The shareholders sold out to the Illinois Central for $80 a share. Morgan was furious. Ever since then he considered Harriman a schemer not to be trusted, a "punk," a "little pad shover," someone always seeking terms, as Morgan's son-in-law put it, "a little better than other people's." Morgan's dislike for Harriman, however, was animated not so much by their conflicts in business but by what Morgan perceived as Harriman's focus solely on the letter of the law. Morgan believed the spirit of the law was just as important, perhaps more so.

In 1894 Harriman sued Morgan's firm to block its plan to reorganize the bankrupt Erie Railroad. Harriman thought, rightly so, that the plan was unfair to one class of Erie bondholders, though he personally held a relatively small amount of Erie securities. Harriman volunteered to head the bondholders' protective committee. He lost in the courts but months later Morgan had to revise his plan anyway because the Erie's earnings were lower than expected. Why did Harriman make such a fuss? Surely because he felt the plan was unfair, perhaps because he couldn't resist picking a fight no matter how small the stakes, or perhaps because he commuted on the Erie into New

York City from Arden, his estate of 9,300 acres in the Ramapo Highlands fifty miles north of Jersey City, an estate that grew to twice the size of Manhattan Island. Then, in 1897, Harriman beat Morgan at his own game. Morgan had his chance but passed on reorganizing the bankrupt Union Pacific, calling it "two streaks of rust across the plains," only to see Harriman come out of nowhere to grab a place on its executive committee and take control of its refinancing. In just three years he transformed it into one of the most profitable railroads in America, paying 10 percent on the par value of its common stock. In the refinancing and rebuilding, some people found him brusque and rude. One admirer, Otto Kahn of Kuhn, Loeb, sympathetically referred to him as a master of what Whistler called "the gentle art of making enemies." For Morgan, however, it was not a laughing matter. Christian gentleman though he aspired to be, Morgan was said to have "never been known to forgive an affront"; he surely struggled to forgive the "little pad shover." Harriman never dined at Morgan's home.

Coming out of "nowhere" was a role Harriman preferred; he was secretive, furtive, calculating. He was the fourth of six children, cold and a bit distant like his father who scratched out a living of a few hundred dollars a year as an Episcopal minister at a country church in Hempstead, New York, and late in life was a bank bookkeeper. His mother was the daughter of a respected physician, and only a modest inheritance from her side of the family enabled the Harrimans to move into a larger home.

Harriman would have taken Morgan's "pad shover" insult as a compliment, because it was how he learned the business as a teenage messenger on the New York Stock Exchange in the early 1860s. He began at the bottom of the totem, a "runner" carrying securities twice a day between the Exchange and the clearinghouse. Before the stock ticker was invented in 1867, boys like Harriman carried pads of paper from the Exchange to brokers with the prices of stocks and bonds written in pencil. He was one of the few who could recite prices on his pad from memory, and he gained an intimate feel for how to value a security.

A contemporary described Harriman later in his career as someone who could "take up a conversation at a point where it had ceased months before, and his knowledge of the details of the legislation, litigation, and conferences was as fresh in his recollection as if they had only that moment been brought to his attention." He became a notoriously impatient listener, drumming his fingertips on desktops, gnawing his mustache with his bottom teeth. He developed an annoying habit in business meetings of asking a question and

Edward H. Harriman, head of the Union Pacific and the Southern Pacific, master of the "gentle art of making enemies," Morgan adversary and mastermind of the plot to seize Hill–Morgan's
Northern Pacific. UNION PACIFIC RAILROAD MUSEUM.

then, in his wispy voice, interrupting the answer with his next question. When
his bile was up he would end a question with, "answer me that!" Like Hill, he
worked at a plain, rolltop desk stacked with papers. He abhorred dictating letters because stenographers—he employed an army and they were said to work
in relays—couldn't keep up with him so he preferred the telephone, which
brought out the abrupt, snapping side of his temperament.

At home he was "Henry," affectionate, fun-loving, boyish as husband and
parent. He revered his wife, Mary, and their three daughters and three sons
born between 1881 and 1895 (including Averell, future U.S. ambassador to the

Soviet Union and to Great Britain and governor of New York). One of the family's doctors recalled when Harriman would meet for business with colleagues at his home; the meeting might stretch into the afternoon but when "the children's hour came, the men and affairs gave way to his children." The death in 1888 of his second son, Harry, at age five of diphtheria scarred Harriman for life. Perhaps he immersed himself in railroading to forget the pain.

At work he was "Ed" or "Ned" and later, publicly, the officious "E. H." He didn't go looking for fights in business but, "stiff-necked to a fault," if he happened upon one it was almost impossible for him to stay out of it. He became known later in his career as Hill's equal for control of the western railroads, but aside from a trip to Fort Worth in 1890 he had no real firsthand experience with the west until he was forty-eight. In August 1870, the same month Hill signed a contract to run a steamboat business on the Red River toward Winnipeg, Harriman borrowed $5,000 from an uncle to become, at age twenty-two, member number 281 on the New York Stock Exchange. He was the only one of the four principals in this story to set foot on the floor of the Exchange. To survive as a floor trader one needed sharp elbows, an in-your-face attitude. No surprise he liked to box as a boy, and despite his puny build was quick and cunning.

For the next decade, as railroad stocks dominated the Exchange, he became, and always remained, a creature of Wall Street. He profited as a "piker," or small-stakes commission broker, from the speculation of others on even the slimmest of margins, through all the stock-plunging episodes of Jay Gould and Daniel Drew and all the market-shaking events—the Chicago fire of 1871, the Boston fire of 1872, the financial panic of 1873 and six-year depression that followed, and "Deacon" White's plot to corner the anthracite coal market in 1874. He became a student not merely of the earnings of railroads, their operating expenses, their charges for depreciation, their deductions for construction, the nature of their assets and liabilities, but he also had the "infinite capacity of taking pains" to look behind the balance sheet to the true condition of the roads themselves.

Unlike Hill, Harriman essentially was friendless. There was one exception and she became the love of his life. He married into money and social status. Mary Williamson Averell, perceptive and wise beyond her years, was the daughter of a bank president and railroad owner in Ogdensburg, New York. Her father, William, put his new son-in-law on his railroad board. Harriman also bought and rebuilt a rundown railroad of thirty-four miles that led to a harbor on Ontario Bay, and sold it to the Pennsylvania Railroad for $200,000.

In 1881 Harriman leapt from brokerage to railroad finance, connecting through old New York money to the Illinois Central, the nation's first land grant railroad. It had been built in the 1850s by New York merchants and controlled and operated into the early 1880s by wealthy merchant William Henry Osborne, who made his fortune trading in the Philippines and bought the Illinois Central when it was almost bankrupt in the mid-1850s. The Illinois Central under Osborne, beloved for dependable dividends, was a darling of New York society, owned in large blocks by blue bloods such as the Astors, Goelets, and Cuttings. He had a summer home in Garrison, New York, next to U.S. Secretary of State Hamilton Fish, former governor of New York and former U.S. Senator. Osborne was comfortable in that society, and in the early 1870s he chose Fish's twenty-one-year-old son, Stuyvesant, to be his secretary. Young Fish, lumbering, personable, well connected, joined the Illinois Central board a few years later. When Osborne died in 1883 Fish gradually assumed working control of the railroad and became its president in 1887.

Fish met Harriman when they socialized among the wealthy at the Travelers Club on Nineteenth Street in New York City. They also were together on the board of the railroad owned by Harriman's father-in-law. Fish now turned to Harriman to sell bonds to finance the Illinois Central's extension south of St. Louis toward New Orleans. Two years later Harriman's firm became the railroad's financial agent and conduit to the capital markets. Fish put Harriman on the board as part of his plan to use the railroad's sterling credit to finance aggressive extensions.

Many railroads had to go into the bond market, paying interest of 7 to 8 and as high as 10 percent. The Illinois Central with its sterling credit inherited by Fish, soon with his new agent Harriman, could sell bonds at three and a half percent interest at par, and did so through the 1880s and 1890s. "If you buy a small railroad capable of earning six percent with the proceeds of a sale of three-and-one-half percent bonds," wrote John Moody and George Kibbe Turner in their perceptive "Masters of Capital in America," "you make a profit of two and one half percent a year; and when transactions run into the tens of millions of dollars, profit of this kind mounts up."

In a few years, the Illinois Central through Harriman was "buying railroads with three percent bonds; that is, he was paying about one third the price for his capital that many a large railroad had been paying only twenty years before." Fish and Harriman used three and a half percent money to extend the Illinois Central through acquisitions from 2,000 miles of track in 1883 to

5,000 miles in 1897. Harriman gained more influence by buying a large block of Illinois Central stock and persuading a Dutch investor in the Illinois Central to name him proxy for his firm's shares. During all these years plodding through the minutiae of railroad finance there was, in the memory of those who knew him then, not a single sign of "greatness," nor a single close friend.

When Harriman took control of the Union Pacific in 1898 he borrowed Fish's private Illinois Central car and put it at the head of a special train of Union Pacific cars with a locomotive at the rear so he could get a firsthand, front-car view of the entire Union Pacific system. He and five other Union Pacific officers departed Union Depot in Kansas City and, traveling only during daylight, covered the 6,200-mile system in twenty-three days. Nothing escaped his attention. "He noticed everything," said one colleague, "he asked you about everything." He asked at one stop why the water pipes, which supplied the engines at each station, were only four to six inches wide. On the last day of the survey, when they reached Denver, he told his associates he had just wired the Union Pacific office in New York to buy 5,000 shares of Union Pacific preferred for his account, and he bought large blocks of Union Pacific common for months. He asked the board for immediate approval to invest an astounding $25 million in new equipment and improvements.

In his first ten months as head of the railroad Harriman scrapped more than one thousand Union Pacific cars. And he did take care of those water pipes, not only replacing them with pipes twelve inches wide but also buying bigger tanks to hold more water. Now it took fifty-three seconds, not two or three minutes, to water the Union Pacific's engines. That saved one minute and thirty nine seconds for every train, times how many water stops for every Union Pacific train every day, every week, every month, every year? Harriman fixated on every last penny of waste, on the waste of needless movement of cars at terminal facilities, the waste of cars that could be built wider to carry more if only the gauge of track were wider, the waste of one-track roads that could carry traffic in only one direction at a time instead of double-tracking, the waste of idle tracks in the summer that could be carrying coal, the waste of coal burned by idling locomotives. "The train makes money when it is going somewhere, when it is carrying something that somebody wants," he once wrote. "When it stops it ceases to make money and becomes a losing proposition."

Harriman was intuitive and self-confident, with a lighting-swift, analytic mind. Unlike Hill he had no talent, finesse, or appreciation for communicating with large audiences. He rarely put pen to paper, perhaps because he had

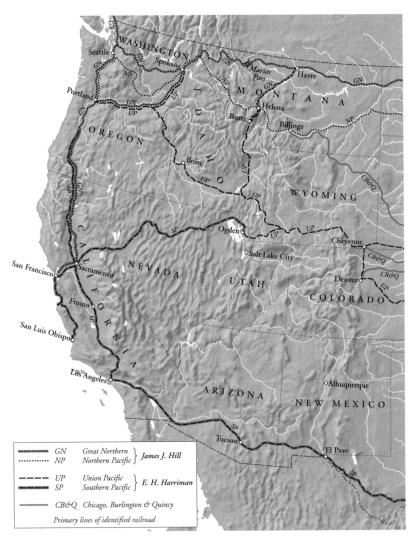

Harriman's and Hill's routes across the western United States. SOURCE: FINANCIAL REVIEW, 1898.

no feel for writing. "It's a great big opportunity for us doing," he once wrote. He is known to have given only one speech, and to have written only one opinion piece—and that was when his back was against the wall in a bitter dispute with President Roosevelt in 1907 over federal regulations. He regretted having left it to "subordinates to explain things to the general public . . . we have got to come out in the open and tell people the railroads' side of the matter." But

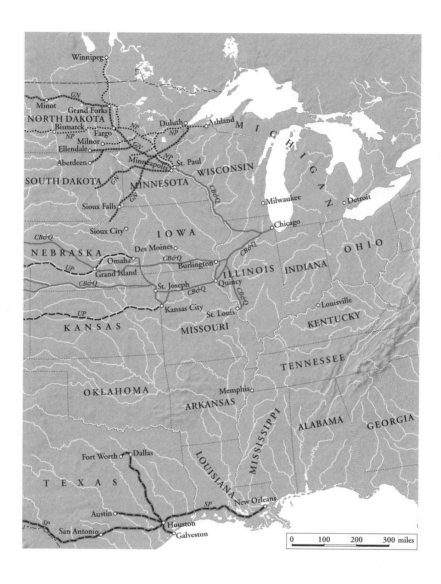

it was too little, too late; he died two and a half years later. He relied heavily on the telephone and telegraph because they enabled him to work fast and left little or no paper trail. In his mansion at Arden there were, by one estimate, one hundred telephones, sixty linked to long-distance lines. "What the brush is to the artist, what the chisel is to the sculptor," said one writer, "the telephone was to Harriman."

By century's end, even after two decades in railroading, despite his masterful revival of the Union Pacific, Harriman was largely unknown, hidden behind the balance sheet. His was not then a headline name, one had to search for it buried in news stories.

On April 3 Harriman wouldn't have been able to see the *Teutonic* glide down the North River because of the low clouds and rain, but he knew Morgan was departing for Europe at this hour, and that for eight days on the North Atlantic Morgan would be beyond the reach of cables, out of touch with his headquarters at "the corner" of 23 Wall Street and Broad. For another two months, moreover, Morgan's contact would be limited to trans-Atlantic cables. And so, this hour triggered the next step in Harriman's audacious plot. He had to protect his territory from Hill's invasion. The Burlington, soon to be in Hill's hands, threatened him at both ends of his landlocked Union Pacific. On the west it competed for his mining traffic. On the east, the Union Pacific's tracks stopped at the Missouri River at Omaha. From there across Iowa and Illinois it depended on other railroads for transport to Chicago and for freight and passengers from the east. This was exactly where the lineament of the powerful Burlington webbed out over the western Mississippi Valley, right in Harriman's face, gathering in the abundance for shipment east and west.

By pursuing the Burlington, Hill had inserted himself into its turf war with the Union Pacific; he had barged into the gentlemen's club and tipped over the "community of interest" card table. Harriman had to make him pay for it. If Hill got the Burlington, the "point of his plow" would be aimed squarely at the heart of the Union Pacific, which then might lose all the eastbound freight it got from the Northern Pacific and all the westbound freight it got from the Burlington. If Harriman got the Burlington he could fence Hill out of the southern territory that produced the cotton and other freight Hill needed to fill his empty westbound trains.

Harriman had tried to buy enough of the Burlington's widely dispersed shares on the open market to at least gain a seat on its board. That failed. He had tried to negotiate an outright purchase or some alliance with Charles E. Perkins and Burlington's board. That failed. So, now he would try to get the Burlington through another door—seize it in an unprecedented stealth raid of the common and preferred stock of the publicly traded company that would own half of it, the Northern Pacific, bankrupt twice the last three decades but now "re-Morganized" with Hill as its largest individual stockholder. If Harriman couldn't get the cream, as was said, he would go after the cow. Or as one editor later put it, the bass had swallowed the minnow but the pike would swallow the bass.

Morgan himself had always insisted that to keep the peace each railroad system should develop its own territory. It should not invade a neighbor's "sphere of influence." Where, however, did one sphere end and another begin? The Burlington's ambit overlapped two strategic spheres in the Midwest and West, rich in natural resources. It was in this contested land, some of the most fertile soil on earth, which some called the amorphous "middle border" but essentially was Illinois to central Nebraska, where the greatest battle in the history of American railroads was to be fought.

Mr. Schiff: 27 Pine Street, New York City

As he had done almost every day the past four years, often many times a day, Harriman picked up the transmitter of one of the dozens of silver candlestick telephones in his office this April 3, 1901. He talked to the man who would lead the attempt to seize Hill–Morgan's Northern Pacific, his financier and investment banker, Jacob Schiff. Schiff was two blocks away at his office on one of the lower floors of the thirteen-story granite headquarters of Kuhn, Loeb & Company, a block north of Wall Street at 27–29 Pine Street, second most prestigious thoroughfare in New York's financial district.

The past quarter century, Schiff had become the "Jewish grand duke" of American finance, rising to head the investment banking firm, second only to Morgan and perhaps even superior. The era's most respected financial writer called Kuhn, Loeb "the most intelligent banking firm in the country." Schiff and his tribe of intermarried German Jewish bankers had reorganized, refinanced, and restored to profitability dozens of railroads, all driven into debt trying to protect themselves from competitors by building systems requiring enormous capital and credit. As proxy for European investors, Schiff with Kuhn, Loeb could deliver that capital and credit. However, beyond their sizeable fees, which normally totaled, like Morgan's, at least 10 percent for underwriting, there was another price to pay: to protect their investment they often demanded a voice in governance.

With his elegantly trimmed white goatee, large blue eyes, and small, plump hands, Schiff was every inch patrician. He was only five foot two but carried himself with such equipoise that he created an illusion of height and could fill a room with his presence. He was a giant of intellect, financial acumen, self-discipline, patience, and diplomacy; a forceful, demanding, sometimes petty, often tempestuous personality. "Behind the gray suede glove," someone said of the Kuhn, Loeb crowd, "there was an iron fist."

Schiff descended from rabbis, Talmudic scholars, scientists, and merchants in Frankfurt, Germany, back to at least the early seventeenth century and perhaps further: the *Jewish Encyclopedia* said the Schiff family had the longest continuous lineage of any Jewish family of its time, back to the thirteenth century and the city's ancient Judengasse ("Jews' alley"). In his more expansive moments, Schiff even claimed ancestry to King Solomon, David, and Bathsheba.

Schiff was the third of five children, born January 10, 1848, to Clara (nee Niederhofheim), a woman with an independent streak, and Moses Schiff, a stockbroker on the Frankfurt Stock Exchange. As a boy he showed an "extraordinary single-mindedness." The Germans called it *Pflicht und Arbeit* (duty and work). After carefully saving $500 he gravitated from Frankfurt to other large financial centers, first to New York at age nineteen where he cofounded a small brokerage firm, six years later to London where he joined M. M. Warburg of Hamburg as their representative to the London & Hanseatic Bank. Then in Frankfurt he met Abraham Kuhn. With his brother-in-law, Solomon Loeb, Kuhn had trod the path of so many successful German Jewish immigrants in America in the mid-nineteenth century, from peddler (many of whom extended credit) to merchant (in their case, making blankets and pants for the Union Army) to private banking in New York City, founding Kuhn, Loeb & Company in 1867 at 31 Nassau Street.

With a referral from Kuhn, Schiff connected with Loeb. His timing was perfect. There was only one major source of capital after the Civil War for New York bankers, and it was the banking houses and bourses of London, Berlin, Paris, Frankfurt, and Amsterdam. This put a premium on a smart young financier from Europe who had cultivated contacts along that axis. Further, he joined the tribe. At Kuhn, Loeb, as with other Jewish firms of the time, "the family was business and the business was the family." Abraham Kuhn and Solomon Loeb had married each other's sisters; the pattern continued for forty-four years after they founded their firm. Every partner of Kuhn, Loeb was related by blood or marriage to the Kuhn, Loeb, and Wolff families. Only five months after joining the firm in New York, Schiff married the senior partner's daughter, Therese Loeb. Solomon and his wife Betty gifted them with a brownstone at Park and Fifty-Third. In just a few years, still a junior partner and not yet thirty, he was speaking for the firm.

Schiff spoke German with his family at home, wrote in German to his family and friends in the homeland, and spoke English with a thick German accent, but like a character patterned after him in a 1905 novel, "he knew English thoroughly like a scholar—a German scholar." His letters, penned in an elegant and forceful cursive, had a smooth, aristocratic tone, with a weakness for flattering and patronizing favored clients. Unlike wealthy New York gentiles, who tended to keep to themselves, he was an inveterate stroller to both synagogue and office, not just for exercise but to gather market intelligence and chat with customers, in the footsteps of the legendary German Jewish peddlers who rose to the heights of American finance such as the Seligmans and Lehmans. He often walked in his rapid, short stride the three miles from his home on Fifth Avenue at Seventy-Fourth Street on Central Park all the way down to Fourteenth Street where he would board a horse-drawn hansom cab to the financial district. He was an exuberant hiker and bicyclist, and kept a trim figure in his frock coat and linen ascot ties, with a special touch of class: a fresh rose daily in his lapel.

Schiff never had a private secretary, kept his own calendar, and attended to every letter addressed to him. He was prompt to a fault. Nothing made him angrier than to arrive on time for a meeting and find others absent. He waited ten or fifteen minutes and then left. In his vest pocket he carried a small silver notebook holding two ivory tablets. "Whenever anything occurred to him that he wanted to do," said his brother-in-law Paul Warburg, "the little tablets would come out and he would quickly write down a memorandum on them. When he had accomplished the particular thing he had noted, he would run a line through it, and in the evening the tablets would be covered from top to bottom." Before going to bed he would review the day's notes and wipe the tablets clean for the next day.

Paul D. Cravath, senior partner of Kuhn, Loeb's law firm, found Schiff to be a "peculiar combination of gentle kindness and uncompromising severity... his conscience set very high standards for his own conduct and he held himself to a rigid adherence to those standards... and that made him uncompromising in applying to others the standards he so rigidly applied to himself." The wealthier Schiff became the more he pinched pennies, logging every phone call, saving string, recycling business letters for scratch paper. Sensitive to anti-Semitism ("Hebrew speculator" or "Hebrew tipster" were in common use), he avoided showy displays of wealth; he liked to travel in Pullman style, had a summer retreat on the New Jersey coast, but did not own a

Jacob Schiff, "Jewish grand duke" of American finance and head of Kuhn, Loeb & Company. Caught between Harriman and Hill in their battle for the Northern Pacific, he mistakenly thought "all paths would unite on the mountain top." PHOTOGRAPH BY PACH BROTHERS. COURTESY OF MINNESOTA HISTORICAL SOCIETY.

yacht and could well have afforded a larger, more ostentatious Fifth Avenue mansion. He had left his German homeland and its overt anti-Semitism but he was always wary of it just below the surface in America. Two years before the Northern Pacific corner he may have been aware of Harold Frederic's novel *The Market-Place* and its racist description of Jewish mannerism.

Schiff was an astute judge of markets, investor psychology, the complex maze of all manner of securities and bonds. With Schiff at the helm, Kuhn, Loeb became the so-called house of issue for railroads, the nation's largest corporate borrowers, through underwriting (helping guarantee an offering's success by pricing for risk), negotiating (commission sales and lending), and contracting (buying an entire "sure bet" offering).

Schiff liked to say he wasn't a railroad man but that was just a front; he had an encyclopedic knowledge of American railroads and their securities, operations, and management. Unlike Morgan, he knew them firsthand, from the rails up. He had personally surveyed thousands of track miles from coast to coast with his client railroad owners, chatting up brakemen and engineers, painstakingly forging an intimate working knowledge of all major American railroads. He seemed to carry a detailed map of their systems and geography in his head.

At age twenty-nine in 1877, Schiff arranged his first financing for a railroad, the Chicago & North Western, earning a fee for Kuhn, Loeb of $500,000. This was two years before a forty-two year old J. P. Morgan handled his first significant transaction for Vanderbilt's New York Central. By 1881, at only thirty-four, Schiff was named to the board of the Erie Railroad and so began his practice of joining the boards of the major railroads that Kuhn, Loeb financed. To ensure vigilance, Schiff didn't much trust firsthand surveys of railroad properties whether he or some outside expert did it. There was no substitute for eyes and ears at headquarters. "To form a more proper judgment about the management and resources of a road," he wrote his European mentor Ernest Casell, "an investigator ought to stay at the operating headquarters for several months, so that he can report intelligently about possible weaknesses in management and remedies therefore." By 1885 he was the undisputed head of Kuhn, Loeb, styling himself the master conciliator who could bring together opposing forces and mediate peace for mutual profit. A formal dinner, quietly engineered by Jacob Henry Schiff, should be able to resolve almost any dispute. "On the mountain top," his father used to say, and Jacob liked to repeat, with a biblical ring, "all paths unite."

Giving every appearance of inflexible moral rectitude, Schiff like Morgan tried to weave his religious principles into the way he did business. When he read Sirach 5:8 from the Torah he must have taken it personally, "Do not depend on dishonest wealth; for it will not benefit you on the day of calamity." There was, to be sure, a practical benefit: trust, honesty, and reputation were the coin of the realm in investment banking. He faithfully lived the Torah's principles of worship, public service, and acts of kindness; he tithed all his adult life and gave tens of millions to charities.

Schiff sprinkled his letters with biblical allusions, to Noah's flood or Moses looking down on the Promised Land. He read every morning from his orthodox prayer book, pacing the rooms of his home. Family, strictly bound with religion, had to be walled off from business by obsessive regimen, what German Jews called *Familiengefühl*, literally "family feeling." He revered his parents, always marked the days of their deaths, and carried their faded photographs in his wallet. Dinner with his wife, son Mortimer, and daughter Frieda began at 6:30 *sharp*, especially Fridays. "I have made it a rule," he said, "to spend Friday evening exclusively with my family, and I can under no circumstances vary from this."

So every Friday evening Jacob and Therese gathered in a circle with Morti and Frieda in the drawing room of their long, narrow three-story home at 932 Fifth Avenue facing Central Park. Jacob blessed the children and in German said grace before their formal Sabbath dinner: "Our God and Father, Thou givest food to every living being. Thou hast not only given us life, Thou also givest our daily bread to sustain it. Continue to bless us with Thy mercy so that we are able to share our plenty with those less fortunate than ourselves. Blessed be Thy name for evermore. Amen." He also said grace after meals. Even when Morti and Frieda were grown and married, Schiff stopped by their homes the night of Hanukkah to make sure candles were lit and prayers said.

He strictly observed the Sabbath—no letter writing, no reading business mail or market quotes. He was less strict with kosher diet laws but didn't eat forbidden foods, and he fasted for Yom Kippur. This April 3, 1901, he was preparing for Passover at sundown, marking the deliverance of the Jews from slavery in Egypt. He likely attended services in the evening conducted by his fiery rabbi, Dr. Joseph Silverman, at Temple Emanu-El, the synagogue and sanctuary where the Schiffs had worshipped with the city's other prominent Jews for twenty-six years.

Temple Emanu-El ("God with us") was the wealthiest Jewish congregation in New York City, thus the most influential in the world. It stood socially prominent on the northeast corner of Fifth Avenue and Forty-Third Street, in all its Gothic and Moorish splendor with its twin towers 140 feet high, brown and bright-yellow brick and sandstone, and roof tiles in lines of red and black. Architect Leon Eidlitz had designed it to evoke Spain's golden age, when Jews served as ministers to both the Muslim caliphs and Christian royalty, and to symbolize the growing prominence of Jewish merchants in America.

Emanu-El was Reform in liturgy and ritual (no yarmulkes on men's heads, no Bar Mitzvah, no separation of men and women) not by accident. It wanted to assimilate, Americanize, reach out to Gentiles across religious boundaries.

Schiff was comfortable in this Reform atmosphere because it allowed him to work out his own code of conduct. This yearning to assimilate reflected his love for America and all it stood for: the freedom to earn one's material success, the pursuit of "happiness," freedom of speech and religion, respect for individual rights and property rights, the richness of ethnic diversity. For his soul and his people (whom he called his "co-religionists") it was the true promised land. That is why Kuhn, Loeb—sandwiched between two British insurance company buildings on the south side of Pine, two doors from the rear of the so-called Sub-Treasury and just around the corner from Morgan—proudly and prominently flew not the firm's colors but the American flag. Schiff was an unapologetic patriot. He once invited some forty financiers to a lunch at which Max Warburg, brother of the Felix who married Schiff's daughter, spoke briefly about events in Europe and his hope for America. When Warburg sat down, Schiff whispered to him, "Too short and not optimistic enough."

He had no appetite for a Zionist state. He was a Jew second, American first, a "faith Jew" not a "race Jew." He could be "entirely loyal" to only one country. "Be Americans above all else," he told his fellow "co-religionists" late in his life, when Zionism was in the air. "True Americanism does not mean only to fight for one's country, but also . . . to serve your country in your daily life."

Morgan, who had referred to Schiff as "that foreigner," could be openly antagonistic toward Jews and had a mean, anti-Semitic streak but Schiff seemed to be the only German Jewish banker he respected as a peer. Morgan even apologized to Schiff for trumping him in a contest to buy a coal company and tried to make amends by offering him a large share of the transaction. Like everyone else, however, Schiff carefully deferred to the Great One, addressing him always as Mr. Morgan. He even asked his permission before embarking in 1895 on the greatest, riskiest undertaking of his business career, refinancing the bankrupt Union Pacific. Schiff tried to get Hill interested in it in the early 1890s but Hill, his hands full building the Great Northern to Puget Sound, said he couldn't see honor or profit in it. Morgan and his partners studied the property carefully. Morgan himself served briefly on the committee representing Union Pacific's bondholders but, frustrated by all the government briar, deemed the project hopeless. It turned out to be the biggest strategic blunder of his career for it was the last great expanse of American railroad geography left for him to consolidate and reorganize, the broad arid land west of the Missouri from Nebraska to Oregon.

Morgan, however, was not a visionary. He dealt with reality. All he could see was an unpopulated desert. He was oriented east. He never really "got" the West the way German Jewish financiers such as Schiff and the house of Speyer (Central Pacific and Southern Pacific) did. For Jacob Schiff and Edward Harriman, then, the way to the Pacific suddenly lay open. The Union Pacific turned out to be for them, and their bondholders and stockholders, "the greatest single railroad fortune in the world."

In October 1895, after being approached by the personal counsel of George J. Gould, son of the late Jay and head of the Denver & Rio Grande and Missouri Pacific railroad systems, Schiff formed a committee to draft a plan to reorganize the Union Pacific, pay off its federal debt, retire the railroad's securities, and create a new capital structure and rebuild the road. The Union Pacific's physical property had deteriorated but the earnings potential of its geography was undervalued. When it went bankrupt in October 1893 it had 8,167 miles of track. By 1895 it had shed unprofitable branches and slimmed to 4,469 miles. The first attempt to reorganize it failed in early 1895 but now the stars and the markets were aligning. The economy had a pulse again. Mining in the Rockies would revive and so would freight volume on the Union Pacific. William McKinley—seventh of nine children, son of an iron furnace manager from rural Ohio, Antietam veteran, former congressman and Ohio governor, devout Methodist, resonant orator, temperate, morally earnest—was on his way to the presidency, pro-tariff and for a gold-backed dollar. He would be good for business. "Markets are better than maxims," he was quoted saying, and who could disagree? He was called "the most popular man in the country," more so than Morgan.

Throughout 1896, Schiff and his committee labored to persuade lawmakers, regulators, editors, and Union Pacific's shareholders that their plan was best for all concerned. They would give to each class of the company's securities a claim to interest prorated to the system's expected earnings. They would issue preferred stock that would pay a dividend only if the road earned it. Common stockholders, in the Morgan style, would help pay for the reorganization with a stiff fee for every share they owned. Sound as their plan was it encountered an annoying, mysterious resistance. Who was behind it?

Morgan? No, said Morgan, it wasn't him but he would find who it was. A few weeks later he summoned Schiff to his office. "It's that little fellow Harriman...that little two-bit broker," said Morgan, "and you want to watch him carefully. He's a sharper."

Schiff first encountered Harriman in 1884 after Harriman joined the Illinois Central board. Ten years later, under Harriman's watch, Kuhn, Loeb marketed some Illinois Central bonds and helped it acquire the Chesapeake, Ohio & Southwestern. Then in the winter of 1896–1897 Schiff and Harriman met several times to discuss Harriman's need for the Illinois Central to have access, as the Chicago & North Western had, to the Union Pacific at Council Bluffs in western Iowa. It was perhaps during these discussions that Schiff, as he recalled it, asked Harriman if he was behind the resistance to his Union Pacific reorganization plan:

HARRIMAN: I am the man.

SCHIFF: Why are you doing it?

HARRIMAN: I want to reorganize the Union Pacific myself.

SCHIFF: But how are you going to do it? We have all the bonds in, and what means have you to reorganize the company?

HARRIMAN: The Illinois Central Railroad ought to have that property. In the Illinois Central we have the best credit in the world...I am stronger than you are.

SCHIFF: Well, you will have a good time doing it, Mr. Harriman, but in the meantime what is your price?

HARRIMAN: There is no price to it. I am interested in the Union Pacific Railway and I am determined to take charge of the reorganization.

SCHIFF: Are there no terms on which we can work together?

HARRIMAN: If you will make me chairman of the executive committee of the reorganized company I will join forces with you.

SCHIFF: That is out of the question. Mr. Pierce [Winslow, counsel to

George Gould who brought the Union Pacific plan to Schiff] is to be chairman of the new company. I think he deserves it.

HARRIMAN: Very well, Mr. Schiff, go ahead and see what you can do. Good day.

Then sometime later that spring of 1897, Schiff called on Harriman to explain again why Pierce should run the plan:

SCHIFF: If you will join with me, I will put you on the executive committee as soon as the company is reorganized. Very likely, if you prove to be the best man on the committee, you will get the chairmanship.

HARRIMAN: All right, I'm with you.

In June, Harriman took a $2.2 million share in Schiff's underwriting syndicate (investing $1.1 million more a year later), and the same month traveled across Iowa, Nebraska, and Colorado to see the country himself. A reader of the *Wall Street Journal* in 1897 would notice what Schiff and Harriman knew. The Union Pacific was not two streaks of rust. Its reorganization committee already had reinvested much of the railroad's surplus into new rails, bridges, and cars. The Union Pacific was in "as fine condition . . . as anything in the West."

Early Sunday morning, October 31, 1897, under a gray sky over the broad and open prairie a special train of private cars from New York arrived in Omaha at the Union Pacific headquarters terminal. Off stepped Schiff and other members of the reorganization committee for what was billed as "the greatest auction sale ever held in America," the federal government's unloading of the Union Pacific Railroad. Schiff's committee was the only bidder but he was anxious nonetheless. He had carefully studied the Union Pacific for four years before deciding to embark on a reorganization plan, but he paced the floor of his hotel room that night wondering if after a quarter-century career in railroad finance he had finally bit off more than he could chew.

The next morning he was present with five hundred others for the legal ceremony at the Union Pacific's local freight house at Ninth and Jones. The government auctioneer spent forty minutes reading in a quiet monotone, scarcely audible a dozen feet away, the published notice of sale for the railroad's line and property from Council Bluffs, Iowa, to Ogden, Utah. The only bid was for $58,564,932.76, the total price eventually $81.5 million.

Harriman quietly joined the Union Pacific board the following month. Hill in St. Paul scanned the list of the new Union Pacific board members. He knew them all, except one. "Now, who the hell," he asked, "is Harriman?"

Much to his delight Harriman found himself in a power vacuum on the board. "Let me be but one of fifteen men around a table," he once said, "and I will have my way." And he did. He was elected chairman of the executive committee May 23, 1898, and became unquestioned head of the Union Pacific. With his certainty of purpose Harriman could synchronize a directors' meeting so "all their pendulums would swing together." Schiff was there by his side, on both executive committee and finance committee, from 1899 through 1906.

The next three years Harriman, under Schiff's financing plan, revived the Union Pacific in an astounding turnaround. During that time it did spend the $25 million Harriman had requested on new track and better equipment, more than twice what the Atchison, Topeka & Santa Fe spent during that time even though it had 70 percent more miles. The Union Pacific laid 42,000 tons of heavier rail on 400 miles of track in just sixteen months. The capacity of its freight cars doubled. Its net revenue doubled in three years. It spent sixty-two cents to earn a dollar of revenue in 1896 and fifty-three cents in 1902. By the end of its 1899 fiscal year on June 30 it had net earnings of $14 million and a cash surplus of $11.4 million. A year later it had $20 million in net earnings and it began paying dividends again. In 1898 it carried 476,000 tons a mile; in 1901, 664,000. In 1899 it regained its "lost outlet" to Portland on the Pacific Coast by buying back the Oregon Short Line and gaining control of the Oregon Railroad & Navigation Company. This, in effect, made Harriman's Union Pacific a northwest transcontinental. It not only competed directly with both Hill's Great Northern and the Hill–Morgan Northern Pacific but it cut off their access to the western tail of the Union Pacific.

Schiff's path crossed Hill's in 1886. Hill had bought and rebuilt what was originally intended to be a south-to-north railroad between St. Paul and the Canadian border. When he pivoted west toward the Pacific he needed more aggressive financing, and for that he leaned on his head of finance, the astute, well-connected Scot immigrant John Stewart Kennedy, who, with little formal education, had made his fortune with Hill and risen to the heights of railroad finance. Kennedy had to find a way to finance the construction in an overbuilt, overbonded railroad market. Hill always wanted to be his own banker, relying first on the cash surplus in his railroad's treasury and then, if necessary, going to his own stockholders, who numbered scarcely more than a hundred in the early 1890s. When all else failed, he forced himself to go to investment bankers, but preferred conservative, low-profile Boston money. Kennedy persuaded him the time had come to go to New York. They needed Kuhn, Loeb for its credibility with European investors, with Baring Brothers and Rothschilds in London, with the Banque de Paris, with Hope and Company and Amsterdamsche Bank in Amsterdam, and with the Warburgs in Hamburg.

Schiff's first offering of bonds in Europe for Hill's railroad oversubscribed five or six times. The next year he sold another $2 million for Hill and Kennedy. He used his success in these offerings to demand a take-or-leave option on large amounts of future extension bonds. It was vintage Schiff: always attaching strings, provisos, and conditions to any offer. In philanthropy, he is said to have invented the matching gift. In 1891, Hill hosted Schiff and other investors on a tour of his railroad to the Rockies. Later that year, Kuhn, Loeb bought 7,500 shares of the Great Northern's preferred stock for $5 million, Schiff joined the board and remained on it through the end of 1901, then helped raise a loan of $500,000 for Hill to help country grain elevators buy wheat and hold it for farmers' accounts until prices rose later in the season. When Hill needed to finance the last major extension to Puget Sound he turned not to Kuhn, Loeb but to his friend Gaspard Farrer of H. S. Lefevre, London, perhaps for better terms.

Hill was a client of Farrer, Morgan, and the First National Bank's George F. Baker, though Schiff liked to say "but I am his friend." In 1894 they were close enough that Schiff could write Hill a prescient, detailed letter encouraging him to find a way to acquire the Northern Pacific and merge it with the Great Northern. Hill showed his appreciation in personal ways: giving Schiff's daughter Frieda and her husband Felix Warburg a sable cape and matching ponies for their wedding; hiring Schiff's son Morti to intern at Hill's offices in St. Paul and Duluth. Hill chose to have his Great Northern office in Schiff's New York building, only a few floors apart. Even during the Northern Pacific corner and panic many in Wall Street couldn't believe Schiff and Hill were opponents. It is testimony to Schiff's ego and his efforts to cultivate Hill that two years after the Northern Pacific corner and panic he sent him as a New Year's gift a large formal photo portrait of himself, as if he expected Hill to frame and display it. Some in Hill's circle didn't trust Schiff and didn't hesitate to share their feelings with the boss. Hill's loyal lieutenant, Edward T. Nichols Jr., who had his Great Northern office in the Kuhn, Loeb building, confided to Hill in 1894 that he suspected Schiff had misled him and that Kuhn, Loeb, besides offering Great Northern bonds in Paris as Schiff said they would, had sold some of them short in London and then delivered them in New York, pocketing the arbitrage.

On that fateful day in the spring of 1897 Schiff had to put personal relationships aside and make the most agonizing business decision of his career. Stay loyal to Hill or join Harriman to reorganize the Union Pacific? Schiff, for whom reputation meant everything, chose Harriman, for whom "managing" reputation meant so little. Schiff had crossed the Missouri River but perhaps also his personal Rubicon. Or maybe not. Perhaps he thought he could juggle both Harriman and Hill as clients; he remained, after all, a board member of both Harriman's Union Pacific and Hill's Great Northern. He knew, however, how delicate the balance of power would be in the consolidation war sure to come.

In his private moments perhaps he worried that if the reorganization of the Union Pacific succeeded it could set him on a collision course not only with Hill but with Morgan too. Schiff already had an ominous hint of this. The day before Morgan departed for Europe, a procession of supplicants strode into Morgan's white marble, six-story temple of finance at 23 Wall Street, next door to the Stock Exchange.

Morgan's office—where he would frown, mumble, harrumph, grunt orders, puff on his cigars, abruptly snatch at papers, and otherwise intimidate everyone around him—was on the first floor down a dark, narrow corridor, beyond folding doors, past the partners' area with its rolltop desks, mahogany walls, and high ceiling. Working at his paper-free desk with the door open, he was separated from observers only by a glass partition.

Among those granted an audience in the two days before Morgan left for Europe were those intimately involved in creating the new U.S. Steel: Schwab of the Carnegie Steel Company, Gary of Federal Steel, Converse of National Tube, Roberts of American Bridge Company. He even took time to visit with the notorious stock plunger John Warne Gates, chairman of the board of the American Steel and Wire Company. He could hardly stand to be in Gates's presence, so incensed was he with his boorish manners, high stakes gambling, whoring, and profanity, especially his market manipulation. It was perhaps at this meeting he told Gates, as the *New York Herald* reported it, "You will not be taken into the directorate of the United States Steel Corporation, Mr. Gates. Your reputation is of your own making and you are responsible for it. Good day, Mr. Gates."

Jacob Schiff also asked to meet with Morgan on April 2. He wanted to petition one last time to have Harriman's Union Pacific share in a third of the Hill–Morgan purchase of the Burlington, in cash of about $65 million or in joint bonds. Morgan refused to meet with him. Schiff, now firmly with Harriman, was shuttled instead to Bob Bacon who told him in so many words it was too late. Morgan was too busy to see him. Schiff said he told Bacon this was a "grave mistake." He repeated a warning he gave Hill a week later, that he should expect the consequences. The Union Pacific "would have to protect itself." The train had left the station.

3

THE END OF THE
"DAYS OF SMALL THINGS"

In just two years Edward Harriman had done what many, including J. P. Morgan and James J. Hill, thought impossible. He took control of and refinanced the federal government's foreclosed Union Pacific and began rebuilding large portions of its track and operations. It was a sort of secular fulfillment of Isaiah 40:4, "The uneven ground shall become level, and the rough places a plain." Harriman restored it to profitability and saw its common stock grow sevenfold from 5⅞ a share on April 3, 1897, to 48½ on January 2, 1900. He began the new year pursuing its strongest competitor to the east, the Chicago, Burlington & Quincy.

The Burlington system was the product of a half century of diligent, measured growth reflecting its New England roots—never growing too far ahead of settlement, always well-capitalized, conservatively managed. Ten of its eleven board members were Boston men. They disdained New York financiers, preferring to issue new bonds or refinance old ones through the capital of their shareholders rather than surrender any influence or control to Wall Street. Its founder was the French-born John Murray Forbes, descendent of a Scottish clergyman and son of a Boston merchant. Forbes had gone to China at age seventeen in 1830 and made a fortune cultivating access to the Hong merchants, intermediaries to the imperial court, and becoming a banker, broker, insurer, and freighter for foreign trading firms. When they overextended, lacked cash to pay their debts, and panic ensued, young Forbes learned the importance of a conservative, strong capital position. "Ship only if the chance of gain is very great but above all the chance of loss very small," he wrote. "Risk in trade at sea no more than you can afford to lose in that season." Returning home to Massachusetts he became a venture capitalist, investing in land, iron, and coal with shrewd timing.

The panic of 1837 wiped out railroads financed with state debt. The advantage swung to private investors, and Forbes bought the securities of railroads in Massachusetts, Maine, Connecticut, New York, and Pennsylvania. In 1845, he and others from Boston, then the center of railroad capital, bought the bankrupt Michigan Central Railroad Company from the State of Michigan. With the Forbes group as absentee owners in Boston but with operators and stockholders on the scene (for market knowledge and to appear locally owned), it gradually extended the line south of Lake Michigan, then into Chicago in 1852 just as it was emerging as railroad capital of the nation. "Imagine a deep black soil, almost every acre of which can be entered at once with a plough," Forbes wrote a colleague, "now for the first time opened to a market by railroad."

Burlington, Iowa, sat in a favored spot on the Mississippi in southeastern Iowa to accept this "enormous crop." It had no eastbound river to transport crops to Chicago but it did have the Burlington & Missouri River Railroad. The Forbes Group bought an interest in it and by 1856 linked Chicago, Burlington & Quincy with 210 miles of track to create the backbone of what became known as the Burlington. Forbes and his investors, however, were 1,200 miles away in Boston. They needed a manager on the ground in the west. Forbes chose to groom his nineteen-year-old nephew, Charles Elliot Perkins, for the job. Son of a Unitarian minister from Cincinnati, young Perkins had been a clerk in a fruit store and then moved to Burlington to work in the treasurer's office for the railroad. He was promoted to paymaster, assistant treasurer, superintendent of the Burlington-Ottumwa line, then to vice president, named to the board in 1875 at age thirty-five, and became head of operations west of the Missouri. He was a company man, a systems man, and long before it became standard process he created the position of auditor of statistics, "to judge whether we are getting all we ought to get, and spending as little as we ought to spend." He was portly, stout as a barrel, double-chinned, and sported a heavy mustache that obscured his mouth and gave him, in formal portraits at least, a blank, taciturn expression. He had a rumpled, unmade bed look, walked with a cane and always wore a suit, waistcoat, gold chain, and floppy brimmed hat to work. He was shy and reflective by nature, but if crossed he had a belligerent streak, as the unions discovered.

Perkins succeeded Forbes as president in 1881, when the Burlington was earning revenue nearly three times that of ten years earlier and continued to pay an 8 percent dividend. Transporting hogs, cattle, and grain east and lumber, coal, salt, building materials, and merchandise west, the Burlington under Perkins steadily pushed west into the territory of Jay Gould's Union Pacific, to Kansas City, St. Joseph, Omaha, Denver, Cheyenne, and Billings. By 1883 it was one of seventeen railroads serving Chicago, but it was a virtual granary on wheels, shipping 41 percent of all corn shipped through the city, 34 percent of rye, 33 percent of wheat, and 21 percent of oats. From 1875 to 1881, it doubled its track to 2,800 miles and almost doubled it again the next seven years to 4,900. It embedded itself into the culture of the plains, introducing alfalfa as a commercial crop in Nebraska and selling two million acres to twenty thousand settlers in the 1870s. It was a lifeline to the cities for settlers on the prairie, such as novelist Willa Cather who grew up in Red Cloud, Nebraska, a town built on the Burlington with a depot that received eight Burlington passenger trains a day. "The railroad is the one real fact in this country," says a character in one of her novels, "That has to be; the world has to be got back and forth."

Forbes and Perkins were one of the great partnerships of nineteenth-century railroad expansion—the marriage of Forbes's "eastern liquid capital, skilled and experienced in railroading" and Perkins's western enterprise and local management. During the 1880s Perkins from his Burlington, Iowa, office and Forbes from Boston looked northwest and found Hill a natural ally with a mutual interest. Hill and his financier Kennedy needed to broaden the capital base of their railroad to keep it independent and protect it against bear raids on its closely held stock. They also needed an alliance with a Chicago-based road. At Hill's request in 1883, Perkins and a group of Boston investors rode with Hill along his tracks from St. Paul into the Dakota Territory. Perkins later called it "probably the snuggest and best of the properties lying beyond St. Paul, with every mile of it in the best wheat country." By 1886 the Burlington had completed a double-track between Chicago and St. Paul. Hill leased land to the Burlington for a freight yard, gave it track rights to Minneapolis, and bought shares in the enterprise on the open market. The Burlington reciprocated by adding thirty-six investors in the Hill road and a Forbes nephew joined Hill's board: twenty-six-year-old Henry Minot.

For all its success, however, and despite all its investing in steel rails, lower grades, pneumatic signals, oil-testing machines, power air brakes, and automatic couplers, its intensive building in its natural markets, and its strong capital position and low debt, the Burlington never could summon the will

The initial target in the Harriman–Hill battle was not the Northern Pacific but the key to dominance in the West, the Chicago, Burlington & Quincy, run by systems-man Charles Elliot Perkins, who reported to a risk-averse Boston-based board. COURTESY OF MINNESOTA HISTOR-ICAL SOCIETY.

to control its own destiny by building to the Pacific Coast. The Burlington's big decisions were made in Boston, where its board convened on the seventh floor of the gray-white marble Sears Building overlooking the old State House. They decided to stop at the Rockies. Thus the incessant rumors that the Burlington would be the Pennsylvania Railroad's path to the Pacific. Were he not handcuffed to Boston, Perkins would have built to the Pacific himself, which was why he so envied Hill's ambition and independence. "Hill is in many ways a wonderful man, not only a prophet and dreamer, but he has a very natural facility for figures," he wrote to Boston investment banker Henry Higginson in late 1901. "He is a great man—there is no mistake about that."

Over the course of fifteen tumultuous years beginning in 1886—as the railroad industry endured rate wars, overbuilding, government rate controls, violent battles with labor, a four-year depression, and economic revival—Hill and Perkins built a bond of trust. They had the same principles: conservative, hands-on, intolerant of waste, relentless in their quest for efficiency, careful stewards of their properties, evangelists for diversity of revenue. "Our business will rest on solid foundations of agricultural, mineral, lumber, cattle and mercantile products," Hill wrote in 1886, "covering so wide a territory that any local failure of the one would not greatly affect any of the others, leaving us in a position to expect a good, steady average traffic at all times."

It was "good, steady" that enabled the Great Northern and the Burlington with their strong cash reserves to survive the panic of 1893 and the four-year depression. By then, however, the world had changed. Perkins had seen it coming since at least 1879 when he wrote, "sooner or later the railroads of the country would group themselves into systems and . . . . each system would be self-sustaining." By not building to the coast, the Burlington had chosen not to run one of those systems. It forced itself to rely more than ever on one state, Nebraska, and one commodity, corn. It had more track in Nebraska than any other railroad, more tracks there than it had in any other state. When the Nebraska corn crop all but failed in 1894 Burlington's gross revenue dropped by a fifth. Two years later with a bumper Nebraska corn crop, Burlington's gross revenue shot up $10 million. That was not exactly "good, steady" and Perkins and his board knew it. It had record earnings in 1900, and 1901 promised more of the same. Side tracks along western railroads were filled with freight cars, a sure sign of prosperity. How long could that continue? The Burlington, by limiting its path west, had concentrated its risk; it was one crop failure away from trouble.

There was another reason for the Burlington to sell itself. Consolidation, the grouping into regional systems, was in the air. To avoid the chaos of price wars and overbuilding that had seized the industry in the 1880s and early 1890s, the nation's largest, strongest roads had to influence or control competitors who had "cut rates almost to the price of axel grease." Customers such as Standard Oil and Carnegie Steel had eroded ("demoralized" as was said then) railroad rates. They demanded and got discounts (rebates) for high-volume business, a perfectly legitimate demand except that they were granted secretly and often at competitors' expense. Standard Oil was in many ways a creature of railroad rebates.

Responding to populist outrage over secret rates that seemed to favor large companies at the expense of small producers, the federal government made railroads the first regulated industry. The Interstate Commerce Commission, created in 1887, required the public posting of all rates (forbidding secret deals) and mandated that rates be "reasonable and just." It also forbade "pooling," the railroads' tool for ending rate wars by acting as if one company, sharing revenue based on percentage of traffic, though penalties at first were rare. The Sherman Anti-Trust Act of 1890 has been called "the first effort to control the economy at large." It forbade restraint of trade, whether reasonable or unreasonable, even though at first there was no federal agency to enforce it. Many states forbade the merger of parallel, competing roads. Then in March 1897 the U.S. Supreme Court on a five to four vote outlawed railroad traffic alliances.

The railroads finessed an entirely legal way around these barriers, enabling them, as someone said, to "drive a coach and four" through the Interstate Commerce Act. Operating costs were so high, profit margins so slim, that if railroad capital, profit, and dividends were to be protected, said Vanderbilt's Chauncey Depew afterward, "there will have to be concentration of control." Perhaps it was Morgan and Hill who came up with the idea. After the U. S. Supreme Court blocked their merger of the Northern Pacific and the Great Northern in 1896, they and their associates bought just enough Northern Pacific stock, some 35 to 40 percent of its shares, to have a dominant voice on Northern Pacific's board to enable them to control its rates. Morgan also surely supported the heads of the two major eastern trunk roads to make common cause, just as he did with them in the mid-1880s. Sometime in late 1898 or early 1899, William K. Vanderbilt, the Commodore's grandson and head of the Morgan-influenced New York Central, approached Alexander J. Cassatt of the Pennsylvania Railroad. Instead of competing, Vanderbilt offered, why not cooperate? If they invested together in competing railroads they could minimize rate wars for almost all northern railroad traffic from the Atlantic to the Mississippi. If Morgan joined them their influence could cover the south as well. Vanderbilt and Cassatt came to an agreement, never codified or signed.

Someone, no one seems to know who, chose an innocuous term to describe this understanding: "community of interest." It was one of those airy phrases that could mean everything and nothing and had even been used in the mid-1890s to describe employee profit sharing. In this case, however, Cassatt and Vanderbilt meant it as code for "community of ownership," a backdoor way to pool revenue, not by sharing it but by industry self-policing, strictly enforcing published rates. Broker Henry Clews called it "the new communism of capital." Morgan denied it was his idea but it bore his stamp of harmony, order, and efficiency over wasteful chaos, combination over competition. The interest of one would be the concern of all. It was, in a way, the affirming of property rights. Morgan himself defined it as "the principle that a certain number of men who own property can do what they like with it." Wasn't that America? It also could house a happy paradox to pacify Main Street investors. A handful of railroad capitalists, with two or three exceptions, could run most of the U.S. railroad system, but the majority of the stock of those railroads could still be purchased in small blocks by stockholders of modest means.

Jacob Schiff, an advocate for the principle, summed up its rationale before a government commission.

> It is human nature that every man tries to get ahead of his neighbor...When one carrier makes a rate of transportation the shipper goes to a competing road to cut under the rate, and the result has been more dangerous to the weaker interests of the country than any possible advantage derived from the anti-pooling legislation...If one road is injuring the other by reducing its rate of transportation and the other road has to meet that cut it stands to reason that the earnings of both are less. Thus the property suffers, and the railroad men are unable to pay high wages to their working force. If the stockholders of the one road hold stock in the other—not necessarily the controlling interest—they will not vote to take any action to reduce the values of their holdings. This is community of interest.

Almost overnight, with little public fuss, through "community of interest" the Pennsylvania Railroad and its subsidiary, the Pennsylvania Company, quietly became a sort of eastern railroad and coal trust. It bought 16 percent of the stock of the Chesapeake & Ohio (also jointly owned by the New York Central). It bought 24 percent of the Baltimore & Ohio (with significant investment from Hill). It bought 30 percent of the Norfolk & Western (with the New York Central), and part of the Long Island Railroad. The New York Central, likewise, bought control of the Lake Shore, the Boston & Albany, and the Michigan Central. The Wabash bought the Western Maryland. The Louisville & Nashville and the Atlantic Coast Line bought the Georgia Railroad. Harriman's Union Pacific bought the Alton, the Kansas City & Southern, and set its sights on both the Burlington and the Southern Pacific. Hill and his Great Northern partnered with Morgan to control the Northern Pacific and Erie. Almost every board of a major railroad, except Hill's Great Northern, was stacked with directors from other roads.

Practical pooling—through community of interest—replaced prohibited pooling of revenue. Formal traffic agreements became informal. The Eastern mergers alone were said to have covered eventually about 85 percent of the nation's railway miles. The New York Central and the Pennsy in just two years controlled 55,000 miles of railroad, about a quarter of the nation's tracks. Demand for railroad stocks soon outstripped supply, lighting the fuse for an explosion of stock prices, a "community of disaster" and the Northern Pacific corner. Into this froth, railroads issued even more stocks and bonds: $67 million worth in 1898, rising to another $434 million in new securities in 1901.

Propelled by "community of interest," America's railroads by early 1901 had swiftly consolidated into six super-regional systems: the Vanderbilt lines under the umbrella of the New York Central system in the Northeast (including the Chicago & North Western), the Pennsylvania (including the Baltimore & Ohio and the Reading), the Hill–Morgan lines of the northern tier (the Great Northern, Northern Pacific, and the Erie) and the Morgan-influenced southern system, the Gould lines (Missouri Pacific, Denver & Rio Grande), and the Harriman roads including the Union Pacific (and Southern Pacific, Kansas City & Southern), soon to be followed by the Moore brothers (Chicago, Rock Island & Pacific).

Time had run out for the Chicago-based roads. They could no longer escape "community of interest." The "days of small things," as Perkins put it, would soon be over. Linked as he was to his Boston board, this phrase undoubtedly refers to the famous passage from Edward Bellamy's utopian time-travel novel *Looking Backward* (1888), set in Boston in the year 2000. "The railroads had gone on combining till a few great syndicates controlled every rail in the land," says Bellamy's guide to the future, Dr. Leete. "The small capitalists, with their innumerable petty concerns, had in fact yielded the field to the great aggregations of capital, because they belonged to a day of small things and were totally incompetent to the demands of an age of steam and telegraphs and the gigantic scale of its enterprises . . . The epoch of trusts had ended in The Great Trust." Perkins confided to his daughter years later he feared someday he would end up as an office boy for Harriman or Hill. His board knew it, too. It set a price for its property: $200 a share, at a time when the Burlington was selling for about $140 a share.

Harriman now used the credit of the Union Pacific to pursue the Burlington just as he used the credit of the Illinois Central to buy the Union Pacific. He made overtures to the Burlington's number-two man, Robert Harris, in the summer and fall of 1899. Then he put a full-court press on Charles Perkins. At Harriman's request, they first met in January 1900, probably in Chicago, when both he and Hill perhaps were unsettled by unfounded rumors that the Burlington might want to build or link to the coast, after all. Perkins was wary and resolute from the start. He could afford to be. Hill was his preferred partner, his natural alliance, and the Burlington would be a far better fit with the Great Northern and Northern Pacific. He could play Harriman against Hill. Further, his board was dead set against Harriman. There also was something about Harriman's manner that probably annoyed him: the impatience and abruptness, the lack of finesse, the Napoleonic imperiousness. Perkins didn't like to be bullied or pressed. He could relax and share a joke and a cigar with Hill, but his discussions with Harriman had an icy formality. The Burlington is not marketing itself for sale, he told Harriman. It has no desire to be part of the Union Pacific. Harriman: What do you believe Burlington's stock is worth? Perkins: at least $200, in cash, period.

Harriman and Schiff plotted their next move. Weeks passed. Harriman asked to meet again. They did so on March 15, 1900, in Chicago, with Harris present. Harriman offered $140 a share in cash or $200 a share in Union Pacific 3 percent bonds. Perkins quickly dismissed both. Harriman asked to meet again the next day when he offered only $150. Perkins declined and repeated: $200, cash. At Harriman's request, they met a fourth time in Chicago, on April 21. This time, Harriman brought master conciliator Schiff with him, who said in so many words, well, Mr. Perkins, perhaps now is not the right time for an alliance between your system and ours. If you and your board, however, are someday inclined to discuss such a matter we ask only that you consult us first. The Burlington would never begin such a discussion, Perkins snapped, because it is not for sale nor does our board want to consider any alliance with the Union Pacific.

Perkins, however, could read a railroad map as well as anyone. The rejuvenated Union Pacific threatened to lure traffic from the Burlington in Nebraska and Colorado. It also had reacquired control of the line from Ogden, Utah, to Portland, Oregon, up to Puget Sound, the line built to avoid the limit Congress had put on the federally chartered Union Pacific. The Burlington had only two choices: build to the coast or merge into another line that did. Harriman and Schiff, in effect, had put the Burlington in play. "I believe Schiff and Harriman have some big combination in mind, and perhaps in hand, and there can be no doubt about the value of the CB&Q to any scheme for combining roads west of Chicago," he wrote on May 31, 1900, to Boston financier Thomas Jefferson Coolidge, who sat on the Union Pacific board with Harriman and Schiff and, in those days of interlocking directorships, also was on the Burlington board, lone director in favor of the Harriman offer. "The CB&Q cannot control any such combination without taking risks which I do not suppose our present stockholders want to take."

Three weeks after Perkins wrote Coolidge, Schiff took the next step. He and Harriman convened in Schiff's office in New York with two others to form a syndicate to buy Burlington's stock on the open market. One of those two was thirty-seven-year-old George Gould, the indecisive, self-indulgent, party-going son of the late Jay Gould, who had been, in many ways, the first western railroad visionary. After Jay Gould died in 1892, his son guided the Missouri Pacific, with significant investment from the Rockefellers, through the depression of the 1890s, sat on the Union Pacific board and its executive committee (as Harriman sat on his Missouri Pacific board), and was buying the Denver & Rio Grande, perhaps aspiring to extend to the Pacific.

The other man in the room with Harriman, Schiff, and Gould was small, inscrutable, mostly silent, elegantly dressed, with dark, penetrating eyes. Fifty-one year old James Stillman was president of the National City Bank, predecessor to today's Citigroup, and a member of the Union Pacific executive committee. In fact, Stillman's financial commitment to the Union Pacific reorganization was almost as large as Schiff's and Harriman's. He personally invested $5.8 million in Union Pacific bonds to pay off the purchase price, 60 percent more than Harriman and almost as much as Kuhn, Loeb.

Stillman's domineering presence at this meeting represented the extraordinary financial strength of the Harriman machine extending well beyond the Union Pacific treasury. Stillman now played a decisive role in Harriman's empire building, and Harriman in turn was on his board. If Harriman had wanted to pay $200 a share for the Burlington, Stillman's bank could have summoned the capital to buy it many times over. Groomed to be president by the legendary merchant prince Moses Taylor when National City Bank was the bank of choice for cotton merchants, Stillman had built it in the past decade into the nation's largest private reservoir of cash. It was chief depository for the City of New York, on its way to being America's first billion-dollar bank in assets, and held about one of every seven dollars on deposit among New York City's sixty-one banks. A decade later its financial resources would have made it the ninth largest state in the union.

Stillman was of Puritan New England stock, son of a cotton merchant, elected to succeed his father on the board of National City Bank in 1883. The next year he became a director of the Chicago, Milwaukee & St. Paul Railroad where he met fellow board member William A. Rockefeller. City Bank became the bank of the merchants of food (Armour) and oil (Rockefeller), where Standard Oil stashed its tens of millions in cash reserves. William Rockefeller became its largest shareholder, and Stillman's daughters cemented the alliance by marrying Rockefeller's sons.

Stillman's office with his paper-free desk was only a few doors from Morgan's on Wall Street. He had enormous personal influence, sitting on the boards of forty-one companies. He had met Harriman five years earlier, but Morgan had cautioned him to be wary and Stillman had, in his words, "steered clear of him." Harriman's revival of the Union Pacific, however, gave Stillman new insight into his ability. By 1899 he was part of a syndicate with Harriman, Schiff, and Gould that bought, in "community of interest" fashion, the antiquated, poorly managed Chicago & Alton Railroad, quadrupling its market capital by issuing stock, declaring an immediate 30 percent dividend, but also rebuilding virtually the entire road, increasing its net earnings 80 percent, and significantly lowering its rates. The perception of the deal seven years later as looting, instigated by a vengeful President Roosevelt and the Interstate Commerce Commission, haunted Harriman the rest of his short life.

Secretive like Harriman, Stillman moved in the shadows, rarely, if ever, speaking in public, concealing every maneuver. His blank, melancholy expression recalled an Oscar Wilde line: "For he to whom a watcher's doom is given as his task, must set a lock upon his lips, and make his face a mask." In Stillman, however, Harriman found a confidante. One evening between acts at the Metropolitan Opera, he entered Stillman's box and asked if he could see him for a moment. They walked to the cloakroom, then to a brougham that took them to Harriman's home at 1 East Fifty-Fifth. Harriman escorted him to the library where they sat and smoked cigars. Stillman asked what it was that Harriman wanted to discuss. Harriman replied with a sigh, "You must have been tired of that opera. I know I was, I thought we might pass the time better at home."

Like Harriman, Stillman kept his distance from Morgan who, it was said, never set foot in Stillman's office or home. He was a reticent loner by nature and now, indeed, did live alone. He had left his wife of twenty-five years in 1894. It was a bitter, vindictive separation. He cut her off from their five children and sent her to Europe for what turned out to be an exile of twenty-five years, though her name remained in the New York Social Register as Sarah Elizabeth Stillman.

He was a bundle of idiosyncrasy. He sometimes shaved three times a day, took an hour to dress, and was said to have glass-enclosed closets holding hundreds of pairs of shoes, suits, gloves, and ties. He would send dozens of eggs back to the kitchen for breakfast until four were boiled just right. In later life he dined alone at home in silence with a printed menu, footmen behind his chair, giving each entree a numeric score. He fawned over favored bank clients but disdained underlings. Stenographers froze in his presence to take dictation; one woman, it was said, fainted with pencil in hand.

Hill had Morgan but Harriman had even deeper pockets with Stillman and "Will" Rockefeller. Hill's longtime financial backer Gaspard Farrer, later of Baring and Company, summed it up when he wrote Hill a few years later that Harriman "has not a tithe of your grasp of transportation matters, and does not pretend to have, but in many other ways he is monstrously able . . . I can see no outfit that will at all be able to balance or cope with the particular interests of his moneyed associates." Farrer was not alone. One New York newspaper editor predicted in early February 1901 that if Hill tried to take on the Rockefellers and the Vanderbilts in a consolidation battle in the Northwest, "he would meet his Waterloo inside of sixty days."

Even with the financial might of Stillman, however, Harriman and Schiff couldn't crack the Burlington nut. Perkins must have been amused by their naïveté. The Burlington was one of the western world's most broadly held securities. Many of its shareholders had inherited the stock, dispersed widely across the United States and Europe, tucked in the safety deposit boxes of households, producing healthy, annuity-like dividends. Hill said the Burlington's books showed the average holding per stockholder was sixty-eight shares. It would be very difficult if not impossible to buy control, especially if one wanted to offer only $140 to $150 a share. Further, how could they think so many small individual stockholders would part with the time-tested certainty of its 8 percent dividend without the imprimatur of the man who had been the railroad's successful president for two decades? Charles Perkins to them was, indeed, Mr. Burlington.

The Burlington began 1900 at $124. By June it was at $131. There were 984,461 shares outstanding. By the first week of June, covertly using designated brokers to scour every investment house and large shareholder in America and Europe, Schiff and Harriman had come up with only 70,000 shares. Six weeks later they could buy only 10,000 more. By July 25 they stalled at 80,300, only about 8 percent of the stock outstanding. It had cost them $10 million. Harriman persisted. After a meeting he called in Chicago of the heads of Midwestern railroads on Sunday, August 12, he stepped aside with the Burlington's number-two man, Harris, and bluntly repeated that the Union Pacific and Burlington should merge.

About three weeks later Harriman took the train north to Perkins's summer home in New Hampshire, the first of two journeys there to see if Perkins at least might entertain a proposal to have one or two directors of the Union Pacific on the Burlington board and vice versa. Back home on the train he went both times, empty handed. By mid-September 1900, the Burlington had settled back to $124 a share with daily trading volume of only about 6,700 shares. Harriman and Schiff gave up in early November and began selling off the Burlington shares at prices from 130 to 140⅝. They dissolved the pool on December 21. By then, however, a tectonic plate had shifted in the industry. The Burlington suddenly moved off Harriman's center stage.

On Wednesday, August 15, 1900, a private railroad car of the Southern Pacific inscribed "Oneonta II" pulled by an engine of the New York Central departed Raquette Lake in the Adirondacks through the forest of northern New York. It carried a black mahogany coffin decorated in silver with bronze handles, carrying the body of seventy-nine-year-old Collis Potter Huntington, who had died two days earlier after a late night game of whist at his summer home on Pine Knot Camp. Huntington was born before the first railroad was chartered in the United States, raised in the valley of Poverty Hollow in Connecticut, peddled goods from a horse cart as a teenager, then went west to sell mining tools to gold diggers from a tent in Sacramento.

Huntington had financed and built with Leland Stanford, Mark Hopkins, and Charles Crocker the Central Pacific from Sacramento to Promontory, Utah, part of the nation's first transcontinental (linking with the nation's eastern

railroads). He then organized a subsidiary he called the Southern Pacific, originally to extend south from San Francisco to protect his flank against competitors with designs on California. The next two decades he bought and merged
twenty-six railway systems, stretching from Portland, Oregon, through San
Francisco and Los Angeles to New Orleans, the only western transcontinental
linking the Pacific and the Atlantic, via the Gulf of Mexico. It was, however, a
mess of a system, dysfunctional, haphazard, and poorly managed. Huntington confessed little knowledge of how to run a railroad. He bribed politicians
and enriched himself through the railroad's inside construction and finance
companies.

The train carrying his body wound to Utica and then Albany and into
Grand Central Station in New York City, and his body was brought to his grave
at Woodlawn Cemetery. He had warred against waste on his inefficient railroads, treating every four-penny nail like a spike, but he chose for his eternal
rest the most expensive mausoleum ($250,000) ever built at that time in the
United States.

The Southern Pacific, which Harriman knew he could improve, could
give him lines right through cotton country from New Orleans to Texas and
Arkansas, but he wanted the Huntington lines less for the Southern Pacific,
which didn't pay a dividend, than for the Central Pacific, which could give
the Union Pacific its natural extension from Ogden into San Francisco. About
a month before Huntington died, Harriman spent a final few days with him
and his associate Edwin Hawley at Huntington's camp on Raquette Lake.
Harriman, who six years earlier personally loaned Huntington $2.5 million
to keep his business afloat, now wanted Huntington's Central Pacific as his
entry into California. Over my dead body, Huntington may have thought. He
got his wish. Now, with Huntington gone, his shares passed to his widow and
nephew. In December Harriman negotiated personally with banker James
Speyer and Hawley, Huntington's chosen agents.

In January 1901 Speyer and Hawley sold the shares to Kuhn, Loeb who
in turn sold them, for a handsome fee, to the Union Pacific, giving Harriman
working control of the Southern Pacific, in "community of interest" fashion,
with 37½ percent of its outstanding stock. To pay for it the Union Pacific issued
$100 million in 4 percent bonds convertible to stock anytime before May 1906.
The new securities flooded the market but, fortunately for Harriman and
Schiff, they were issued into a rising economic tide. Investors bought it all
in a month. Hill and Morgan must have noticed: Harriman couldn't possibly

need all the proceeds just to buy control of the Southern Pacific. He was up to something else. Harriman used $40 million of the proceeds to buy Huntington's stock. The balance stayed in the Union Pacific war chest.

Meanwhile, Hill paced the sidelines, obsessed with gaining working control of the Northern Pacific from Morgan's voting trust. More than a decade earlier he had flirted with trying to buy it himself, but took the more conservative course and built his own line to the coast first. "The more I think it over the more I am convinced that the thing to do is to 'take the bull by the horns' and get control of the Northern Pacific," he had written George Stephen, president of the Bank of Montreal, in 1889, "and by one stroke settle all questions at once." But then came the panic of 1893, the bankruptcy of the Northern Pacific, his attempt to buy it derailed by the courts, and the Morgan "voting trust" control.

The death of Morgan's railroad mind, Charles Coster, in March 1900 accelerated the timing. Hill, who met several times with Morgan two months later in England, was getting impatient, pestering. Morgan was getting annoyed. Hill, however, had legitimate gripes. He and his associates believed they had lived up to their part of the agreement. Hill initially had bought from Morgan some 300,000 shares of Northern Pacific stock at $16 a share, a price Hill claimed was higher than what the shares later sold for, an investment he said he didn't need then or now, though his holdings soon proved fantastically valuable.

Through that investment Hill had improved the Northern Pacific's reputation and became its single largest individual shareholder. In exchange he had to stand by as Morgan's caretakers—whom he accused, in so many words, of incompetence and deceit—invested his money in what he considered "useless construction" and worthless branch lines (one to a nine-hundred-foot-deep coal shaft in Montana that never found a working vein), and failed to consult him before making decisions that affected the Great Northern, such as unilateral rate cuts. The problem was Morgan never set a date for giving Hill working control of the Northern Pacific. He promised to do it "within a reasonable time." Hill felt that time had come.

Into this acrimony stepped a mediator, a confidante and business associate of both Morgan and Hill. Sixty-one-year-old George Fisher Baker was the unquestioned dean of New York banking, president of the First National Bank of New York, called the "Fort Sherman" of banks. He had helped found it in 1863 as a mere twenty-three year old, and became its president in 1877. Also, as a venture capitalist he had bought and rejuvenated several railroads, and now, among America's half dozen wealthiest men, served on the finance committee of Morgan's new U.S. Steel, on the board of the Northern Pacific, and on the boards of some thirty banks, railways, and insurance companies.

After the panic of 1893 when fear seized the markets, Hill had sought a loan from Baker's First National for $300,000. "'I will send you by express tonight what you asked for,'" Hill remembered Baker as responding. "'If you actually need more I will take off my coat and go to work.' That transaction and that reply won me to George Baker for life. I would rather have his friendship and I would rather have his judgment in time of panic than that of all the other men between Trinity Church and the East River." At a word from Baker, it was later said, "the 20th Century would halt on its tracks." Indeed, the railroad came to Baker's door. When he built a mansion farther north at Ninety-Third and Park he had his own underground railroad siding in the basement where a train could stop to attach his private car.

One day in the fall of 1900 Baker casually mentioned to Morgan that Hill regretted his falling out with Morgan over the Northern Pacific and would like to mend things. "Yes," replied Morgan, "I should think he would." A private rapprochement was arranged. On the rain-soaked late afternoon of Monday, October 8, 1900, Hill and Baker climbed aboard Morgan's yacht, *Corsair*, anchored at the New York Yacht Club Station on the North River at the foot of Eighty-Sixth Street. They joined Morgan and Bacon for dinner amid its polished maple, lace curtains, and humidors of Cuban cigars. The windows of the *Corsair* glowed in the harbor darkness as they talked long into the night not only about the Northern Pacific but about the need for the Northern Pacific and the Great Northern to control their destiny in the Midwest, especially Chicago.

Morgan had been an intimate part of the Vanderbilts's New York Central for more than two decades. He knew how vital it had been for that system to extend west to Chicago in the late 1870s when it bought the Lake Shore. He now believed it was time for the Great Northern and Northern Pacific to do the same east to Chicago. Time was of the essence. Harriman would not settle very long for having his Union Pacific end at Council Bluffs on the east or depend merely on a traffic alliance with the Vanderbilts's Chicago & North Western across Iowa and Illinois. He also needed to control his access to Chicago. As Morgan later said, "if somebody wants a thing another man wants it, too."

Morgan said to Hill and Baker that night he thought they should pursue the St. Paul. It could be a joint purchase by the Great Northern and Northern Pacific for two reasons: to tie the two northern tier lines closer together, and to halve the debt burden of the purchase between them. Even so, Hill said the

George Fisher Baker, president of the First National Bank of New York, banker–confidante of Morgan and Hill and board member of the Northern Pacific and U.S. Steel. PHOTOGRAPH BY UNDERWOOD & UNDERWOOD. COURTESY OF BAKER LIBRARY, HARVARD UNIVERSITY.

Great Northern would have to earn at least another $10 million a year to afford it. Morgan volunteered to finance the purchase. The meeting ended at two a.m., and Hill and Baker climbed out onto the dock to get some fresh air. The sky had cleared, the stars were out, the Palisade cliffs of New Jersey rose high and black across the North River. They walked up and down the long dock in the dark, talking sotto voce, their breath fogging in the chill night air. Baker was a curious hybrid: conservative banker and venture capitalist. The banker side of him worried the St. Paul was too big a bite. "I was thinking about your statement to Mr. Morgan about the St. Paul," said Baker, "You know, J. J., ten millions would be a very large increase in annual earnings." Hill replied with a laugh, "Why, George, that's all right. I didn't dare tell him what I really thought. It will be a great deal more than that."

Less than a month later, November 6, 1900, McKinley vanquished William Jennings Bryan for the second time in four years. The next morning at the Stock Exchange the public galleries were jammed to capacity for the opening bell at 10 a.m. When it rang it unleashed a din of howling and shrieking, some 750 traders jamming the floor, a fourth more than normal. The market ignited with huge gains in a burst of optimism. There was so much buying some brokers had to turn away orders. Everything was up. The bears had nowhere to hide. Call loans were as low as 1 percent. On the curb market, Standard Oil rose twenty-five points over its old record high of 650. "This country is entering upon an era of prosperity," said veteran Exchange member Arthur A. Housman, "that has never been seen. We are the greatest exporting country in the world. We are going to be greater . . . The opening of our new era is . . . a renaissance of investment and speculation." Whispered to be "Morgan's broker," Housman the incurable optimist had founded in 1885 what became the oldest direct predecessor of Merrill Lynch, building his personal fortune during the first four McKinley years.

The following Saturday Hill boarded a train in St. Paul for New York. As Hill's private car rolled east through the night on Monday, November 12, Henry Villard, tortured by his Northern Pacific failures, immobile for days after a series of strokes, unconscious for almost a week, died just after midnight at age sixty-five at his country home near Dobbs Ferry, New York. He and his wife, Fanny, had made one final tour over the Northern Pacific route the previous year. That morning, Hill strode into the lobby of marble and onyx of the Hotel Netherland at Fifth and Fifty-Ninth, his preferred location in New York City, on the plaza off Central Park and checked into his room. Shortly after two p.m. the voting trust that had controlled the Northern Pacific since 1896 voted to dissolve itself. Morgan cabled Hill, "many congratulations."

Morgan would transfer his minority control to Hill, who now at last could have a free and direct hand in making it more efficient and profitable. The numbers were there for all to see. Morgan and Coster, for all their effort the past four years, were merely short-term asset managers. The Northern Pacific tracked across more supposedly fertile, mineral-rich soil in many areas than the Great Northern, but Coster couldn't make it perform to Hill's standards. The two railroads covered about the same distance, but for the 1898–1899 fiscal year Hill's Great Northern carried 72 percent more tons of freight, 18 percent more tons per mile, had 23 percent more freight density, and 21 percent more average tons per train, all at rates per ton mile 14 percent less than the Northern Pacific.

The New Year dawned with wild enthusiasm in the streets and in the stock market. Some hundred thousand gathered on Broadway near midnight to welcome 1901 with the gonging of Trinity Church's bells in the financial district. The White House doors were thrown open that day to one and all, and President McKinley spent three hours shaking 5,350 hands. On the New York Stock Exchange the next morning, with rumors of more mergers, volume was up 10 percent from the last full trading day of December. Banks and investment houses were heavy buyers of the coal railroads ("coalers"), the farm railroads ("grangers"), and the western transcontinentals ("Pacifics").

The focus of all this trading was Chicago. Every major Chicago-based system was in play. Traders, speculators, and investors laid their bets and traded rumors. Which system would Hill–Morgan pursue? The Rock Island and the Wisconsin Central routes into Chicago from the Twin Cities weren't direct enough for Hill. The Chicago & North Western was out of the question. It had long had a traffic alliance with Harriman's Union Pacific across Iowa and Illinois, was heavily influenced by the Vanderbilts who liked things just the way they were, and had no direct link to Kansas City. That narrowed it to the 6,400-mile "St. Paul" and the Burlington, both with direct routes from the Twin Cities to Chicago along the Mississippi River.

Morgan had urged Hill to go after the St. Paul. Never mind that it was known as the "Standard Oil" road (William Rockefeller owned a large number of its shares and been on its board almost two decades). Never mind it had parallel and competing tracks with the Great Northern in some areas, bound to bring a lawsuit from the State of Minnesota if the two lines tried to merge. Never mind the pork packer Philip D. Armour, another major shareholder and board member, thought it was worth far more than it really was. "Every man who holds 100 shares of St. Paul," he said while running a "bull pool" on the stock, "has a joint account with God Almighty."

The St. Paul also was vulnerable to consolidation. Like the Burlington and the North Western, it had no desire to build to the coast, relying instead on traffic from Hill's lines to the north and Harriman's to the south. It could give Hill

Chicago, Kansas City, and Omaha, but Hill still far preferred the Burlington not just because he knew Harriman wanted it or because of its strength in Iowa and Nebraska or because of its Chicago dominance but because of its western tail. At Grand Island, Nebraska, the Burlington swung eight hundred miles northwest to Billings, Montana, where it could connect directly with Hill's Northern Pacific and provide a link to the Puget Sound. Hill, however, was still in Morgan's yoke. He dutifully went through the motions with the St. Paul.

On Friday, January 4, the great bull run on U.S. railroad stocks became a stampede. Many investors owning stocks on margin used their paper profits as margin to buy even more shares. In his *Letters from a Self-Made Merchant to His Son*, George Horace Lorimer likened it to wading around the edge of a swimming hole. "It seems safe and easy at first, but before a fellow knows it, he has stepped off the edge into deep water . . . trading on margin means trading on the ragged edge of nothing." The St. Paul, which one could have bought the previous June for $108 a share, rose over 9 percent from 145 at the open to 158½ at the close, on a huge volume of 251,200 shares. A single block of 12,000 St. Paul shares traded hands. The Northern Pacific rose 6⅛. The Burlington gained 3⅞ to 143¼. Trading volume set a record: 1.8 million shares, 13 percent higher than the Monday after McKinley's reelection in November. The "ragged edge of nothing" looked very alluring. J. P. Morgan and Company announced it had acquired control of the Central Railroad of New Jersey, including the shares of the Central owned by Baker's First National Bank of New York, giving Morgan effective control of the entire U.S. trade in anthracite coal.

The following Sunday evening, Hill's horse-drawn carriage rocked down the hill through a light snow from his Summit Avenue mansion to the red brick St. Paul Union Depot, a block from the Mississippi River. There he boarded the Burlington to a Chicago transfer for meetings in New York with Morgan and the St. Paul's chairman, silver-haired Roswell Miller. A few hours earlier, the sixty-eight-year-old Armour ("I am just a butcher trying to go to heaven"), died of pneumonia at his home in Chicago. Traders, however, already had bid the St. Paul's stock even higher. Hill called rumors that he was trying to buy it "nonsensical rubbish."

As Hill's train rolled toward New York on Monday, the market passed two million shares traded. A block of 15,000 shares of Rock Island changed hands. The Burlington rose another 3⅞ on heavy volume and wild rumors. Harriman might join its board. The Union Pacific had already bought it. Union Pacific interests "might appear in Burlington management." The Pennsylvania or the

Baltimore & Ohio might buy it. Some investors sold their St. Paul shares and invested the proceeds in the Burlington.

The market caught its breadth as Harriman called a meeting for Saturday morning, January 19, at his offices at the Equitable. Ten leaders of railroad finance and operations came together to form what they called the Railroad Advisory Committee. Extending from "community of interest," they signed an agreement to settle pricing differences peacefully within boundaries set by Interstate Commerce Commission. Beneath the surface, however, was an undercurrent of suspicion and self-interest that belied "community of interest." The principals were together in Harriman's conference room for what unknowingly was a dress rehearsal for the war to come, first for the Burlington and then for the Northern Pacific. Schiff and Stillman likely flanked Harriman on one side of the conference table, Hill and Bacon with Morgan on the other. The timing of this meeting and its organizing by Harriman make one suspect it also was his ploy to try to persuade Hill and Morgan of the pricing advantage in sharing ownership in the Burlington.

Given Morgan's disdain for Harriman it was a miracle he even deigned to come to his office. Likewise, Hill and Harriman had a bitter, mutual contempt. The animosity ran so deep Hill often couldn't bring himself to refer to Harriman by name, identifying him obliquely as the "Union Pacific interests" or "the southern people." Now they were jockeying secretly not just over the Burlington. They still had not resolved their dispute over how to divide the traffic and territory where their roads came together in a tangled mess in the Spokane–Portland–Seattle triangle at the doorstep of the Puget Sound. In a preview of their battle for the Burlington and the Northern Pacific, Harriman didn't want to divide the territory and favored a traffic alliance with Hill. Hill felt an alliance could be ruled illegal and was thus "more apt to lead to trouble than to avoid it." He threatened to build his own line from Spokane to Portland. There they stalemated—Harriman the parson's son always seeking some compromise at mid-field, Hill ever the "zero sum" wager of total war, taking no prisoners. Between them stood the pacifist Schiff.

It may have been sometime around this meeting in New York that Hill later claimed he told Harriman directly what he might be up to. "So as to remove any ground for the charge that we were working secretly to acquire the CB&Q," he wrote to his longtime finance advisor John Stewart Kennedy the following May, "I said to Harriman in January [1901] that if he at any time heard that we were conferring with the CB&Q Board of Directors looking to the joint acquisition of that property, I wanted to be the first one to tell him that we intended to take the matter up seriously." So much for "community of interest."

A week later the market turned again to the St. Paul. "The Street is full of rumors that the St. Paul deal has made good progress," said the Wall Street Journal, "and may be announced at any time." The St. Paul rose two points on Friday, January 25, six the next day, and then Monday, January 28, it led the market, rocketing twelve points in the first hour, declining five and a half, then adding two points. It closed at 154¼, its volume equal to the five other most active stocks, three times as many as any other active stock.

Reporters gathered outside a room where Morgan, Hill, and the St. Paul chairman Miller were conferring. Miller admitted weeks later "there was a time when it looked as if" Hill and Morgan might buy the St. Paul. Like many of his peers, however, Miller was conflicted by "community of interest." He was on the board of the Union Pacific with the Harriman clique including Otto Kahn, Schiff, Gould, and Stillman. Even in that, Miller was torn. Harriman's Union Pacific favored the St. Paul for freight but the Chicago & North Western for passengers. Further, he must have sensed if his negotiations with Hill went nowhere, then Hill would look for another partner, and it would be the Burlington. Then the St. Paul would have no choice: it would have to build to the coast or be boxed in by those who did. This put even more pressure on Harriman–Schiff to at least get a piece of the Burlington.

Behind the scenes a most unlikely figure, James Henry "Silent" Smith, a Wall Street broker and director of the St. Paul, suddenly shed his nickname and stepped forward to oppose a Hill–Morgan purchase of the St. Paul. As inheritor two years earlier of $50 million from the estate of his banker uncle, an early builder of the railroad, little Mr. Smith had been a shy, withdrawn bachelor who recently had taken a turn for society, where he was spotted at flamboyant parties, on yachting excursions, in his box at the Metropolitan Opera, and coaching in Central Park. He was in no sense a business leader but likely a front for the Rockefellers and Harriman. Hill–Morgan's only recourse now was buying St. Paul shares in a rising market, risking war with the Rockefellers.

By Thursday morning, January 30, the Wall Street Journal reported "St. Paul Deal Dropped." Hill returned to St. Paul. He could now resume his pursuit of the Burlington. He knew Schiff and Harriman had tried to buy a voice in it the previous year. Sometime that month Schiff told him so. What Schiff hadn't told him, but what Hill certainly suspected, was that Schiff and Harriman hadn't given up.

4

THE BATTLE FOR THE BURLINGTON

The evening of Saturday, February 9, 1901, Stuyvesant Fish was in many ways at the peak of his career. He had been president of the Illinois Central Railway Company for fourteen very successful years. Patrician, a bit smug and self-absorbed, he presided over an elegant black tie dinner celebrating the fiftieth anniversary of America's first land grant railroad. It was held in the ornate banquet room of Chicago's Auditorium Hotel, in the city's grand Romanesque complex of opera house, theater, convention hall, and offices. Chicago was snowbound. The second storm in a week had blocked all railroads in and out of town. Drifts banked several feet high against the hotel's gray granite at Congress and Michigan Streets, facing the snowscape of Grant Park and the endless gray expanse of Lake Michigan.

Amid palm trees and tables festooned with roses and violets, the din of the orchestra and a cloud of cigar smoke, 156 tuxedoed guests dined well, courtesy of the railroad's refrigerated cars: Blue Point oysters; filet of black bass *Rockelaise*; saddle of Southdown mutton *Tyrolienne*; asparagus with sauce *mousseline*; sherbet *Andalouse*; roast Philadelphia squab on toast; croustade of fresh strawberries; and fancy ices *en surprise*. Fish was at his oratorical best, celebrating the railroad's illustrious history—born when Chicago had fewer than thirty thousand people—noting it had been a client of attorney Abraham Lincoln, transporter of Union soldiers and supplies to the front during the Civil War, agent for cultivating "the Grand Prairie," shipper of the bounty of the West through Chicago to the East and Gulf Coast.

The distinguished audience of civic and business leaders included the presidents of ten railroads. One was Harriman. In those days when the government sanctioned not just "community of interest" among railroads but ignored conflicts of interest among its management, he remained on the board of the

Illinois Central and head of its finance committee. Fish singled him out for praise: "The measure of success which has been achieved by the Company in the last twenty years, with regard to its finances, is due to no man more than to the Chairman of our Finance Committee, Mr. Harriman [Applause]." Through the warm glow of all this good cheer it was impossible to conceive that in just four years a nasty public dispute would erupt over Fish's alleged self-dealing in company funds, with no board knowledge, fueled in part by his daft wife's extravagant spending. Harriman then seized control of the Illinois Central board, ousted Fish as president, and bought the railroad for the Union Pacific.

On this celebratory evening, however, all that was unimaginable. Harriman hosted table number ten near the dais, one of the many speakers who took the program well into Sunday morning. "Gentlemen: I know how difficult it is to make an extemporaneous address without careful preparation," he said, "and as I have had so little to do for the past two weeks or three weeks I have been preparing mine [Laughter]." Discreetly absent this evening among the ten railroad presidents, perhaps not even invited, were Hill and Charles E. Perkins. Five days earlier, the sixty-year-old Perkins had resigned as Burlington's president after twenty years but would remain chairman. Harriman's "so little to do" quip was code for the announcement six days earlier. The Union Pacific had bought control of the Southern Pacific, giving it a direct route to San Francisco, a virtual monopoly on local traffic in California, thereby eliminating one of its transcontinental competitors. This alliance reordered the power structure of the western railroads, stoked speculation of even more railroad mergers, further bulled the stock market, and helped make Union Pacific the most traded stock of the year. Its common stock began the year five weeks earlier at 82⅛. Two days before the announced purchase of the Southern Pacific it closed just short of 88. The day after the announcement, it closed over 90 for the first time and the next day it closed at 94.

With the new week, Harriman and Hill resumed their dance with Perkins. There was one difference. Harriman never let price stand in the way when he wanted something badly enough, but for some reason he wouldn't budge from his low-ball offer for the Burlington. Perhaps it was Schiff's influence. He was too much like Harriman, always wanting a better deal than anyone else. Hill and Morgan were willing to bargain and, ultimately, ready to pay full price. "When Mr. Hill said we must pay $200 a share," Morgan said later, "I say certainly, pay it." Hours after the banquet tables were cleared, Harriman and Perkins met Sunday somewhere in the Auditorium complex. Harriman made another half-hearted offer. The Union Pacific wanted to buy half the Burlington's stock. Perkins took it as an insult, quickly rejected it.

During the meeting Perkins was handed a message. Hill, who first approached the Burlington's executive committee the last week of December, wanted to see him tomorrow in Chicago. At that meeting on Monday, February 11, Hill offered six shares of Great Northern valued at $193 each for every seven of the Burlington, valued at $140. Perkins rejected it and repeated $200 a share in cash, period. They agreed to meet again soon. Hill wanted to bid higher. He cabled Morgan two days later: "Had long meeting with the president of the CB&Q. Think I can arrange to purchase control and possibly entire capital...I can take no further action for both companies [the Great Northern and the Northern Pacific] until you advise me your desire to act together as understood in New York" (referring to his meeting with Morgan, Bacon, and Baker the previous October on Morgan's yacht).

Morgan and Hill rarely signed contracts between each other, preferring handshakes and telegrams. Morgan tended to judge a person's character by intuition; he instinctively trusted Hill. "He believed more in men than in measures," his church rector said of Morgan. "Once he found the man he was looking for...he was willing to trust him far." Morgan cabled back to Hill the next day permitting him to use his name in discussions with Perkins: "I am distinctly in favor of the business in which you allude on fair terms. You can say to the president if you so desire that I am working with you and shall do everything in my power to carry out any contract that can be made, but come what may I wish you to understand distinctly that until I tell you to the contrary, which is not likely, I am acting with you in good faith to carry out what was agreed to in New York of October last." Rumors percolated. That same day, buried in the *Wall Street Journal*: "A St. Paul [newspaper] yarn says the Burlington and Northern Pacific will be consolidated." Two days later, Perkins met in Chicago with Northern Pacific president Charles Spangler Mellen, a Morgan manager, who proposed a long-term traffic contract between the two systems. Perkins was agreeable but said such a contract should be for five years. Nothing came of the discussion but the market began to swing from the St. Paul to the Burlington as Hill–Morgan's target. Trading on the Exchange revved up in the last hour on Friday, February 15. There were rumors that "Chicago investors," led by notorious plunger John W. "Bet a Million" Gates, were buying heavily into the Burlington, which closed up 4¼ on thin trading. Hill worried: were Schiff and Harriman buying Burlington shares again to block him and Morgan? Yes, the Burlington's Perkins told him, he'd heard rumors that Schiff and Harriman recently bought 100,000 shares of Burlington on the open market. The next Monday, February 18, the *Wall Street Journal* reported the Burlington had stopped laying track in Wyoming. Was this a signal it no longer controlled its destiny? Three days later Hill was said to have begun surveying an extension into Nebraska, the Burlington's heartland. Then another rumor, perhaps a diversion by Hill: was he planning a five-month Mediterranean cruise?

Momentum swung to the Burlington and the whole market rose. Veteran Exchange member Jacob Field, a quiet, reserved munchkin, not much more than four feet tall, watched the St. Paul close at 150 and the Burlington at 145¾ at 3 p.m. on Tuesday, February 19. "Jakey's" world was confined to Wall Street. He knew little else. It was said someone once asked him what he thought of Balzac (the French novelist), and he replied, "I never deal in dem outside stocks." But what he knew of stocks had made him rich. He now bet a fellow member $10,000 (about $250,000 today) that a share of Burlington would be higher than a share of the St. Paul in thirty days. Two days after Field made his bet, the Burlington announced Perkins had retired as president, succeeded by George B. Harris. Perkins, later named chairman, said he was resigning because of ill health, later disclosed as kidney disease. The market, however, took it as a signal: the Burlington was in play. Several of its largest shareholders in Boston were said to be buying more of the company's stock on the open market, assuming Hill and Morgan would get control.

Twelve days after his last meeting with Perkins in Chicago, Harriman dined with him and two other Burlington board members, chairman F. W. Hunnewell and J. Malcolm Forbes, son of the Burlington's founder, the late John Murray Forbes. Harriman told them he suspected Hill and Morgan were buying Burlington stock on the open market. He hoped the Burlington board could designate someone to negotiate with him. Perkins demurred. He wanted to give Hill more time to counteroffer because he sensed Morgan was backing him. "If Hill means also Morgan and the Northern Pacific," Perkins wrote Hunnewell, "then that would be the stronger and safer place for us to land."

There were other reasons. Harriman's bonded debt was higher than Hill's. Hill's geography had more potential for population growth than Harriman's. Hill had the timber resources of the Pacific Northwest. West of the Missouri, especially at Billings, Hill could move more two-way traffic than Harriman. Hill's Great Northern and the Northern Pacific had been competing against each other in relative peace the past twenty years and had been offering the Burlington, and other roads, joint rates to ensure more through traffic. Hill, a more effective persuader than Harriman, might have an easier time selling regulators on a full alliance of the Great Northern and the Northern Pacific than the cranky Harriman could with the Union Pacific and the Southern Pacific. If the Burlington went with Harriman, however, then Hill could always build from Sioux City to Denver and Omaha and lure traffic from the Burlington, anyway.

Harriman went around Hill and approached Morgan. If the Union Pacific and the Northern Pacific could buy the Burlington jointly, said Harriman, then he would reconsider a traffic deal in the Spokane–Portland–Seattle triangle that would be acceptable to Hill for a path for the Northern Pacific from Spokane to Portland. Traders and the *Wall Street Journal* kept floating rumors that the Pennsylvania was still interested. Some traders were using the *Journal* to float the rumor of a joint offer for the Burlington from the Union Pacific and the Northern Pacific. Union Pacific and Burlington shares seemed to be rising in tandem. Wasn't that proof the Union Pacific somehow would have a role in the Burlington?

If the Burlington didn't get the offer it wanted then it certainly had the resources, didn't it, to build to the coast if it wanted to? But did it want to? Was $200 a reasonable price for the Burlington? Hill privately thought so, in fact he thought it a bargain. "If I had $100,000,000 in bonds on one side on a table before me," he was said to have told a Northern Pacific director who doubted the Burlington's earnings power, "and the Burlington contract on the other side, and was told I could have either one, but not both, I would not hesitate to reach out for the contract. Then I would try to get the bonds, but the Burlington contract would be first."

On Sunday, March 3, Morgan and Carnegie announced the birth of U.S. Steel. Baker of the First National Bank joined the board with Morgan, as did Morgan's Bacon. To "manage" the offering of his new U.S. Steel on the New York Stock Exchange—in other words, to create demand—Morgan retained James Robert Keene, the legendary market manipulator, trader, and manager of investment pools, held in fear and reverent awe throughout American finance. "He did not bet on fluctuations," said one Wall Street observer, "he made them." Keene was tall, lean, and wiry, with delicate hands and a goatee. He favored black Victorian frockcoats and a derby hat, and had an intensity in his gaze it was said could stop a freight train. His office off the floor of the old Exchange was a nine-foot-square "private den" that one trader said was "pitch dark but for the electric light," with one tiny window for air and "a little hole, about the size of a man's fist, cut through the partition" that separated his office from those of his brokers. When he talked with a guest he had a nervous habit of fingering the tape as it spooled from the ticker. He insisted on formality. His son called him "Mr. Keene."

Born in London in 1838, a merchant's son, Keene came to America at age fourteen, invested in mining companies in California and Nevada, made a fortune on the San Francisco Stock Exchange, made another fortune in railroad stocks after a brief panic of 1877, locked horns with Jay Gould, lost a fortune trying to corner the Chicago wheat market in 1880, regained his fortune on sugar stocks, and then in the 1890s built his reputation as a market maker and pool manager, and as one of America's premier breeders of thoroughbred race horses. For his services to Morgan during the first offering of U.S. Steel stock on the market, Keene was said to have earned $1 million. The two thus were wed forever in U.S. financial history. Morgan discreetly kept his distance; Keene never met him in person.

Now, in March 1901, as he prepared to manage the U.S. Steel offering for Morgan, Keene's name was first mentioned publicly with the Burlington, as orchestrator of a pool buying its shares. The birth of Morgan's U.S. Steel had multiplied the wealth of owners and investors in Federal Steel, National Steel, National Tube, American Steel and Wire of New Jersey, American Tin Plate, American Steel Hoop, American Sheet Steel, and the Carnegie Company. These so-called Chicago and Pittsburgh crowds, enriched by paper profits from the new U.S. Steel, unleashed millions more in speculative dollars into the stock market, much of it into the Burlington and other railroad stocks.

The morning after the U.S. Steel announcement, on the steps of the U.S. Capitol, Roosevelt took the oath of office as vice president in a drizzle followed by McKinley in a downpour. Awaiting McKinley in Congress were even larger majorities than his party had before. The next day Burlington rose 2⅞ with another 1⅛ the next day, hitting a high of 156⅜ but easing to close just above 149 on heavy volume. Keene was not a member of the Exchange and executed many of his trades through the brokerage firm of his son-in-law, Talbot J. Taylor. He was said to be behind the heavy buying in Burlington the last hour of trading on Wednesday, March 6, as the Burlington and Northern Pacific both closed strong on deal rumors.

Hill was anxious. Schiff and Harriman weren't going to sit back and let him have the Burlington without a fight. But what could they do? Morgan

Legendary market manipulator James R. Keene, who led the Hill–
Morgan buying of Northern Pacific on the New York Stock Exchange
on Monday, May 6, 1901. "He did not bet on fluctuations," said one
observer, "he made them." KING'S VIEWS OF THE NEW YORK STOCK
EXCHANGE, 1897–1898.

was leaving for Europe in three or four weeks, and Hill had to sew things up
before then because Morgan would be gone perhaps two or three months.
Hill left for New York early the first week in March, may have met en route
with the Burlington's Perkins in Chicago, and arrived at Grand Central station
in New York Friday evening, March 8. He checked into the Hotel Netherland
and learned the Burlington had risen a point for the day in moderate trading.
Word was now firm on the Street and in the *Wall Street Journal*: $200 a share was

the Burlington demand. If Harriman or Hill paid that it would be a remarkable 33 percent premium to its current market price. More remarkable, the Burlington's earnings' capacity seemed to more than support it. Could Hill and Morgan offer bonds backed by the Great Northern and the Northern Pacific that could generate annual returns of 8 percent or more to persuade Burlington stockholders to part with their shares, which had consistently returned at least 7 percent a year during many of Perkins's twenty years as head of the railroad? The shareholders would follow Perkins. If he said yes, they would sell.

Hill tried to stem speculation to keep the price down. "I don't own a share of Burlington stock and have not owned any for years," he told reporters, "and am not engaged in any deals with the Burlington or any other property." But the Burlington kept rolling. It rose two points Monday, March 11. The next day it rose a half point, closing at 151¼ and crossing the St. Paul, which closed at 149⅝. Little "Jakey" Field won his $10,000 bet in just eighteen days.

The Burlington kept rising. Up five-eighths on Wednesday. Up three-eighths Thursday. Up two and one-half Friday. Then on Saturday, March 16, with the Exchange open for trading for only the customary 10 a.m. to noon, it rocketed five and one-half points on heavy trading, crossing 160 for the first time. It had taken forty-seven days since the start of the year to go from 140 to 150, then only five to get to 160. It was rumored that an offer to guarantee Burlington shareholders an annual return of 7 percent had been refused and that large Burlington shareholders were behind some of the buying themselves, convinced the stock would go much higher and that the dividend could be increased.

Chairman Kennedy's whack of the gavel opened trading Monday morning, March 18. At his office on 120 Broadway Harriman paced the floor, surrounded by his telephones and tickers. He hadn't met with Perkins for almost a month and apparently had made no further attempt to contact him. Schiff was at his office at 27 Pine, agonizing over rumors that Hill was close to a deal with Burlington. Morgan and Bacon were at the corner of Wall and Broad, raising another $25 million in cash to help finance U.S. Steel from a syndicate including the Moore brothers, Baker's First National Bank, Stillman's National City Bank, William Rockefeller, and Kuhn, Loeb. Hill was at his Great Northern office on the ninth floor of Schiff's building. Traders crowded the Burlington post on the floor, yelling, gesturing, pushing. Hill watched the ticker. By the close at 3 p.m. Burlington was up again by 2⅜ to 162⅝ on heavy volume. Hill sent an urgent wire to the Burlington's Perkins asking for another meeting. Burlington rose again the next day, up 3⅛ to a record 166¾.

On a warm, rainy Sunday, March 24, Hill quietly checked out of the Hotel Netherland in New York. He took a carriage to Grand Central station and a train to Boston, arriving on one of some thirty tracks funneling into the long shed of the city's new South Union Station with its triumphal Roman arch on Causeway Street. Charles Perkins was there to greet him the next morning at the Hotel Victoria, the red terra cotta landmark that gave the Back Bay its medieval, almost Moorish, look. They spent much of the week in secret talks. The ticker at the Victoria showed Burlington closing down 2⅜ Monday on lighter volume. There were rumors of profit taking by the "Harriman interest." There was talk that Baker's First National Bank was using some of the $23 million from its sale of the Jersey Central to Morgan to buy Burlington shares on the open market for Hill and Morgan. Was Hill using this as another lever to persuade Charles Perkins to sell?

Schiff later wrote that he and Harriman believed Hill–Morgan and their agents had been buying large lots of Burlington "irrespective of price" as early as January or February. Schiff and Harriman had been able to accumulate only about 80,000 shares of the Burlington the previous year but now there was a rumor that Morgan, through various brokerage houses, had pried loose between 200,000 and 300,000 shares, contrary to what the Burlington board thought possible. Hill denied it eleven months later under oath, saying Morgan had told him "neither the Northern Pacific nor his firm, nor anyone connected with it, could or would buy a share of the Burlington pending the negotiations."

Trading opened volatile Tuesday, March 26. Short-sellers were thought to have built large positions in Burlington and other stocks. Then, near the end of trading, the bearish mood snapped. Had reporters spotted Hill and Charles Perkins together at the Victoria? Rumors swept the floor that Hill and Morgan had gained control of the Burlington. Burlington and Northern Pacific leapt in frantic trading. Burlington closed up 4¼, to 167⅜. Northern Pacific rose 4⅝, closing over 90 for the first time. Both rose again Wednesday and Thursday. Virtually unnoticed was the Great Northern. Its thinly traded preferred stock, paying a healthy 7 percent dividend, had been as low as 145 the previous year. On March 11, 1901, it had hit 208, driven higher partly because Hill had just raised $25 million for reinvesting in the company's operations and granting stockholders an extra dividend of 5 percent.

On Friday, March 29, Hill telegrammed his wife, Mary, with their daughters on the *Wacouta* on the Potomac. He was back in New York at the Netherland. He had ended his negotiations with Charles Perkins earlier in the day. Then he and former U.S. Senator Edward O. Wolcott, the Burlington's Denver-based legal counsel, in Boston almost two weeks working on the Burlington deal, had "hurriedly departed" for New York. U.S. Steel common and preferred had their debut on the Exchange with Morgan's agent, James R. Keene, and his team masterminding a rise for the common from its initial $38 to $55 in a few weeks. Traders piled into Burlington, sending it up almost six points in heavy trading to a record 174⅞. Profit taking sent both Burlington and Northern Pacific down a fraction on Monday, April 1, but the bulls took over again the next day. Burlington rose 5¾. Northern Pacific followed, up 1¾ to 96⅜. Perkins watched the Burlington cross 180. He penned a note to Hill at the Netherland. His demand was still an all-cash offer: "I hope you will not forget that the C.B.&Q. Directors will not take the responsibility upon themselves of recommending *any* securities and that it is therefore necessary to have a cash alternative."

5

"PEACEMAKERS"

ARMING FOR COMBAT

What were Harriman and Schiff doing while Hill maneuvered? They watched the Burlington start the year at $140, close over $150 on March 11, over $160 on March 16, over $170 on March 29, and well over $180 on April 3, the day Morgan departed for Europe. Hill and Morgan assumed Harriman was preoccupied with buying the Southern Pacific. Union Pacific had announced the purchase February 1, and Harriman and his managers must have been devoting much of their time to absorbing it. Given the size of the Southern Pacific, how could Harriman have time for anything else? Hill and Morgan assumed their large minority interest in the Northern Pacific, thought to be around 35 percent of the combined common and preferred shares, was enough for a controlling voice. Perhaps another 5 to 10 percent of the shares were held by parties aligned with them, such as George F. Baker, John Stewart Kennedy, Lord Mount Stephen, Edward Tuck, Dan Lamont, and other Northern Pacific board members. Hill claimed he warned Harriman in January not to be surprised if the Great Northern and the Northern Pacific approached the Burlington board. If Harriman seriously had wanted to go after the Burlington he'd have done it by now.

Hill and Morgan were wrong on all these counts. Throughout March, Harriman and Schiff with Stillman weighed alternatives. Stillman likely brought with him to these meetings the man who may have helped direct their thinking away from the Burlington and toward the Northern Pacific. He was Stillman's personal legal counsel, trusted adviser, alter ego, closest friend and business associate for more than a quarter century, the ingenuous corporate lawyer John William Sterling. Stillman, who had a habit for nicknames,

97

affectionately called him "Lord John" because among his clients were several titled Englishmen (including Hill's close friends Lord Strathcona and Mount Stephen). Sterling, six years older than Stillman, came from a seafaring family in Connecticut and was a Yale graduate, admitted to the bar in 1867. In the mid-1870s Stillman sent him to Texas to do legal work on his father's estate. His law firm, Shearman and Sterling, had its offices in the headquarters of National City Bank, and Sterling had done work for the bank well before Stillman became president in 1891.

The ideal client, Sterling once said, is "a very wealthy man in very great trouble," and very many of them paid millions for his whispered counsel. Throughout the 1870s and 1880s Sterling built a high-profile practice, representing Jay Gould, James Fisk, the Rockefellers, and Standard Oil. In 1897 it was Sterling who urged Stillman to buy the Third National Bank, the purchase that vaulted National City to number one in assets in New York. He also schemed a plan enabling Stillman's federally chartered bank to avoid the capital and cash reserve requirements of the National Bank Act and legally conduct almost any kind of business. To do this he had National City create an affiliated company, under the bank's control, chartered by the State of New York. National City Bank financed this new affiliate by declaring a 40 percent dividend on its $25 million in capital stock. To pay the dividend the bank assigned three trustees to organize and hold in trust all the voting stock of the new affiliate, whose charter required that its trustees be officers of National City Bank.

Sterling and Stillman became inseparable, meeting several times a day and often dining together in the evening at the Union League Club. Sterling lived at 912 Fifth Avenue facing Central Park, just around the corner from Stillman's home with its large windows, gray stonework, and pillars at 9 East Seventy-Second Street. Sterling, high-strung, chain smoker, fast walker, was just as eccentric as Stillman. He had a habit of making appointments at odd minutes, 3:17 rather than 3:15 p.m. He dined in the same chair at the same table six nights a week at the Union Club. Despite his family's nautical roots, he feared water and dreaded even the ferry, and because of that never traveled abroad. He was introduced to Stillman in the 1870s by a cotton broker named James Orville Bloss. Sterling never married, but it was "Blossy" who became his law partner and live-in companion for the next half century. Sterling was a fanatic for security; he feared burglars (he routinely had his valet check under his bed) and his large home bristled with locks and gates, iron bars on the windows, and an iron door to his bedroom. He even locked his door when he was in his office at Wall and William streets, a small space stacked with papers, where he sat at his desk in a small, armless revolving chair.

Sterling was known never to have shorted a stock or bought on margin; he always paid in cash for his investments and never spoke at public gatherings. In small conferences, however, he could be "bold, fearless and aggressive," more intuitive than analytic. Given his penchant for maneuvers such as the end-around of the National Bank Act, Sterling may have been the one who floated the idea of a raid on the Northern Pacific. Or perhaps not. Harriman was a bold enough thinker, still a trading "sharper" from his days on the Exchange, and already had tried something similar a year earlier with the Burlington. The idea, fraught with peril, very likely unsettled the cautious Schiff. Wherever the idea came from it had for Harriman instant appeal. He was a young boxer again. It could be a "haymaker" of a punch, a bold Napoleonic strike into enemy territory, the stuff of legend. No one had ever tried to seize control of such a large public company.

There was one other principal in the plot: sixty-one-year-old William Avery Rockefeller, head of Standard Oil in New York since 1865. He had an appetite for market raids and promoting stocks. He couldn't keep his eyes off the tape of the ticker near his office window on the thirteenth floor of the Standard Oil Building at 26 Broadway, the Renaissance revival tower with setbacks that curved with the lower tail of the street. He smoked cigars and had a weakness for gambling, yachts, costume balls, and fast-trotting horses. Indeed, he did have a horse in this race, actually two. If Harriman and Schiff could seize the Northern Pacific then his Chicago, Milwaukee & St. Paul railroad could finally get a cheap path to the coast. He also had to protect the St. Paul against a Burlington that would be backed by Hill–Morgan. Unlike his older brother, John D., known for his analytic mind and Baptist probity, "Will" was a natural salesman, a friendly charmer; as Ida Tarbell described him, "open-hearted, jolly, a good story-teller... not a man to suspect or fear." Stillman and Rockefeller, like Harriman, both had an aversion for public speaking, and a phobia for newspapers, and they preferred to hide behind their wealth. "I like William because we don't have to talk," Stillman once said, "Often we sit fifteen minutes in silence before one of us breaks it."

Hill and Morgan had working control of Northern Pacific, but like most of their peers with other railroads, including Harriman, they didn't directly own a majority of its shares. They didn't think they had to. Open market raids of any size and scope were extraordinarily difficult to pull off. Burlington had proved an impregnable fortress. Northern Pacific was different. It was believed that about 60 to 65 percent of its shares were in the market. A sizeable quantity of those were traded in large, speculative blocks by the "plungers," the big speculative investors, with their buying and selling widely disbursed.

Three of Harriman's allies in this meeting had an extra advantage—an insider's "community of interest" knowledge of the Northern Pacific. Stillman was still on its board and had been since the Northern Pacific was reorganized in 1896, when he, Schiff, and William Rockefeller were part of its refinancing syndicate. One can imagine the conversations among Harriman, Schiff, Stillman, Sterling, and Rockefeller about the Northern Pacific going something like this:

How many shares of Northern Pacific common are outstanding? 800,000. Worth about $80 million.

How much do we estimate Hill–Morgan directly own of the common? Not quite half. $35 to $40 million.

How many shares of preferred are outstanding? 750,000. Worth about $75 million.

How much of the preferred do we estimate Hill–Morgan owns? Certainly well less than half.

How much do we need to get control? We believe if we can obtain a majority of the common and preferred combined and a majority of the preferred, because the preferred have voting rights, that we can gain control of both the Northern Pacific and the Burlington with it because Hill and Morgan intend to house the Burlington corporately in the Northern Pacific.

How does the preferred differ from the common? The preferred is really a fixed income security. It pays a set dividend that does not rise or fall with Northern Pacific's earnings. When Morgan reorganized the Northern Pacific in 1896 he wanted the preferred issued largely in lieu of bonds, to improve the Northern Pacific's balance sheet. We believe the preferred, however, has the same voting rights to elect the board as the common, so when we buy Northern Pacific we will buy both the common and the preferred. We believe a share is a share in terms of gaining a majority.

How long would it take to accumulate this majority? We think we could do it in a month, taking most of April.

Won't our heavy buying of Northern Pacific shares in such a short time drive up its price so Wall Street will suspect a takeover attempt? We don't think so, if current conditions continue, and there's every sign they will. The bull market still has plenty of legs. The U.S. economy and exports are booming, talk of more railroad mergers will continue to bull railroad stocks. Any rise in Northern Pacific will be camouflaged by a rise in the entire market. We simply can give our brokers the order to buy at the prevailing market price all Northern Pacific offered.

How do we disguise our buying? We will leave no fingerprints. We will distribute orders to purchase Northern Pacific shares to a number of unrelated brokerage firms that cannot be traced to us. We also will look for opportunities to sell some shares back into the market and then buy them back later, to mask our buying and moderate the price.

What is our message to the market to explain the rise in the Northern Pacific? The Northern Pacific's purchase of the Burlington will make the Northern Pacific a more efficient, profitable system and more than justify a material rise in its stock. Our brokerage firms should just keep repeating: the Northern Pacific has the Burlington (in street slang, the "Nipper's" got the "Q,") and they're rising together.

What about Northern Pacific insiders, sympathetic to Hill and Morgan, who hold large blocks? We think some of them will want to sell, or can easily be persuaded to do so, in a fast-rising market and take their profits. They may fear Northern Pacific can't possibly go any higher.

When should we start buying? It's now late March. We should start buying as soon as we can. Our window of opportunity is open.

We spent June and July last year on a goose chase for the Burlington and stalled at 8 percent of the shares. What makes you think this will be any easier? We believe it's held by only about 5,000 to 7,000 investors. The Burlington has at least twice that number of owners. We believe many of these Northern Pacific shares are "lying loose" all over the United States and Europe because its turbulent history still types it as a volatile bankers' stock, a thirty-year legacy of enormous federal grants of land, which mostly could not sustain settlement, and to the stock-and-bond jobbing of Jay Cooke and Henry Villard. A large percentage of Northern Pacific common and preferred is institutionally held, not widely dispersed among small investors. We know where most of the large blocks are. We can buy them directly from the holders without having the purchases go through the exchanges on the open market where they would be publicly recorded immediately. There are many shares in Europe, as much as 20 percent or more.

Where in Europe? We know a large percentage of the preferred is still held in Germany, where they were sold through Deutsche Bank in Berlin to pay off the bonds of the old Northern Pacific. Deutsche Bank, J. P. Morgan and Company of New York, and Drexel and Company of Philadelphia were the three underwriters of the May 1896 Northern Pacific Railway reorganization voting trust. Kuhn, Loeb doesn't have branches in Europe but has close relationships with all the major houses: Baring Brothers, the Rothschilds, and the Bank of Montreal in London, the Banque de Paris, Hope and Company and the Amsterdamsche Bank in Amsterdam, and of course, the Warburgs in Hamburg. Mr. Schiff believes his relationships with Deutsche Bank in Frankfurt and Berlin will be particularly valuable.

Why do the Germans want to sell their Northern Pacific now? They can make a substantial profit at today's prices. Many of them also are against the Burlington deal, some angry enough that they've organized mass meetings and protests. They believe the Hill–Morgan guarantee of an 8 percent return to Burlington shareholders through collateral trust bonds creates an obligation that could jeopardize the market value of their Northern Pacific stock because Hill–Morgan is using Northern Pacific assets as collateral for the Burlington bonds.

Will a rapid rise in the Northern Pacific attract a growing number of short-sellers who believe it overpriced? Maybe, but that's a chance we'll have to take. If we can get a majority of the common and preferred by late April or early May that question will be academic.

Are Bacon and Hill suspicious? We don't believe they are, yet. They're preoccupied with other things. Hill is focused on the Burlington. So is Lamont of the Northern Pacific. Morgan is focused on U.S. Steel and the threat of a coal miners' strike. Morgan heads for Europe Wednesday, April 3. He'll leave Bacon in charge. He and Steele are focused on the Burlington and U.S. Steel. Bacon has never been tested in a situation like this. George W. Perkins is new, only there a month and still full time with New York Life.

How do we fund the purchases of Northern Pacific? We have more than enough financing from four sources: the treasury of the Union Pacific (we still have about $60 million in our war chest from the sale of the 4 percent convertible bonds), the treasury of the Oregon Short Line (a subsidiary of the Union Pacific), the several millions we netted last year when we sold our shares of the Burlington, and of course, we have Mr. Stillman's National City Bank with Mr. Rockefeller.

There was one other concern. Let's return, someone may have said at this meeting, to the risk that buying could drive the price of the stock up and what this could do to the shorts. We all know there is a real risk of leaks. Insider information is bought and sold every day. There is no law against it, no government agency to monitor it. What if Hill–Morgan find out about our buying before we acquire majority control of the stock? What if there's a fight for the remaining shares on the market? Morgan would stop at nothing. He has virtually unlimited financial resources and influence. There would be hell to pay. In other words, what if we and Morgan end up causing a corner?

Harriman, Schiff, Stillman, and Sterling were all in their fifties, Rockefeller in his early sixties. They were old enough to remember all the notorious corners the past four decades, caused by vanity, greed, or revenge, and all the nasty publicity those corners attracted, with reputations tarnished or ruined. They were all young men in 1863, and Harriman was an impressionable fifteen-year-old messenger boy on Wall Street when Commodore Vanderbilt cornered the stock of his New York & Harlem Railroad. He did it not so much for financial gain but to teach a lesson to the crooks on the New York City Council who repealed and reinstated a franchise law to manipulate the stock of his railroad for their personal benefit. They remembered five years later when Vanderbilt tried to corner the stock of the Erie Railroad against Jay Gould and Jim Fisk. They remembered a year later when Fisk and Gould tried to corner the gold market, escaped unharmed, but caused the financial ruin of many in what came to be called Black Friday. They remembered John B. Lyon and his clique trying to corner the cash wheat market in 1872, squeezing the shorts from eighty cents a bushel to a dollar and sixty-one cents, followed by a violent price break that pushed one of the perpetrators to suicide. They remembered "Deacon" White's corner of the Delaware, Lackawanna & Western Railroad in 1884 that netted him an estimated $1 million and his disastrous encore in 1891 when he tried to corner the corn market and lost about $3 million. They remembered Cincinnati banker E. L. Harper serving a ten-year prison term after using the bank's funds in 1887 to try to corner the wheat market. And most recently, they remembered what happened to young Joe Leiter, the Harvard graduate, son of a wealthy colleague of Marshall Field, and a crony of Gates, who tried to corner the wheat market. With his father's money, Leiter began buying wheat in April 1897 at just under seventy-three cents a bushel; in a year he owned contracts for more than thirty million bushels when the price rose as high as a dollar eighty-five cents a bushel. He could have cashed in by selling when world demand was highest but held on too long. On June 13, 1898, after Phil Armour unleashed his supply of wheat into the market, the price for a bushel broke to eighty-five cents. Leiter's father paid some seven million dollars to bail out his son, and Armour, designated agent by the banks, took over the Leiters' cash grain.

Were they willing to risk having their names on a list of "corner" infamy with Fisk, Gould, Deacon White, Lyon, Harper, and Leiter? They believed their motive was not revenge, vanity, or greed. All they wanted was the common good, to buy and merge railroad properties, eliminate redundant management, reinvest in operations, increase efficiency, and be able to reduce rates. They believed their motives to be honorable, just as Morgan's were for creating U.S. Steel. The shorts were the greedy ones, trying to get something for nothing. If a corner develops wouldn't it be obvious to everyone who caused it: the gamblers, the speculators, the shorts? They were simply going to buy publicly available stock on the open market.

They weighed risk and reward. Harriman made the call. Schiff began orchestrating the buying in late March through various brokerage houses. Northern Pacific common's daily trading volume was 18,400 on Monday, March 25, the day Perkins and Hill first met at the Victoria Hotel in Boston. The next four trading days it spiked to 95,700, 156,700, 126,100, and 69,400, respectively, rising $10 a share to close at 98 on volume of 130,100 the day Morgan left for Europe. No one thought it unusual. The whole market was rising. Why shouldn't Northern Pacific?

Harriman and Schiff must have smiled as the *Wall Street Journal* dutifully kept parroting brokers and traders with Kuhn, Loeb's message about the inevitable rise of the Northern Pacific. On March 30 the *Journal* reported: "It was agreed that control of Burlington by Northern Pacific would be greatly to the advantage of the Northern Pacific and would amply justify a material rise in the stock." April 3: "Northern Pacific ought to be greatly benefited by ownership of the Burlington." April 8: "Insiders repeat the statement that Northern Pacific is going to be materially benefited by control of Burlington and will show this benefit in the price of the stock." April 10: "Northern Pacific will probably rise on the Burlington deal, as it will be considered the principal beneficiary of the purchase." April 11: "Some of the interests which have been long of Burlington are selling that stock and buying Northern Pacific on the ground that the principal advantage of the acquisition of the Burlington will be to Northern Pacific." A skeptic might ask: Since when did an acquirer's stock rise merely on predictions of what it hoped to achieve with an acquiree? Harriman–Schiff scarcely could contain their amazement.

Even Hill seemed to be unknowingly promoting their cause by optimistically justifying the rise of the Nipper. Or was it Kuhn, Loeb planting rumors about him? On April 9 the *Commercial Advertiser* said, "Mr. Hill was quoted as predicting 125 for Northern Pacific common within a few months." And a week later, more embarrassing for Hill, "Intimate friends of Mr. Hill were quoted as being more bullish on Northern Pacific common than on any other stock on the list."

Thursday morning, April 4, 1901, Hill left his family on the *Wacouta* and took the B&O train to Grand Central Station in New York where he changed trains for Boston to meet with Perkins of the Burlington to try to seal the deal. The market opened wild and erratic with heavy buying and then bearish selling and sharp declines. Trading was so intense and prices swung so widely on the same stocks from one point on the floor to the other that order takers couldn't keep pace, "buyers and sellers were lost or forgotten," disputes erupted. When the bears threatened to dominate, some thought they saw the invisible hand and the "masterly manipulative genius" of James Keene at work, orchestrating bullish rumors. *They're going to put up Copper. They're going to make a movement in Steel.* "What constitutes the mysterious 'they' is never stated," said the *New York Herald*, "and no one apparently stops to ask; but when the stock moves the speaker is regarded as an oracle, and if it does not move, which is sometimes the case, the explanation is prompt:—'They're not ready to move it yet.'"

On Keene-made rumors, New York Central closed up 5, the Pennsylvania up 2½, Amalgamated Copper up 8⅜. The *Wall Street Journal* said Hill and Morgan had increased their offer to the equivalent of $198 for each share of the Burlington in 3½ percent collateral trust bonds, for an annual return for Burlington shareholders of 7.7 percent. Hill negotiated all day on Good Friday with Perkins in Boston, then returned to his wife Mary at the Netherland in New York early Saturday morning, went to bed and slept several hours. Newsstands carried headlines that day, a portent of trouble from the least likely source. McKinley had appointed an old pal, corporate lawyer Philander Chase Knox, to be U.S. attorney general. Pulitzer's *New York Evening World* called him a "distinguished practitioner" of "trust lawlessness." In ten months, to the astonishment of Hill and Morgan, he turned out just the opposite.

Easter Sunday, April 7, dawned cold and windy with threatening, low clouds. The Hills made their way via carriage nine blocks down Fifth Avenue in slanting rain to St. Patrick's Cathedral for the 11 a.m. Pontifical High Mass. Hill was a nominal Methodist but often on the "twice a year" days he dutifully tagged along with his faithful Catholic wife. The bells had tolled for a half hour, some 10,000 worshippers filling every pew, by ticket only, in a sea of lilies, roses, azaleas, and daisies, the main altar ablaze with candles.

Hill must have daydreamed through the drone of the High Mass, his mind wandering to the evening. He was to have dinner at George Baker's four-story, double row-house mansion at 256–258 Madison Avenue between Thirty-Eighth and Thirty-Ninth, four blocks north of Morgan's home on Murray Hill. Lamont of the Northern Pacific was to join them, then at midnight Hill and Baker would board a train at Grand Central to Boston for more negotiations in the morning. Baker, Hill, and Lamont had tried to suppress the Burlington rumors to keep its stock price down but they had failed. Their negotiations had leaked all over the street, with what the New York Herald later called "the blowing of horns and the beating of drums." And now their dinner this evening was going to be compromised, too. In Harriman's presence a few days earlier, Baker had let slip that Hill was coming to his home for dinner Easter Sunday evening.

No sooner had they finished dinner than the doorbell rang. It was Harriman and Schiff. They weren't aware Baker and Hill were headed to Boston again in a few hours, but may have suspected it. This was their last chance to persuade them to make some "community of interest" concession to the Union Pacific for the Burlington. Morgan would be in Liverpool in just a few hours, back in cable contact. They were escorted into Baker's dark-paneled mansion, past eighteenth-century tapestries, paintings of the Barbizon school, Persian rugs, cabinets glistening with jade and Japanese enamel, and into the library with its hefty, upholstered chairs. This wasn't going to be a discussion. It would be a confrontation. Hill had a nervous habit of playing with a small sack of rough stones he carried in his pocket. Perhaps Schiff now could hear them clicking.

Schiff reviewed for Hill, as Schiff claimed later in a long posterity letter to Morgan, that sometime in the last half of March, though he never said when or where, he and Harriman had "interrogated" Hill about reports "freely circulating" that Hill was trying to get control of the Burlington. Schiff said Hill had denied to him these reports, that Hill told him he had no interest in Burlington stock or in buying the company. Schiff said he accepted Hill's answer because "I could not believe that a man whom I had known and with whom I had been closely associated for some fifteen years, whom I had never wronged, but whom I had shown friendship without reserve, and whom I believed to be my friend, would willingly mislead or deceive me."

Schiff essentially was asking, Why did you lie to me? I had to do it, Schiff recorded Hill as saying, because I knew of your relations with the Union Pacific. Schiff naively had thought somehow their friendship or "community of interest" would cause Hill to make the interests of his competitors equal to his own. We ask you again, said Schiff, not to conclude your negotiations with the Burlington until you can protect us against its further invasion into "our" territory. Is there still some way the Union Pacific can be part of your purchase of the Burlington? Schiff said Hill responded with "platitudes." Whatever they were, they meant "no." Harriman bristled. "Very well, then," he said, "this is an invasion of Union Pacific territory, a hostile act, and you will have to take the consequences."

Harriman and Schiff, of course, did not mention they had secretly tried to buy at least a voice in the Burlington themselves. Nor did they concede that Hill was merely trying to buy a railroad well established in Harriman's so-called territory years before Harriman bought control of the Union Pacific. Hill may also have mentioned that various state laws prevented the Union Pacific from owning all or part of the Burlington because they were parallel lines, competing in the same territory. That may be true, said Schiff, but we can finesse that through something short of ownership control, just as your Great Northern, J. J., has with the Northern Pacific.

The clocks in the Baker mansion showed it was time for them to head for Grand Central to catch a train for Boston. Harriman and Schiff, however, were not about to let the meeting end. They followed Baker and Hill out the door, down the dozen or so front steps, and into the carriage. The argument continued all the way to Grand Central. By Baker's account, the four kept arguing all the way to the platform right until the train began to move. Baker and Hill boarded and it disappeared down the tracks.

The battle lines were drawn. All the agreements to try to avoid rate wars, all the reorganizations and mergers to avoid destructive competition, had ended with the prospect of "violent combat among the peacemakers." There was something else that rankled Harriman and Schiff, perhaps left unsaid in their "conversation" at Baker's that evening. It was what Hill and Morgan supposedly were willing to pay for the Burlington. Two hundred dollars a share had been rumored all over the papers for the past month as Burlington's demand. Harriman and Schiff sensed Hill and Morgan were willing to pay it. If they did it would be a "damned fool price," as someone said later, because Harriman and Schiff knew it would set a new, unreasonably high valuation for future deals.

The next morning, Monday, April 8, the market opened with heavy selling as profit-takers sent most stocks down, including the Burlington, the St. Paul, and the Rock Island. The bulls took over before noon and Northern Pacific showed strength. One brokerage firm bought 5,000 shares of Northern Pacific, which closed down 1¾, and the Burlington dropped 3¼ to 182½. A newspaper claimed Hill was at his New York desk "bright and early" in meetings, but it was a feint; he and Baker were in Boston with the Burlington's Perkins.

At his desk at Kuhn, Loeb's offices on Pine Street that Monday, April 8, Schiff recalled the heated words of the past evening at the Baker mansion and in the carriage to Grand Central. For the first time in his three-decade career he was headed for a bitter public fight with a favored client backed by the world's most powerful private banker. His firm's huge financial stake in the Union Pacific, however, had to come first. He did not want to burn his bridge with Hill but for his client, for the contemporary record, and for his place in history, he felt a need to communicate to Hill his view of the situation. Hill wouldn't listen to Harriman but perhaps he would to Schiff. He was wearing, impossibly, six hats: Harriman ally, Union Pacific board member, Great Northern board member, financier of the 1896 Northern Pacific reorganization, competitor of Hill's, friend of Hill's. He pulled out a sheet of folded, embossed Kuhn, Loeb stationery, bordered in black to commemorate the recent death of partner Abraham Wolff. He penned "Personal" in black ink at the top and then wrote in his elegant cursive:

> Dear Mr. Hill:
>
> Lest you might misunderstand my position and sentiments, it is proper that I should say to you, that wherever our business interests may place us, I feel it is too late in our lives to personally go apart. Friendships have little value, if they are only determined by personal interest and go to pieces on the first clashing of interest; on my part, I can assure you, this will never be the case, as far as my esteem and attachment for you are concerned.

I have never had in anything so large an interest as in the Great Northern Co., to which I have held on until now, under every condition, these many years, because of my implicit faith in you. I have always spoken frankly to you, and I say now to you, that the manner in which this proposed acquisition of control of the Burlington has been proceeded with has not been in the best interests of the Great Northern shareholders. Since you have deemed it well that the Burlington be controlled partly by the Great Northern Co., your judgment, as to this, is to me final, but I am afraid you have permitted others to induce you, because of the personal advantage and profit they will get therefrom, to pay an exorbitant price, rather than to follow lines through which much might have been saved to the companies which acquire control.

As to the Union Pacific, it must take care of itself, as it will be able to do, but in any event, I want to feel that nothing has come between us, for I would truly be less happy if such could ever be the case, and I am

As ever, your friend,

Jacob H. Schiff

The market opened strong Tuesday morning, April 9, with Burlington hitting a record 188½. Northern Pacific was strong with large-block purchases and there was strong buying throughout the day of the St. Paul, the Atchison, and the Rock Island. Burlington finished up 3¼, Northern Pacific up 2. At the Netherland Hill read Schiff's letter. He pondered Schiff's words and then sat down to pen a three-page reply in his own strong, forceful hand. He used some of the same obscure language that had sounded to Schiff like the "platitudes" Hill had used at Baker's mansion:

My dear Mr. Schiff

Your kind note of yesterday received for which I am greatly obliged. I beg to assure you that the long years of intimate and friendly association between us, which while growing out of business relations has long since sunken so deeply into my life, that no act or thought of mine can ever knowingly destroy or impair the feeling of affectionate friendship which I hold to both yourself and those who are nearest to you.

I have missed your counsel in the CB&Q matter very much, but I felt with the knowledge I had of the situation that any discussion of the subject between us would only lead to mutual embarrassment. However, I took occasion to say to Mr. Harriman a day or two after my arrival [in New York in January] that if he should ask me if there was any truth in the rumor that the Gr Nor or Nor Pac were working for control of the "Q" I could not say the rumor had no foundation. I wanted Mr. Harriman's first information to come from me.

I have worked hard in the interest of peace and harmony for more than two years, but I sometimes find without much success. When the So. Pac. matter was on the table I did all I could to help the interest of yourself and friends. If I had said the word "yes" the control would have been much more secure, regardless of what the outcome might have been.

I have for years considered the Burlington as our nearest ally in case of any attempt concerning territory beyond St. Paul to the South, and as late as when the "St. Paul deal" was being considered, you will recall my saying to you that we would not pay above a certain figure, as I really preferred the Burlington at a higher price. You said it would be very difficult to do anything with the C.B.&Q that your friend [Harriman] had tried it and given it up, as impracticable. There was no opposition to our buying the St. Paul and I assure you my astonishment is very great at the position of the Nor. Pac. [Union Pacific?] today. It could not legally take a single step toward its control of the C.B.&Q west of the Mo. River. Our discussion with the Board of that Co. develop [?] as one of the strong privileges [?] of that Co. the fact that they can build a much shorter line to San Francisco, with lower grades and with 3 1.2 % money. They have a connection over the Nor. Pac. with the Puget Sound country, and do not desire to extend in that direction.

There are already four lines from the East to Washington and Oregon, and only two to California. We do not need any more through coastlines. Therefore I was strongly of the opinion that a control of the CB&Q by the Gr. Northern + the NorPac. would remove any object for extending to the Pacific and insure the greatest harmony. However, I find myself mistaken.

Whatever is done allow me to assure you in all sincerity that I will always be not only ready but desirous to consider the situation of our neighbors as well, of our competitors. I like peace, and am not ashamed or afraid to work for it, in every consistent manner. On the other hand, I do not think the time has come when we must acknowledge that we have no rights which our neighbors claim for themselves, or such as we are willing to accord to them. Again, thanking you I am ever faithfully yours,

Jas. J. Hill

That afternoon, April 9, Hill took a carriage down to the financial district to be nearby for a board meeting of the Northern Pacific, and he conferred late into the afternoon with Baker on the Burlington talks and the motives of Schiff and Harriman. On Wednesday the 10th, a week after closing over 180, the Burlington closed over 190, up 5¾ on heavy volume. Northern Pacific rose with it, up 1¼, closing at 97⅞.

At 8:41 Ireland time that evening, after a stormy passage of eight days, the twinkling lights and tall stacks of the *Teutonic* were visible through the darkness from Cork Harbor as the steamer glided into port at Queenstown (Cobh). No reporters were allowed on board "owing to the presence of Mr. Morgan." Exhausted, he had played his favorite card game, Miss Milligan two-deck solitaire, and slept most of the voyage. A cordon of detectives waited for him at the pier at Liverpool for the ride to London in a private train car. There was good reason for the security; Scotland Yard was investigating numerous threats on his life, namely letters written to him blaming him "for the present distress among British workingmen." His son Jack Jr. was there to meet him at Eustis Station where Morgan hurried through a crowd of reporters to his private carriage and drove off with his grandsons on his knees. They headed for the former London residence of Morgan's father, the five-story double crème-colored mansion at 13–14 Prince's Gate facing Hyde's Park, where Morgan for tax reasons now housed much of his art collection.

Profit-takers seized the market in New York, sending Burlington down 3¼, and Northern Pacific down 1¾ on heavy total market volume of 1.7 million shares. Brokerage firms were buying Northern Pacific in large blocks: 2,500 shares, 3,000, 4,000. Did Hill and Bacon see the *Wall Street Journal* that morning? Front page, above the fold, it pointed to dark clouds: Northern Pacific's acquisition of the Burlington "threatens to antagonize Union Pacific [which] is not taking social action, but the interests back of Union Pacific are very powerful and their disapproval is not a matter to be taken lightly...Hints were given in various quarters that all was not well, and that powerful interests might make themselves felt before long in the money market."

If Hill and Bacon were worried about Harriman and Schiff retaliating they gave no sign. Hill's mind was on leaving town and heading west. For years he hoped to take his old friend and investor, Edward Tuck, a member of the board of the Chase National Bank (Hill's properties were its single largest depositor), on a personal round-trip tour of the Great Northern from St. Paul to Seattle. Tuck retired from banking in 1881 and had lived in France, first as a diplomat and then with John Munroe and Company, the only American bank in Paris at the time. Then, as an expatriate philanthropist, he had become a sort of unofficial U.S. ambassador to France, later giving his extensive art collection to the Petit Palais and having a boulevard named after him near the Tuileries. He owned a lavish apartment on the Champs Elysees, a country estate in Rueil, a winter villa at Monte Carlo. He was a noted raconteur and wit and he and Hill enjoyed the banter of camaraderie. Tuck had made a hobby of investing in and channeling European investors into Hill's Great Northern and was to have been one of the primary investors in Hill's aborted purchase of the Northern Pacific in 1895. Hill postponed his trip home twice that week, on Wednesday and again on Thursday. Was he waiting for final cable approval from Morgan on the Burlington?

The market closed on Friday, April 12, with Burlington up 1, just below 190, Northern Pacific up 1⅛ to over 98. Morgan was at his Old Broad Street office in London meeting with English bankers, then reassured British ironmasters that U.S. Steel had no intention of driving them out of business. Hill and Tuck departed New York's Grand Central station for St. Paul in Hill's private car, the cars of his vice president Darius Miller and chief engineer John Stevens, and a combination express-baggage car. Hill also brought his oldest son, thirty-one-year-old James Norman. Tuck brought his young nephew, Amos French, a vice president of the Manhattan Trust Company and son of the late Francis Ormond French, associate of Jay Cooke during the 1873 panic and a former president of the Manhattan. Hill, Tuck, and young Amos were now all on the Manhattan board.

As their train sped through the countryside of Pennsylvania and Ohio the morning of Saturday, April 13, there was strong buying during the two-hour session. The Burlington deal pushed up volume and prices for the Rock Island, the St. Paul, and the Union Pacific. Broker Harry Content, known for his connections to James R. Keene and Morgan but probably trading that day on his own account, bought 8,000 shares of Northern Pacific, perhaps as many as 20,000 in all. In twenty-two days, Content would stalk the floor of the Exchange for every possible share of Northern Pacific for Morgan and Hill. The rate on overnight call loans reached 6 percent but Morgan, acting as the Central Bank before there was one, was said to have wired orders to his New York office that money should be kept relatively easy. The Morgan firm supplied all overnight loan demand at 5 percent.

Hill's private four-car train pulled into the 700-foot-long iron and glass shed of the St. Paul Union Depot early Sunday morning, April 14. After the long winter, it was, as Mary Hill wrote in her diary, "a most perfect day." There were strollers and carriages up and down tree-lined Summit Avenue on the bluff where the Hill's huge brownstone mansion overlooked the city and the Mississippi River valley. At 1:50 the next afternoon under a crystal-clear sky, Hill's four-car private train eased out of the St Paul Depot shed carrying Hill, son James, Tuck, French, Miller, and Stevens pulled by a Great Northern locomotive. It had been eighty-seven years since George Stephenson of England, a coal man like Hill, invented the steam railway locomotive but its fundamentals and "mechanical honesty" had not changed: fire-burning coal creating gas and steam—pushing through valves, powering cylinders, rotating pistons, pushing side rods, churning wheels. The ten-wheel steam locomotive that pulled the Hill train for part of the trip likely was one of ten Hill ordered two years earlier from one of America's oldest, most respected manufacturers of steam locomotives, the seventy-year-old Rogers Locomotive Company of Paterson, New Jersey, what Hill knew as belonging to the Class E-3 "Passenger Engine 900" series. He took special pride in impressing Tuck and French with its efficiency, power, and endurance. Build it once and build it right, indeed. It wasn't sold for scrap until the 1930s.

Hill probably could rattle off its dimensions from memory. Engine and tender weighed 115,000 tons. The engine cylinders were eighteen by twenty-six inches. The boiler was over five feet wide, designed for 210 pounds of pressure per square inch. The firebox was nine feet by three feet. The engine, with a heating surface of about two thousand square feet, held 243 heating tubes each two inches in diameter. The tender held 4,500 gallons of water and eight tons of coal. The driving wheels were six feet in diameter with cast-steel centers, the truck wheels three feet in diameter with wrought-iron plate centers and steel tires. Hill was so impressed with his Rogers locomotives he had recently hired a Rogers's superintendent as a consultant.

Based in St. Paul, the train was run by Hill's best crew: conductor C. McCormick in charge, the "president's engineers" John Kilbain and Peter J. Olson, who had made this run with Hill two years earlier, and firemen W. C. Gardner and C. C. Jordan. All were ready to relieve each other every 200 miles or so in eight-hour shifts. Everything had to be perfect and polished for the boss: Pins and bearings snug? Valves and side rods well lubricated, free of clogging grease? Boiler foaming efficiently, free of scum and oil? Their passage west would take four days across 1,823 miles, five states, four mountain ranges, across right-of-way granted by Congress through nine Indian nations, over or along ten major rivers, and across three time zones to Seattle.

In New York, the market opened higher. Northern Pacific touched 100, then backed off to close at 99⅜, down ⅛. Bacon, paying no visible notice, was in Boston addressing restless stockholders grumping that the guaranteed bonds offered them would not produce a high enough return to make them want to part with their stock. Schiff and his team scavenged the globe for Northern Pacific shares. They had 150,000 shares of common, 18.75 percent of the shares outstanding. They needed 400,000 for a majority. They had 100,000 shares of Northern Pacific preferred, 13.3 percent of the shares outstanding. They needed 375,000 for a majority.

For the next six days, as Hill and his troupe wheeled west, as Morgan foraged the art galleries of London, Schiff's agents kept shopping: quietly, secretly, 10,000 here, 20,000 there, in New York, Boston, Philadelphia, Chicago, Berlin, Frankfurt, London, Amsterdam, Vienna, and Paris, slowly loosening Hill–Morgan's grip on the Northern Pacific. They planted rumors to throw their adversaries off the scent. "A story circulated today," said one New York newspaper, "that the Kuhn–Loeb–Harriman interests had sold to the Hill–Morgan party a big block of Burlington accumulated by the former below 150. This was taken as indicating that the success of the [Burlington] deal was assured, and also that the Union Pacific had nothing to fear from the deal." Wrong, on both points. A few days earlier another false rumor, perhaps by Kuhn, Loeb, floated to explain the rise in Northern Pacific: its board was considering an extra dividend, perhaps worth as much as 5 to 10 percent more to the market price of the common stock, in Wall Street slang, "melon-cutting." There was no melon. There would be no cutting. Northern Pacific didn't have surplus earnings to return to shareholders.

That Monday afternoon, April 15, the Hill train crossed St. Anthony Falls over the Mississippi in Minneapolis on the serpentine Stone Arch Bridge that Hill built in 1884 to resemble a Roman aqueduct. From Anoka north to St. Cloud they followed the east bank of the Mississippi, dotted with rafts of timber floating to the mills, and rolled out onto the greening prairie and dairy farms of central Minnesota, brick and clapboard depots of German settlements blurring past, curving around lakes so abundant one observer said it felt like "being at sea on a railway train." At Fergus Falls they met the Red River of the North as it plunged from the valley into rapids. Dusk came at Fargo. They sped north into the night under a waning moon across a "limitless expanse of unfenced fields, of growing wheat and stubble field," past shadows of hay stacks and grain elevators "everywhere on the horizon like ships at sea."

They crossed the Red River into the heart of the number-one hard wheat region of Grand Forks into North Dakota, where Hill began his dramatic push west fifteen years earlier. He had bought 7,000 acres of this land twenty years before in Kittson County, Minnesota, for a bonanza wheat farm he called Northcote, where it was said you could plow seven or eight miles straight through the clay and sandy loam without a twist or turn. It was a smart investment, but his dream for the Great Northern was that someday he could look out into the darkness along his railroad on the northern plains and see lights glowing from one small family farm after another, each with 160 homesteaded acres. The answer, he thought, was "dry farming," coaxing wheat and alfalfa from the arid soil by plowing deep to push moisture up to the root of the wheat, then tamping the soil to trap moisture. Rotate crops. Irrigate. Fertilize. Immigrants were flooding into the northern Great Plains by the thousands, wide-eyed families with their steerage trunks gathered at railroad platforms, not just from Europe but native-born Americans from the east and south; a month earlier, an estimated 2,400 had departed one weekend from St. Paul on four trains on the Great Northern and the Northern Pacific. "Enormous areas of fertile soil," Hill called this, "like opening the vaults of a treasury and bidding each man help himself." He had been right so many times. This time he was never more wrong.

Hill and his guests slept through the night, curtains closed. Firemen Gardner and Jordan sweated and shoveled coal from the tender into the intense red glow of the firebox. The locomotive's solitary headlamp was a lonely glowing dot in an expanse of black on the prairie. Past shelter belts of box elder and all the huddled little settlements as they neared the geographic center of North America. Great heaps of buffalo bones at station after station.

Dawn came in western North Dakota across the ocean of prairie grass, giant cottonwoods, buttes, and the first flowers of spring: wood's rose, bluebills, leopard lilly. They set their gold pocket watches back an hour at the Missouri River near Williston, 614 miles from Saint Paul and 1,168 to Seattle, ninety-six years to the day that Meriwether Lewis and William Clark arrived at this point.

In New York, the Burlington rose 6¼ and closed at 194⅞. Northern Pacific common closed over 100 for the first time in the stock's history, 103⅞, up 5½. Hill may have noticed something unusual. During the last seventeen trading days, Northern Pacific common's daily volume had averaged almost 80,000 shares, more than twice its average daily volume earlier in the year. One brokerage firm today bought 10,000 shares of Northern Pacific common. Many others, however, seeing Northern Pacific over 100, and who bought it a $10, $30, or $50 a share, took profits. One unidentified Morgan associate around this time sold 35,000 shares. Someone else at Morgan sold 10,000. Brokerage firms secretly retained by Kuhn, Loeb happily scooped it all up.

Morgan wasn't paying attention. He was reported to have just bought Thomas Gainsborough's *Georgiana, Duchess of Devonshire*, in London. It had, for him, great sentimental value. His father wanted to buy it a quarter century earlier in London, but a thief broke into Thomas Agnew's Bond Street gallery and stole it. Six days before Morgan sailed for Europe, the same thief, criminal mastermind Adam Worth, surrendered it after two years of negotiations to William Pinkerton at the Auditorium Hotel in Chicago for $25,000 ransom. It was shipped back to Agnew's on Bond Street where Morgan bought it via cable sight unseen, refusing to reveal the price. "Nobody will ever know," he was quoted saying. "If the truth came out I might be considered a candidate for the lunatic asylum." The rumor was $125,000 to $150,000.

Where the Yellowstone flows into the Missouri the Hill train followed Lewis and Clark, past Fort Buford where Sitting Bull had surrendered. It crossed into the ranch country of eastern Montana, with herd after herd of cattle, buffalo, sheep, and horses dotting low buttes and green meadows of hay to the horizon. It was there fourteen years ago that some nine thousand Great Northern workers, many of them Irish, shoveled a roadbed two to three feet high, built bridges, and laid 550 miles of steel track west from Minot in six months, an average of three and a quarter miles of track a day, including a Great Northern record eight and one-tenth miles in one day. On those same tracks along the Milk River, Hill's train gradually rose at Chinook into a valley surrounded by the Bears Paw mountains, where Nez Pierce Chief Joseph had surrendered. When Hill was building west on this stretch thirteen years earlier, tribes ceded more than nineteen million acres to the federal government along the line, reducing the Fort Berthold Reservation in North Dakota by 60 percent and the Blackfeet's land in Montana by 80 percent. Lamont was President Cleveland's executive secretary at the time, perhaps helping grease the Congressional wheels for Hill.

The Hill train slowed into the Great Northern station and locomotive shops at Pacific Junction (later Havre) thirty-five miles from Canada for water and coal and to dump cinders. Halfway to Seattle, they were at the Great Northern junction that struck out southwest toward the mines and waterpower of Great Falls, Helena, and Butte. Straight on and flat they rolled west the next one hundred miles across plains green, gold, and brown, past cattle ranges and wheat farms. Near Cut Bank, wheat fields gave way to grassy plains, less water, and drier soil, and they entered the Blackfeet Reservation, catching their first glimpse of the distant Rockies.

It was there twelve years earlier that Hill parted company with Lewis and Clark's trail. Jefferson's orders were to explore the Missouri River, so they followed it south. Hill, however, needed a direct route west for his railroad and he was desperate; both the Canadian Pacific to the north and the Northern Pacific to the south already had crossed the Rockies. Hill commissioned his rugged, resourceful chief engineer John F. Stevens to find the pass, and now here was Stevens himself in the car with Tuck and French describing for them, matter-of-factly, how he did it. In December 1889, first with a Salish guide and then alone, he had followed the Marias River, as the Salish had for centuries. In handmade snowshoes strung with rawhide he pushed through waist-deep snow in a blizzard at forty below zero to the summit where he could see the course of the Marias winding west. It was the lowest pass across the Montana Rockies, 5,200 feet above sea level, a 1 percent grade on the west, a 1.8 percent grade on the east. It shortened Hill's route to the coast by one hundred miles, no tunnel needed.

The train climbed the barren granite slope into the wind and snowpack of Marias Pass across the Continental Divide, through deep, misty forest, and across the trestle bridge over the Flathead River canyon. It descended the western side through deep snow, past the rail villages of Libby and Troy, and over the whitewater of the Kootenai River, "sea green in the pools." Crossing over Columbia Falls, it rolled down the foothills into Whitefish, Montana, west of the Divide, shielded at last by the Rockies from the dry wind of the eastern plains. They pushed on through the night, gaining another hour into the Pacific time zone, across the Idaho panhandle and sagebrush plains of eastern Washington along the Columbia River basin. The train paused in Spokane for water and coal, passing the wheat-shipping centers of Coulee City and Dry Falls then on a trestle bridge over a gorge eight-hundred feet deep called Moses Coulee.

Dawn came in the broad, fertile Wenatchee Valley of central Washington where Tuck and French saw, rising from volcanic ash, row after row of apple trees ready to blossom. This fall the Great Northern would transport the first commercial shipment of Wenatchee Valley apples west to Seattle for export to Asia. Surrounded by marsh with deer and elk, they were 120 miles from Seattle. They passed a railroad construction camp called Leavenworth and ahead, past hillsides where they could spot mountain goats, loomed the northern Cascades, an ascent of 3,000 feet in just a few miles. At Rock Island, they crossed over an 875-foot trestle bridge that Hill's crews had built almost a decade earlier.

The Rogers locomotive and its four cars scaled the Cascades against the downdraft of the Chinook winds, past granite cliffs, through Tumwater Canyon, rock lilies in bloom, the roaring spring melt and spray of the Wenatchee River, glaciers of snow and ice. At Madison, the Great Northern tracks made a 180-degree loop over the Tye River. Here again, eleven years earlier, Stevens followed the water. He found a creek in the eastern foothills of the Cascades he was certain would lead to the lowest, flattest pass. He climbed and trudged for miles and at one point crawled on hands and knees over sharp ridges to follow the Wenatchee River and the shortest course over the Cascades to the summit near Wellington. Hill's crews built a series of switchbacks, three on the east side, five on the west, the last spike driven January 3, 1893, in the final gap of seven miles from St. Paul to Seattle. Then the switchbacks were replaced by a two-and-a-half mile tunnel, opened just five months earlier. The tunnel shot so straight through the bore that inside it Tuck and French would have been able to see a faint dot of light at the end. To make the passage the Hill train had switched to an electric locomotive, because steam and hot engine gases in the tunnel could asphyxiate.

Down they sped on the western side as the path opened to the Pacific, through dense pine and fir, the mud of spring, over the Foss River trestle bridge at Skykomish, descending slowly through the Great Northern settlements of Index, Gold Bar, Sultan, and Snohomish. On the New York Stock Exchange, trading seemed quiet, Northern Pacific closed down 1⅝ to 102¼.

As the Hill train neared Puget Sound, a portent appeared in the "Wall Street Gossip" section of the *Commercial Advertiser* in New York. It was a clue to the Harriman–Schiff scheme: the move up in Northern Pacific buying was thought to be caused by "brokers understood to be acting for prominent interests identified with the largest bank in the city." That was National City Bank, run by James Jewett Stillman.

Hill wanted to have his guests in Seattle late Wednesday night, April 17, but they lost five hours due to slow tracks on mushy spring soil. Then a mudslide blocked the train as it approached Everett, Washington, on Port Gardiner Bay and the mouth of the Snohomish River north of Seattle. At 5:15 a.m. on Thursday, April 18, Hill's train slowed through the darkness just before dawn along the rail corridor through the Elliot Bay waterfront south of downtown Seattle and pulled up to the canopy of the Northern Pacific's neglected little rail depot. Hill, who had given Seattle its first direct rail link to the east, apologized for the shabbiness. Work had begun the previous September to clear the site for a union passenger depot and freight warehouses. There were plans to tunnel under downtown, Hill explained, and build a new station at King Street. His dream of global transport did not stop at the water's edge: Seattle was his gateway to Asia. In June a year earlier he had proposed to stockholders the building of Great Northern's own line of Pacific steamers.

In Boston, Hill's lawyers with Morgan's Bacon and Steele had finally agreed that morning to terms with Charles Perkins and his board to buy the Burlington. They sweetened the pot by raising the annual guarantee on the joint Great Northern–Northern Pacific bonds for Burlington stockholders from 7.7 percent to 8 percent, pricing them at 200 at 4 percent rather than 220 at 3.5 percent for every $100 of Burlington stock. The market drew comfort; the deal appeared done. The Burlington and the Northern Pacific both closed up a fraction, the latter at 103 with trading volume moderate enough not to attract attention. Total market volume was strong, almost 1.7 million shares traded.

Hill's train spent only a few hours in Seattle, long enough to load coal and water, go through the roundhouse, and begin its return east. Hill wanted to show Tuck and young French what the Great Northern could do; he sent orders to clear the tracks, stop only for coal and water. He wired to St. Paul he wanted "fast time" home. They passed through Everett, just north of Seattle, at 12:05 p.m. There was not, as myth has grown around this trip, any urgent business for Hill to get back to in St. Paul or in New York. Northern Pacific common's trading volume was up significantly, yes, and it had crossed 100 but that was not compelling enough to cause him to rush back in a panic. He simply wanted to show Tuck and his European investors how the quality and efficiency of the Great Northern's tracks, engines, cars, and facilities translated into speed to market for its freight customers, more revenue for the railroad, and a better return for investors.

Tuck and French, in a way, were a proxy for oranges. Just the past Tuesday, March 26, fourteen Great Northern refrigerator cars carrying 5,000 boxes of oranges from the Southern California Fruit Exchange had left Seattle at 1 p.m. They arrived in Minneapolis at 11 a.m. that Friday in first-class condition, their temperatures varying only four degrees from 44 to 48. The trip took sixty-five hours, considered a record time of almost twenty-eight miles an hour, deducting for station delays, and it came to be called the "orange special." Hill would have argued, by the way, that it was a perfect example of the need for lower rates for long hauls and a guaranteed "through rate" for the shipper, which meant lower retail prices for oranges. Short hauls naturally were more expensive: they required more handling of freight and switching of cars relative to their volume.

Hill's train stopped at Spokane where Stevens's and Miller's private cars were uncoupled. They were now just Hill's private car and the baggage-express car pulled by the Rogers locomotive. On Friday, April 19, under a moonless sky spangled with stars, Hill ordered Chief Engineer Olson to pick up speed over a straight, flat shot. Like a jockey and his racehorse, he wanted to put the new Rogers locomotive through its paces on a fast track. "This would be a good chance," he told Olson as they approached Cut Bank, "to see what he [the Rogers locomotive] could do." With Olson at the controls, the train roared toward the dawn across north-central Montana. For the next 126 miles, from Cut Bank to Pacific Junction, Montana, to the delight of Tuck and French, the needle on the meter of the locomotive's console passed 55 miles an hour, then 60, 65, 70, 75, and 80, to reach a top speed of 84.6 miles. The engine vibrated so much that fireman Gardner couldn't stand up in the cab; he shoveled coal sitting down.

Like Hill's locomotive, the market opened with a strong surge in New York and kept building. Then, out of nowhere, with no sign of it during the week, it leapt to a plateau of higher prices that seemed to catch everyone off guard. Buying erupted on the floor at a dozen posts at the same time. Shouting scrums of traders roiled around the posts of the railroad stocks. Every important stock on the list rose, even Canadian Southern up 10½, Lake Erie & Western up 5, Pacific Coast Railroad up 5½. The St. Paul ignited on rumors it was underpriced and might soon follow Burlington into a merger, closing up 4⅞ to 163¾. Stocks traded not just by hundreds or thousands but tens of thousands. The last sale in Union Pacific common, up 4 for the day, was recorded by the ticker at 10,000 shares at a post-1897 record of $100 a share. The intensity of it reminded many of the previous record volume after McKinley was reelected in November, and then again January 7. Trading set a record of 2.2 million shares. When stop orders and unrecorded transactions were added it probably would near 3 million. What caused it? That Hill had the Burlington and that could set off more mergers? Rates for call loans as cheap as 3 percent? Rumors that strikes against iron and steel companies were unlikely? No one was sure. Northern Pacific, however, hid in the weeds on light volume, up only a quarter to 103¼.

That evening, April 19, Morgan departed London by private railroad car, crossed the English Channel to Le Havre and arrived in Paris. The next afternoon at 12:55 p.m., Hill's train steamed into the St. Paul depot, completing the return trip of 1,823 miles in a record running time of forty-five hours and fifty minutes, nineteen hours faster than normal, consuming one hundred tons of coal. Hill said he could have made it home five hours faster but all he had to do was get to St. Paul in time for Tuck to catch the evening train to Chicago so he could depart New York for Paris on Monday.

The Rogers locomotive eased to the platform and some two hundred Great Northern employees cheered as Hill stepped from the train. His secretary, George C. Clark, thrust a telegram in his hand. Hill opened the envelope and read it. It was in cipher from the Northern Pacific's Lamont. "Is it Louisa Pomegranate to Comport Hopingly Nursery Wooden?" (Is it your plan to come here [New York] next week?) Lamont was right to ask the question. Northern Pacific stock was lifting with velocity, but neither he nor Hill had connected the dots. There were no alarming trends on European exchanges, trading was dull on the Berlin Bourse. Hill decided to stay in St. Paul a few more days. In Boston, Charles Perkins announced he favored accepting the Hill–Morgan offer of $200 a share in guaranteed 4 percent bonds from each Hill road for every $100 par value in Burlington stock. Morgan agreed to include in the purchase price a cash payment of $50 million for smaller Burlington shareholders who didn't want the bonds.

On the same day, Great Northern's board, with assent from Northern Pacific, voted to empower Hill to buy 96.79 percent of Burlington's shares by issuing bonds and scrip valued at $215 million, committing Great Northern and Northern Pacific to debt payments of $8.72 million a year. In the end, Perkins and Hill–Morgan split the difference. Perkins got his $200 a share but mostly in bonds not cash. Harriman must have been outraged. A month earlier he offered $200 a share in 3 percent Union Pacific bonds and cash. The Great Northern and the Northern Pacific would become joint owners of the Burlington, each owning half its stock. The long-independent Burlington, pride of provincial Boston wealth, had finally sold out, through Hill–Morgan, to New York's Wall Street.

The board voted ten to one to sell. The lone dissenter was the only New Yorker, James H. "Silent" Smith, the multimillionaire New York society *arriviste* who had opposed Hill–Morgan's approach to the St. Paul three months earlier. Thus began the decades-long demise of the two other Chicago-based lines, the Rockefellers's St. Paul and the Vanderbilts's North Western, neither immediately wanting to build to the Coast or wanting to partner with a transcontinental to get there. Hill later compared them to "Ginx's Baby," the satire about a poor foundling in nineteenth-century England who became the object of competing do-gooders. The St. Paul and the North Western would both remain, said Hill (contradicting his April 9 letter to Schiff), "nobody's child . . . until they build to the Coast, which I hope they will do, and also that they will build to Puget Sound. The addition of the business of two such lines to Puget Sound would greatly help that seaport and would enlarge the whole business, and in the end would do us much more good than harm."

Attention shifted to the spectacular, inexplicable rise in the Union Pacific. From the first day of trading in January to April 18 when Hill headed back home from Seattle, Burlington rose 38 percent, Northern Pacific 23 percent, and Union Pacific 22 percent. From April 18 to May 1, Burlington rose 2.5 percent to almost 199, Northern Pacific common rose 12 percent to 115, but Union Pacific common rose at a pace two and a half times that, another 29 percent to 129. Its daily average trading volume during that time was almost four times greater than that of Northern Pacific: 260,000 versus 66,000.

As the Hill train entered Minnesota, the galleries were standing-room only at the Stock Exchange long before the opening, jammed with men and women from uptown, even spectators from the country come to see what everyone expected would be a morning of spectacular Saturday trading condensed into two hours. Minutes before 10 a.m. the floor was filled with traders, buzzing that early advances had held in London. Everyone on the floor was in place, the messengers, the members bunched around the stock posts, the reporters and telephone boys poised along the walls.

Chairman Kennedy, every eye on him, dropped the gavel, and "with a roar and a rush the groups surged up tight about the posts, brokers reached over one another, jumped and yelled." Tickers could not at first absorb the electric rush of volume. Only two quotes appeared on the ribbon in the first three minutes. "Then the machine whirled away, showing prices up as much as a point and a half in big lots. Traders jumped into pandemonious mobs, leaping, gesturing, fighting." It looked like a "bull panic," setting a record for Saturday's two-hour trading session, 1.15 million shares with some 30,000 shares changing hands the first ten minutes. Even the little granger railroad, Chicago & East Illinois, rose a phenomenal twelve points. Fifteen thousand shares of Union Pacific changed hands in one trade. Trading volume surpassed the previous week's record.

Were buyers pushing up Union Pacific because Hill had the Burlington, and the Union Pacific would pursue the St. Paul or the North Western? That alone couldn't account for Union Pacific's amazing rise the last half of April. Were Harriman and Schiff buying Union Pacific shares on the open market, perhaps with insiders such as Stillman, Rockefeller, and Gould, to protect it from a takeover, or perhaps to divert attention from the rise in Northern Pacific? Street rumors, followed by headlines, turned to William K. Vanderbilt. Were the Vanderbilts going to create a transcontinental? They controlled the New York Central, giving them direct access into Chicago. They had controlling influence of the Chicago & North Western from Chicago west into Omaha. Could they then buy the Union Pacific out from under Harriman and become a true transcontinental? Unlike his famous grandfather the Commodore, however, William K. lacked the motivation and moxie to act alone, the rumors went, so perhaps he was an agent of...Morgan? Did Morgan want to create a Vanderbilt transcontinental a la U.S. Steel? If he did, surely he couldn't leave it to the overwhelmed Bacon to orchestrate such a risky venture while he was vacationing in Europe?

Hill bid good-bye to Tuck and young French and began the week of April 21 back at his desk in St. Paul, running his railroads, keeping his good eye on the ticker, communicating with Bacon, George Perkins, Lamont, and Baker via telephone and coded cablegram. He still had not persuaded himself he needed to go to New York. His job was to run the railroads not second-guess Wall Street. Perhaps he didn't want Morgan getting wind that he was interfering with his partners Bacon, Steele, and George Perkins. He had to be careful; reporters would try to read signals into his New York presence.

"Can come last of week," he cabled back to Lamont on Sunday, "if I can do any good." Lamont responded the next day, "Mr. Bacon thinks it desirable that you come as early as practicable." Bacon wanted him in New York only, it seemed, to help "execute necessary papers" to determine the portions that the Great Northern and the Northern Pacific would contribute to the $50 million cash payment to Burlington shareholders who didn't want the bonds. There was not a single mention of suspicion about the rise in Northern Pacific.

The week began with the market on fire. On Monday, April 22, the Exchange set a record for volume, 2.3 million shares. An estimated 100,000 shares traded the last hour. Looking back months later, one broker in New York pinpointed April 22 as the day on which "the big men were moving." A great backlog of orders flowed into the Exchange that had accumulated over the weekend due to a blizzard that had dropped a foot of wet snow from Canada to Tennessee and east to the Atlantic, severing wires to brokerage firms in Chicago, Cleveland, Detroit, and Pittsburgh. Most of the active stocks declined but, said the *Wall Street Journal*, "the sentiment of Wall Street leaders is still confident on the long side." Exports, imports, railroad traffic, and consolidations were booming. The U.S. economy was awash in money for investment and speculation. Stocks of some large industrials boomed even more than railroads. Standard Oil remained number one in the total market value of its stock. The "market cap" of General Electric, created nine years earlier by Morgan, was higher than any railroad. Colorado Fuel and Iron had risen fifty points in less than a month.

Volume was high again Tuesday, 1.8 million shares traded. Mrs. Astor's Four Hundred was distracted from the ticker. One of Stillman's daughters, Isabel, walked down the aisle of St. Bartholomew's Church at Madison and Forty-Fourth in a creamy white satin gown with a bridal veil of Brussels lace on the arm of one of William A. Rockefeller's sons, Percy. The market declined the next day with losses of one to three points, but volume again surpassed two million shares. Union Pacific accounted for almost a third of it, rising almost nine points to 107¼ on record volume of 663,000 shares, two-thirds of all the company's common shares outstanding, the most shares ever traded to date for one firm in one day on the Exchange. More than a third of those shares traded in two furious hours. In less than ten days it would be at 133. Another record was set, the largest single block of shares ever traded on the Exchange, 25,000 U.S. Steel common. Hill was quoted in the *Wall Street Journal* denying that his purchase of the Burlington was destructive of "community of interest" or a hostile act. The *Journal* wasn't so sure: "It is easy for hostility to spring up when actions seem to belie words."

Stoked by the Burlington deal and rumors of more mergers, there was enormous buying from Chicago money and foreign interests the next day in Atchison, B&O, Northern Pacific, Southern Pacific, the St. Paul, and Union Pacific, accounting for more than half the total two million shares traded. Some banks and brokerages feared the market was overheating. Prices were too far ahead of values. More worrisome, even peculiar as the *New York Herald* said, there was not a shred of news "bearing thereon." Some brokers required customers to provide more margin, some demanded full cash for more speculative stocks. Some commission houses drastically cut their borrowing. The rise in stock prices, said the *Journal*, "has brought into the market a great many people who, starting with small lots of stock, have increased their lines out of profits . . . Men who have 200 shares have 1,000. They are the men who carry bull markets too far ahead whose enforced selling makes Wall Street panics."

In Paris, Morgan prowled for more art. He strolled into the gallery of the Austrian art dealer Charles Sedelmeyer at 6 Rue de la Rochefoucauld in the Ninth Arrondissement on the right bank. There he bought the Raphael altarpiece *Madonna and Child Enthroned with Saints* from the Colonna Gallery, signed contracts to buy paintings by Reubens, Titian, Nattier, and Morland, and bought Renaissance portraits of the Virgin and Child. Twelve years later at his death the Raphael piece was considered the most valuable in his collection; he was rumored to have paid $500,000 for it, more than Britain alone ever paid for a single painting.

In route to Seattle, Hill had gazed out the window of his private car at prairie and farm field, forest and mountain, river and gorge. He had been reflecting on the future of his railroad and his country. On Friday, April 26, he climbed the stairs to his second-floor office (never using the elevator) in the Great Northern building at Third and Broadway on the Mississippi in St. Paul. A blustery spring wind rattled the windowpanes. He sat down at his rolltop desk and penned a letter to his old friend, Lord Mount Stephen, former president of the Bank of Montreal and one of his three original "associates" in buying the bankrupt St. Paul & Pacific Railroad almost a quarter century earlier.

"We have been making railway history pretty fast for some time, in our part of the country," he wrote, "the United States has grown in population since 1790 at the rate of about doubling every 30 years. Since the close of the Civil War, the increase has been over 41,000,000. If we maintain anything like the above rates, and I see no reason why we shall not do so, we would have a population of 150,000,000 by 1930." He wasn't far off. The U.S. census by 1930 was almost 123 million, by 1950 more than 152 million.

It was now after 2 p.m. Central time. The New York Stock Exchange had closed for its last day of trading in its old building, shrouded in scaffold, ready for demolition. Trading volume, a proxy for the stupendous growth of the nation's economy, had long since outgrown the space. Volume had tripled from 1896 to 1899, this year it would nearly double again. Tom-toms beat as the Exchange clock ticked toward 3 o'clock. The floor was jammed with some eight hundred brokers, many old timers, some of whom hadn't been on the floor for ten or fifteen years, gazing up at the familiar frescoes. "Got to take one more look across these old boards," said one. The galleries were deep with spectators on three sides, including many women in their new spring dresses. One of them in the packed gallery, "very handsomely dressed," was said to have fainted into the arms of a man who carried her to an open window for fresh air. "Oh dear, where am I?" she asked, when she regained consciousness. "Oh yes, how did Southern Pacific close?"

When President Rudolph Keppler tapped his silver and ivory gavel to close trading, brokers heaved snowflakes of scissored memos into the air. Then came a loud boom as four large pans of powder ignited for a flash photograph. Dozens of workmen immediately began packing furniture and removing telephones. Horse-drawn vans and trucks clogged Broad Street. Demolition crews stood ready. There would be no Saturday trading as the Exchange moved to its temporary quarters of a portion of the floor of the New York Produce Exchange, a five-minute walk south from 10 Broad Street.

In St. Paul, a clerk came into Hill's office and handed him a note. Northern Pacific common had jumped 3 points to 108¾, up 7½ for the week. More alarming was the volume. It began the week on Monday at 27,274 shares traded. Tuesday, 39,250. Wednesday, 74,000. Thursday, 78,050. Today, its fifth highest daily trading volume of the year, 129,900.

Hill had many reasons to head for New York this weekend. Bacon and Lamont needed him to work out the cash details of the Burlington offer. He had wanted to depart Saturday so he could visit Monday with banker Grant B.

Schley, brother-in-law of George F. Baker, who was negotiating some matter for him with Harriman and Gould, but Schley had to leave New York and the meeting was canceled. Ever the vigilant father, Hill also wanted to be in New York to bid farewell to daughters Clara and Rachel. They were headed for France on the *Kaiser Wilhelm der Grosse*, eventually to join their older sister "Mamie" in Aix-le-Bains, where perhaps they would get a glimpse of the great Morgan.

Hill had another, unspoken, reason to go to New York. The three-point rise in Northern Pacific common, on volume almost five times that of the previous Monday, convinced him that in Morgan's absence he needed to be at "the corner" with Bacon, George Perkins, Steele, and Lamont. All railroads were lifting in this rising tide but the Northern Pacific, especially its trading volume, was lifting more than most. Was he worried the forty-year-old Bacon was too junior to handle all this alone? On Saturday he may have learned of a front-page rumor in the Wall *Street Journal*. Was word leaking of the Harriman–Schiff plot? One analyst had linked the increased buying of the Northern Pacific to the Union Pacific, but few took him seriously. "There has been for several days what was called Union Pacific buying in Northern Pacific," said the *Journal*.

On Saturday night, April 27, lightning haloed across the valley of the upper Mississippi River; there was a low rumble of thunder from the west. White-bearded Archibald Guthrie, loyal Great Northern colleague of Hill's for more than two decades, drove him down the hill at dusk to the St. Paul Union Depot. Hill boarded the overnight Burlington express for Chicago where he would change trains in the morning for New York and board a drawing-room car on the New York Central's Lake Shore number six.

Schiff apparently was expecting him, too. "For Jacob message received," Hill cabled his assistant Edward T. Nichols, "Expect to be in New York Monday." He had no way of knowing he was embarking on what would be the two most chaotic weeks of his life. A market cyclone was gathering strength that would threaten his control of the Great Northern, the Northern Pacific, and the Burlington. It was about to create or wipe out the wealth of thousands of speculators and bring the New York Stock Exchange to its knees.

6

"THE WEAK LINK IN YOUR CHAIN"

Monday morning, April 29, 1901, hundreds of members of the New York Stock Exchange led by President Keppler marched in two columns five blocks south down New Street from their shuttered building on Broad, through the east entrance of the New York Produce Exchange at 2 Stone Street, up a short, narrow stairway on the south side, and onto the expansive second-floor trading hall, their temporary home for the next two years. The hall was 221 by 140 feet, larger than any arena in the city except Madison Square Garden, staked out with the trading posts and the giant quotation board moved from the old Exchange. The hall's expanse of a fifth of an acre was bathed in sunlight from its huge arched windows and its skylight of stained glass sixty feet above. On the north end of the hall several long marble tables held displays of large bowls of flour, one of the commodities of the Produce Exchange. The traders, boys at heart, could not resist, and flour throwing erupted. The Produce Exchange members joined in and soon all were caked in billowing white dust, anointing the guests in their new home.

The stock traders found their space cramped and congested. Their allotted portion of the floor at the south end measured about 12,000 square feet, 200 smaller than their old home. They were separated from the Produce Exchange trading by a thin, heavy wooden partition eight feet high. Spectators crowding the public gallery above would have to crane their necks even for an obstructed view of stock trading because they were at the north end of the hall overlooking the wheat pit. The stock traders' old home had entrances onto the floor on three sides with plenty of room for brokers, clerks, messengers, and customers to pass. Their temporary space at the Produce Exchange had only one entrance, on the east.

There was abundant light and air, something the traders didn't have in their old home, but when the sun beat down through the huge skylight on a warm day it could melt the starch in a trader's collar and drench his shirt in sweat. Since the stock market had become national entertainment, it was fitting the Produce Exchange still used old calcium lights. They flamed bright with the same cylinders of calcium quicklime used in theaters and music halls. Stock trading truly was in the "limelight." It had taken six weeks to install wiring for the Exchange's 450 private broker telephones and 650 Western Union cables. Over the weekend workmen used a thirty-foot crane to reassemble on the east wall the huge, electric "annunciator" board that alerted any of the five hundred members on the floor by assigned number, with electronically operated flaps, when they were wanted on the phone or at their office. The Exchange employed "annunciators" who operated the electronic buttons, signaled by an attendant who stood at the entrance and called out members' numbers. A new service was added outside: automobiles for transporting brokers and traders to and from their offices.

Befitting the noble aspirations of the American market, the Exchange was a masterpiece of commercial architecture. Its campanile clock tower was visible for miles, a beacon for at least the ideal of "just and equitable principles of trade." Designed by George B. Post and opened in 1884, the Exchange faced the Bowling Green and Battery Park with grace and elegance, standing where two and a half centuries earlier there were cattle sheds with roofs of straw, thatch, and old Dutch tiles that served as the Market-velt-Stegie, the embryo of market trading in New Amsterdam. The building evoked the Italian Renaissance in dark red brick with light-toned granite, in terra cotta bas-relief on its façade were shocks of wheat, ears of corn, and windrows of oats.

Chairman Kennedy stood at the podium high above on the Whitehall Street side of the building, "like a swallow's nest on a cliff," as the seconds ticked toward 10 a.m. The small gallery for spectators on the north wall was jammed, a sea of messengers in Confederate gray uniforms lined the trading floor. Among the observers was a distinctly American touch: "Reddy" the bootblack, a familiar presence at the old Exchange for more than forty years, was given a prominent post at the rail. At 10 a.m. Kennedy whacked the gavel, setting off a "continuous roar from hundreds of throats" from the floor. Trading erupted from pent-up demand after Saturday's holiday and snowstorm delayed executing Friday's high volume. Telephones and electronic call buttons malfunctioned. One large brokerage virtually closed for the day, its telephones dead. Traders were confused by the location of the new trading posts. Clerks from the arbitrage houses had to plow their way back and forth

New York Produce Exchange on a quiet day, temporary headquarters in 1901 for the New York Stock Exchange, site of the May 9 corner and panic. MUSEUM OF THE CITY OF NEW YORK/ART RESOURCE, NY.

through mobs on the floor to get to their offices. At 10:30 trading opened for commodities on the northern end of the floor for the Produce Exchange. The competing roars were deafening, stocks at one end and commodities at the other, heard a block away on the other side of Bowling Green. Some traders found the smaller space so cramped and intimidating they refused to step onto the floor.

There was enormous buying the first hour, 740,000 shares trading, an Exchange record. At precisely 10:30 a.m., as the market boomed, a special train carrying President McKinley, "the high priest of prosperity" with his sickly wife, Ida, and an entourage of forty-three including cabinet members, pulled away from Washington Station. The track was provided courtesy of the Southern Railway, and the cars, at no cost to the White House by the Pullman Company, had interiors of carved mahogany, vermillion and gold, a glass dome over the barber shop. The president had begun a six-week tour across the southern and western United States, to end after a summer hiatus at the Pan-American Exposition in Buffalo in September. This day McKinley's train glided through Manassas, Culpepper, Charlottesville, Lynchburg, through the valleys of the

Rapidan and the James and into Tennessee. Crowds lined the tracks all the way to the city limits of Washington, packing the stations on the route just for a glimpse of the president, "hat in hand, carnation in his buttonhole," waving from the rear platform. He was fifty-eight years old and had 138 days to live.

By noon, trading volume surged past 1.1 million shares. Buying was extraordinary across the board, especially Northern Pacific common, Union Pacific common, New York Central, People's Gas, the steel stocks, and the "Granger" and the "Pacific" railroads. Chicago investors were said to have bought over 300,000 shares in the first hour alone, with London investors buying 100,000. There were renewed rumors: Was the Rock Island almost cornered? Was the source of the buying a major commission house on the Street? "Vanderbilt brokers" were still said to be buying Union Pacific and Chicago & North Western on merger rumors. After all, five New York Central board members were on the North Western board, controlled by the Vanderbilts. Some major Wall Street houses were thought to be buying Union Pacific for Marshall Field of Chicago, a North Western director. Perhaps the North Western would take over the Union Pacific and guarantee 5 or 6 percent on Union Pacific shares?

Chairman Kennedy gaveled the session closed at 3:00 p.m.; exhausted traders cheered, the floor littered with paper. Many traders, drenched in sweat, retreated to the basement baths. Trading volume set another record at 2.7 million shares. There were such long delays recording transactions that some observers thought as many as some 100,000 shares traded had yet to be recorded. Northern Pacific rose a stunning 10¼, closing at a new high, 119, on record volume. Union Pacific common rose 11 to 118¾. Trading in U.S. Steel, Union Pacific, and Southern Pacific was more than a third of the volume. Southern Pacific buying was thought to be from 26 Broadway, headquarters of Standard Oil, on rumors of protecting the property against anti-Harriman raiders. "Some of the Union Pacific people are said to be buying Northern Pacific," said the Wall Street Journal, "although no reason is given. The rise is a mystery."

The Stock Exchange itself had become a more expensive place to do business. On this day someone bought a seat on the Exchange for a record $66,000, almost double what one sold for two years earlier. There were warning signs on the Street of an overheated market. A sheriff walked into the third floor offices of the F. A. Rogers and Company brokerage firm at 38 Wall Street and served papers to close the branch after several clients failed to pay margin calls and the branch was unable to pay depositors' claims.

Hill arrived in New York around noon, checked in at the Netherland, quickly caught a carriage down to the financial district. His jaw must have dropped at the 10¼ rise in Northern Pacific common. Random speculators and plungers could account for some but not all of it. What was behind it? He noticed something even stranger. Northern Pacific preferred this day crossed $100 a share for the first time. It began the year at 87½ but didn't cross 90 until March 27. Then it took off, jumping 2¼ points in one day, April 9, just two days after Harriman threatened Hill at Baker's mansion on Easter Sunday night that he would have to "pay the consequences" for the "hostile act" of buying the Burlington. It kept rising steadily in fractions day after day. On this Monday, April 29, it was up another 1⅝. Since it guaranteed only a 4 percent dividend and the board was expected to retire it next January, it should have traded more as a conservative banking play than the common stock. Yet, it was up a mystifying 15 percent since the beginning of the year. Hill couldn't figure it. He flitted from one office to another—huddling with Bacon and George Perkins at Morgan headquarters, with Lamont next door in his fifth-floor office of cherry wood and marble wainscoting in the U-shaped Mills Building of brownstone and red brick, and at his own office on the ninth floor of Schiff's building on Pine Street on the back side of the Sub-Treasury from Morgan's. Burlington's directors sent a letter to the company's stockholders recommending they accept Hill's offer. Lamont and the Northern Pacific's directors met on this day, too, holding their regular May meeting a few days ahead of time to accommodate schedules.

Undetected, meanwhile, the enemies had breached the Hill–Morgan fortress. Apparently, no one at Morgan or Northern Pacific could discern from their stock transfer books the enormous extent of Harriman–Schiff 's buying. Kuhn, Loeb—known on the Street variously as the "German crowd," the "German clique," the "Deutsche Bank crowd"—had covered its tracks, buying the largest blocks of shares through brokerage firms direct from owners, outside the open market. If Hill scanned the past Saturday's hour-by-hour trading of Northern Pacific common in the New York newspapers looking for a pattern or clue he would have found none. In hindsight it seems such an elementary precaution, especially in the "community of interest" era when owners were expected to buy stock in each other's companies for mutual vigilance; especially since Hill himself publicly had made large personal investments in both the Erie and the B&O. Perhaps he trusted too much in the power and influence of Morgan. He wasn't alone. Raid a *Morgan* property? Unthinkable. No one did think it, except Harriman–Schiff.

Monday melted into Tuesday, some red-eyed traders stayed awake through the night to gather around tickers in hotel lobbies to see how London would open at 4 a.m. New York time. One report called it perhaps the most excited day ever in "Americans" at the London Stock Exchange (scene of the original mania for railway stocks in the mid-1840s), with its great granite dome a hundred feet above Capel Court. British traders were again going crazy for U.S. railroad stocks, and there was high initial volume in U.S. Steel. A crowd of excited short-sellers lingered in "the House" well into the evening.

Taking its cue from London, New York opened in a frenzy at 10 a.m. The roar of traders on the floor took on a sort of animal sound. One reporter described it as "a deafening noise without any articulated sounds except from time to time a long-drawn-out 'Boohoo, oo-ooh,' which is quickly drowned by a shrill 'Aye, yigh, yigh.' . . . These are the cries of the bulls and the bears." If one got close enough, the howling could be deciphered, the faces read, and one could see, as writer Edwin Lefevre re-created in his 1907 novel *Sampson Rock of Wall Street,* that the "eager ears" of the traders "were listening to the voices of those who were selling or buying . . . taking in all the externals of the trading, receiving a thousand little impressions in a fraction of time, so that they too might buy or sell according to their logical, but unanalyzed impulse." *Seven-eighths for a thousand! Sold! A hundred at eight! Any part of a thousand at eight! Three-quarters for two thousand! Seven-eighths for five hundred!*

Tuesday, April 30, went down in history as the "million every minute day." From 10 a.m. to 3 p.m., five hours of "furious trading," an average of $1 million worth of stock traded every minute. More than a million shares traded in one hour, an average of 16,700 shares a minute. In one fifteen-minute period, almost a half a million shares changed hands. It was so chaotic "buyers in one portion of a crowd were paying in some instances as high as $2 a share more than buyers in the same issue not three feet away." Buy orders poured into New York brokerages via telegram and cable from Europe, all across America, especially the Midwest and West, and Canada. U.S. Steel hit a record 55, up 2⅛ on 700,000 shares traded, the preferred closed at 101, up 2. Broker Talbot J. Taylor alone accounted for a purchase of 100,000 U.S. Steel common.

Burlington touched 199⅞. New York Central gained 5, Atchison & Topeka 3¼, Alton 3¾, Erie 3⅜, Missouri Pacific 1¼. More than 400,000 shares traded in Atchison on rumors that the Pennsy, which rose 2¾, was after it as its link to Asia. A "strong bull pool" was said to be buying Louisville & Nashville, which funneled the freight of Cincinnati, St. Louis, and Louisville south through Memphis, Birmingham, Pensacola, and New Orleans. Profit-taking hit Northern Pacific, down 4, and Union Pacific, down 1⅞. Volume surpassed 3.2 million shares, to be the record for the year, almost a half million shares higher than the record the day before.

In the middle of the "million every minute," vows were exchanged uptown. At noon, Miss Adele Neustadt, daughter of Mr. and Mrs. Sigmund Neustadt, entered the parlor of the Neustadt's home at 24 East Sixty-Ninth Street in a gown of white satin. The Reverend Doctor Gustav Gottheil, chief rabbi of Jacob and Therese Schiff's synagogue, Temple Emanu-El, united her in marriage with Schiff's son, Mortimer. Harriman and his wife, Mary, were there to witness the vows. So was one of the ushers, Schiff's loyal junior partner, Louis A. Heinsheimer, who, in just four days, would be an intermediary between Harriman and Schiff, the three bound together in the most historic of Wall Street phone calls. After the wedding, everyone, including the Harrimans and the William Rockefellers, were driven in a convoy of varnished carriages down to Sherry's at Fifth and Forty-Fourth Street for a reception in its opulent Versailles-style ballroom designed by Stanford White.

Hill, who once showed young Morti the ropes as an intern at his office in St. Paul and did the same for Stillman's son Chauncey, was nowhere to be seen. He was never one for the silk of New York society but now he kept his distance for another reason: this was no time to encounter Schiff and Harriman. He had, besides, family obligations. With the market in a frenzy and the Schiff wedding underway, the spring rush was on for Europe. Hill was caught in the crush of some three thousand people on the northern end of the Cunard pier on the North River, trying to board the *Kaiser Wilhelm* to say goodbye to his daughters Clara and Rachel, headed for France. He pushed through the crowd only five minutes before sailing and had to present identification before officers realized who he was and let him on board.

In Boston, Perkins of the Burlington watched the ticker spool out the trading volume and price of Northern Pacific with great unease. He dictated a typewritten letter to Hill, including a copy of the circular mailed to all Burlington shareholders on the proposed sale of the company. He also commented on the startling rise in the price of Union Pacific common, mentioned rumors of a possible three-way deal among the Union Pacific, the Chicago & North

Western, and the "St. Paul," and told Hill that the Burlington, in the face of a stronger Union Pacific, could not "afford to be fenced out of Colorado and Utah or California." Near the end of the letter, almost as an afterthought, he wrote, "I see there has been great buying of Northern Pacific, and high prices. Is not that situation the weak link in your chain?" He did not know Hill was in New York at the Netherland, so he addressed it to Hill's Great Northern office address in St. Paul. The letter never got to Hill in time. It arrived in St. Paul on Friday, May 3.

Bacon came ever so close this day to discovering the plot. By scanning the stock transfer books of Northern Pacific, he could see certain brokerage houses were buying thousands of shares of Nipper common and preferred on the open market. None of these purchases, however, could be traced explicitly to Kuhn, Loeb, which also was orchestrating the selling of some Nipper shares to disguise the plot. Despite all this masterful camouflage, Bacon, to his credit, still was suspicious. But not suspicious enough. In his April 30 cable to Morgan he said he suspected the buying was being done somehow on behalf of Harriman–Schiff merely "with intention at least asking for representation" on the Northern Pacific board, a common "community of interest" practice.

Had Hill warned Bacon of Harriman's "you will have to pay the price" threat? There is no evidence he did. Did Bacon alert Hill or Lamont to the suspicious buying of Nipper shares? If so, Hill and Lamont did as Bacon did. Nothing. Bacon perhaps was unable to probe deeper because he lacked a trader's instincts. Further, his attention was spread thin. In addition to managing U.S. Steel and pursuing the Burlington, Morgan and Company had announced a deal the previous day to buy Great Britain's Leyland Line, the world's largest hauler of steamship freight. The firm also was marketing British war consuls to help finance Britain's war to colonize the south of Africa.

On Wednesday, May 1, Morgan and Company happily sold more than $1 million worth of Northern Pacific shares in the ordinary course of business, because the stock was trading far above its intrinsic value. Sometime in April, one Northern Pacific stockholder had sold some $3.5 million in Northern Pacific shares to Harriman brokers before he received a telegram from Hill asking him not to do it, for reasons that remain a mystery. In late April in London, Donald Alexander Smith, one of Hill's three associates in buying the bankrupt railroad that became the Great Northern, now honored as Lord Strathcona for his role in building the Canadian Pacific, was eighty-one years old and selling certain investments. He saw Northern Pacific common trading in London around $111 a share and through his attorney asked Hill "whether it would be advisable to take advantage of the market and dispose of some of his Stock." The attorney's letter did not reach Hill until Monday, May 6. Lord Strathcona held tight for Hill. "I have word from Mr. Hill," he wrote, "not to part with my stock or be disturbed by a little flurry." He held 30,000 shares of Northern Pacific common, for which he later was offered $700 a share. It would have meant a profit of $20 million, more than a half a billion dollars today. In a few weeks he would be offered much more. Smith's attorney was John Sterling, the lawyer behind the Harriman–Schiff plot.

Some of Hill's friends sold their Nipper shares innocently into the market and later were mortified at being duped. "I cannot tell you how sorry I am," Charles Ellis, a friend of Mount Stephen and Gaspard Farrer, wrote to Hill from London, "I sold all my N.P. shares thinking this was nothing but a mad gamble . . . But of course we were all in the dark . . . I would sooner have thrown the money into the sea than look as if I had sold away for the sake of profit."

Most embarrassing of all was the story of a Northern Pacific insider, the self-important scientist and financier Edward D. Adams. He was a member of the railroad's executive committee, agent of Deutsche Bank in New York City in the Northern Pacific's reorganization of 1896, and pioneer proponent of the commercial advantages of alternating current for electric power. A large portion of Deutsche Bank's holdings of Northern Pacific common were said to be in his name. A large part of that stock, if not all of it, found its way into the hands of Kuhn, Loeb. Adams, however, did not stop there. Sometime between April 11 and April 19, when Morgan was in London, he was thought to have "short-sold" between 5,000 and 7,000 shares of Northern Pacific at an average price of $95 a share, and then later had to eat the difference between that price and the eventual settlement price with Morgan and Company, a loss to Adams of between $275,000 and $385,000, excluding what he had to pay for overnight call loans for borrowing the stock, at one time as high as $700 for every one hundred shares loaned overnight. Perhaps it was the Northern Pacific curse of Henry Villard. Adams was living in one of Villard's mansions on Madison Avenue at Fiftieth.

Estimates were that by May 1 the value of the Hill–Morgan holdings in Northern Pacific common and preferred had shrunk from $40 million to a perilous $26 million. Using Kuhn, Loeb's extensive European contacts, many of the Northern Pacific shares Schiff contracted to buy were in large blocks from holders in Berlin, Amsterdam, and London for delivery in New York.

Schiff later claimed in his letter to Morgan in mid-May that he and Harriman never really wanted to take control of the Northern Pacific, and through it the Burlington. They merely wanted to "be in a position to exercise a potent influence" over the management of both systems and obtain a board position on the Burlington. The buying activity of Kuhn, Loeb throughout April and into early May, however, shows the opposite. They were not just after "potent influence," they were seeking majority control. Six years later, testifying before the Interstate Commerce Commission, Harriman admitted as much. If he'd gained control of the Northern Pacific in 1901, he said, it would be ten years ahead of where it was in 1907. When told of Harriman's remark, Hill was quoted, "My! Mr. Harriman has got control of time, too, has he?"

After nine days in London and twelve in Paris buying art and making business calls, Morgan likely departed Paris on Wednesday, May 1, for Aix-les-Bains in the shadow of the Alps in Savoy, southeastern France. He and his sister, Mary Burns, would have traveled in a rented "PV" (Private Varnish) railroad car, and with them for company was a thoroughbred collie Morgan bought in Paris. They probably hitched to the Savoy Express at the Gare de Lyon station, its lattice of steel and glass completed a year earlier for the World Exposition.

The nine-hour journey to Aix covered 350 miles. It was Morgan's preferred springtime destination, and for centuries since the Romans it was a haven for the rheumatic, anemic, insomniac, gouty, gastric, neuralgic, stressed, and arthritic. At thirty miles an hour, Morgan's train crossed the Marne, through the wooded valleys of the Yeres, and across the plateau of la Brie, descending into the Seine valley, through the Forest of Fontainebleau, though Dijon, Macon, Amberieu, and Culoz. Then it swung around to the vista of the Grand Revard mountains and the graceful bend at the foot of Lac de Bourget, past fields of figs, almonds, Roman ruins, and into the little train station at Aix.

Morgan proceeded via private carriage through the narrow cobblestone streets of Aix up into the wooded countryside and onto a crushed gravel path, stopping in front of a large, butterfly-shaped canopy of wrought iron and glass, the entrance of the lavish pastel-yellow and cream-colored Regina–Grand Hotel Bernascon. It was in art nouveau style, the last word in elegance, opened just a year earlier by the great French hotel capitalist Jean-Marie Bernasconi of Lyon. Built into a forest sloping up to the Alps, the Regina–Grand was six stories, 250 rooms with "*lumiere electrique, ascenseurs luft.*" With two wings flanking a central garden, steep slate roof, square towers, and carved windows with ornate blue grillwork, it had a "magnifique vue" of the Alps from its back and the lake in front.

Morgan was early enough in the spring to be ahead of the crowds, ready for his daily routine that helped him forget steel, railroads, coal, and oil. If he did as custom among pilgrims to Aix, he began in the morning conveyed to the thermal baths draped behind drawn curtains in the privacy of the traditional Aix sedan chair covered by a steep tent of striped canvas. He would have received the *douche,* as Mark Twain did a decade earlier, when "two half-naked men seated me on a pine stool, and kept a couple of warm-water jets as thick as one's wrist playing upon me while they kneaded me, twisted me . . . I came out . . . feeling younger and fresher and finer than I have felt since I was a boy."

Then back Morgan would have been carted, shrouded in his sedan chair, to the Regina–Grand, "rapidly dried, wrapped in flannel sheets and blankets . . . lifted into bed, still swathed like a mummy." He may have perspired in the steam baths with only his sweating head visible as he sat in a wooden box, or may have been immersed in thermal baths of sulfur water at 114 degrees Fahrenheit or submitted to the therapeutic exercises popularized by the Swedish physician Jonas Gustav Zander. Morgan then would have lunch, reply through his secretary to his daily stack of letters and telegrams, embark for motor-cab rides with his sister, Mary, into the surrounding foothills and valleys, perhaps to the village of Annecy with its "old, crooked lanes" and "curious old houses that are a dream of the middle ages," and then back to the Regina–Grand for dinner. The day would end with a cigar and a lighthearted game of bridge and much banter at a hundred francs a point.

Between thermal baths and bridge Morgan must have noticed the alarmingly high volume and remarkable rise in the price of both Northern Pacific and Union Pacific stock. Coded cables ensued between Bacon in New York and Morgan's son, Jack, in London. The elder Morgan may have won a bid of five spades at bridge that evening in Aix, but it never occurred to him he was losing control of a railroad.

7

THE CONSEQUENCES

OF A "HOSTILE ACT"

On Wednesday, May 1, the day Morgan is thought to have arrived in Aix, the New York Stock Exchange went crazy again for Union Pacific common. It opened up nearly two points. Then it rose in a cyclone of bid and ask; with frantic, sweaty mobs of traders swaying, waving, screaming, pushing. Up and up, rocketing nine points in just minutes. In one span of five minutes 32,000 shares of Union Pacific changed hands.

Otto Loeb, a widely known trader, bought Union Pacific at 118½ and sold it a half hour later at 129, pocketing $40,000. Broker H. G. Campbell, known to be an agent of Harriman, sold 30,000 Union Pacific on the rise, perhaps signaling Harriman thought it was the top. One customer ordered his Union Pacific to be sold when it was at 122 or 123, but to his delight when the order was executed it was at 128. It closed at 122⅛, up 13 for the day, on volume of more than a half million shares, almost one of every five Exchange shares traded. New York Central closed up 7, the North Western up over 5. There were large purchases of many other railroads. Brokers "howled and shrieked in the execution of their orders," said the *Wall Street Journal*, "even the messenger boys seemed to have caught the fever, for they rushed about, oftimes aimlessly, or so excited that they failed to remember the purpose for which they were sent." Many clerks worked through the night to catch up on orders. Some leading commission houses, short on clerks, refused to take some orders.

Brokers were so swamped that posts on the trading floor were tacked with buy and sell offers scrawled on paper slips: "We want 5,000 Steel common. Jones & Co." One broker wanted to sell 250 shares that would have been valued at $21,000. He couldn't find a specialist in the stock to take the order so he pinned a signed note to the specialist's post. It went ignored. Red-eyed clerks worked until three or four in the morning; many had no place to sleep. The eight-story Stevens House on Broadway at West Twenty-Sixth, where they had once found beds, was filled; so were all three hundred rooms at the Astor House on lower Broadway. It was said one big commission house handled so much volume that in April it hadn't closed its main office for a single hour day or night. The Exchange fined some commission houses for mistakes in their clearing sheets.

The rush of orders made it impossible for some traders on the floor to place orders with specialists in certain stocks, even a half hour before trading began. There were reports that none of the specialists in twenty active stocks on Tuesday, April 30, could execute all their orders without making mistakes. They sometimes had to buy or sell a big lot and "trust that [they] would get even on [their] over-purchases or oversales." One commission broker said he had stop-loss orders in twelve stocks and three orders for more than 1,000 shares, each to be executed at the market and the open, but he couldn't place them with specialists and "had to take a chance on executing them all himself." The tape ran so far behind, prices changed so fast, that orders to be executed at a set price had little or no value. Orders "at the market" became the rule. Brokers advised customers that any "stop loss order" was at their risk. The federal government reaped enormous revenue from the frenzy: a tax of $2 (charged to the customer not the broker) on every hundred shares traded. A clerical army of hundreds licked and pasted tax stamps on about a million traded certificates for the year in New York City alone.

Rumors mushroomed on Union Pacific. Was Vanderbilt conferring with Morgan in Paris? The New York Times blared "UNION PACIFIC CONTROL LOST BY E. H. HARRIMAN," claiming Chicago investors Marshall Field, J. J. Mitchell (Gates's banker), Norman B. Ream, and others had bought control of the Union Pacific on behalf of the Chicago and North Western with the aid of William K. Vanderbilt to protect the North Western's transcontinental traffic and its Eastern connections threatened by Hill's purchase of the Burlington. The story wasn't true. What was true was the unprecedented buying of railroad stocks by individuals, banks, brokerages, insurance companies, and railroads buying the stock of other railroads. Reducing the floating supply of railroad stocks made it even easier for speculators and "plungers" to manipulate prices.

For many small investors it was a new sensation; building wealth not by working for it, or by saving it, or by making and selling something of tangible value but rather by trading in mere paper, certificates of shares of stock that represented only the hope of future value based on the projected earnings of the companies that issued stock. There had never been a time, said the *Wall Street Journal* on May 1,

> when so many people were interested in Wall Street...Many persons scattered throughout the country who have been worth from $100,000 to $1,000,000 in years past have had that wealth in mills and shops. It was wealth but not Stock Exchange collateral. Combinations of industrial companies have transferred this ownership into certificates of stock, and great numbers of persons have found their possessions liquid assets instead of fixed assets. They have sold the certificates which they received and bought them again. They have learned to trade in stocks. They have discovered that their certificates are good collateral available for borrowing money for trading purposes...With it all the need for caution is great.

How could there be caution when asset values were rising so dramatically? It was pure profit. There was no income tax, no capital gains tax. The nation's prosperity became a sort of "moral hazard" safety net for stock gamblers. What was the risk of buying on rumor or fable? If you lost one day you could win the next. Economic growth and rising markets would save you. Someone else could pay for your risk. "Where is there anything to worry about?" asked James R. Keene. "Prosperity is still vigorously asserted on every side. Good-times do not disappear off-hand."

The euphoria made Schiff, ever cautious and vigilant, very uneasy. Ever since McKinley was elected he had watched the market inflate beyond what he felt were reasonable values. As early as September 1, 1897, he had written his friend in London, the respected banker Robert Fleming, that "the revival which you and I have been looking for has come with a vengeance, and already at this early stage speculation is threatening to run away with good judgment. The time appears not too distant when almost any printed certificate, no matter what it represents, will command a market...it is already necessary to exercise considerable caution."

On the ferry boats and the elevated in the morning, the coffee shops at lunch, hotel cafés at night, the chatter was stock tips. Mobs gathered from 3:10 to 3:20 every afternoon in the arcade of the Empire Building on Broadway at Rector, steps from the Stock Exchange, for the first evening newspaper editions with stock quotes and market analysis, some of the news dictated by reporters direct to composing rooms an hour before the market closed. Hearst's *New York Journal* called it "the delightful anaesthesia of gold getting...money dementia." Brokerage houses overflowed with people off the street who found they could "acquire wealth without labor." Lawyers, grocers, physicians, teachers, waiters, chorus girls, and clergymen all were equal at the foot of the ticker. The smoke of the fanciest Perfecto cigar mingled with that of the cheapest "Pride of the Sewer." Boys dashed from one end of the huge blackboard to the other, up and down the ladder on wheels, chalking the latest prices—some changing minute to minute—shouted to them from someone at the ticker. Half a dozen telephones chimed with buy or sell orders. A cheer erupted: Atchison up 2¾! Speculators scoured the brokerage house's "dope book," filled with the latest gossip.

"The air was almost unbreathable for the innumerable 'tips' to buy or sell securities or insecurities of all kinds," wrote Edwin Lefevre. "The brokers, the customers, the clerks, the Exchange door-keepers, all Wall Street read the morning papers, not to ascertain the news, but to pick such items as would, should, or might, have some effect on stock values. There was no god but the ticker, and the brokers were its prophets." Someone heard of a manicurist who left her job after netting $3,000 to $5,000 on stock trades. The butler of Sara Delano Roosevelt was said to have overheard a stock tip at the Roosevelt mansion in Hyde Park, quit his job, and staked his savings on the conversation.

A new economy seemed to have dawned. Many Americans awoke to find themselves rich. One could buy, for instance, almost two hundred dollars worth of gold with just one share of Burlington, a stock that could have bought only about half that gold a mere four years ago. "Are there tickers in Heaven, I wonder?" asked reporter Charles Henry Webb in the *New York Times*. One conservative banker said a customer from an uptown hotel called him to buy 10,000 shares of a certain stock. "I asked the man," said the banker, "did he know anything about the stock. He had a balance large enough on our books to insure us against loss, but I wanted to know whether it would be wise for him to go into a stock so deeply. He replied, in a matter of fact way, that it was all right, and that he believed the stock was worth more than it was selling at. So I had to execute the order."

For the first time women in numbers were visiting commission houses, although some, such as Harry Content's firm—a male stag club of black leather chairs, red mahogany desks, and cigar smoke—refused them. A reporter observed fifty to seventy-five women, in their tailor-made, narrow skirts (covering ankles), high collars, and blouses with puffed sleeves, gathered around four or five stock tickers in one brokerage house. "There's U.P. 125¼," he heard one woman say, "I bet it goes to 127. Mr. So and So told me at the Waldorf last night that it would go to 128 before the market closed this afternoon." She said to a young man with an order pad, "Buy me fifty shares of U.P. at the market."

There always seemed to be a broker to encourage buying and selling for the standard fee of $12.50 for every hundred shares traded. There were even so-called small margin shops, accepting as little as 5 percent down on a stock purchase, some as little as 2 or 3 percent, blurring the line between speculation and gambling. It was all reminiscent of the women from the West End of London who came into the city in 1720 at the height of another bubble to pawn their jewels for stock "to have a flutter in South Sea shares."

The market had its shadowy underworld: the infamous bucket shops lining lower New Street between Broadway and Broad, especially in one building on Wall Street called Hell's Kitchen. These were the "fake exchanges," unregulated betting parlors, with a stock ticker and a large blackboard where the latest quotes were chalked. They looked legitimate, with lounges, daily newspapers, and pretentious names like the New York Commission Company. Men (only) put up 10 percent, bet on a stock, and were given a receipt with a time-stamped ticket showing the number of shares they "purchased" and the price per share. The money never went to the Stock Exchange, it stayed in the shop. If the stock lost 10 percent of its value in a day, based on the market price, the shop won the bet and "closed out" the trade. If the stock went up the trader went to the window to collect. Tipsters and touts retailed rumors. "Psst. Flip Beaner," one would whisper, meaning buy Manhattan Elevated Railroad. They advertised in newspapers with lines like "CONFIDENTIAL CLERK to prominent operator knows of good dividend-paying stock that will yield good profits. Address Profits 185."

The afternoon of Thursday, May 2, only a block north of the Produce Exchange, police raided a bucket shop, arresting the owner, a former Pullman car conductor, and seven others for "conducting a gambling house pure and simple." Some New York bucket shops ran wire circuits across the Northeast and into the West; one didn't even accept street trade but ran solely as a national wire business. Many relied on traveling solicitors who roamed towns and cities, chatting up the local Western Union man who could, for a fee, provide a list of speculators in the town who stock-gambled via wire. To turn a profit, 90 percent of a bucket shop's traders had to lose. An erratic, volatile market was a bucket shop's dream; a steadily rising stock market, such as this one, was death to profits. To hedge their bets, some large bucket shops even bought directly into the market through the New York Stock Exchange, to sell enough of a certain stock to drive down its price.

Easy money tempted wage earners throughout New York's financial district. Clerks and secretaries sold confidential information about the stock of their company gleaned from correspondence they took in dictation from their bosses. Brokers executed orders on a one-point margin. Managers of "discretionary pools" promised gullible clients a 10 percent return. Brokerage clerks ignored company policy and formed investment pools with their wages, appointed one or two colleagues to deal with a broker and let the broker pick the stocks or "picked their own horses." In Chicago it was said that hundreds, perhaps thousands, of clerks at the Stock Exchange and the Board of Trade were taking out loans to buy stock on margin. "Every one of the boys who can raise the coin," said one clerk, "is trying to 'rag' off a bunch of money." An official of the Denver & Rio Grande railroad said he knew of a clerk at a brokerage house, earning $25 a week, who made $90,000 in the months after McKinley's reelection, presumably on information overheard at work.

In the countryside there were said to be some villages, too small to have a ticker, where farmers and merchants gathered around blackboards chalked with quotations obtained by telephone from the nearest town. If you didn't want to gamble on stocks there were other ways to feed your habit. One New York gaming merchant said he sold more roulette wheels the last few months than for years before, many to people who kept them in closets in their downtown offices and pulled them out to play at lunch or late in the afternoon.

Even McKinley called the prosperity of America at this time "almost appalling." Somehow, just short of appalling could be tolerated. Jewelers, haberdashers, milliners, department stores, hotels, restaurants up and down Manhattan were flush with business. "A man goes down to Wall Street in the morning," said one jeweler, "and cashes in $1,500 or $2,000 before 3 o'clock, and he naturally feels like loosening up. Nothing is too good for him and the best is sometimes not good enough." The city's premier makers of evening gowns were rushed as never before, two to three months behind on orders. Women of means who steamed to Europe usually had their gowns made "on the other side," but now wanted them made in Manhattan, including a growing number of wealthy women ("birds in gilded cages," went the song) from Philadelphia, Baltimore, Pittsburgh, Cleveland, Chicago, Omaha, and Denver whose husbands were new U.S. Steel millionaires. *Life* magazine called them the "new Fortunatuses," men with "swollen wallets" who had washed off the soot of Pittsburgh and now were buying everything in sight in New York, Paris, and London: pictures, furniture, *objets d'art*, mansions, estates. One "old operator," old enough to remember Black Friday 1869, said he hadn't seen so many new faces on the Street as in the last few months, some from as far away as Seattle.

The new money from the west, from National Steel Company, American Tin Plate Company, Federal Steel Company, American Linseed Company, Chicago Street Rail Company, and Colorado Fuel and Iron Company poured into New York. "I often think," said one Manhattan gown maker, "that there is no one to whom a fashionable woman grows more confidential at times than to her dressmaker, with the possible exception of her doctor or her father confessor. We have simply marveled at the stories we have heard of the money that some of the male attaches of our customers have been making. It is one long marvelous tale of gold."

Almost every steamship sailing out of New York harbor up to August 1 had every berth reserved. Carriage makers and Maiden Lane jewelers were overwhelmed. Prestige hotels were booked nights in advance. In one of the large hotels there were three beds in some rooms, cots were hauled up in elevators, some hotel parlors became dormitories. Just try getting a table at the Waldorf-Astoria, Delmonico's, Rector's, or Stanley's! Private dining parties jammed hotels and restaurants, booking weeks in advance. Customers insisted on pricier fare: the finest wines, please, not just whiskey and beer, sweetbreads instead of ham. American beauty roses once were luxuries for tables, but now customers wanted orchids, violets, and pansies. The manager of the Hoffman House at Broadway and Twenty-Fifth—where the nudes in Bouguereau's *Nymphs and Satyr* behind the bar seemed to come alive if one drank too many slings and toddies—said the amount of gold and silver coins and currency passing over the counters was "simply prodigious."

When the gavel came down and trading ended at 3 p.m. on weekdays and at noon on Saturday the ginning of interest in buying and selling stocks didn't stop. Clerks stayed at their desks processing orders, but the traders, and the money, moved uptown. Carriages, "hacks," and "automobiles" lined up in the narrow alley leading from Beaver Street to the Produce Exchange court. The traders and brokers went to the Hoffman House, to the Hotel Manhattan on Madison Avenue at Forty-Second Street, with its portico and columns of Green Island granite, its walls of ornate friezes and Tiffany's iridescent Favrile glass mosaic, mother of pearl and gold. They went to the ten-story Hotel Martinique in the French Renaissance style at West Thirty-Second and Broadway on Greeley Square in the theater district.

They packed the lobster palaces lining Broadway, the "great white way" of street lamps and electric lights between Madison Square and Longacre Square (soon Times Square). They poured into Bustonoby's at Thirty-Ninth, Café Martin, Shanley's with its silver and pewter tankards, and Café des Beaux Arts at Forty-Second and Sixth Avenue, where you might spot songstress Lillian Russell or financier "Diamond Jim" Buchanan Brady, said to be making millions from rigged equipment contracts with the Northern Pacific through his friend, president Charles Mellen. Next to Shanley's was the premier lobster palace, Rector's, with its two-story yellow facade and huge griffin standing guard at Broadway's first revolving door, which swept you into a huge main hall and a second floor, 175 tables and sixty waiters in white ties and vests. It was a "green and yellow wonderland of crystal and gold" and floor-to-ceiling mirrors so everyone could see if that really was Lillian or Diamond Jim who just walked in.

The big money, however, came by carriage up Fifth Avenue to between Thirty-Third and Thirty-Fourth Streets to what became known as "Uptown Wall Street." It converged on the city's premier hotel: the original Waldorf–Astoria of brownstone baroque, symbol of America's new economic might, designed to bring, as Oliver Herford said, "exclusiveness to the masses." The approach to the hotel, the world's largest and most elegant, was on Thirty-Fourth Street, where carriages, and soon motor-cabs, arrived under a vaulted, columned green canopy spangled with electric lights.

Guests streamed into the grand lobby through a giant glass revolving door past the front desk, a long parabola with an army of staff, into "a vast, glittering iridescent fantasy." Before them spread a wide, three-hundred-foot long corridor with marble of amber and deep-cushioned chairs and sofas. The corridor, which came to be called Peacock Alley, was the hyphen in the Waldorf–Astoria, running between the hotel's most famous spaces, the Palm Room and the Empire Room. Statuesque beauties paraded in flowing gold and silver gowns with high "empire" waistlines just below the breast, in flamboyant Merry

The Waldorf–Astoria, circa 1901, "uptown Wall Street" at Fifth
Avenue and Thirty-Fourth Street. "Hell is empty," said one broker,
"and all the devils are here." *Museum of the City of New York/Art
Resource, NY.*

Widow hats with boas and ermine furs. It was entertainment enough for visitors to stroll the grand corridor and be part of it all: the Astor dining room
with its carved dark walnut from the Astor mansion, the tapestries, paintings,
chandeliers, French lamps of hammered brass, the frescoes, marble and onyx
mosaics. The hotel's jewel was the Astor gallery with a snowy replica of the
Soubise ballroom in Paris in Louis XV style. Its vast main floor, almost the size
of a city block, was like a theater where the actors and the actresses were the
audience.

Peacock Alley, connecting the Empire and Palm rooms of the Waldorf–Astoria, "a vast glittering, iridescent fantasy," after-hours watering hole for brokers, traders, and speculators and a symbol of America's new economic might in 1901. MUSEUM OF THE CITY OF NEW YORK/ART RESOURCE, NY.

Along the corridors, speculators conferred in private apartments and lounges. They huddled two and three deep around the four-sided standing bar, watering hole for brokers and traders, politicians and bankers, or at the billiard tables in the south café. Ladies gathered in the Empire Room from 4 to 6 p.m. for tea (or for Scotch poured discreetly into teacups). Pages in tuxedoes glided past calling for Mrs. or Mr. So and So. In the Palm Garden, the city's most lavish restaurant, white tie and tails and evening gowns were mandatory, and waiters were fluent in English, French, and German. Only one other ticket was as hard to get as a table at the Palm: a box at the Metropolitan Opera.

Morgan once had his headquarters at the Waldorf–Astoria. James R. Keene lived there in 1901 at $100 to $150 a day merely for the privilege of a parlor and bedroom. So did the master "plunger," John W. Gates, who ran a Chicago-based pool in Northern Pacific stock. He rented a suite at the Waldorf, banged on the elevator doors for service, cursed reporters who crossed him, and held court in a leather armchair at a round oak table playing bridge at a hundred dollars a point and poker in the Men's Café if the market was quiet. The vulgar Gates had become a walking myth. Had he really bet on which rain-drop would reach the bottom of a window, or the weight of the next man to enter the room? The wire services claimed he won a million dollars after his horse, Royal Flush, won the Steward's Cup at an exclusive English racetrack (his winnings were more like $600,000). He was known to walk around with a roll of $16,000 for pocket money. Bernard Baruch said he saw him place a million dollar bet in a game of baccarat at the Waldorf (or was that the game's total chip count?) So, what was he betting on now? Union Pacific? Gates managed investment pools, won and lost millions on the Chicago Board of Trade, the New York Cotton Exchange, Brazilian coffee, Texas oil, and the Kansas City & Southern Railroad. He made his fortune selling barbed wire in San Antonio and St. Louis, merged seven Illinois factories into one company and then added seven steel mills to create the American Steel and Wire Company. In the main corridor of the hotel, he once had a conversation with his colleague John W. Lambert and his lawyer Max Pam. It enabled him to sell his steel and wire company for $120 million to Morgan, who absorbed it into U.S. Steel.

The original Waldorf opened March 13, 1893, seven months before the Union Pacific and the Northern Pacific went bankrupt, just as the economy crumbled into a four-year depression. The hotel was conceived by John Jacob Astor's son William Waldorf Astor, realized by his right-hand man Abner Bartlett, designed by architect Henry J. Hardenberg, but made a reality by a genius of hotel management, the Prussian immigrant George Boldt who, with his wife Louise, knew what appealed to women and gave the Waldorf its cache. They stationed female concierges in offices on each floor to communicate directly for guests to the kitchen, housekeepers, and the main office. Boldt would not hesitate to cash a check for a guest, even an unfamiliar one, because he believed people "didn't go to the bad for a small check." That was why the Waldorf sometimes carried up to $100,000 in its safes and won the everlasting loyalty of its customers.

The Astoria Hotel opened next door to the Waldorf on November 1, 1897, the day Jacob Schiff stood anxiously in the crowd at the federal government's foreclosure sale for the Union Pacific in Omaha. Combined they became the Waldorf–Astoria, seventeen floors and a thousand rooms. Boldt became a friend of J. P. Morgan and so did the Waldorf's first employee, maître d' Oscar

Tschirky. He was never a chef nor had he ever cooked a meal for the hotel but he became supervisor of appetites and gastronomic tastes, orchestrated private banquets, "friend of gourmets and epicures," as his son put it, a "confidant of swelldom." He invented the use of plush rope to restrict the capacity of the Palm Room and created the Waldorf salad. When Morgan dined at the Waldorf he insisted Oscar supervise the meal and allowed no one else in his private dining room to serve him. "Oscar of the Waldorf" managed a staff of fifteen hundred, and routinely strolled the dining rooms trying to greet every guest by name. To be addressed by name by Oscar Tschirky at the Waldorf–Astoria was, well, you had arrived.

The prime movers at the Stock Exchange during the day became Peacock Alley's glitterati after hours, in whispered conversation or loud laughter in the corridors, lounges, the billiards room, around the four-sided bar. All the major brokerage firms had offices with tickers just off the smoking room where one could buy or sell stocks, some open into the night if Exchange volume was high. The arbitrage houses, doing a business via their leased, private wires with the bourses in western Europe, sometimes circulated order takers throughout the main floor as early as 4 a.m. when the London stock exchange opened at New York time.

The mere presence of James R. Keene, manager of investment pools, attracted a knot of bystanders hoping to overhear market tips. A waiter would be pumped with questions after he left Keene's presence. "What is Mr. Keene talking about?" asked one speculator. "Talking about?" replied the waiter, "Why, don't you see he is talking with Mr. Follansbee. He never talks anything but horse with him." Waiters tended to be more diligent serving a table of brokers, hovering closer, keeping the glasses filled, pretending to ignore the gratuity. "It's not that they love cash tips less," said someone, "but they love stock tips more." A veteran director of American Steel and Wire who frequented the Waldorf–Astoria noticed "as soon as you begin to talk stocks your waiter is right at the table, and as soon as you quit he makes himself scarce."

Every trading record downtown pumped more money through uptown's arteries. The queue of varnished carriages grew longer outside the front portico, customers and sightseers jammed Peacock Alley, the hotel's restaurants were at capacity. Oscar had to order more plush rope as cordon when the tables filled. The Waldorf–Astoria was where Keene and Gates, Housman, Field, the Wormsers, the Baruchs, Frothingham, and all the managers in investment pools gave every active stock a story because the "story" drove the stock. Traders for these pools sometimes tried to bribe reporters to bull their stock, offering them "calls" for a number of shares a few points higher than the current market. Commission houses threatened to cancel subscriptions to "bear" newspapers. As John Durand wrote two years before the crash of 1929, "a good rise on increasing volumes is the best advertisement a stock can have...all the news purveyors make it their business to supply the public demand for some plausible explanation...a stock which merely goes up and stays up is attractive to nobody—it must have reactions, even if these are created by selling...the ticker is the market's greatest publicity agent." The second-best agent was the pool's press agent. For Wall Street reporters, college educated though some were, speculating in stocks was a constant lure; most earned only about $2,000 a year, $5,000 at most.

On Thursday, May 2, after days of record volume, the Exchange was strained beyond limit. Many specialists in major active stocks were overwhelmed. The Union Pacific specialist had quit so no one was available to watch limit orders or stop orders on the company's stock. Anyone who wanted to buy or sell Union Pacific had to do so "at the market" not knowing what the price would be when the order was executed. That hardly adhered to the Exchange's hallowed mission of encouraging "just and equitable principles of trade." Investors had to watch the tickers themselves but the tickers were running so far behind there were no reliable, real-time prices. Worse, there weren't enough tickers. After McKinley was re-elected some brokerage houses put two or three more machines in their offices. Houses that tried to order more machines now were told it would take at least two to three weeks for delivery.

Some houses tried to restrict trading with little success. Everyone was working late, short of sleep. Some specialists were working through the night and still running two or three days behind on recording transactions. There were reports of Exchange members so exhausted they were taken home to recover. "If they had had to carry home their gains every night," said *Life* magazine, unable to muster empathy, "they would have long ago succumbed, but luckily they can dump the accumulations of each day in the banks and go home light." Some brokers circulated a petition asking that Saturday, May 4, be an Exchange holiday to get an extra day's rest even if it meant forfeiting commissions. The attempt failed. There was too much money to be made.

Since Monday, April 29, twenty specialists had quit dealing in specific stocks and by Thursday there was likely to be only one specialist left on the trading floor, trading for U.S. Steel alone. "My dear boy," a broker from one of the older, more conservative commission houses told a reporter, who asked him where the market was headed, "when a man is in a wagon behind a runaway team the best thing to do is to clutch the back of the seat, hang on and make no predictions."

The volume kept coming. More than 2.8 million shares traded hands on May 2. Northern Pacific dropped a point on modest volume. Union Pacific closed down 1⅜, a feverish 545,000 shares traded. No one could say for certain that a syndicate had been formed to gain control of it and, if so, who comprised it, but the energy seemed to be running out of the story, especially with Harriman finally speaking: "I have not let go of any of my holdings of Union Pacific. There is really nothing new to be said on the subject. There is no news." The most important trade of the day never appeared in the papers. A treasurer for one of the Northern Pacific subsidiaries decided it would be a good day to sell 13,000 shares of Nipper common at the prevailing market price of about $115 a share, for an estimated $1.5 million. The buyers presumably were brokers working secretly for Kuhn, Loeb. Bacon, Lamont, and Hill were none the wiser.

The market seemed to need a merger story to replace it so attention shifted to the Atchison, Topeka & Santa Fe (the "Atch"), the 7,700-mile system heavily owned by Edward Julius Berwind, founder of the Berwind Coal Mining Company, the nation's largest holder of bituminous coal, and a Morgan man. The Atchison ran from Chicago through Kansas City and Wichita, through Fort Worth, Houston, and Galveston to the Gulf, west to Colorado mining country, and into San Diego. It rose almost 11 points on astounding volume of 556,000 shares on rumors it was the natural transcontinental link for the Pennsylvania and that Pennsy insiders were the largest holders of Atchison stock. Some thought the Atchison rumor was being retailed in part by the Berwind pool to drive the stock up. The pool was thought to have begun buying Atchison a year earlier when it was selling for $20 a share. Now it was at around $90—outrageous, many thought, for a railroad that didn't even pay a dividend, only five years out of receivership.

The rise in the once-bankrupt Union Pacific, meanwhile, helped mint a batch of multimillionaires such as Arthur Orr of Chicago. He had bought 10,000 shares in 1898 for around $20 a share and now sold them all at 131, netting him, it was estimated, more than $1 million. Charles Head Smith—flamboyant plunger in Chicago grain, crony of Gates, owner of Kentucky racehorses, racetrack gambler, barely in his forties—also chose to get out of Union Pacific on May 2. Like Orr, he bought 10,000 at about 20 three years earlier and hung on to it even though it hadn't paid a dividend much of that time. His patience was rewarded. He also sold it that day, netting $1.3 million. The previous year his three-year-old colt and the pride of Chicago, Lieutenant Gibson, won the Kentucky Derby but this year Smith skipped the Derby entirely. He knew it was time to get out of Union Pacific in early April when he visited his broker in New York. The broker left the office for a few minutes. Smith sat in his chair, running the ticker tape through his fingers. A young woman rushed in, thinking him the broker, and said, "Please buy me all the Union Pacific you can." "Why do you want to buy Union Pacific?" Smith asked. "Papa says buy it all if you can," she replied.

Six blocks north of the Produce Exchange at 120 Broadway, the board of the Equitable Life Assurance Company was holding a regular meeting May 2 at the company's headquarters building, where Harriman had his office. The board was headed for disarray, the company rudderless after the death two years earlier of its legendary founder Henry B. Hyde. His twenty-five-year-old son, the extravagant Francophile and playboy James Hazen Hyde, only three years out of Harvard, was now chairman of the board and seriously out of his depth. "I have wealth, beauty and intellect," he may or may not have said, though it did sound like him, "what more could I wish?" Harriman, perhaps tempted by the Equitable's investment capital, was elected to the board that morning where he joined other railroad owners and financiers including Schiff, Chauncey Depew of the New York Central, Alexander Cassatt of the Pennsylvania, Boston's T. J. Coolidge, a board member of the Union Pacific and Burlington, and William Van Horne of the Canadian Pacific.

Schiff's involvement in the Equitable exposed him to a huge conflict of interest. While he was head of the board's finance committee, Kuhn, Loeb sold to the Equitable 16 percent of the stock it acquired for its investment funds, despite a New York state law forbidding corporate self-dealing. Furthermore, on that morning, at young Hyde's recommendation, the board voted for Hyde to personally lend to Harriman's Union Pacific $2.7 million on collateral for purchase by the Equitable of 36,000 shares of Union Pacific stock, the largest block of stock the Equitable had ever accepted as security. Harriman and Schiff, who used the proceeds to buy more Northern Pacific stock, then gathered piously a few hours later with other board members and a large crowd in the arcade of the Equitable building for a ceremony honoring the late Henry B. Hyde on the second anniversary of his death. A cord was pulled removing a canopy of Stars and Stripes from a seven-foot statue in dark bronze of Hyde by John Quincy Adams Ward, sculptor of the Washington bronze on the steps of the Sub-Treasury two blocks away. Hill, who later served on the Equitable board for a short period and then resigned before it blew up, was paying little attention. He took the train up to New London, Connecticut, to observe the building of his ocean cargo ships.

The market opened Friday, May 3, and profit-takers took control, the kind of day the traders said was for the "shaking out of dry bones." Rumors of a takeover of Union Pacific had grown stale, so had rumors of a takeover of the Atchison. Call money for overnight loan rose to as high as 8 percent as brokerage houses tried to dampen speculation. The market opened down in early trading but before noon turned buoyant with fresh buying.

Then, as a *New York Times* reporter said, "from a disguised source selling started." Perhaps it was the rumor planted by bears that President McKinley had been shot in New Orleans. Atchison broke from 90 to just above 80. Rock Island dropped from 169⅞ to 161. Missouri Pacific from 115 to just under 109. Baltimore & Ohio lost 6. The St. Paul fought the current and rose 2¼. Union Pacific common closed down 7⅜, Atchison down 9¾, both on heavy volume. Northern Pacific dropped 8, Rock Island 8⅞, Missouri Pacific 6¼. Trading volume was over three million shares. Three-fourths of the 175 listed stocks closed down, the first big sell-off since McKinley's re-election. The volatile ups and downs were too much for the weak heart of one John Kee, who collapsed and died at 1:45 p.m. while watching prices decline on the quote board at an uptown brokerage.

Hill had been in New York since Monday, conferring with Bacon, George Perkins, Baker, and Lamont, concluding the Burlington purchase, avoiding Schiff and Harriman. Perhaps something he or Bacon's stock specialists saw in the transaction data convinced them he had to confront Schiff. More likely it was Schiff who contacted him, perhaps because he believed he and Harriman finally had majority control of Northern Pacific's preferred and common and could use it as leverage with Hill, perhaps also to avoid forcing Morgan to go into the open market to buy more shares, which could panic the market.

Either way, sometime the morning of Friday, May 3, Hill went to Schiff's office. The air would be cleared. Hill had been turning over in his mind the threats Harriman made against him at Baker's home three weeks earlier, Easter Sunday evening, that Hill's purchase of the Burlington was an invasion of

Union Pacific territory, "a hostile act," and that Hill would have to "take the consequences." He remembered the words Schiff had used in a letter to him the following day, that the Union Pacific "must take care of itself, as it will be able to do." Harriman did not make idle threats. It was not *if* he would retaliate but when. Knowing Harriman, when he did it wouldn't be merely a glancing blow. What did "consequences" and "take care of itself" mean?

If Hill was at his desk he didn't have far to go to see Schiff. Hill's ninth-floor office was only about six elevator stops above Schiff's in the Kuhn, Loeb building. Schiff would have been in the reception area to greet him. He guided him formally by the arm into his office and closed the door with its frosted glass window. Schiff wasted no time. As he later re-created his version of this meeting in a letter to Morgan, Schiff told Hill that Kuhn, Loeb with the Union Pacific had spent $60 million buying the common and preferred stock of Northern Pacific. Our group, he said, now holds 420,000 of the 750,000 preferred shares. We also hold 370,000 of the 800,000 common shares. That is more than 50 percent of the common and preferred combined. Just this morning, said Schiff, we bought a block of 35,000 preferred shares from a Morgan associate who was unaware of our effort and who sold us the shares without informing Mr. Bacon. With that sale and with what Kuhn, Loeb has been able to purchase we believe we control the total of preferred and common. We intend to combine the Northern Pacific, Great Northern, and the Burlington with the Union Pacific and the Southern Pacific.

Hill was thunderstruck. This would be a western railroad version of U.S. Steel. Schiff continued. We would like you, J. J., to run the whole thing for us. You can name the terms. We would provide general direction when needed. We also offer you irrevocable power of attorney over the combined system for ten years. But, Hill countered, you can't get control, thinking of what he assumed was the 35 to 40 percent he thought he and Morgan still controlled. That may be, said Schiff, but we've got a lot of it. That makes no difference, said Hill, a combination of such size, involving the Burlington which parallels the Union Pacific, would be challenged immediately by all the affected states and ruled illegal. The U.S. Supreme Court had already ruled Hill couldn't own the Northern Pacific directly because it was a parallel competitor of his Great Northern and would violate Minnesota law.

At one point, Hill remembered, a door opened. In walked Harriman. He and Schiff had choreographed the whole thing. Harriman said something to Hill like, "You are the boss. We are all working for you. Give me your orders."

They were, in effect, asking Hill to throw Morgan overboard. The chutzpah was stunning. Schiff had observed Hill's growing impatience with Morgan's delays in ending the Northern Pacific voting trust the last few years. He may have misread it as a breach of trust between the two, which it wasn't. Now Harriman and the Rockefellers were trying to use Hill in their vendetta against Morgan. "During the time of their supposed control [of the Northern Pacific]," Hill wrote Mount Stephen a month later, "they boasted how they would show the world that Morgan & Co. were not the only financial house in America."

In his testimony in the Northern Securities case three years later Hill cloaked himself with honor, "I simply said that it was not necessary to bribe me to do the fair and respectable thing toward so close a neighbor as the Union Pacific; and on the other hand I could not be bribed to do wrong in any way." Throughout the meeting, as Hill recalled it, Harriman appeared, commented, departed, and reappeared again "repeatedly," as if on stage cue.

Why did Schiff and Harriman tip their hand to Hill? Merely to force him to put a Union Pacific director on the Burlington board? Allow their interests to have a third share in the purchase? Avoid having to buy even more Northern Pacific stock, which could squeeze the short-sellers and panic the market? Was Schiff trying to salvage his relationship with Hill? Then how to explain Harriman–Schiff's stated plan to merge their lines with Hill's? Hill had no time to speculate on their motives. He probably tried to look calm but underneath was in full panic. His life's work was on the line. If Harriman gained control of the Northern Pacific he also would control the Burlington. That would give him control of four of the six major western railroads. Hill's Great Northern would be left isolated, pinned against the Canadian border. Now *he* might be Harriman's office boy.

Schiff had betrayed Hill to Harriman. Perhaps, however, there was still time for Hill to stop them. One can imagine him flying down the three flights of stairs, breathing heavily for his sixty-three years, down the front steps, past the Lancashire Insurance Company Building, breaking into a running walk (he "glided along the streets," someone said of him, "with all the agility of an Indian") past the rear of the Sub-Treasury, left and slightly downhill at Nassau, past horses and pushcart vendors, the spire of old Trinity Church up Wall Street to his right, past the bronze Washington, dodging pedestrians and carriages to Morgan's headquarters, "the corner" at Broad and Wall. He would have leapt up the eight marble steps beneath the columned Greek pediment with its huge American flag, barreled through the heavy front doors, through

James J. Hill, still agile in his early sixties, may have looked like this as he sprinted from Schiff's office to Morgan's with the news that Harriman and Schiff apparently had seized control of "his" Northern Pacific. COURTESY OF THE MINNESOTA HISTORICAL SOCIETY.

the railed vestibule, past clerks and counters (all male), down a dark, narrow corridor with marble pillars, into a hushed, carpeted space of mahogany and glass where the partners sat, breathless into Bacon's office. The diligent Bacon was stunned by the news as was his colleague George Perkins. So was George Baker, who later confessed that for the first time in his life he feared he was in water much deeper than he preferred.

Quick, Hill probably said (or yelled), where are the stock transfer books? Bacon and Perkins summoned assistants. Everyone began pouring over ledger columns of trades to determine if Hill–Morgan indeed had lost control.

It apparently was then that Hill recalled the legal charter of the reorganized Northern Pacific of July 1896. He had been an intimate part of the refinancing syndicate behind that reorganization and remembered the conditions under which the stock of the new Northern Pacific was issued and how it was to be retired. Hill knew the preferred shares amounted to a loan from stockholders and could be retired at par by the board any January 1 before 1917. They were a key part of the Morgan reorganization, distributed in exchange for the old Northern Pacific's bonds, partly a legacy of debt owed German investors from the tumultuous Villard years. Morgan's own firm, then called Drexel and Morgan, had inadvertently helped seed the collapse of the Northern Pacific by buying millions of those risky Northern Pacific bonds (perhaps today rated "junk") at a premium from Deutsche Bank twelve years ago.

The election of the Northern Pacific board, dominated by Morgan men, was fixed for October 1901. Therefore, to maintain control it was not a matter of owning a technical majority of the common and preferred combined. Whoever owned or voted for a majority of the common alone could postpone the election of a new board until January 1, 1902, when the preferred could be retired and the current board could keep control. Hill, apparently, was the first to remember this key clause in the reorganized Northern Pacific charter but he couldn't have been the only one. Others surely knew it, too, including Morgan's chief counsel, Francis Lynde Stetson, who also was general counsel of the new Northern Pacific in 1896 and certainly signed off on the charter; Morgan lawyer Charles Steele; Bacon, Baker, and Lamont, all of whom were on the Northern Pacific board; and perhaps also Hill's allies John Stewart Kennedy and Lord Mount Stephen, both of whom were in the financing syndicate.

Schiff, however, was the master of conditional promises. He wasn't yet convinced of the legal power of the majority of the common to retire the preferred but was still trying to lever Hill into compromise. He invited Hill to dinner that Friday evening, May 3, at his home at 932 Fifth Avenue at Seventy-Fourth. Hill accepted. It would buy him time while Morgan's men counted their Northern Pacific shares. It also played to a Hill strength. When he wanted to be evasive, he could be bilingual. Double talk was his second language.

It happened to be Sabbath eve, which meant dinner at 6:30 sharp with Schiff's wife and children, preceded by gathering in a circle with Jacob blessing each member of his family and then reciting grace in German. After dinner with the family, Schiff and Hill talked in private amid the red damask and dark marble. Schiff seemed to want reconciliation. He offered Hill a lifeline with a string attached: we will stop buying Northern Pacific stock if you will just give Harriman a seat on the Burlington board.

Hill was too coy to say absolutely no. He could not, however, trust Harriman outside the Burlington boardroom (any more than Harriman could trust him). How could Hill trust him inside? Hill knew Harriman already had shown, first with the Illinois Central and then with the Union Pacific, that once he got on a board he could work his will with it. Hill may never have said so in so many words to Schiff that evening but Hill would never make that mistake with Harriman.

The two talked on and soon it was ten o'clock, Schiff's bedtime. As he had done so many times before when Hill was a guest, Schiff's butler Joseph would bring Schiff orange juice on a tray at ten and say, 'Mr. Hill, your taxi is waiting." Hill would say, "Send it away" and back he would dive into his monologue. As a full moon rose over Manhattan, the two went back and forth until almost midnight in stalemate. An exasperated Schiff considered the meeting such a waste of time and Hill so annoyingly vague, he never told Harriman about it. He had observed Hill many times this way in their fifteen-year relationship—feigning, dissembling, disguising his real intent behind an affable facade, appearing to honor "community of interest" but not believing it for a second. Hill had allowed Schiff to be on the Great Northern board for about a decade but Schiff soon learned Hill was keeping him at arm's length from his strategic thinking and the Great Northern's books. Harriman and Schiff naively assumed Hill would see it in his best interest to keep the peace. Now Harriman had lost patience even with Schiff's ability to lever Hill. All paths would not unite on this mountaintop. They were headed for the trenches.

Sometime during this evening, while Hill and Schiff argued past Schiff's bedtime, Harriman felt a sharp, intense pain in his abdomen. Pale and drawn, weighing only 130 pounds even in good health, he withdrew to his bed at his Manhattan home at 1 East Fifty-Fifth. The pain throbbed in his abdomen through the night and into the morning. Doctors were contacted. He would have to stay in bed.

8

DECISION AT TEMPLE EMANU-EL

Saturday morning, May 4, dawned clear and crisp in Manhattan. It would be a very pleasant morning to walk to the synagogue. Jacob and Therese Schiff, in their Sabbath best, left their Fifth Avenue home facing Central Park and began their customary stroll down the thirty-one "short" blocks to their synagogue Temple Emanu-El at Fifth Avenue and Forty-Third Street. They knew all the landmarks by heart; the mansions four, five, and six stories, many designed by Richard Hunt Morris or Stanford White in flamboyant châteaux and castle styles. Historian Frederick Lewis Allen later called this multimillionaire's row the "little world of magnificence . . . an island set apart from the common life of the country." Windows were open, curtains billowing, everyone inhaling the fresh spring air; the sort of air that, said one writer, "surprises you. It is cool, but it is not sharp. It is warm, but not flat. It is mellow, and yet fresh."

The mile and a half that Jacob and Therese walked that morning showcased more wealth than anywhere else on earth: the Stillman mansion at Seventy-Second, the beaux-arts Lenox Library, the mansions of the Whitneys, Havermeyers, Goulds, and Mrs. Astor; the elegant hotels beginning at Fifty-Ninth—the Savoy, Netherland, St. Regis, and Gotham—the Harrimans, Rockefellers, Vanderbilts, and St. Patrick's Cathedral at Fifty-First, then the restaurants Sherry's and Delmonico's, and looming ahead at Forty-Third, the familiar slender twin towers of Temple Emanu-El, the spiritual home of the Schiffs for more than a quarter century.

Passing from daylight through the huge arched front doors into the temple, they entered a soaring, vaulted space that could seat eighteen hundred worshippers on the main floor and five hundred in the rear gallery. The Moorish effect gave the interior a floating, hypnotic feel, with dazzling stained glass, columns sixty feet high, and walls of light stone lifting higher

Above left: Jacob and Therese Schiff as they might have appeared that star-crossed Sabbath morning, Saturday, May 4, 1901, walking down Fifth Avenue to Temple Emanu-El. LIBRARY OF CONGRESS, PRINTS AND PHOTOGRAPHS DIVISION, BAIN COLLECTION [LC-DIG-GGBAIN-30017]. *Above right:* Temple Emanu-El synagogue, Fifth Avenue and Forty-Third Street, New York City, the world's wealthiest, most influential synagogue. It was the spiritual home of the Schiffs, where Jacob decided to overrule Harriman. MUSEUM OF THE CITY OF NEW YORK/ART RESOURCE, NY.

and higher to brilliant geometric patterns of red, blue, vermillion, yellow, and white, all gilded in gold. The vaulted, arched ceiling was a heavenly deep blue with diamonds of stars. The columns and arches behind the pulpit climbed to pinnacles over the doors of the Ark, made of black walnut, intricately carved.

Jacob and Therese strode up the aisle and settled in their rented pew, no. 316, probably near the front but not conspicuous, among the familiar faces of so many wealthy German Jewish families they knew so well, the Loebs, Wolffs, Seliegmans, Herzogs, Kossins, Hoddmans, Froelichs, Schulhoffs, Lehmans, and Frankheimers.

Sometime late Friday or early Saturday May 4 morning, after furious counting Hill and Bacon discovered that the Great Northern and Morgan and Company and their friends together held only 260,000 shares of Northern Pacific common of the 800,000 outstanding, compared with Schiff's claim that Kuhn, Loeb and the Union Pacific held 370,000 of the common. That meant Hill–Morgan safely needed another 150,000 shares to have a majority of the common. Harriman–Schiff needed only 40,000. Hill urged Bacon to cable Morgan immediately at Aix. Bacon consulted with partners Charles Steele and George Perkins, and cabled Morgan in code with something like "Harriman–Schiff claim majority NP common & preferred. Majority common can retire preferred & retain board control. Urgent permission needed buy 150,000 common Monday." Bacon also cabled Morgan and Company's London office and said it was essential they "or friends should not sell any NP common at any price without consulting J. P. M."

Hill circled the wagons, cabling his financier friends Gaspard Farrer of Baring Brothers, Lord Strathcona, Lord Mount Stephen, all in London, and Edward Tuck in Paris, asking them to hold fast, don't sell, and help fund purchases of more Northern Pacific shares. They all eventually cabled their support but not soon enough for the anxious Bacon. He kept asking Hill if they had responded, and finally Hill replied, "Damn it, Bacon, don't worry. My friends will stand without hitching." They did.

Harriman had spent a restless night in bed. He had always been frail, tended toward rheumatism, and this time his sharp pain proved to be symptoms of chronic appendicitis, which in this era could be a dangerous, life-threatening infection. He also was in mental torment. Schiff and all the best legal counsel money could buy, no less than five eminent legal authorities, were unanimous in reassuring him that a majority of the common and preferred combined, which they now believed they had, would ensure control of the Northern Pacific. They also surely noticed that the railroad's 1896 charter could be interpreted as providing that a majority of the common stockholders had the power to retire the preferred shares on January 1 of any year. Regardless, Harriman may have thought, why not be absolutely sure we have a majority of the common? What's another 40,000 shares for peace of mind? As he recalled later, that the common could retire the preferred on January 1 "bothered me somewhat." Odd phrase, that. Perhaps Harriman found it difficult in retrospect to admit he had relied too heavily on legal counsel and had overlooked the loophole Hill exploited.

It was about mid-morning Saturday, May 4. The Exchange would open at 10 a.m. for trading until noon. Harriman was bedridden, unable to stand much less get to his office. He grabbed one of his candlestick telephones but couldn't reach Schiff, who either was on his way to or inside Temple Emanu-El. He did reach Louis A. Heinsheimer, a forty-one-year-old junior partner at Kuhn, Loeb. Born in Cincinnati in 1859, he was a nephew of cofounder Solomon Loeb and a company lifer. By 1901 he had worked with Schiff almost a quarter century, first as office boy, then clerk, then as a "power of attorney" and, the past seven years, as a partner. He had a quick wit, was an astute trader, one of Wall Street's most respected authorities on bonds, but stayed mostly behind the scenes. He had a habit of standing at the stock ticker, nervously shifting his weight one foot to the other, lost in thought as he tried to divine meaning behind the numbers. He remained a bachelor, living with his mother in a row house at 17 West Seventieth, but later built one of the grandest mansions of the time in Tudor style on fourteen acres in Far Rockaway, Long Island, an enclave for wealthy Germans, then more elite than the Hamptons. "Never have I found a man," said Schiff later, "who was more unselfish, and more ready to please everyone... he had a very keen mind and sound judgment, and as a worker was indefatigable."

Harriman's voice was a weak, pained whisper over the phone but his instructions to Heinsheimer were short and clear: buy 40,000 shares of Northern Pacific common at the market before trading closed at noon today. "All right," said Heinsheimer. He hung up the phone and knew immediately he needed Schiff's review and approval before making that large a purchase. Every second counted. He had to get to Schiff at Temple Emanu-El. Some historians have mistakenly assumed Schiff didn't make a decision on the Harriman order that day because he didn't want to violate the Sabbath. Nothing could be further from the truth. "A man does not become a great banker," wrote political scientist William Letwin, "by letting business slide while he prays."

Whether Heinsheimer was two miles from the synagogue at his row house west of Central Park or four miles away at Kuhn, Loeb's offices downtown is not known. Nor is it known how he got Schiff's attention after he entered through Temple Emanu-El's giant front doors. He would not have embarrassed Schiff by marching down the aisle and disrupting sacred space on a matter of commerce. The heads of investor–worshippers would have bobbed up from prayer books. It would be more discreet and practical to summon

Schiff to the vestibule so he could deliver Harriman's order in person. Perhaps he scribbled a note for an usher.

Heinsheimer whispered Harriman's order and waited for what he thought would be Schiff's quick approval. Instead, Schiff paused. Then he nodded, "no." The purchase would not be necessary, said Schiff, and he would take full responsibility for the decision. Schiff never explained why he overrode Harriman's order. Did he believe more buying would raise the price of Northern Pacific further, escalate short-selling, and perhaps panic the market and inadvertently corner the shorts? Did he think Kuhn, Loeb and Harriman didn't need the extra shares to gain control? After all, Schiff and Harriman wouldn't have spilled the beans to Hill the previous afternoon if they hadn't done their counting and weren't confident of the strength of their ownership. Did Schiff not want to do business on the Sabbath or perhaps risk having a Jewish firm blamed for greed that could send prices higher and overheat the market? Did he simply get cold feet? Did he not want to antagonize Morgan and Hill further and risk losing any opportunity to compromise with them for his and Harriman's benefit? After all, investment bankers were supposed to build and strengthen bridges to clients, not burn them. Did he still think he could persuade his old friend Hill to give Harriman a place on the Burlington board? Perhaps he had interpreted something Hill had said at his home the previous night as sounding like Hill might lean that way. Schiff never explained why he said "no." Heinsheimer returned to the office or his home. He did not call Harriman back. Schiff would have to do that.

As Schiff worshipped at Temple Emanu-El, trading opened with strong rumors of a three-way merger of Union Pacific, the St. Paul, and the Chicago & North Western—pushing the St. Paul up 7½ at the close to 184¾. Almost a million shares traded in only two hours, about a third of it equally for the St. Paul, the Union Pacific, and the Atchison. Northern Pacific common sat quietly, up three-quarters, closing at 110 on trading of only 22,500 shares. Many other stocks were down. James R. Keene, from his office nearby on the fifth floor of the Johnston Building on Broad at Exchange Place, told a reporter that given the recent "excessive speculation," the sell-off actually was beneficial. "Railroads which for years past have suffered under the blight of excessive competition," he said, "are now controlled by wiser and more conciliatory counsels. As a result of this, prices have appreciated and should appreciate in the future." He was right about appreciation but Harriman and Hill were not headed for any "conciliatory counsels."

Bacon had sent Morgan the urgent, coded telegram sometime after noon Saturday, New York time, and for added secrecy, apparently, sent it from his home at 1 Park Avenue at Thirty-Third. It was evening in Aix. Morgan was standing probably in white waistcoat, Ascot tie and wing collar, in the carpeted central hall of the Regina–Grand. A clerk handed him the envelope with the coded cable from Bacon. Morgan read it and perhaps thought to himself various unprintable expletives about Harriman and Schiff. He and Hill had spent the better part of twenty years, together and separately, pursuing and propping up the rickety Northern Pacific. Morgan himself had refinanced it twice in thirteen years. He and Hill thought they controlled it. Now they would have to pay grossly inflated market prices to do so, if even that was possible.

Morgan strode immediately to the concierge and dictated a reply to Bacon in code: Buy "at any price." He later described his feelings that night in the hotel lobby when he received the telegram, portraying himself as usual with a certain undefined moral duty,

> We had organized the Northern Pacific; we had placed all the securities of the Northern Pacific, and I knew, as I had always supposed, that there were people, friends of ours and other people, who practically held enough Northern Pacific—we had always supposed we had with us people upon whom we could depend to protect our moral control of the property. And consequently, when the news came to me, I hadn't any doubt about the fact of the matter. And at the same time the news came so strong—whoever had acquired it—I felt something must have happened. Somebody must have sold. I knew where certain stocks were, and I figured it up. I feel bound in honor when I reorganize a property and am morally responsible for its management to protect it, and generally I do protect it.

Financier John Stewart Kennedy, a partner of Hill's in the founding of what became the Great Northern and a friend of Morgan's for four decades, happened to be at the Regina–Grand with Morgan and reassured him, "Whatever you want done I want done with my Northern Pacific."

Morgan's response reached Bacon sometime early Sunday, May 5. Bacon and Hill, meanwhile, found the situation dire: Harriman and Schiff had acquired some 46 percent of the common, some 56 percent of the preferred, or a combined 51 percent. With the green light from Morgan, Bacon quickly called Keene Sunday morning and retained him to orchestrate the buying beginning Monday morning at 4 a.m. London time and 10 a.m. New York time of every possible share of Northern Pacific common that Keene and his forces could get their hands on, up to 150,000 shares "at any price."

Keene mobilized for Monday not only as a Hill–Morgan agent but also now had insider information to trade, if he wished, on his firm's own account. The Harriman–Schiff camp was in limbo. Schiff must have had a difficult time keeping his mind on matters spiritual when he returned to his pew at Temple Emanu-El. Perhaps he had glanced up at the starry vaulted ceiling and prayed for deliverance from what he feared might be a stock market Armageddon. He surely would have to call Harriman as soon as he and Therese returned to 932 Fifth Avenue. He could not possibly have waited until Monday. But, he did. At least that is how Harriman remembered it. Amazingly, no one at Kuhn, Loeb—not Schiff, not Kahn, not Heinsheimer—called Harriman back Saturday or Sunday to tell him Schiff overruled him. Did they not want to call Harriman because he was sick in bed? Did Harriman's doctors fend away phone calls? Did Schiff delay to block Harriman's influence? It was left to Harriman to have to call Heinsheimer back Monday morning.

Harriman's reaction is not recorded, but when he did talk to Schiff it must have been an uncomfortable conversation. Harriman tended to speak in a low voice, but when he got upset or surprised he would be speechless for a second and then yelp "Wow-wow-wow!" He must have "wow-wowed" this time when Schiff told him of his decision. Schiff, however, appears to have convinced Harriman that not buying another 40,000 was the right call. They must have concluded that a majority of the common and preferred was what mattered.

More importantly, Schiff must have counted carefully. Perhaps he persuaded himself and Harriman that they also had a majority of the common. Morgan and Hill could not possibly find enough of it on the open market to get a majority without buying shares that had been shorted and didn't exist. Perhaps Schiff told Harriman he could see what was coming. Morgan's men were going to go into the market Monday and overheat it with indiscriminate, ham-handed buying and cause a calamity that would bring down the market. Let them do it and then let them take the blame. We can take the high ground. As Harriman claimed under oath a year later at an Interstate Commerce Commission hearing on railroad rates, "I don't think there was a contest...We made no contest for the control of Northern Pacific. We purchased a majority of the capital stock. We purchased prior to the supposed contest and no stock was acquired during the panic in May."

Schiff, however, still needed all hands on deck for Monday morning trading. To lead Kuhn, Loeb into battle he turned to Otto Hermann Kahn, a junior partner twenty years younger than Schiff, part of the firm's third generation united by blood or marriage. Kahn had joined the firm four years earlier after marrying Abraham Wolff's daughter, and worked almost exclusively with Harriman on the Union Pacific reorganization the next two or three years. He met Harriman in 1894 when Harriman was head of finance for the Illinois Central, but it was during the Union Pacific project that he was mesmerized by Harriman's intelligence and boldness. Schiff had a purely business relationship with Harriman, Kahn's was hero worship.

Kahn in many ways was Schiff's opposite. He worked on the Sabbath, and considered becoming Catholic; he thought Jesus, St. Paul, and St. Francis were the three greatest figures in history. He played, quite well, the piano, cello, and violin as a boy, and became a connoisseur of music. At Harriman's urging, he joined the board of the Metropolitan Opera and later played a major role as its chairman in creating its golden era.

He also was, unlike the self-effacing Schiff, addicted to publicity. He knew reporters by name, greeted them cordially, hired public relations pioneer Ivy Lee to guard his reputation, and in 1901 began collecting newspaper clippings about himself in a scrapbook that eventually grew to twelve bound volumes each gold-stamped OHK. For Kahn, however, the volumes stood not for his ego but for a principle, which he understood as well as Lee. He later criticized high finance for its "cult of silence ... nothing could be better calculated to irritate democracy, which dislikes and suspects secrecy and aloofness." The "fierce light" that Tennyson said "beats upon the throne" also beat upon Morgan, Hill, Harriman, and Schiff. Like Schiff, Kahn was a master conciliator. "Gentlemen," was his standard greeting in his mellow voice, then, with a slight dramatic pause, he would add, "Good afternoon." He had a brilliant talent for phrasing a complex problem with crystal clarity. Perhaps he learned from Schiff how to diffuse a tense negotiating session right at the start. He would disarm his opponents with such a generous opening concession they couldn't help but agree to his conditions. A quarter century later, six years after Schiff's death, Kahn absolved Harriman of causing the corner and panic. Was he obliquely blaming Schiff for his decision at Temple Emanu-El? Kahn simply referred to "certain circumstances beyond [Harriman's] control which I am not now at liberty to relate . . . the time for telling that story has not yet come." The truth was Schiff had let Harriman down at the worst possible moment.

Sunday, May 5, turned out to be the first warm day of spring. Tens of thousands of New Yorkers, from the lower East Side tenements to the mansions of Fifth Avenue, flocked to Central Park from early morning to sunset for picnics, games, and boat rides. Maître d' Oscar Tschirky of the Waldorf–Astoria, whom one trader guessed had netted up to $50,000 on Atchison common, took his family on a pleasure cruise up the North River to his farm at New Paltz, New York. Keene and Schiff huddled in their war rooms in the financial district. Many investors spent the day lost in the newspapers. They would have seen the byline of reporter J. J. Conway of the *New York Sunday Journal* who claimed to have gotten an exclusive interview with Morgan in Aix, quoting him saying, "The United States can solve every commercial problem if we give it time. The country can supply all the markets of the world . . . All these combinations are steps in an advance of a great movement that will distinguish the twentieth century."

Many investors also must have spent the weekend worrying themselves into a conservative, perhaps even short-selling, frame of mind. It had been, said the *New York Herald*, "the most colossal week of speculative trading in the world's history." This was the sixth month of an unprecedented run-up in railroad stocks since McKinley's re-election. Was it the top? It certainly seemed so to *New York Sun* financial reporter "Philip King" (pen name for the Street's most influential financial writer, thirty-six-year-old Daniel Fiske Kellogg, said to have a pipeline to Morgan himself). He wrote in the Monday morning, May 6, edition:

> Railroad stocks of the country are selling at prices which represent advances of from 200 to 900 percent [since McKinley was elected in 1896], and which in the great majority of instances, afford returns to the investor of less than three and one-half per centum annum, or less than that of the first mortgage bonds upon the properties . . . It is not a good omen for Northern Pacific, for instance, that its surplus for the nine months from July 1, 1900 to March 31, 1901, after charges and allowance for dividends upon both classes of stock, and deduction of the earnings of the St. Paul and Duluth road, which entered the Northern Pacific system at the beginning of the period, is over $1,000,000 less than for the similar time in the preceding year.

Some brokerage firms already were paying the price. On Saturday night a Chicago firm was forced to liquidate, caught in an ever-rising market with too many short positions. Another Chicago firm went under four days later for the same reason. There was more fuel for short-sellers. Some New York bankers were wary of what they considered the inflated values of certain stocks. "Three or four blocks of stock of a very large financial institution in this town were refused as collateral all around the Street," one banker was quoted saying, "I would not take them, and...the presidents of the very large banks whose stock was offered refused to lend to them...The prices at which the stocks were quoted were altogether too high and all out of proportion to their actual worth." National City Bank stock, once at 325, now traded at 800, Standard Oil had gone from 500 to 815, the Bank of New Amsterdam from 600 to 1,400.

Someone was rumored to have bought Colorado Fuel and Iron a few weeks earlier on the advice of no one less than the president of the company, and then sold the shares May 1 for a profit of $500,000. Former congressman Jefferson M. Levy was said to have netted $3 million, Jacob Field $5 million, and Oscar of the Waldorf–Astoria boasted he had made on trades "almost as much as the chief room clerk." A Pennsylvanian who made money in lumber and then bought stock in the steel companies that were absorbed into U.S. Steel was overheard at the Waldorf–Astoria claiming he used the proceeds to buy 11,000 shares of Union Pacific and sold them in three weeks netting $250,000. A quiet investor from San Francisco, George Whittell Sr., was staying at the Waldorf. He had inherited millions in real estate and his father-in-law owned the San Francisco Water Company, and had made millions more since November on National City Bank, Standard Oil, Atchison, and Union Pacific.

Then there was flinty, eighty-four-year-old Russell Sage, former partner of the late Jay Gould, stock trader and money lender whose railroad empire once spanned 15,000 miles of track. He had prospered in four panics, 1857, 1873, 1884, and 1893, and was looking for similar profits by lending call money in this bull market. He was certain it was headed for a panic. He had made a fortune many times over on puts (a contract to sell a stock at a specific price during an option period) and calls (a contract to buy a stock at a specific price during an option period). He also invented conversions: placing puts and calls on the same contracts, protecting his upside and downside, then asking an exorbitant rate for the call option. London commission houses were taking a lesson from old Russell. They were selling call options to New York traders on American securities who held them until the great rise in the market began and then "called" them from London at enormous profits.

Sage claimed never to have understood the value of Hill's northern tier railroads. Why would anyone want to live in that cold country? He once bought Northern Pacific common at $8 a share and sold it at $15 and that was enough for him. Sage, in a way, was right. There was nothing to justify the 30 percent rise in Northern Pacific common since the start of the year, especially with the added debt of the Burlington purchase. What if crops failed this summer? Part of the spring wheat crop had failed the last year, cutting into the Northern Pacific's gross earnings with no commensurate cut in expenses. What if business took a dive again? The Northern Pacific, with its dwindling surplus, would be on the hook with the Great Northern for the Burlington debt.

Under a clear sky with the temperature in the 50s, a stream of carriages queued traders and brokers to the east entrance of the Produce Exchange on Monday morning, May 6. There was little news or rumor to move the market. There was, however, an ominous poem. On the newsstands that morning you could open Hearst's *New York Journal* to page 2. There you could find a new poem by Edwin Markham, "The Wall Street Pit," which read in part:

> I see a hell of faces surge and whirl
> Like maelstrom in the ocean—faces lean
> And fleshless as the talons of a hawk—
> Hot faces like the faces of wolves
> That track the traveler fleeing through the night . . .
> Is Babel come again with shrieking crew
> To eat the dust and drink the roaring wind?
> And all for what? A handful of bright sand
> To buy a shroud with and a length of earth?

After what would have been his customary breakfast of brandy and black coffee, Keene quietly entered the building but never appeared on the trading floor. Since he was not a member of the Exchange he would direct buying operations for Hill–Morgan in his whispered, high-pitched voice from the office of his son-in-law, Talbot Jones Taylor. Harry Content was ready to run the floor operation for Keene. Known as the "prince of brokers," he had survived the panic of 1893 and would still be an active broker in October 1929.

Content descended from Dutch Jews from Amsterdam who came to Manhattan in the early nineteenth century. His father, Noah, also was a broker and member of the Exchange. At age fifteen in 1876, Harry earned three dollars a week as a quotation boy for a curb broker; five years later he was making $20,000 a year, and by 1881 had bought himself a seat on the Exchange. He made a fortune buying and selling on both sides of the sugar corner in 1893, bought a townhouse on Park Avenue, a country home in Elberon, New Jersey, a 110-foot yacht, and entertained lavishly, often in the company of Diamond Jim Brady. Content always wore an "unfailing mask of good nature," an inscrutable smile, smoked cigarettes in a gold-tipped holder, and wore a fresh flower in the lapel of his double-breasted Prince Albert. His infamous colleague Thomas Lawson in his novel *Friday the Thirteenth* described a character based on Content as "a handsome, miniature man, with a fascinating face lighted by a pair of sparkling black eyes . . . with a black moustache parted over white teeth, which when he was stalking looked like those of a wolf."

Content's phone operator was twenty-one-year-old Leonard A. Hockstader of Philadelphia, a recent Yale graduate whose father had found him an entry-level job with Taylor's brokerage firm at the Exchange. Hockstader would send buy and sell instructions on the floor to Edward Loudon "Eddie" Norton of the Street and Norton brokerage firm. "Experience, astuteness, and adroitness," the *New York Times* said of him later, "these are Norton's characteristics . . . equally known is the honesty of the man." In other words, Keene needed someone of integrity, someone who would not, in the midst of chaotic trading, scalp a stock in his own self-interest.

The thirty-eight-year-old Norton was one of the most popular traders on the Exchange, "good looking, good natured," of slender build and angular face. The San Antonio–born son of a merchant, he traced his lineage to the early seventeenth century and Nicholas Norton, a Mayflower passenger. Eddie and his stepfather, Henry Allen, opened a brokerage firm in the Produce Exchange district at the foot of Broadway in 1884. Two years later Norton became a member of the Stock Exchange at age twenty-two and they moved their headquarters to 31 New Street, a block from the Exchange. In the early 1890s they helped lead bear runs against the Distillers Securities Corporation (the "Whiskey Trust") and the American Sugar Refining Company (the "Sugar Trust"), using the proceeds to bull the stock of James M. Waterbury's overextended National Cordage Company.

When the stock of National Cordage plummeted from 140 to 70 a share in early May 1893 it kicked off the four-year depression that took Allen's firm down with it that month. Seven years later, Norton formed Street and Norton with William Greene Street. They soon became Morgan favorites, just in time for the big bull run of the last two McKinley years, between the "hay and the grass," as Norton liked to put it, especially in railroad and steel stocks. Norton was the trader who just a few weeks earlier had sold, on behalf of Keene and Morgan, 150,000 shares of U.S. Steel preferred in a single day. On the morning of May 6 his buying was backed by the deep pockets of the Morgan treasury, including cash from New York Life, courtesy of Morgan's George Perkins, who continued his dual employment with both firms. Otto Kahn of Kuhn, Loeb never crossed paths with Keene at the Exchange; he came through another entrance and met with his floor manager, the young Al Stern. The Keene–Content–Norton strategy (as with Schiff and Kahn) was to try to hide trades by not dealing with a specialist in Northern Pacific, or even dealing with the "two-dollar brokers" on the floor, but rather to distribute orders secretly through large wire houses.

London opened at 4 a.m. New York time on heavy buying of American stocks including Northern Pacific, which shot up four points at the open to 114⅜, a signal of what was to come in New York. Chairman Kennedy gaveled the New York session open at 10 a.m. In the first ten minutes, Northern Pacific common—which began the year at 83⅓ and had closed Saturday at 110—opened at 114 on a sale of 500 shares. The next trade was at 116½. By the end of the first hour, it was at 120. Then two hundred at 121⅝. Two thousand at 121¾. Two hundred at 121⅞. One thousand at 122. Five hundred at 122⅛. Thirty-two hundred at 122¼. Two hundred at 122⅜. Three hundred at 122½. Twelve hundred at 122⅝. One thousand at 122¾. Fifteen hundred at 122⅞. Two thousand at 123. Heavy buying pushed it to 123¼ before noon. "There was," said the *New York Herald*, "not a word of news to justify it." What *was* behind it, then? Had a large short position in the "Nipper" scrambled to cover? Or was it an attack *against* the shorts? Then, word spread. Street and Norton was acting for an unnamed client with an unlimited buy order for Nipper common. "Take everything that's offered," Norton was heard saying. No haggling over eighths and quarters.

Nipper common dropped two points. Then, about 1 p.m., the shorts began to panic. There was what one reporter called "one of the most sensational exhibitions of stock market fireworks seen on the New York Stock

Exchange in many moons." The gallery was packed with spectators leaning over the north railing trying to see the traders at the south end over the eight-foot partition, "a struggling mass of humanity...now surging this way and now that, now with many arms a-waving and now with few, now howling and shrieking as though a mob were let loose and now the voices moderating so that in the distance they sounded only like the hum of many bees."

There was "one great football scrimmage" at the Nipper post. Bedlam seemed to vibrate the building. In the confusion, one trader mistook a sell order of a thousand shares for a buy order. Two hours later he discovered his mistake but found the stock had risen seven points. So he sold 2,000 shares at the higher figure, half for himself and half for his customer, each netting about $7,000. One trader bought 1,500 shares of Northern Pacific common at about 11 a.m. for $117 a share and sold it three hours later for $130 a share, netting $19,500. Elbows flew, fistfights erupted among mobs of messenger boys trying to get their trades verified at the commission windows. Windows were smashed. The Exchange had to staff the stations with security officers to keep order.

Norton escalated the buying. His order that morning from Keene was to buy 150,000 shares of Nipper common "at any price," but for tactical purposes at least up to 125. The price rose above 120 before he could fill half his quota. Norton rested at around 120. When he did some shorts judged it the top. This was their value to the market: pessimists doubting optimists. They began to sell Nipper short. They were wrong. Norton started buying again. Eight successive trades pushed Nipper common up 2¾ to 124½. Then sixteen consecutive trades each at a higher price. Then to 125½. Then an amazing leap to 133. It fell back to 128, a thirteen-point margin in about ten minutes.

Minutes later, an *Evening Post* reporter spotted Hill on Wall Street bounding up the front steps two at a time into the Mills building, perhaps headed for Lamont's office on the fifth floor. "Sold at 125, did it," he replied to the reporter. "I didn't know it had gone so high." The *Herald* thought the short interest in Nipper appeared to "have been shaken out," but it was wrong. Nipper common rose again to 129⅞ and closed at 127½, perhaps from selling by the shorts, but it was almost 18 points above Saturday's close. Its total volume was 371,800 shares—a single-day record for Northern Pacific, almost half its total shares outstanding. The rise made the shorts even more certain that the Nipper couldn't possibly hold much longer at that level. A week later the *New York Times* looked back on these hours and surmised that "every professional speculator began to go short of the stock in free and easy fashion."

This didn't look anymore like merely a brief "squeeze of the shorts." This was worse. Then someone uttered, for the first time, the "c" word. Nipper common "began to mount as on wings," said the *Herald*, "and as the story glided out of countless tickers in the financial district and nimble office boys began to get up the new prices on the boards, the veterans exclaimed in convincing ways, 'Only one explanation for that—they have it cornered!"

But *who* was "they"? And how could a corner be worked on a property with $80 million in securities outstanding? Who had pockets that deep? Standard Oil? Reporters demanded a statement from Street and Norton. "We received an order over the telephone," was all the firm said, "and we absorbed nearly 150,000 shares." In a diversion, Keene's traders also had sold some of the preferred Kuhn, Loeb brokers snapped up. Kuhn, Loeb had not yet realized the preferred could be retired by a majority of the common. In fact, continuing to buy Nipper preferred turned out to be—after Schiff's tipping his hand to Hill, and after Schiff's decision at Temple Emanu-El—Schiff's third tactical error. That was what Hill meant when he told Mount Stephen via cable, "We are letting enemy think they have control." The more Nipper preferred stock that Kuhn, Loeb bought the less opportunity they had to buy any Nipper common. Farrer told Hill via cable from London that "brokers who usually act for Jacob [Schiff] here continue buying all preferred offering."

Nipper common inflated the whole market. Total volume was 2.3 million shares. Atchison rose 2⅞; Union Pacific up 1⅝; the St. Paul up 1. Call money rose to 10 percent ($1,000 to rent 100 shares for 24 hours) then settled at 4 percent. One bank was said to be requiring not only the usual 20-point margin but another $30 on each $100 requested for overnight loans. There was one estimate that some $20 million was lent on the Exchange in overnight call money at 6 to 9 percent. Street and Norton, buying Northern Pacific in blocks of hundreds and thousands throughout the day, now had bought at least 150,000 shares of Nipper common. Perhaps it was as high as 180,000. Halle and Steiglitz, and Rogers and Randolph each bought 40,000. But for whom? The *New York Tribune* thought it was all bought for Vanderbilt. Whoever Street and Norton was buying for, it was a record on the Exchange for trading by one firm in one day. They were known as a "pool broker," buying for a syndicate. The firm also was known to be a Keene broker. But who was Keene buying for? Not possibly for Gates or the Moore brothers. Were some plungers working together through Keene to try to put the screws to those who had built a large short interest in Northern Pacific? One report said Norton was buying for Keene who was buying for the Northern Pacific–Great Northern–Burlington interests. But why?

Hill told one reporter, innocently, he thought maybe the Northern Pacific was going up simply because some investors thought it was undervalued. Was the Nipper rising because some German investors were betting Northern Pacific would merge with Canadian Pacific, which closed up 9½? Was there a "large banking interest" behind the buying not previously associated with Northern Pacific? Had Hill–Morgan and the Vanderbilts agreed to merge the Union Pacific and the Northern Pacific? Might there be an alliance forming among Vanderbilt, Rockefeller, and Harriman–Schiff? If Morgan was behind the buying of Union Pacific shares and Union Pacific was behind the buying of Northern Pacific shares was it some alliance to achieve some sort of off-setting balance of "community of interest"? Was it because Northern Pacific preferred was scheduled to be retired in January, and thus holders of Nipper common would be entitled to all the dividends, perhaps as high as 6 percent? "Mr. Hill has always told friends that Northern Pacific would get 6 percent dividends sooner or later," said the *Journal*, perhaps that could account for the feverish demand for Northern Pacific common. It could, but only for some of it. The heads of railroads and smart floor traders knew the fundamentals of Northern Pacific didn't support the run up in its stock price.

There had to be some other force at work behind the rise of Northern Pacific. No one yet had traced the trading publicly to Morgan and Company or Kuhn, Loeb. On the surface it was Eddie Norton's show. It was true, no one ever waved a flag or rang a bell when it was time to get in or out of the market, but now the traders who had shorted Northern Pacific, betting it would soon go down, kept their eyes on Norton on the trading floor, watching every gesture he made, every expression on his face. When he stopped buying that would signal the market had topped and they would start selling. But all day Monday Eddie kept buying. He knew in doing so he was causing the ruin of many of his fellow traders who had shorted Northern Pacific on their own account; many of them were his longtime friends whom he would have to look in the eye. Someone recalled seeing Norton that Monday afternoon, May 6, standing motionless in the chaos on the floor, tears in his eyes. Some of his colleagues gathered around him. Norton was overheard telling them in a trembling voice, "Boys, I am more sorry than I can tell you, but, by God, I can't help it! It's no fault of mine, believe me."

There was one young trader on the floor this day who knew exactly what was going on. He stood six-feet-three, parted his jet-black hair in the middle, and wore gold-rimmed spectacles. Thirty-year-old Bernard Mannes Baruch was a native of South Carolina, son of a Prussian immigrant who became a medical doctor; his mother was from a Confederate family of thirteen children who lost their plantation during the Civil War. The family moved to New York, Baruch went to college, became a runner on Wall Street in the late 1880s, joined A. A. Housman and Company in 1895 as a partner, bought a seat on the Exchange, and soon became a millionaire trading in the sugar market. Future generations would know him as an eminent American statesman, advisor to presidents, and philanthropist.

Early this morning he was simply another young trader in a high-band collar starting his day before the first sunlight poured through the stained glass skylight of the Produce Exchange, at the arbitrage rail where cables were sent and received from London, profiting from the price differences between London and New York, which tended wider on Monday mornings. At 4 a.m. New York time, Northern Pacific common was selling in London at about ten points below its closing price the day before in New York. It was an arbitrager's dream. Standing next to him was Talbot Jones Taylor, a Stock Exchange member and head of his own brokerage firm. Taylor was married to Keene's daughter, Jessica, and due partly to his father-in-law's largesse, he owned a palatial vine-covered estate that grew to thirty rooms on the Hempstead Plains of Long Island. Like Keene, he indulged his passion for horseflesh as a member of several jockey clubs.

As Baruch recalled years later, Taylor was watching him, pensively tapping his lips with the end of his pencil. Finally, he asked: "Bernie, are you doing anything in Northern Pacific?" "Yes," Baruch replied, "and I'll tell you how to make some money out of it. Buy London, sell here, and take an arbitrage profit." Taylor kept tapping his lips then his forehead with the pencil and said, "I would not arbitrage it if I were you." Baruch did not ask why, assuming Taylor would tell him if he wanted him to know. Baruch then offered to give Taylor some of his previous London purchases. "All right," said Taylor, "you can buy N.P. in London but if I need the stock I want you to sell it to me at a price and a profit that I will fix." Baruch agreed.

Taylor stood there for an instant. Could he trust the young trader to keep quiet? He took Baruch's arm and led him to where they couldn't be heard. "Bernie," he said in almost a whisper, "I know you will do nothing to interfere with the execution of the order. There is a terrific contest for control and Mr. Keene is acting for J. P. Morgan. Be careful and don't be short of this stock. What I buy must be delivered now. Stock bought in London will not do." Baruch held the stock he bought in London. Taylor had given him, perfectly legal in those days, insider information. Traders who had shorted Northern Pacific thinking it would go down were going to be roasted because it was not going to go down. It was going to go up, way up. As it kept rising the shorts would have to liquidate their shares of other stocks to raise the cash to cover their short positions on Northern Pacific. When they did that the whole market would collapse. So Baruch would hold on to his Northern Pacific and sell some other stocks short, anticipating the panic.

The less fortunate brokerage firms, with no Talbot Taylor whispering in their ear, were trying to play the same game but instead were shorting Northern Pacific. Houses such as Ladenburg, Theimann and Company, Von Hoffman and Company, and the Wormsers were playing the arbitrage game between London and New York on Northern Pacific and generating about $50,000 or more a day in revenue. That evening through all the premier uptown hotels, the Hoffman, the Manhattan, the Imperial, the Martinique and through the Palm Garden room and up and down Peacock Alley at the Waldorf–Astoria rumors swept that Morgan and Keene were behind the Northern Pacific buying because they wanted to teach the shorts a lesson. It was rumored that not only was call money up to 10 percent but Stillman's National City Bank had stopped lending to brokers.

On Tuesday morning, May 7, Norton went into the market for even more Northern Pacific common for Keene and Hill–Morgan. There were few shares available. Brokerage houses, which had loaned out Northern Pacific to the shorts, began demanding delivery. Northern Pacific common opened with a trade of 500 at $127\frac{1}{2}$. The next eleven trades it ran up to $130\frac{1}{2}$. It jumped quickly in furious trading to 133. By noon it was at $135\frac{3}{4}$, rising eight points in only two hours. Then to 140. Then $143\frac{1}{2}$. At one of the large brokerage houses near the Stock Exchange the public room had only one ticker. The crowd around the machine became so large shortly after 11 a.m. that someone had to read off the prices as they came over the tape. By noon some shorts, worried Northern Pacific could go even higher, tried to buy more shares to cover their short positions.

That put even more upward pressure on the stock. Other shorts thought Northern Pacific now was headed down so they bought more shares of it short. This added even more volume. Some commission houses refused to take any short-selling orders for Northern Pacific on any terms. One called for delivery of Northern Pacific shares it had bought. That panicked some short-sellers who had to sell other stocks to raise cash to cover their Northern Pacific short positions. Northern Pacific preferred was just as scarce. One brokerage firm received a customer order to buy 10,000 shares of Nipper preferred at the open at 103. The broker yelled himself hoarse on the floor and could buy only 300 shares. He bought another 300 at 104 for the same customer and then gave up. Nipper preferred rose seven for the day, closing at 110.

At 1 p.m. on Tuesday afternoon, May 7, Nipper common hit 145, then a sharp drop to 140. Then, said the *New York Herald*, like Antaeus of Greek myth who wrestled Hercules, it gathered "fresh vigor from its fall" and rose again. Seven hundred at 142½. Two hundred at 143½. One hundred at 143⅞. Six hundred at 145. Five hundred at 144½. Eighteen hundred at 145. Two hundred at 146. One hundred at 146½. One hundred at 147. One thousand at 147½. Six hundred at 147. Five hundred at 147½. Three hundred at 148. One hundred at 147½. Eleven hundred at 148. One thousand at 148½. Four hundred at 149. Three thousand at 149½. One thousand at 149¾. Norton, Keene, and Content, on behalf of Hill–Morgan, thought they finally had their 150,000 and stopped buying. The shorts then resumed their covering. The gong sounded. The last shout of "Sold!" echoed across the arena. Nipper common closed at 143½ on volume of 231,400 shares, up 16 for the day, up 33½ for two days.

There now were thought to be only 46,000 available shares of Nipper common to meet the commitments of short-sellers. A line had been crossed. More shares of Northern Pacific had been bought than existed. Those who still held blocks of Northern Pacific now offered to lend them at 15 percent interest or to sell them at 17 points above the closing price of 143½. Harriman–Schiff definitely had a majority of the preferred and common combined. They and Hill–Morgan both believed, as well, that each had a majority of the common. Some of that stock, however—how much, no one knew—came from short-sellers who had sold what they didn't yet own. About 100,000 more shares of Northern Pacific had been sold than had been printed. The Northern Pacific shorts had been cornered. Neither Hill–Morgan nor Harriman–Schiff had any desire to sell them any shares, concerned they might find their way to the adversary. Under the Exchange's rules, a seller had to deliver sold shares to a broker by 2:15 p.m. the following day. The market closed at 3 p.m. Panic was in the air. The brokerage firm of Moore and Schley, thought to be agents of Morgan, became the first to call for delivery the following day of Northern Pacific stock certificates from the shorts.

Before the market had closed, but after Norton stopped buying, he walked around the floor with a list of traders who had borrowed Nipper common from Street and Norton. "I haven't got another hundred shares to lend," he said, "but I'm perfectly willing to renew loans with everybody at fair rates." After trading ended he met in the southeast corner of the floor with arbitrage sellers. They represented holders of Northern Pacific in European capitals who had sold their stock but had to borrow equivalent shares to cover delivery the day after the sale, until the certificates arrived in New York after the eight-to-ten-day Atlantic crossing.

The shorts who needed stock to deliver to those to whom they'd sold it were caught, said the *Herald*, like "a fawn who should get playfully between the mouth of a sporting rifle and a grizzly bear." In addition to the overnight call loan rates the "arbs" and the "shorts" now would have to pay a premium for renewing their loans, a certain percentage of the par value of the stock. The bidders shouted at Norton: "I'll give a thirty-second for 500 shares of Nipper common!" "A quarter for 500!" "Three-eighths for 200!" "Half a thousand for Nipper!" "I'll give 1 percent for 2,000 Northern Pacific!" Hands shot up. The mob of traders began to surge and scream: "I only want 200, a pitiful little 200. I'll give 4 percent for it." One broker ran around the edge of the crowd yelling, "Lift me up, will you? Lift me up! I'm little and I can't yell loud enough."

Dusk settled over the city, lights glowed throughout the financial district. Hill, Bacon, Steele, George Perkins, and Baker were at Morgan and Company. Somehow, Harriman was back at work. It had been only seventy-two hours after the pain in his abdomen had been so intense it had kept him in bed at least through Saturday morning. What was his doctor's diagnosis? Was he on medication? He must still have been weak and drawn. It was all kept from the newspapers. But there he was, fully present and in the fight, at the offices of Kuhn, Loeb with Schiff, Stillman, Gould, and William K. Vanderbilt's son-in-law Hamilton McCown Twombley. Baker tried to mediate, as did Lamont. He was among the first to warn Hill a year ago of the Stillman–Harriman alliance.

The corner now was obvious. Panic selling was inevitable. Perhaps it was Lamont or Baker, or both, who urged both sides to settle fast. Sometime Tuesday, May 7, Harriman cabled Morgan in Aix asking him to suggest a settlement. Later in the evening reporters staking out the Hotel Netherland spotted Hill and surrounded him. He shrugged his shoulders like an innocent bystander. "I have not bought a share of Northern Pacific in six months," he told a reporter. "I'm the president of the Great Northern, you know, and I'm not interested in Northern Pacific. I don't know anything about Mr. Morgan's relations to the road—we are two separate individuals." And to another, "I have not been engaged in any such contest...This movement in Northern Pacific shares appears to me to be the outcome of a speculative craze." And to another, "My dear sir, we [the Great Northern] never had control, we don't want control, and under the law we could not have control. Really, I have had no more to do with this than the man in the moon." It was a magnificent, wholly convincing performance.

A year later, testifying in a trial stemming from a lawsuit related to the Northern Pacific corner, Hill said at the time of the corner he owned about 60,000 to 70,000 shares of Northern Pacific common worth about $7 million, making him its single largest individual shareholder, and he estimated his friends owned another $14 million. Morgan and Company was said to have owned $20 million. Hill cabled Mount Stephen, "We have the present board and will elect the next one if our friends stand firm." They did stand firm but it was too late to save the market. The panic was just around the corner.

9

"HELL IS EMPTY AND
ALL THE DEVILS ARE HERE"

The gavel came down. A roar erupted. A great, brawling, sweaty mob of traders stormed the Northern Pacific trading post on the floor of the Exchange Wednesday morning, May 8. Nipper common opened at 155. Three hundred shares quickly traded at 159. Ninety-five hundred at 160. A thousand at 165. Two thousand at 170. A thousand at 175. Two thousand at 180. The five hundred telephones just off the floor were all ringing at once, a lunatic jangle of buy and sell.

One broker, Cornelius W. Provost, had an order from a customer to sell 1,000 shares of Nipper common. He sold when it hit 180. There was a sharp, violent break to 150. Provost then covered a short position on Nipper common at 150, netting his customer a profit of $30,000. Another broker, John Manning, had similar luck. He sold 1,000 shares of Nipper common to a frantic bidder at 180. He started to write the sale on his pad but before he could scribble the buyer's name Nipper common broke downward and he bought the thousand shares at 160, turning a profit of $20,000 in less than one minute. Down it went to as low as 145. During the rise to 180 those who had shorted it now had to dump other stocks to raise cash to cover their deficit in Northern Pacific. Union Pacific fell 8½, U.S. Steel 7, and Amalgamated Copper 12.

Robert Bacon authorized James R. Keene to lend some Northern Pacific common to the shorts to stabilize the market, but it was a finger in the dike. Northern Pacific kept rising. As other stocks tumbled Northern Pacific shot up again to 167½ and closed at 160, fifty points higher than Monday's open. A bulletin from an unnamed source inched out over the tickers: "We can state authoritatively that James J. Hill has not sold one share of his Northern Pacific stock."

At 120 Broadway, Harriman reported to the Union Pacific board on Kuhn, Loeb's purchases of Northern Pacific so far. The board gave approval to buy more as needed. It was a meaningless vote. There was no Northern Pacific available. Short-sellers were, in effect, bidding against each other to buy enough Northern Pacific to cover their commitments to deliver. One trader loaned 1,000 shares of Northern Pacific at 35 percent interest, another at 45 percent. An hour later, Northern Pacific shares were being loaned at 85 percent. The sell-off became a route. Northern Pacific was the only stock on the Exchange to finish with a net gain for the day. The St. Paul closed down 15⅛, Delaware & Hudson down 13, Lackawanna down 9¼, Pennsylvania Railroad down 6⅝, Missouri Pacific down 8½, Union Pacific from 130 to 112½. The gavel closed trading at 3 p.m., but the Exchange tickers, circuits overloaded like a twitching muscle, kept recording sales until 3:26 p.m., the longest time the tape had ever been behind.

An animal mob of short-sellers roamed the trading floor looking for Northern Pacific shares to borrow overnight, confronting any broker who walked onto the floor. The mob pinned one broker against the railing around the floor and he yelled, "Let me go, will you? I haven't a share of the d—d stock. Do you think I carry it in my clothes?" Another broker was slammed against the arbitrage rail with enough force to break his ribs.

At about this time, Otto Kahn dispatched his young floor manager, Al Stern of Herzfeld and Stern, onto the floor to do as Eddie Norton had done, offer to loan some shares overnight to show there was no concerted effort to squeeze the shorts. In his excitement, however, Stern lost his head. Unlike Norton who did it quietly, Stern yelled a line to the traders that prefigured by three decades a scene from a Marx brothers' movie. "Who wants to borrow Northern Pacific?" he yelled, "I have a block to lend!" He was offering the shares, furthermore, at only 1 percent interest versus the prevailing market of 7 percent.

Bernard Baruch watched what happened next and years later described the mayhem: "The first response was a deafening shout. There was an infinitesimal pause and then the desperate brokers rushed Stern. Struggling to get near enough to him to shout their bids, they kicked over stock tickers. Strong brokers thrust aside the weak ones." Hands were waving and trembling in the air. "I want a thousand, give you two percent!" "Three percent for 500!" "Three and a half for 200!—three and a half—three and a half—four!" "Four and a half for 300!" Almost doubled over on a chair, his face close to a pad, Stern began to note his transactions. He mumbled to one man, "All right, you get it" and to another "For heaven's sake don't stick your finger in me eye." One broker took Stern's hat and beat him over the head with it to get his attention. The traders nearly climbed over each other to get to him. "Mr. Stern is a young man of medium size," wrote one reporter, "and he was almost carried off his feet by the rush of excited men." The mob followed him to a telephone booth and trapped him inside while he yelled into the receiver. After Stern had loaned the last of his Northern Pacific he staggered from the floor, pale and disheveled. For the right to borrow a hundred shares of Northern Pacific overnight one now had to pay a premium of 45 percent, or $4,500.

At first both Morgan and Kuhn, Loeb didn't want to lend Northern Pacific shares to brokers, fearing the shares would end up in each other's accounts. They soon realized that if they didn't they would bankrupt the brokerage houses acting for the short-sellers and also the arbitrage houses, which could not deliver stock until the steamers crossed the Atlantic in eight to ten days from London. It was rumored that one international banking firm was short 25,000 shares of Northern Pacific and another was short 20,000, liabilities respectively of $25 million and $20 million. Many prominent houses were short 5,000, and one conservative brokerage firm on Broadway was short 6,000. Kuhn, Loeb and Morgan told the "arbs" they would lend them "flat" the stock they were short, not charging a premium. "At first sight this might look like a magnanimous act," said the New York Times, "but really it is shrewd, sound business... To have exacted onerous premiums from London sellers, caught innocently in this awkward position, would have aroused a storm of hostile criticism abroad sure to react injuriously here." Even Kuhn, Loeb admitted it was just protecting its European profit: "If legitimate holders of securities abroad cannot sell them here without being subjected to the afflictions which speculators who sell short bring upon themselves, how long would foreigners interest themselves in our market?"

Both sides realized the battleground no longer was on the trading floor but in the corridors of investor and broker opinion. It wasn't how much Northern Pacific either side owned but how much others believed they owned. It also was about what could and should be done to rescue the shorts from a disaster that could bring down the whole market, hundreds of brokerage firms, and the investments of hundreds of thousands of retail stockholders.

Late Wednesday afternoon, Schiff took the offensive. "Is it true," a reporter asked him, "that the Harriman syndicate, including your firm, now have control of the Northern Pacific?" He replied, "We think we have." In words Schiff and Kahn chose carefully, Kuhn, Loeb said it and Harriman "have absolute physical and numerical control of the stock. This stock was not bought in the open market. It was known where the large holdings were and they were secured. The preferred stock has the same voting power as the common stock. We have an absolute majority of the stock, including the preferred and common." Those key words, "absolute physical and numerical control," meant that even not counting "shares" bought from shorts who didn't actually own what they sold, Kuhn, Loeb and Harriman still thought they had a majority of actual shares.

This was a first of its kind—an accidental "corner." It was not intended to extort or squeeze the shorts and compel them to cover their positions by liquidating their other stocks, thereby causing a collapse and then bottom buying by the perpetrators. This was a "natural" corner, two forces buying shares of a company's stock for voting power. Kuhn, Loeb claimed J. P. Morgan and Company had proposed that the two firms pool their Northern Pacific holdings and loan shares pro rata to the shorts at some mutually determined rate. The Morgan firm denied making any such offer. It was adamant that it "has held and now holds control of the Northern Pacific Railroad" and that it "actually has a majority of the stock in hand and at its disposition." Schiff and Harriman, it said, "had bought a quantity of Northern Pacific stock that on paper figures up to a majority of the total issue. A great deal of this stock was sold to the Harriman syndicate by persons who did not have it in their possession but gambled on the chance of getting it in time for delivery."

That evening at the Netherland Hill accused speculators and shorts of causing the corner. "It is all ghost dancing," he said. "There are cliques and parties there that are always ready to rush in and buy or sell as the case may be upon the slightest provocation."

Desperate brokers and speculators couldn't bring themselves to go home. They had to stay close to the latest rumors. They jammed the corridors and restaurants of the Waldorf–Astoria, the Hoffman House, the Imperial, and the Manhattan far past midnight into Thursday, looking for hope and solace . . . and shares of Nipper common. Traders ran back and forth from the hotels' telephone booths. "Hell is empty," said one of the brokers, who had spent the day pressuring customers short Northern Pacific to liquidate their other positions, "and all the devils are here." It was easy to tell winners from losers; the latter were in black tie trying to look happy, the former were in tweeds, dining quietly and "swallowing magnums." If Northern Pacific could go from 110 to 160 in three days, how high could it go tomorrow? A rumor swept the corridors that some frightened shorts had already bid 230 for

Nipper common. Whoever was fighting for control of the stock could easily, said one newspaper, "jam it up to 500." A wild curb market among frantic shorts for Nipper common became a free-for-all in the corridors of the Waldorf–Astoria. At 7:30 p.m. someone bid $200 a share and 400 shares traded hands. A few minutes later, someone paid $25,000, or $50 a share, simply for the overnight loan of 500 shares of Nipper common.

Scotch and soda somehow was no longer enough for brokers in the Waldorf–Astoria cafés. The head bartender claimed he served more champagne that night than any time since the two hotels opened as one, four years earlier. Every broker and trader of any repute seemed to be at the hotel, including the Wassermans and the Housmans. Hill's friend, President Henry W. Cannon of the Chase National Bank, was there, too.

The plunger Gates had postponed his trip that day to Europe. He was seated in a far corner of one of the cafés in a cloud of cigar smoke talking intensely with his lawyer, the thirty-six-year-old legal prodigy Max Pam. An Austrian immigrant, self-taught in the law, Pam made his fortune helping Gates organize the American Steel and Wire Company two years earlier, then struck it rich again when they sold the company to U.S. Steel. Gates was watching "every move of his companion's face as if trying to recall something he had forgotten." It was whispered at the Waldorf that a Morgan employee had set Gates up with a false rumor of an imminent bear raid on Northern Pacific. Gates reportedly fell for it and persuaded many of his "Chicago crowd" to short Nipper common. Gates denied rumors he was short no less than 60,000 shares of Nipper common at 50 points below its May 8 closing price or that he had lost $3.5 million in the crumbling market. He did, however, compare himself to a dog that had been kicked so many times he walked sideways.

Gates also was seen with Arthur Housman, John H. Davis, and a few other noted brokers. They were heard discussing whether Russell Sage's comments about the overheated market had been a self-fulfilling prophecy. "I tell you what let us do," said one of the group, "Let us make old Sage a 'sporty' offer for 30 shares of Missouri Pacific, to be called in five months at 105. Let's offer 2 percent for the call." The others thought a moment and someone said, "Well, that's all right. I will go in for 10 shares." Another said, "I will take 10." The one who made the original offer said, "Well, count me in for the other 10." A bystander remarked, "I thought these fellows were big operators, but here they are haggling over 10 share lots." Said another, "When they say 30 shares they mean thirty thousand."

Everyone waited for some word of hope from Morgan across the Atlantic. No one was going to sleep until the ticker in the bar or café told how London opened at 4 a.m. A rumor swept the Waldorf: Keene is meeting at 10 p.m. at the hotel with people from both Hill–Morgan and Harriman–Schiff. Keene was not there; he had slipped out to a dinner party.

At the White Star Line pier at West Tenth Street sometime during the night, trunks from London were unloaded from the S.S. *Majestic* and S.S. *Servia* under tight security. They carried certificates for thousands of shares of Northern Pacific stock from London arbitrage houses, destined for the account of arbitrage houses in New York for signing and delivery in the morning. They had borrowed them from Kuhn, Loeb, which would now add them to what Schiff believed would be his side's majority control. Another steamer, the *Oceanic*, had just left Liverpool with another 40,000 to 50,000 shares.

The tickers in their glass bell jars clicked to electromagnetic life in the Waldorf–Astoria shortly after 4 a.m. on Thursday, May 9, 1901. Everyone had the same question: How is London? Then came the brassy, whirring, clicking sound. *Ticky-ticky-ticky-tick.* Someone reached out for the thin reed of hope spooling from the ticker's steel springs and wheels: the three-fourths-inch wide ribbon of paper with stock symbols and quoted prices. "The letters and figures used in the language of the tape," someone once said, "are very few, but they spell ruin in ninety-nine million ways."

London opened with some improvement. The St. Paul was up 6¾. Norfolk & Western up 5¼. Union Pacific common up 1½. Union Pacific preferred up 3⅜. U.S. Steel up 1¾. Atchison & Topeka up 1½. And then, Northern Pacific common . . . down 27½. Was there hope for the shorts? Now all attention turned to the Produce Exchange. The Northern Pacific "corner" was made in America. It would have to be unwound in America, not at Capel Court or even at the Produce Exchange but in the war rooms of Kuhn, Loeb and J. P. Morgan and Company, a block apart on either side of the Sub-Treasury and the bronze Washington.

Morning dawned gray, rain pooled in the streets, umbrellas were up. The American flag atop the Produce Exchange's tower fluttered at half-staff for a deceased member. Another tense meeting was underway at the Equitable Building at 120 Broadway. Harriman, Schiff, Rockefeller, and Gould were there. So was Stillman, not just as an ally of Harriman–Schiff or head of National City Bank but as a representative of the New York Clearing House, the medium for all transactions among New York banks and thus in a position

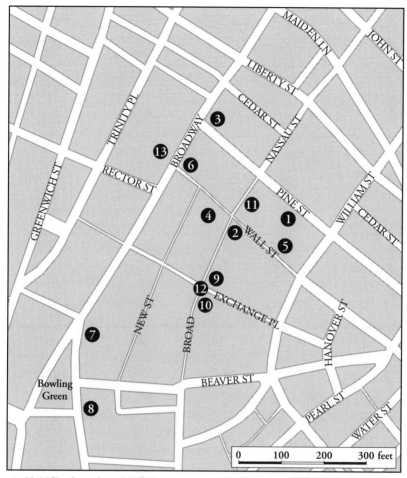

1. 25–27 Pine Street: James J. Hill (Great Northern) and Jacob H. Schiff (Kuhn, Loeb & Co.)
2. 23 Wall Street: J. P. Morgan & Company
3. 120 Broadway: Edward H. Harriman (Union Pacific)
4. New York Stock Exchange
5. 52 Wall Street: James J. Stillman (National City Bank)
6. 2 Wall Street: George F. Baker (First National Bank)
7. 26 Broadway: William A. Rockefeller (Standard Oil)
8. New York Produce Exchange
9. 23 Broad Street: Daniel S. Lamont (Northern Pacific)
10. 30 Broad Street: James R. Keene
11. Sub-Treasury Building, Washington statue
12. Curb Market
13. Trinity Church

The financial district of New York City, circa 1901.

to offer some relief to commission houses and to the shorts. Bacon was there as the only representative of Hill–Morgan. Kuhn, Loeb offered "to join with Morgan & Co. in loaning Northern Pacific, or are willing to enter into arrangements for cancelling purchases of Northern Pacific pro rata or otherwise to do what can be done to relieve the existing situation if it can be done without altering the relative position of the two interests." Bacon, suspecting the offer was a ploy to compensate for Kuhn, Loeb's short positions, rejected it.

At the Produce Exchange, anxious, weary faces gazed up at the podium as 10 a.m. approached on Thursday, May 9. The gavel came down and at first there was a collective calm, something like prayerful reverence. Then screams of bidding. Northern Pacific common, which closed the previous afternoon at 160, jumped to 170 on the first trade of 500 shares. The panic built. Two hundred shares sold at 175. Three hundred at 180. Down to 170 on 200 shares. A sudden leap in one trade of 300 shares to 190. More than one million shares traded in the first hour. Northern Pacific passed 200. Then 210. The floor held its breadth for a few seconds and traders broke into a roar "akin to the approach of a hurricane." Then 225. Then 280. Then 300. Then, a heart-thumping plummet to 230. Then back up to 300. Before 11 a.m. it hit 400. Traders climbed over each other to buy and sell, shouting obscenities that couldn't be repeated "in a bar room of even a second class." Just off the floor, the faces of men in brokers' offices turned "ashen, wild-eyed." Exchange members who were short of Nipper had to keep bidding for it because if they didn't deliver the stock on time they would violate Exchange rules, lose their seats, and be barred from the floor. Under New York law, a brokerage could be declared bankrupt if stock it sold was not delivered on time.

No one watched the quote boards. Mobs built around every ticker with their mounds of paper ribbon coiled on the floor. There was simply no Northern Pacific stock available. Overnight call loan money jumped to 60 percent. Broker H. P. Frothingham, always with a Cheshire cat smile, a boutonniere, and a dollar to lend at whatever the market would bear, moved in for the kill, quickly loaning a total of $10 million to desperate shorts at an extortionate 60 percent rate. From his office at Nassau and Liberty Streets, Thomas Fortune Ryan knew a marketing opportunity when he saw one. The 60 percent call loan rate so appalled him he announced that his Morton Trust Company would offer $3 million in call loans not at 60 percent but 6 percent. Commission houses mandated that any sales of Northern Pacific shares must be for cash only and same day delivery. There was a rumor that trader Arthur Housman had dropped dead on the floor, but before it could be denied it had been wired to London. To prove he had a pulse, Housman went to the Exchange and offered $1 million in call money at an undisclosed rate and sold out the offering.

At about this time, broker George I. Malcolm said a client came into his office and gave his partner a certificate for one hundred shares of Northern Pacific common. The partner telephoned Malcolm on the floor of the Exchange asking for its current price. Malcolm said $400 and the client told Malcolm's partner to sell. Malcolm returned to the Northern Pacific post on the trading floor and found Nipper common at $600. He offered the certificate for a hundred shares at $700 a share but there were no takers. He offered it at $650 and a broker bought it at that price but another broker stepped in at the same time and also offered $650. Both claimed the purchase was theirs and left it to Malcolm to decide. He couldn't, and neither could any broker nearby who had watched the bidding. Malcolm and the two buyers agreed to flip a coin. "The broker to whom I thought I sold it lost," he recalled. A sale that was to have been worth $40,000 became $65,000 in less than four minutes.

Now came what Hill later called "that wild hour." Sometime after 11 a.m. Northern Pacific common hit 700. Many in the gallery clinging to the railing for a view of the floor or the quote boards went pale, frozen in fear. It was only a matter of time. They were going to be wiped out. It meant the "destruction of a city of shimmering castles in the air." Two or three women spectators, languid in the chaos, scanned the trading floor from the gallery with opera glasses as if in a box at the Met. Traders and messengers jammed in the single corridor, unable to move on or off the floor. Messenger boys and clerks from the brokerage houses pushed into the mob, trying to deliver transaction slips when every second meant thousands of dollars.

A record number of extra messenger boys, estimated from 2,500 to 3,000, had been hired for that day and still couldn't handle the demand. Some were given as many as twenty-five order messages at a time to deliver to any one of 1,500 offices in the Wall Street district for stock trades, bank deposits, certified checks, or stock certificates. The messengers were not an entirely reliable bunch. Some of their messages, even some of their certified checks, never made it to intended destinations. About two weeks earlier on Broad Street, a block east of the Produce Exchange, a fight erupted after police arrested some vendors for peddling without a license. When the police left, a mob of messenger boys, looking for a free lunch, upset the vendors' carts, sending melons and citrus rolling down the street. The boys stole the vendors' fruit

The May 9, 1901, panic on the "curb" market at Broad Street and Exchange Place, where brokers could buy or sell lots of one hundred shares or less: "They were throwing away their stocks like rubbish." HARPER'S WEEKLY, MAY 1901.

and candy, igniting a violent brawl during which many of the boys lost their messages. One messenger's certified checks for $139,000 disappeared.

At 11:15 a.m. in New York came the trades of the day, the most famous ever in the history of the Exchange. Eddie Norton sold 300 shares of Northern Pacific common—which one could have bought for 25 cents a share on May 25, 1896—for $1,000 a share in cash. The buyer first was thought to be a Standard Oil millionaire or a Chicago plunger. It was later learned Norton had sold 200 shares to an unidentified commission house and 100 to the firm of R. H. Thomas and Company, whose head happened to be a member of the governing board of the New York Stock Exchange and a former president of the Exchange. The 100-share trade made at $1,000 would have represented a loss to the short party, even in the most favorable circumstance, of about $85,000.

The order from the Exchange soon was shouted across the floor: Use of the anteroom off the floor is limited to members of the Exchange or their clerks! For the first time in the Exchange's history, the spectator galleries were closed. "All strangers out," security guards yelled "No one allowed here but members." A rumor spread: uniformed guards also were there to protect brokers on the trading floor from assault by ruined customers. The elevators became death traps, stuffed beyond capacity. They were supposed to carry no more than twenty passengers but carried twice that. The crowd of lunch hour spectators poured back down the narrow stairway, out into the main corridor, and toward a bank of four elevators at the Beaver Street side to try to see the action from the gallery on the south side, but it had been closed too. Automobiles and hacks clogged the east-side court entrance. Even lower Broadway was jammed. Between 11 a.m. and noon, seven of ten Wall Street brokerage firms were said to be technically insolvent. The bucket shops, shellacked in the bull market, now had their day, clearing an estimated $30 million, many customers lost their bets before stepping ten feet from the buy window.

A downpour began. At about noon, plunger Gates was spotted entering the "corner" at Wall and Broad—sloshing through the rain, leaning forward, jaw thrust out, no overcoat or umbrella—where he was said to have had an "excited conference" with Morgan's son-in-law William Pierson Hamilton, a manager of the firm. Had the Morgan men trapped him short in a Northern Pacific "bear" rumor? Given their mutual animosity for Morgan, was Gates scheming with Harriman? Gates, after all, had swooned over Harriman's revival of the Union Pacific, calling it "the most magnificent railroad property in the world." The reporter said he saw Gates rush out of the building crying "No! No!" At the same hour, a hat, coat, watch, and pocketbook were spotted next to a vat of boiling beer at the Bolton Brewery in Troy, New York. Pulled from the suds was the body of the wealthy Samuel Bolton Jr., philanthropist, scion of the founder, said to have lost big in stocks.

Something had to be done to calm the shorts. Kuhn, Loeb announced it would not demand delivery of Northern Pacific stock for the day. At 2:15 Al Stern climbed on a chair on the Exchange floor and yelled the announcement. Minutes later came the same news from J. P. Morgan and Company, approved in a frantic exchange of cables with Morgan in France. Then both firms announced they would not insist on delivery of Northern Pacific common due the next day if the same condition continued, or they would "adopt measures that [would] afford similar relief." This would ease the pressure on the shorts, brokerage houses, and arbitrage houses. In Street and Norton's case it was about 80,000 shares. To caution the shorts, both sides said if they settled with the shorts for Northern Pacific common, it would be at "what will generally be considered a fair market price" or even "at a reasonably low price." The New York Clearing House said Northern Pacific transactions would not have to be channeled through its offices, to make it easier and quicker to settle with the shorts.

As darkness came in London, hundreds of desperate speculators, brokers, clients, and clerks, "haggard and frightened," soaked to the skin in a downpour, ankle-deep in mud, jammed into Shorter's Court outside the closed London Stock Exchange trying to gain some parity with New York prices. It was an impossible task. All sorts of prices were being quoted for the same American securities, and even if a trade was executed it could take ten days to get the certificates across the Atlantic. For that reason, Northern Pacific common had traded in London earlier in the day at 130 when it was being quoted for 500 in New York.

At 2:05 p.m. a breathless messenger rushed into the offices of J. S. Bache and Company at New Street and Exchange Place with a satchel holding 500 shares of Northern Pacific common. They were gathered from Bache customers in Troy, New York, eager to loan them to shorts at the going overnight rate of 50 percent ($5,000 per hundred shares). Bache promised to get them to New York by the 2:15 p.m. daily Exchange deadline. The New York Central express train, the Mohawk, left Troy with the shares at 10:44 a.m. and pulled into Grand Central station at 1:35 p.m., covering 150 miles in two hours and fifty-one minutes.

The "bull panic" became a "bear panic." The selling stampede began. Today it is called a "Minsky moment," named after a twentieth-century economist for the panic dumping of good assets after a euphoric boom heads toward collapse. At first, declines came in a point or two between sales. They grew to breaks of five points, then ten. The downward momentum fed on itself. Chaos engulfed the floor. Then came declines of 15 points between trades. A broker rushed onto the floor shouting "Three hundred Atchison preferred! What's bid?" "40," someone replied. The broker sold it. Atchison had opened that morning at 76 and closed just under 67.

Delaware & Hudson Railroad dropped 20 points one trade to the next. Some young traders, never having lived through anything like this, lost their heads. They sold securities for less than the offered amount because before their bid could be accepted another young broker offered them at an even lower price. "They were throwing away their stocks like rubbish," said one observer, "going crazy because they could not get rid of them faster."

Some veteran brokers tried to restrain the younger ones with arm locks.

They sold because of fright, because margins had been exhausted, because stop orders were reached. "They have plenty of money to pay for a Stock Exchange seat," said one veteran, "but they have no more right to be on the floor than I have to do a trapeze act." It so happened that on this day a record was set for the sale of a seat on the Exchange: $70,000, or three times what a seat sold for only four years earlier, 20 percent more than just a month earlier. It was purchased for a twenty-year-old graduate of Princeton, one George Blumer Schmidt. His mother bought it for him.

The tape was running ten minutes late so there could be no such thing as "selling at the market" because no one knew what the market was. The price of a stock on the ticker was meaningless. A bank clerk ran into a New York brokerage demanding more margin on the brokerage's bank loan. The broker offered the clerk one thousand shares of U.S. Steel to help satisfy the margin call, thinking it was at 40. He looked again: 26. He offered the clerk 500 shares of Manhattan Elevated Railroad, which had been selling at 105. Ten minutes later: 88. U.S. Steel common, which hit a high of 55 nine days earlier, plunged to 24. Its preferred shares, almost 102 nine days earlier, dropped to 69. A wealthy speculator in Chicago, who had gone short a thousand shares of Nipper common at about 100 through a large brokerage firm near the Board of Trade, had to buy the shares back at 350 and lost $300,000. Another top-tier customer guessed the market right but still got burned. He sold 5,000 shares of Rock Island short at 152 just after the market opened and put up cash collateral of $300,000 as margin. Sure enough, Rock Island "blew up," down to 140, down to 138, down to 130. He tried to buy it back at 130, where his profit could be $110,000, but there was such chaos his order wasn't executed for about two hours, by which time Rock Island had risen to 158. His $110,000 profit melted into a $30,000 loss.

A woman in her early sixties dressed in black emerged from a horse-drawn hansom cab on the arm of her butler and made her way to the east door of the Produce Exchange. "What is the latest on Steel preferred?" she asked. She was told it was down to 83, and she burst into tears in the arms of her driver: "God help me, Jackson, I am utterly and completely ruined, I haven't a dollar to my name."

Theodore S. Baron of Brooklyn suffered even more. He had walked into a brokerage office at the Exchange on Monday, May 6, intending to buy one thousand shares of Northern Pacific and one thousand shares of Union Pacific (or 11,000 Southern Pacific, depending on which newspaper one read). At the last moment he changed his mind and turned from investor to gambler, deciding to short both of them. The broker demanded more margin the next day. Baron presented a $25,000 check drawn on the First National Bank of Brooklyn for more than double the amount of his debt and asked to extend his short position another day. The broker refused. The check turned out to be worthless. He was arrested at his home, lost up to $160,000 on his short positions, and lost his partnership in his Baron and Strauss knit goods company. Had he simply bought the stock as he first intended he could have netted over $700,000 on Thursday, May 9. He had learned, the hard way, the maxim of the legendary Daniel Drew: "Don't sell the market short when the sap is running up." This was nothing new for Baron; six years earlier he lost $7,100 gambling on sugar stocks.

Asset values evaporated. American Sugar lost 8⅜, Amalgamated Copper 25, American Tobacco 21. In only one or two hours, Missouri Pacific lost 33, both the Rock Island and St. Paul 30½. Delaware & Hudson nosedived from 163 to 105 on just six transactions in a half hour. Union Pacific dropped from 105 to 89 on just eight sales. Then it dropped to 76 and closed at 90, down 24. Atchison Topeka, down 10⅝. Baltimore & Ohio, down 9. Louisville & Nashville, down 27¼. Manhattan Elevated dropped almost 40. Standard Oil had opened at 800 but by 1 p.m. had dropped to 650. The best stocks fell further than the poorer ones because, as one observer said, "the good ones had further to fall." All stocks fell except Northern Pacific because the ticker was so far behind and the floor was in such chaos that hardly anyone knew what the offering prices were anyway. Price became irrelevant.

While Morgan was preparing to dine at the Regina–Grand in Aix, his U.S. Steel common lost more than a third of its value from 11:30 a.m. to noon, New York time. His were only paper losses. He could wait it out. Another young investor lost his shirt on Morgan's U.S. Steel. Somewhere near the Exchange floor was a slender man of twenty-three, blonde and blue eyed with a smile of perfect white teeth. Jesse Livermore had run away from home in Shrewsbury, Massachusetts, in 1894, posted stock quotes at the Paine Webber brokerage in Boston, and made his first money using trend analysis to win big in the bucket shops—so big they had to ban him.

He started out making money just like Baruch, Keene, and Jacob Field did when they were his age, dealing in so-called small "odd lots," trading in and out of stocks quickly with a small profit on average, known then as "scalping." He fancied himself a "tape reader," intuiting market moves based only on recent price and volume. He had bought 110 shares of Northern Pacific at

80 and sold it at 110. On the morning of May 9 he had almost $50,000 in his brokerage account, owned not a single share of stock, and had been bearish for weeks. He sensed a panic was imminent and when it came there would be bargains everywhere and then a quick recovery. "We were going to have an opportunity to catch them coming and going," he recalled a quarter century later, "not only for big money but for sure money."

At 9:59 a.m. that morning, seconds before the market opened, Livermore filed an order to sell short a thousand shares of U.S. Steel common at $100 a share and a thousand shares of Atchison, Topeka & Santa Fe at $80. The clerk went to call the trade on the floor. When the panic came, Livermore felt vindicated: U.S. Steel and the Atchison plunged. The volume was so heavy, however, it took traders longer and longer to fill their orders. "Fills on orders" were fifteen minutes late, then thirty minutes late, then an hour late, then two hours late. The clerk returned and gave Livermore copies of his fill orders. Livermore's order to sell U.S. Steel short at 100 was filled at 85. The Atchison he wanted to short at 80 was filled at 65. He had bought low and sold high. He was short on U.S. Steel at 85 for a thousand shares and had to cover at 110, losing $25 a share or $25,000. He lost another $25,000 on Atchison. He thought he was trading in real time as if this was a bucket shop, but he was trading in a parallel universe, delayed time. "I was accustomed to regarding the tape as the best little friend I had because I bet according to what it told me," he recalled. "But this time the tape double-crossed me." Livermore had unknowingly written the epitaph of the inexperienced trader who overbuys in a bull market: "He Did Not Know How, and He Could Not Wait to Learn."

At the height of the May 9 panic, journalist Edwin Lefevre staked out one of the commission houses to watch the demise of average speculators.

> Some men will stand by the ticker and, as if fascinated by the horror of their ruin, unable to take their eyes off the tape, gaze on unblink-ingly, hour after hour, each minute seeing them poorer. Others walk up and down the room, smoking furiously, twitching and snapping their fingers...One man stood by the ticker holding in his right hand half a cigar. The light had gone out but he was unaware of it. From time to time he raised the cigar, but as some quotation more disastrous than the previous one appeared on the tape, his hand would stop suddenly, midway to his lips, and then drop to his side. Then, with a quick jerk, he would raise the cigar to his mouth, bite at

it spasmodically, and take it out again. Once his cigar dropped to the floor and you saw him gulp. He walked away from the ticker. At the door he paused. The customer who called out the quotation yelled, "Paul, 50!" [Chicago, Milwaukee & St. Paul Railroad] It was a rally of twenty points from the lowest figure. It meant a difference, in the smoker's view, of $100,000. The man gulped again and walked back to the ticker, picked up the cigar, and began his performance again.

Another customer at the same commission house was "utterly ruined," even in debt to his brokers. "Well," he said, "I didn't know where I would spend my summer... Now I know. I guess I'll take in the air of Central Park."

In another room at the same brokerage the head of the firm and his partner were in their inner office. "Steel, 24" said the senior copartner and then slumped down on a sofa and wept. Former boxing champion Jim Corbett, who was to perform that evening in vaudeville at the Orpheum in Brooklyn, could take a punch but not a panic. He admitted to a reporter he had lost between $15,000 and $18,000. He had bought U.S. Steel common at 54 but lost his nerve and sold at 24. One young man watching the ticker and the quote board at a brokerage firm off the trading floor confessed he had run out of margin and had to take his losses on U.S. Steel preferred. "Oh well," he said, with the air of a casino gambler, "I don't mind. This is all 'velvet,' and so I can afford to lose it. I came down here with only $100 and I rolled it to about $1,200. Well, it's all gone now, and I come out where I went in. I've had my fun and it hasn't cost me anything." In Louisville a stock speculator had sold Northern Pacific common short at 84 a few weeks earlier and had to deliver it this day, with shares he bought for 160. He was thought to have lost $100,000 and the $1,400 he had paid his broker the night of May 7 to carry his short position for a day and the $10,000 he had to pay on May 8 for the same privilege.

An assistant to the president of one of the city's largest banks left his office to catch a train home and was spotted by a friend who asked him if anything was the matter. "Billy, this damn market has done me in. I went in with every cent I saved, and every dollar has been wiped out. I'm going home now to make a clean breast of it to my wife, and we'll try to start all over again. It took me five years to save up what I've lost in the last three hours." Another New York man, who had lost heavily, told of having dinner the evening of May 9 with a friend who had been caught short with a significant number of shares of Northern Pacific. "The dinner was a gay one," he said, "and we talked of the stock market as though it were a Gilbert and Sullivan opera. Finally, my host's wife said to him, 'Did you make any money today, John?' 'No,' he said, laughing. 'Did you lose any?' she asked him. 'No,' he said again, with another laugh, and when he said it I knew that everything he had had been wiped out."

Someone else overheard another man say: "I've lost every cent I had in the world. I don't mind that so much, but I've got to go home now and tell my wife." A broker, whose name was a "byword on the street," told a reporter, "I might as well tell you that at these prices I am insolvent. If they prevail I will not have a dollar in the world where last night I had more than $1,000,000." Harry Content, who helped engineer the Hill–Morgan buying on Monday, still wore his irrepressible smile but somehow missed out on the bargains. He had lost heavily on his own account, perhaps he couldn't liquidate his positions quick enough because of the crush of sell orders. "You couldn't get out of anything" he recalled thirty years later from his office overlooking the graveyard of Trinity Church, "It was the worst day in Wall Street."

During the market free-fall in the afternoon, the Hamburg America Line's steamer *Deutschland* entered the lower bay of the North River carrying, among others, William K. Vanderbilt, who had been abroad since February, and Henry Osborne Havemeyer, founder of the American Sugar Refining Company. A tug ran alongside the steamer and a single copy of an afternoon paper was tossed on board. The passengers rushed for it, mad for stock market news. One passenger said he had sent a dispatch to his brokers before leaving London to hold his stock at all cost. They did. When he reached New York harbor he was $150,000 out of pocket.

A continent away, President McKinley was only remotely aware of the panic. He had spent the day leading a parade through downtown Los Angeles in an open-air carriage covered with white carnations and yellow coreopsis blossoms, drawn by horses in yellow satin harnesses. He stood in the reviewing stand and was soon ankle deep in rose petals, tossed by women from the parade's carriages.

All over the country, small fortunes were made, including in Minnesota, site of Northern Pacific's operations headquarters. A. B. McGill of Fargo, North Dakota, had bought 350 shares of Northern Pacific at $30 a share after it was reorganized in 1896. He had kept the certificates in a safe deposit box in St. Paul. On Tuesday, May 7, he sent them for sale to a bank in New York. They arrived there the morning of May 9 whereupon McGill telegraphed an order to sell. A few hours later he received a telegram: The stock had sold for $300,000, or $857 a share. He netted about $290,000. A "well-known capitalist" in St. Paul had shorted Missouri Pacific on May 8, selling a thousand shares at 102, even though he had to put up $60,000 in margin. His broker filled the order the next day and the customer cleared $11,000.

In Chicago, the talk was all Nipper and no longer of the thirty-two-year-old "corn king," George Harshaw Phillips. He had tried to corner the nation's corn futures market but on April 3, the day Morgan left for Europe, was wiped out and went bankrupt. This day it seemed every train into the Loop on the "El" brought desperate men who sprinted over cedar block and cobblestone to their brokers' offices to cash out or put up more margin. All along the four-block ravine of La Salle, with its "towering cornices" from the Stock Exchange south to the Board of Trade at Jackson, there was panic. Brokerages with their "gilt-lettered" windows were so jammed they issued tickets for admission to customers only. Even those lucky to get inside couldn't get close to the quote board or a ticker. It was almost impossible to get a buy or sell order on the wires to New York. Many brokers were caught short with heavy losses. One young Chicago trader, however, followed Daniel Drew's advice, went with the flow and struck gold. He reportedly bought 2,500 shares of Nipper common at 130 on Monday and sold it out on May 9 at 700, netting $1.4 million. Many Chicago traders simply sat out the storm in safe harbor with conservative, dividend-paying stocks such as American Linseed (the oil used in paint, varnish, putty, and linoleum). It opened the week at 13 and closed May 9 at 14½. One trader compared it to "the man who came safely ashore on a snare drum from the wreck of an excursion steamer, while the lifeboat capsized and drowned fourteen sailors."

In Cincinnati, local Republican boss George B. Cox, a former bar owner who came to power through fraud and bribery, claimed to have bought heavily into stocks after McKinley's re-election and said his paper profits now were $1 million, including $800,000 in April alone. A young man walked into a brokerage house in Philadelphia with a hundred shares of Northern Pacific he bought for $25 a share a few years earlier and received $400 for each share, netting $37,500. At the brokerage firm of C. A. Missing in New York, a customer was short 5,000 shares of Atchison, Topeka common at 88 and ordered his broker to cover at 72, which would net him a profit of $80,000. He covered instead at 47, netting $205,000. In Schenectady, New York, brokers bombarded Peter McQueen with telegrams, begging him to loan them his one thousand shares of Northern Pacific, which he bought only a month earlier at 95. McQueen, recovering in a hospital from a railroad accident, finally tired of the pleas and wired instructions to sell at the market the morning of May 9. His order filled at $700 a share, grossing some $600,000.

At the Waldorf–Astoria, it was said a man who had never invested in stocks had come to the hotel from the West for a vacation. He had, however, brought with him $14,000 in cash. On the advice of a stranger at the hotel he took the money to a broker's office on Wednesday, May 8, and said, "Buy me all the Northern Pacific that will carry at twenty points margin." He bought 7,000 shares. The next morning the man was having a late breakfast in one of the hotel's cafés when his broker rushed in to tell him Northern Pacific was selling at $250. "What should I do?" asked the broker. "Sell it!" said the man. They raced from the hotel to the broker's office. Just as they arrived Eddie Norton's sale of 300 shares of Northern Pacific had gone for $1,000 a share. "Let her go!" shouted the investor. The trade settled at $700 a share. If the shares had been bought at the previous day's closing price of $160 a share, it meant a net of $540 a share or $378,000 in less than twenty-four hours. On a train to New York City the previous week, a young man from Cleveland met an official of the Burlington, who recommended he buy some Northern Pacific, which, he said, "should reach 115, anyhow." When the young man got to New York he bought one hundred shares of Northern Pacific at 107. He sold it May 9 for 700 a share, netting $60,000.

For alert bargain hunters who had cash, including the well-advised such as young Bernie Baruch, the last hour of trading was the harvest. Veteran traders hadn't the slightest interest in Northern Pacific. They seized the hour to buy other stocks at depressed prices to cover positions for their clients who had sold them short. "It was a hard trial," said one Exchange member, "but there was money in it for the rich." If you had bought Standard Oil after it had dropped 150 points to 650 before 1 p.m. you could have sold it near the close on the curb market on Broad Street at 776. Someone bought U.S. Steel common at 29 with $500,000 in cash. It closed at 40 giving the investor a paper profit of almost $190,000 in just a few hours. Some weren't paying attention at all. "I'm not interested in Wall Street," said one Chicago bank president. "All day I've been sitting here attending to my business just as if New York didn't exist. I have not looked at the ticker once . . . We are kept busy enough making loans for commercial purposes."

At his office on Bond Street, old Russell Sage, in his frayed suit, sat in his squeaky, second-hand swivel chair in front of a little stand amid boxes of papers and said to whomever would listen, "I told you so." At the height of the afternoon's panic he was lending money at 40 to 60 percent. He was making money, he told his friends, simply because others were foolish enough to lose it. "It seems outrageous," he told a reporter, "that the eighty millions of people in this country and ever so many in Europe should be excited over a corner in a stock of a one-horse road like the Northern Pacific. I wouldn't take the stock of the road at 50 cents on the dollar now . . . The road runs too near the North Pole to be made to pay."

As fortunes were made and lost, both sides met again early in the afternoon, first at Schiff's office, with Hill and Vanderbilt's son-in-law Twombly, and an hour or so later at Morgan's with Hill, Bacon, Lamont, Twombly, Schiff, and Baker. The volume of trading, more than three million shares, overwhelmed the Exchange again. It took twenty minutes to a half hour through the day to get price quotes from the ticker to brokers' offices. The day's final prices were not reported until an hour or two after the 3 p.m. close. Neither side wanted the uncertainty to linger any longer: the announcement from both sides came shortly after 5 p.m. They would settle all existing contracts for Northern Pacific common at $150 a share, $10 below Wednesday's closing price and only for "brokers who bought stock operating for the opposing interest."

They agreed on $150 but that was all. Both sides still blamed each other for the panic, and did so for years. "This difficulty," said a statement from J. P. Morgan and Company, "is not of our making." It was reported later that Schiff, who met with Harriman several times during the day, was still, even in the midst of the panic, trying one last time to cut a deal with Hill–Morgan over the Burlington. Schiff was thought to have offered that Kuhn, Loeb would sell Northern Pacific shares to the shorts, at a price to be determined later, if Hill–Morgan would treat Union Pacific as an equal with the Burlington in all traffic agreements. It also was reported that on May 9 Schiff argued for suspending delivery dates for Northern Pacific shares much longer than twenty-four hours. This signaled that Kuhn, Loeb didn't want to have a single short-seller fail in delivery of Northern Pacific shares, and that Kuhn, Loeb's control of the Northern Pacific depended on fulfilling those short contracts more so than Hill–Morgan's fulfillment did. Hill–Morgan, which claimed all along it held practically no shorted Northern Pacific shares, declined both of Schiff's offers. In addition, it appears to have been Kuhn, Loeb that pushed for the $150 settlement figure, even though Northern Pacific had closed Thursday at $325.

The agreements to suspend delivery dates and let the shorts cover at $150 were motivated by more than just a desire to save the banks and the commission houses. There were threats of lawsuits. As the bottom fell out of the market, two brokers, one representing a client short only 200 shares of Northern Pacific common, retained a law firm to prepare a ten-page complaint alleging that a basic law of contracts had been violated: Morgan and Kuhn, Loeb could not legally require delivery of shares contracted for because they already had all the shares. Furthermore, didn't both sides know by at least mid-morning Wednesday, May 8, that there was, in effect, a corner? Why did it take them until late the next afternoon to announce an agreement to cover at $150? They rushed the complaint to the chambers of a State Supreme Court justice who promptly signed an order restraining the firms from requiring immediate delivery of shares. The client short 200 shares later was revealed to be the extortionist David Lamar ("the wolf of Wall Street") who had tried to block the Schiff-led purchase of the Union Pacific in 1897 by claiming to President McKinley that he had a letter pledging a higher bid.

Other customers complained that during the panic their brokers cashed out their accounts unilaterally without asking for more margin. Some customers ran the other way when their margins were exhausted, hoping the price would recover. They failed to read the fine print on the back of their ticket order, the legal contract permitting the brokerage to protect itself and cash out the account if the customer couldn't be found or if the customer hadn't advised the broker of his intent to put up more margin on demand. "It is the duty of the speculator to keep in close touch with the market," said one of Talbot Taylor's brokers, "If he neglects to do so he must expect to suffer the consequence." Many did. Some lawsuits stemming from May 9 were still in legal limbo two years later.

As the panic built that Thursday morning, May 9, one large brokerage firm at the Stock Exchange telephoned one of its clients demanding more margin to protect his stock. "All right," said the client, "I'm coming downtown and I'll stop in at my bank and get a check for $25,000 certified." The brokerage assured him that would be enough to carry him. Sometime after noon, the customer called to say he was at his bank, had the check, and would drop it off in an hour. It was then that the market collapsed. On his way to the brokerage firm the customer stopped in a saloon to look at the tape, learned he had lost everything, and went back to his office. The brokerage firm had to eat his loss of more than $25,000. Many firms and their customers had no tangible proof that some transactions were made. During the panic many customers shouted orders to their brokers over the telephone but never got receipts.

There was no sympathy from Finley Peter Dunne's Mr. Dooley. "Crazy come," he said, "crazy go."

About the same time, a syndicate of fifteen New York–based banks announced it was making available a pool of $19.5 million to loan to stock market borrowers, with approved collateral. J. P. Morgan and Company and Baker's First National Bank each provided $2 million for the pool. Stillman's National City Bank, with no savvy for symbolic gesture, was notably absent. The loans would be made at prevailing market rates to prevent speculators from relending the money at higher rates. The bankers' syndicate made its first loan through the pool at the prevailing rate of 60 percent on overnight call loans and the last loan at six percent. The entire $19.5 million pool quickly found customers. Independent of the pool, J. P. Morgan and Company was said to have loaned another $5 million to $11 million at below market rates to prop up deflated stock prices including its own U.S. Steel.

Brokerage houses, on the hook to banks for large loans to fund clients buying on margin, blamed the banks for accelerating the panic. When the margins of brokerage house clients ran out and stock prices began their death spiral, the banks panicked and cashed out huge blocks of stock at fire-sale prices—stock the brokerage house clients had posted as collateral. The brokerage houses, in turn, had to liquidate their client's stocks. The entire fifty-five point drop in Delaware & Hudson, for example, came in just six transactions in a half hour. It was blamed totally on panic selling by a few large banks that had sold their brokerage house clients down the river. If the banks had waited an hour or so they could have made money. Delaware & Hudson soon was nine points above its opening price for the day.

Virtually every major brokerage may have been technically insolvent in the crisis, but not one went bankrupt because of it. Chicago banks, repositories of so much new wealth from the steel mergers, were said to have sent an estimated $20 million to correspondent banks in New York to satisfy margin calls on Chicago brokers, and shipped another $1.15 million in currency to New York brokers. The total was said to be the largest amount of funds ever sent from Chicago to New York for stock market purchases in one day. Lost in the chaos were the conservative New York brokers, and there were many, who didn't fit the "panic" story line. They had been buying in the rising market the last few months but also cashing in paper profits, building a liquid reserve for the collapse they sensed was coming. When the big commission houses, under bank pressure, demanded more margin the afternoon of May 9 these brokers met the calls quickly.

Northern Pacific—the railroad that went under in 1873 at the hands of Jay Cooke, that went bankrupt again in 1893, ruining Henry Villard and crippling the American economy, and then rose once again from the dead, catapulting in market value from $11 million in 1896 to $155 million in 1901—had done it to the market again. Its low for the day was 160. Its high was 1,000. It closed at 325 on volume of only 16,300 shares. If you were short a hundred shares of Northern Pacific common from Saturday, May 4, until the end of trading on May 9 you would have lost $24,500. If you were short a thousand shares you would have lost $245,000. Just before the announcement of the 150 settlement, one short-seller, perhaps fearing that if Northern Pacific could head toward 1,000 once it could do so again, decided to cut his losses and settle for 200 shares of Northern Pacific at $600 a share. Had he delayed his order just five minutes he could have settled at 150 and saved himself $450 a share or $90,000. An individual identified only as the "Morgan broker," thought to be Eddie Norton, later testified he had a list of names, "closely written, two feet long" of shorts who had sold Northern Pacific to him in amounts of from one hundred to 2,000 shares, 70,000 to 80,000 shares in all.

In front of hotels and department stores, outside the station stops of the elevated, the streetwise boy "newsies" from the tenements waved editions of the evening "papes," hollering headlines from Hearst's "Joinal" and Pulitzer's "Woild": "Extry! Extry! Foychuns lahst in stahk panic! Banks cumtahda rescyah!" The richer and the poorer, the shocked and the exuberant, the touts and the kingpins returned to the uptown hotels to trade stories and rumors. Keene, Taylor, Norton, Gates, and the Housmans were all spotted early in the evening at the Waldorf–Astoria.

Guests and visitors jammed the lobby of the Gilsey House, the three hundred room luxury hotel that sat like a six-story baroque birthday cake at Twenty-Ninth and Broadway. Around the hotel's bar made of silver dollars, everyone seemed to have their story for the day. One was told by Long Island native William Read who said he left New York in 1871 as a brakeman on a train and homesteaded in North Dakota's barren Red River Valley, now prosperous in grain and cattle and served by both Hill's Great Northern and the Northern Pacific. "It is the Western country that is enriching New York and the world," he said to anyone who would listen. "Hill's millions have been won in partnership with the Western pioneer, and they were honestly got. They did not come out of the other fellow's pocket, but from the farm and the mine that Hill made possible." He said the speculators who had lost small fortunes could have learned a lesson from a man named Jack Hannihan. Read said he had watched a card game of faro one night in Bismarck in which Hannihan never bet more than a dollar. Another player said to him, "Jack, if you had bet $100 on that queen you would have won just as well." To which Hannihan replied, "By gosh, sir! Jack Hannihan never flies higher than he can roost!"

Morgan's train glided through the night north to Paris. He had left Aix with the market in panic, apparently on an overnight train late Thursday, May 9. Departing from the Gare de Lyon train station Friday morning, his private carriage sped up the Quai along the Seine past the Tuileries and entered the broad expanse of the Place Vendome square. He was surrounded by police and besieged by reporters when he arrived at the Hotel Bristol at 3–5 Place Vendome, home of royalty and aristocrats and fashionable salons, where the owners always reserved for him the premier corner suite. He paused a moment to tell reporters he thought the New York panic was over, then disappeared into the hotel. He rushed immediately to the office of Harjes, Morgan and Company at 31 Boulevard Haussmann to communicate via cablegram with New York. He cabled Bacon to tell both sides if they didn't settle by tomorrow he would return at once to New York. He was reported to be in a "snarling mood." One morning to clear his head he took a carriage to the Bois de Boulogne as the oak, locust, and cherry were just leafing out, and walked the gravel paths deep in thought before his carriage took him to Harjes, Morgan and Company. His original plan was not to return to New York until the end of June, but the events of May 9 made him think about going home as soon as possible. He had reserved a suite of staterooms on the *Kaiser Wilhelm der Grosse*, scheduled to depart Southampton and Cherbourg for New York the coming Wednesday. Then he changed his mind and asked his son, J. P. Jr., to take passage in his place. The market seemed to have righted itself a bit so he felt he could manage things from abroad, and he couldn't risk just now being out on the north Atlantic isolated for eight days and out of touch with cables.

In New York, the lights were on at Kuhn, Loeb long into the evening of Thursday, May 9, but Schiff was not there. In the midst of the chaos at the Exchange that afternoon and in between tense meetings to try to save the market from a catastrophe, the story was told that Schiff had calmly gone to his desk, picked up the telephone receiver, and asked the operator to connect him with the Henry Street Settlement House of Lillian D. Wald. He had first met Wald in 1893 when she was twenty-six and had dropped out of medical school for community service. She had chosen to live amid the filth, odor, and sickness of eastern European immigrants, many of them Jews, crammed into tenements on the Lower East Side. It was the year Wald pioneered public health nursing in the United States by founding the Henry Street Settlement, later known as the Visiting Nurse Society, to provide trained nursing care for the poor in their tenements. The past eight years Schiff and his wife Therese had helped Wald find a permanent headquarters and raised millions for her organization, and Schiff had become a member of the Henry Street Settlement's board.

Schiff was never one to shirk an obligation, even in the midst of a catastrophic market meltdown. Over the phone that afternoon he is believed to have said to Wald, "I think this is the night Mrs. Schiff and I were coming down to take dinner. Is the hour six or half-past six?" He would have taken a carriage from his office up Pearl and over to Madison and then walked up the front steps of the three-story federal-style brick building at 265 Henry Street where Wald would have greeted him. He often ate dinner "with whomever happened to be there," wrote his biographer Cyrus Adler, "and sat in discussions with the men and women around the table." Wald recalled observing Schiff at the Henry House Settlement "having a discussion with a Jewish tailor about a strike. The discussion ended with Schiff putting his arm on the tailor's shoulder and their exchanging Hebrew quotations which obviously placed them upon a footing of equality and cordiality."

Hill left the financial district sometime early in the evening. He had spent some of his day, he told reporters, working on contracts for sixty locomotives. Perhaps he wanted to show he had better things to do and was above it all. He changed into evening attire at the Netherland and walked the few blocks to East Sixtieth just off Central Park through the huge wrought-iron gates of the white marble Metropolitan Club for dinner with Lamont, Baker, and his son Louis, then to the Union League Club at Fifth and Thirty-Ninth. Looking "pale and haggard from lack of sleep" he did not return to the Netherland until 2 a.m.

The hotel's lobby swarmed with reporters to interview him, a dozen assigned to track his every move. Weeks earlier Hill could walk the Wall Street district unrecognized, and was even turned away at the Cunard pier to say good-bye to his daughters. Now he was, without seeking or caring for it, a front-page personality. The newspapers and magazines once portrayed him as "careless of dress, with a long bushy beard, and shaggy hair reaching to his shoulders, in the manner of Buffalo Bill." Now they saw a different Hill: face still tanned from his active, outdoor life but beard carefully trimmed like Schiff's, hair no longer flowing over the collar but cropped shorter, his old black slouch hat replaced with a square-crowned Derby "not of the new style." Did the $150 Kuhn, Loeb had agreed to as a settlement price with the shorts amount, he was asked, to an unconditional surrender to Hill–Morgan, given it was more than 50 percent less than what Northern Pacific had closed at that afternoon? "I am a farmer from the West," said Hill in a performance he had mastered. "I am not concerned with what men are doing on Wall Street...Why should Kuhn, Loeb & Co. send a copy of their announcement to me? They might just as well send a copy to Bishop Potter."

Then, from fatigue or frustration, Hill gave a hint of the rancor that prevailed at the meetings between the two factions as the panic had escalated. It had been a stressful week. He no longer could conceal his animosity for Harriman, Schiff, and their allies. "The struggle was started by people trying to get control of a piece of property," he told a New York Tribune reporter. "They can see the conditions they have created...those who have made them must be responsible for the conditions which they find...They have done things which they ought to be very ashamed of—despicable things...the house of J. P. Morgan & Co. [has] nothing at all to conceal—nothing to be ashamed of." Hill and Harriman both tried the last few years to show professional courtesy. They dined together at the Metropolitan Club. Their wives, both named Mary, called on each other when the Hills were in New York. They sent each other gifts. But in the heat of battle the "act" of friendship between their husbands dissolved.

The financial district awoke Friday, May 10, to survey the carnage. Two European banking houses were rumored to have lost millions, but no banks failed and no large brokerages went bankrupt. It was reported that every check had gone through the Stock Exchange's clearing house without trouble, meaning every brokerage firm on the street was solvent. "The overwrought watchers by many a ticker," said the New York Herald, "only needed a leader to burst into cheer." The economy was unaffected, the stock market recovered. In a perverse way, the market had worked. Rather than a prolonged release of pressure, the "corner" had detonated the speculative bubble with one huge blast. Most Americans, long before 401(k)s, IRAs, and mutual funds, who didn't know what it meant to "short" a stock, went about their business. They viewed it as a rich man's panic. The confidence of small retail

IT WAS FIERCE WHILE IT LASTED!

New York Tribune, May 11, 1901. The Northern Pacific panic lasted only a few hours but it ignited a debate that continues today. What are government's limits on property rights and restraint of interstate commerce? What is better for the common good: competition or combination? How big is too big?

investors, however, was shattered. "So many persons of small incomes have been ruined," said one veteran trader who had survived Black Friday thirty-two years earlier when Fisk and Gould had tried to corner the gold market, "it will be many a moon before the general public will venture again into speculation... thousands of men and women were led to believe that it was easy to make quick fortunes in stock gambling. They had heard of the luck of their friends. They had read in the newspapers of the luck of persons... and they concluded to take a flyer in the Street. Many of them got out by the middle or end of last week and they are richer by the thousands... Many more stayed in too long." By one estimate, losses to the shorts in Northern Pacific were thought to be around $10 million, including the contracts privately settled at $150 a share with J. P. Morgan and Company and Kuhn, Loeb, but excluding the tens of millions in losses suffered by those who had to sell other securities at depressed prices to cover their Northern Pacific short positions.

Everyone was wise after the event. What stunned some observers was that quite a few veteran traders supposedly felt trouble had been brewing for weeks, the symptoms seemed obvious to them (at least in hindsight). Few of them, however, as the New York Times said three days after the panic, "were astute enough, quick enough to take advantage of the opportunities thrust upon them." Few bears profited from the panic because it all happened in just a few hours and the rise in Northern Pacific to 1,000 was ten times what the decline was for other stocks when the panic occurred.

The New York Times estimated a week later that of the Northern Pacific stock still short on May 9 about one-third was covered by purchases in the open market when the price averaged 500. About 4,000 shares sold short were covered at between 500 to 800 or a loss of $2.5 million or more overnight. For Schiff's clients in Europe, who sold Northern Pacific shares through Kuhn, Loeb, it was all a matter of timing. Those who cabled orders to sell their Northern Pacific stock before May 6 through 9 not only missed out on the march to $1,000 a share but had to pay 5 percent a day or more for renting shares pending arrival of the steamers from Europe to New York. Many of Schiff's German countrymen profited greatly when their Northern Pacific preferred was retired on January 1, 1902.

The phrase that stuck, and kept being repeated, however, was "stock gambling." The Stock Exchange had become a casino, no different in results than a bucket shop. The New York Herald called it a "stock gamblers" panic. The people who went "stock mad" or had "ticker fever" were not investors but gamblers. They had profaned a secular temple of commerce. The fools had who shorted Northern Pacific stock, gambling that it would sink fast, selling what they didn't own, had turned the lofty principles of the New York Stock Exchange ("maintain high standards of commercial honor and integrity," "promote just and equitable principles of trade and business") into a joke. Maybe, someone suggested, the governor of the Stock Exchange should temporarily strike from the list any stock that becomes the target of a corner. The Herald said the problem wasn't the corner but the "wickedness" of the "professional manipulators" who inflated values and created "false impressions as to security. They brought to life a monster like that of Frankenstein, which in the end strangled its creator."

Some thought it was just a Wall Street problem, but newspaper reports were filtering in from the provinces that stock gambling had infected Main Street. In Niles, Michigan, cashier Charles A. Johnson had been speculating in a bucket shop across the street from his bank. He lost all his own money and $100,000 in deposits from the First National Bank, which had to close its doors. The Le Mars National Bank in Iowa closed after its vice president used bank deposits to speculate and lost it all. A cashier at the Farmers National Bank in Vergennes, Vermont, stock-gambled away at least $35,000 in bank deposits, perhaps as high as $150,000. In Vancouver, Washington, an audit found that a cashier of the First National Bank had lost $81,000 in bank funds in stock gambling. The cashier and the bank president committed suicide with revolvers.

The shorts and the gamblers who were the inadvertent perpetrators, however, didn't get the headline blame. Neither did the federal government, which had created and perpetuated the Northern Pacific, nor did average shareholders, all of whom had been quite willing to ride the market to the top. The railroad owners and financiers, trying to squeeze inefficiency and waste out of an overbuilt system, were convenient scapegoats for every shareholder's moral accountability. The *New York Times* called them drunken cowboys shooting up a saloon. "If the gentlemen composing the groups known respectively by the names of Mr. Harriman and Mr. Hill," said the *Times* the morning after the panic,

> delude themselves with the belief that fighting for control of a railroad is their own private business and none of the public's, and that the community looks on at the contest with no other emotions than those of amusement and curiosity, it will be prudent for them to get rid of that delusion without delay . . . if panics and disasters such as that which have just convulsed Wall Street and projected a shadow of doubt and demoralization over a financial and business condition of great prosperity and promise are to be viewed as necessary incidents of capitalistic consolidation, then the strong popular disfavor which trusts and consolidations have thus far successfully defied may presently rise to a pitch of anger that will cause them to take thought, not how they may control railroads, but how they may save themselves.

William Jennings Bryan wondered why "a petty thief is severely punished while great criminals go unwhipped." Stock gambling should be outlawed, he said; exactly how he wasn't sure. The *Kansas City Journal* wasn't buying it: if Bryan had been elected, it said, there would be unsound money, no business

Cartoonist William Allen Rogers, nearing the end of his remarkable quarter-century career with *Harper's Weekly*, immortalized the Northern Pacific corner with these illustrations in May 1901. The "lambs" had "shorted" Northern Pacific and had to cash in other stocks at fire-sale prices to cover their short positions. Some observers blamed the "community of interest" interlocking ownership of railroads for creating a scarcity of railroad stocks that led to the speculative bubble.

confidence, and not "sufficient life in industrial or railroad stocks to generate any excitement . . . Wall Street speculation is harmless, except to speculators."

The *New York Evening Post* blamed "community of interest." To gain influence on each other's boards to limit destructive rate-cutting, competing railroads had to buy more and more shares of each other's stock. All this stock was swept off the open market, artificially boosting trading volume, lifting stock prices beyond fundamental values, attracting more stock gamblers. "The 'community of interest' idea had taken possession of the public mind," said the *Post*, "as a limitless source of wealth."

Only a day after the panic, the *Post* went beyond even Bryan:

There is a substratum of socialism in every community, which demands municipal ownership of "public utilities." It wants street railroads and gas and electric lighting works and telephones to be owned by cities and administered in the interest of the consumer. It will very likely want country trolley lines to be owned by the State and operated in competition with the steam railroads. It may demand the taking of coal and iron mines and oil wells under the law of eminent domain. It may impose killing taxes on what it conceives to be dangerous monopolies. It may meet the "community of interest" idea of railroad management with more stringent legislation by Congress and the Legislatures than any we have yet had. It is only a rumbling force now, but is capable of doing vast mischief, both to itself and to those whom it conceives to be inimical to it. Nothing is better calculated to awaken the slumbering giant than such spectacles as we have seen in Wall Street the past few days.

Clergy across the nation thundered from the pulpit at stock gamblers, the little King Ahabs building temples to Baal "to destroy the prophets of truth and justice." Episcopal Bishop William Lawrence in Boston thought he saw an "unreadiness to work steadily for the legitimate reward of labor, an unrest at the moderate and fair returns on capital . . . a fascination in living by one's wits instead of by one's sober thoughts and careful work." The pastor of Grace Methodist Episcopal in New York called stock gamblers "human motes who feel their way through the black underground of selfishness and self-indulgence, and lush up their little piles of dirt." Pastors of some congregations along Fifth and Madison avenues noticed more money than ever pouring into their Sunday plates and suspected some of it was tainted proceeds of stock gambling or the result of "guilty consciences." Word of the panic buzzed among delegates in Philadelphia on May 9 at the annual convention of the Episcopal Church of Pennsylvania. "Northern Pacific is selling at $500 cash" was whispered down the rows. The delegates voted to adjourn early so they could "protect their interests in the stock market."

Where were the howls of righteous indignation from Washington? Some suspected they were muted because some members of Congress were thought to be gambling on stocks. Among those rescued from even greater ruin by the settlement at $150 a share was an unidentified U.S. senator, caught short the morning of May 9 with 10,000 shares of Nipper common at 120. Even with the $150 settlement he would still have been out $300,000. Another story received wide currency: a rumor that an unnamed U.S. senator from the West, dealing either on margin through a local broker or in a bucket shop in the District of Columbia, had lost upward of $100,000 on western railroad stocks. Depending on which account one read, he either was saved by a Senate colleague from the East who loaned him the margin to provide his broker or had lost it all at the bucket shop. The annual salary of a U.S. senator was then $5,000. The principal in the story turned out to be Senator Francis Cockrell of Missouri. His brother-in-law, who reportedly had lost $75,000 in the market, said he had asked Cockrell for help. Cockrell borrowed the money from Senator Stephen Benton Elkins of West Virginia (later to coauthor regulations further restricting railroad rates) to bail out his brother-in-law, who claimed his actual losses were only a few thousand dollars.

There were published rumors, never verified, that Senator Hanna, perhaps even the Northern Pacific's Lamont, were whispering stock tips in Washington as political currency; perhaps even President McKinley and Treasury Secretary Lyman J. Gage had lost money. There was talk in Chicago that former president Cleveland had netted half a million dollars thanks to a tip from Lamont. A few other Lamont friends apparently did well, too, including wealthy Buffalo lumberman and railroad owner Frank H. Goodyear, a confidant of Cleveland, said to have made $85,000 to $165,000. Former U.S. senator Richard Pettigrew of South Dakota, a pro-silver Republican who left the Senate March 4, was thought to have made $100,000 on the St. Paul and another $150,000 on Burlington stock on tips, perhaps from his old friend Hill. Not everyone who got an inside tip could act fast enough. Sometime before Saturday, May 4, Hill advised his old St. Paul railroad colleague Crawford Livingston to buy Nipper common. He told Hill later he wasn't able to place an order for 700 shares on May 4 when it closed at 110, perhaps because brokers were buried in backlog.

Stock pools were said to have formed in many departments of the federal government, into which members deposited from $35 to $100 for investment through local brokers. All these pools were said to have been wiped out in the panic. A number of generals and admirals and their subordinates in the War and Navy departments supposedly trooped down to the district's brokerage houses on government time to "breathe the atmosphere of the market." An employee of the Agriculture Department, whose annual salary was $1,800, was said to have made $20,000 in the market. There was a report that a young woman in the U.S. Treasury, who inherited $5,000 through a life insurance policy, put it all in the stock market. By Tuesday evening, May 7, she was $14,000 to the good. By Thursday, May 9, she was said to have lost it all.

One of the big insider winners was the railroad attorney and former U.S. senator from Colorado, the lusty Edward Olive Wolcott. He was a tall, burly, extroverted orator who "captivated men and women by the charm of his talk, his wit, his manner, and his social accomplishments" in Washington. He had a taste for gambling and billiards, and was often seen behind the bronze doors of Canfield's Casino on Fifth Avenue, playing faro with Gates. He also had a prolific sexual appetite, frequenting bordellos in New York and Denver where he was known as "Edward of Navarre" after a brothel of that name. He had bought five hundred acres of railroad land south of Denver, built a twenty-five-room Tudor-style mansion and conservatories for tropical plants, stocked the property with pure-bred horses, cattle, quail, and pheasant, and diverted water from the South Platte River to form a fourteen-acre lake. He also appeared to have been expert at channeling insider trading information. He had been with Charles Perkins and Hill at the Victoria Hotel in Boston for two weeks in late March as counsel for the Burlington. He was said to have cleared $750,000 on trading in the stock of Burlington, Colorado Fuel and Iron, and the Denver & Rio Grande railroad. New York State Senator Patrick Henry McCarren, a Democrat from Brooklyn thought to be on the take from Standard Oil, was said to have netted the same.

Virtually every daily newspaper across the country the morning of May 10 had "Northern Pacific" in banner headlines. Crowds gathered around the windows of brokerage firms in New York displaying Northern Pacific stock certificates as if they were cultural icons. The market opened so strong Friday morning it was hard to believe there had been a panic. Bargain hunters with cash still smelled value and bet on more mergers among western railroads. London opened with strong advances in "Americans." New York followed, with Amalgamated Copper closing up 10, Burlington 11, the St. Paul 17½, Consolidated Gas 14¾, Lackawanna 16⅜, Interstate Power 11½, Missouri Pacific 13, and Union Pacific 22 in what seemed a vote for a Harriman victory. U.S. Steel, Atchison, and Union Pacific alone accounted for almost half the 1.9 million shares traded. Northern Pacific opened in New York at 150, the settlement price announced after the close the day before, leaped to 200 during the day, and then closed quietly at 150.

At the Waldorf–Astoria one could hear again the "merry click-click" of ivory balls in the billiard room. The lines had disappeared around the bars and the cafés but some speculators couldn't help themselves and bet on whether Harriman–Schiff or Hill–Morgan controlled the Northern Pacific. The early wagers were that Kuhn, Loeb ended up with many of the short contracts and that Hill–Morgan had retained control. The Exchange canceled Saturday morning trading to catch its breath (and push the partition on the trading floor back to give members ten more feet of space), but everyone at Kuhn, Loeb and Morgan and Company worked through the weekend reviewing ledger books, counting and stamping stock certificates.

There was a tense meeting Saturday morning at Harriman's office—Bacon and Steele from Morgan and Company, Hill, Schiff, and Harriman. Perhaps Schiff was still piqued that Bacon had blocked him from seeing Morgan the day before he left for Europe. At one point Schiff said, as Hill recalled it, "We hold control of the Northern Pacific!" to which Bacon responded, just as emphatically, "Mr. Schiff, before you are through, you will find out you don't!" The Burlington's Perkins in Boston told Hill he had it on "good authority" that Harriman's friends still were offering $500 in cash for Northern Pacific common at Boston brokerage houses. Sometime this Saturday morning, perhaps after the emotional meeting at Harriman's, a reporter found Hill walking down the corridor to his office on the ninth floor of the Kuhn, Loeb building. Hill steered the conversation toward the effect of the corner on small investors. He paused and turned half around. The reporter said he saw tears in Hill's eyes.

> Look at the ruin that has been done. I have received lots of letters from friends of mine—men and women—who are not rich, who are comparatively poor. They knew that I was interested personally and largely in my properties, and they had faith in them and in me. Now they are completely ruined, and simply because they have been caught in the vortex of a gamble. Yet they bought their shares in good faith . . . This morning I got a letter from the wife of a friend of mine, telling me of the losses to her family. I repeat that this trouble has not been of my making and no one regrets it more than I do.

Hill spent Saturday afternoon at Morgan headquarters and told reporters that "the people on the corner," the Morgan men, were confident they still had control of the Northern Pacific. Bacon cabled the Morgan office in London on Sunday to confirm their count. It showed Hill–Morgan still short of a majority, with 394,830 shares of Northern Pacific common, or 49.4 percent.

They needed 400,001. They spent the coming week quietly buying 24,580 more shares of the common, mostly in London. By Saturday, May 18, they had enough to claim 52.5 percent of the common. "We appreciate very much," cabled Bacon to Morgan's son Jack in London, "all you have done for us in this miserable business."

Hill knew a key to maintaining control was the loyalty of his old associates, Lord Mount Stephen and Lord Strathcona in London, John S. Kennedy in New York, and his old friend, Edward Tuck, in Paris. Eight years later, at a luncheon at the Winnipeg Canadian Club honoring Strathcona, Hill recalled 1901. Choked with emotion and tears, perhaps embellishing for effect, he spoke of being alone in his room at the Netherland in New York, "my life's work evaporating . . . in black despair . . . the darkest day of my life." There was a knock at the door. A messenger handed him a cable from the eighty-year-old Strathcona in London: "Harriman interests have cabled offering $1,000 a share for use of my Northern Pacific stock at approaching [Northern Pacific's early October board] meeting to which I have replied, 'My stock is in vaults of (such and such) Trust Company in New York at disposal of my friend James J. Hill to whom I am cabling my proxy for use at coming meeting.' For me, the clouds had suddenly parted and glorious sunshine was streaming through, scattering my desolation. I was saved."

Hill's remarks about Harriman and Schiff, appearing Friday morning in the *New York Daily Tribune,* did not sit well with his adversaries. They fired back Saturday morning. In the *New York Herald* they said the only way Hill–Morgan could win was if they resorted to "legal trickery," but of course that would be "undignified" and "Mr. Morgan himself would no doubt frown upon that when he returns." They told the *New York Times,*

Mr. Hill for years has been accustomed to the role of an autocrat. His will has been law, and he carried on things with a high hand. So long as he confined himself to operations in the faraway Northwest no one cared. But when he carried these methods into territory where there was keen competition, it was different. The conditions in the territory which he invaded were very finely balanced. Everyone was working in harmony, the territory of everyone was respected, no one's interests were hurt, and the rates were fairly well maintained. Into this fine web came Mr. Hill with his rough hand when he acquired, or sought to acquire, a Chicago connection . . . We are even now willing to return the control of the road to the other side if they will assure us that our previous request will be granted.

The Union Pacific had no quarrel with the Burlington, they said. It had always been a good neighbor; "Great Northern, on the other hand, has been a bad neighbor. Whenever it has come into contact with other properties there has been trouble."

Perhaps sensing, correctly, that the public mood was coalescing against all of them, Schiff's colleague Otto Kahn was more contrite: "None of us expected that that which did happen would happen," Kahn told a reporter, "and I have not any doubt that we are all a little ashamed of ourselves." Then he added, "I feel sure that the happenings of [May 9] would never have been recorded had Mr. Morgan been in town." Everyone seemed to agree, in private at least. A reporter found Hill Saturday evening in the lobby of the Netherland "serenely lighting a cigar."

On the newsstands the next morning was an inflammatory interview with Hill in the *New York Morning Journal*. He accused Harriman, Schiff, and Stillman of being opportunistic speculators who wanted to line their pockets, not provide better service to customers. He was quoted saying

the Union Pacific men had waited until Mr. Morgan had gone abroad. They did not dare attack the road he had reorganized and brought to prosperity while he was here. . . . They knew that he would protect every man who had invested a dollar in Northern Pacific stock on the strength of his reputation. . . . The property was still under Mr. Morgan's protection—under the protection of his reputation and under the protection of his brains and influence . . . Did the man [Harriman] who tried to buy control of a competitive system, whose main lines were five hundred miles apart from theirs for the purpose of giving better service to the country or for the benefit of the minority stockholders? Or did they want to get that splendid property for the purpose of restraining and restricting a rival? We acted in self-defense. We refused to sell. Even if we had been willing to sell it would be a plain violation of the law for the Union Pacific to acquire control of a parallel and competing line. When the Northern Pacific was offered to the Great Northern the Supreme Court of the United States decided that point. But not one of my friends showed the slightest desire to sell, no matter what the price might be. When Northern Pacific was selling at $1,000 a share a friend of mine, a director of the Northern Pacific road, who owned $1,000,000 of stock, came to my office and said: "I'm sorry for the ruined. I am a very rich man, according to the market prices, but I haven't the slightest idea of selling a share."

On the Sunday this story appeared, with name-calling escalating, Hill was at his office of the Kuhn, Loeb building. He was planning to head up to New London, Connecticut, to be on his yacht *Wacouta* and get a firsthand look at the building of his two behemoth ocean transport steamers. Then he would head back to St. Paul in a week. He did not want to leave town without seeing Schiff to try to smooth things over. Despite all the acrimony of the past week, they still regarded each other as friends. It was possible in 1901 to battle in public and conciliate in private. They also shared a bedrock conservative belief in how to value a railroad. "The true value of all property is its productive power," Schiff once said. "All other value is speculative only."

Hill decided he would pay Schiff a visit. That Sunday, unannounced, he strolled into the offices of Kuhn, Loeb, looking for the man he had publicly accused two days earlier of "despicable things." Schiff was not there. Hill walked over to Schiff's son-in-law Felix Warburg. He asked Warburg about the health of members of the Schiff–Warburg family. And then he asked casually, as if nothing had happened, "How is Schiff?" "Not very happy," said Warburg. Hill paused. "He takes these things too seriously," he said.

10

NORTHERN INSECURITIES

John Pierpont Morgan had left New York thirty-two days earlier, on April 3, dreaming of rare art and thermal baths. Now he was stewing in Paris. While he was dozing under hot towels after massages in Aix, Harriman and Schiff were trying to steal "his" railroad. They would be in a real fix if it hadn't been for Hill alertly remembering that a majority of the common stock could retire the preferred stock and thus keep Morgan's board in control, Even now the outcome was uncertain. To make matters worse, Harriman had publicly embarrassed him, showing the world that Morgan didn't control what he thought he controlled, unmasking him as a corporate imperialist, not as a champion of peace and "community of interest." Schiff had crossed him by siding with Harriman. And Bacon, should Morgan have left him in charge? Now Hill and Harriman were trading insults in the newspapers. A fight had broken out in the schoolyard with the principal gone. *Harper's Weekly* compared Morgan to the little girl in charge of the baby who had just been rescued from the cistern: "Oh! I just took my eye off her for one minute!" If they weren't careful there would be a curse on all their houses. It wasn't the corner that tarnished all their reputations. The public didn't care who owned the Northern Pacific. It was the panic that ensued and the public fear and anxiety it caused. Morgan had to make sure the fighting stopped immediately. If it didn't there would be more uncertainty and chaos in the market. There could be another, even worse, panic. And guess who would get the blame. A court test of the language of the 1896 Northern Pacific reorganization plan was out of the question; neither side wanted that. It would drag on for months of headlines and just prolong the fight.

Morgan didn't stay long in Paris. He needed to be in London where there could be trouble on Monday, May 13, the day scheduled for fortnightly settlement in American stocks on the London Stock Exchange. The British called it "delivery day," when brokers under contract to deliver a stock must do so unless the buyer agrees to delay delivery or agrees to settle for cash. The New York arbitrage houses had picked London clean of Northern Pacific stock on May 9. A survey showed J. P. Morgan & Company or Kuhn, Loeb held every available Northern Pacific share in London; brokers there who sold calls on Northern Pacific for delivery in May apparently couldn't find a single share. If Morgan and Kuhn, Loeb didn't provide some relief, many of London's leading brokerage firms could go bankrupt and it could be worse than the collapse of Baring Brothers in 1890. There also were lawyers advertising in the Sunday New York newspapers looking for speculators who felt brokerage firms had treated them unfairly by calling for more margin and then closing their accounts during the panic.

In New York a flurry of meetings among the principals throughout the day made it appear compromise was in the air. Hill spent the morning and part of the afternoon at Morgan's headquarters at Broad and Wall. Reporters were waiting for him outside his office and asked for his response to the Harriman–Schiff claims that they had control of the Northern Pacific. "I've got nothing more to say about that," said Hill, "but if the gentlemen like their clothes they can wear them."

Harriman spent most of the day at Kuhn, Loeb. Schiff and Stillman knew he was tone deaf to public opinion. They feared the huge chip on his shoulder could cause more chaos and collateral damage to their customers, their business, and the market. He had to be reined in. Thus Harriman obediently strode to the Morgan headquarters at Broad and Wall and conferred with Morgan's men, probably Bacon, Steele, and George W. Perkins. Harriman emerged "smiling contentedly," trying to reassure reporters "things will come out all right." Harriman and Schiff circulated a story that they had no desire to take control of the Northern Pacific from Morgan; their fight, they said, wasn't with him but with Hill. They did nothing to stop stories on the street that Hill's role in the Morgan properties soon would be diminished.

Late in the afternoon Harriman took the elevator to the ninth floor of the Kuhn, Loeb building and met briefly with Hill in his Great Northern office. The encounter lasted just a few minutes. Perhaps at the urging of Schiff, Harriman was trying to open a conversation toward compromise. At about this time he also invited Hill to spend the weekend at Arden, his country estate near New York in the Ramapo Mountains, an overture with all the marks of Schiff, but Hill declined. Hill could not conceal his, and Morgan's, total dislike and distrust of Harriman. He was more angry after Morgan's George Perkins told him that in one of their May 9 conferences Harriman had overstated how much Northern Pacific stock he actually controlled. Later in the month, Bacon warned him that Harriman was making noise about wanting "common methods of management and accounting" for all their roads. It felt to Hill as if they were right back in Schiff's office on May 3 when Harriman had popped his head in to second the motion for combining all their roads. Harriman could dissemble all he wanted, but it was still clear to Hill he wanted to run the whole show.

Sometime that day someone from Kuhn, Loeb told the *New York Times* on behalf of the Harriman syndicate that they believed they had "absolute control" of the Northern Pacific. They claimed that on Friday, May 3—the day Schiff took Hill into his office and closed the door—they had $65 million worth of Northern Pacific stock when Hill–Morgan had only $30 million. They computed that if the preferred on that day was worth $73 million and the common was worth $80 million then the total would be $153 million and a controlling interest would be just over $77.5 million. "It stands to reason," members of the syndicate said, "that Kuhn, Loeb & Co. would have been more likely to secure the $12.5 million necessary to them for the control than the other side to secure absolute possession of $47.5 million of stock or less, which they needed to have a majority."

In London, Morgan got a reality check. The Associated Press reported that the senior partner of London's largest arbitrage firm, R. Raphael and Sons, which just happened to be Kuhn, Loeb's associates in the city, had summoned Morgan, Lord Rothschild, and others to his private home on Sunday, May 12. He told them if the buying in Northern Pacific shares didn't stop then his firm would have to default, meaning an immediate loss to the London Stock Exchange of some 16 million pounds ($80 million). Morgan and Lord Rothschild had no other choice. They immediately pledged to stop buying Northern Pacific shares even though it was contrary to the laws of Capel Court, the London Exchange. Morgan asked R. Raphael and Co. to cable Schiff and tell him Morgan was willing to postpone delivery of shares to the next "settling day" if Kuhn, Loeb would do the same. "We will recommend," said Morgan in a cable to Bacon, "Northern Pacific RR not to close Transfer books or make any change in status quo before 10th June." Schiff agreed. Both sides announced that, with their support, London shorts could deliver Northern Pacific common at 140, and both quietly loaned shares to favored customers caught in the corner. "The whole development of the last few days" said one

London stockbroker, "merely shows how much we are in the power of New York." Morgan was made the hero.

On Tuesday, May 14, Harriman returned to Morgan headquarters where he was thought to have had an "extended conversation by cable" with Morgan in London. In the *New York Daily Tribune*, Harriman and Schiff with straight faces denied there had even been a quarrel: "Whatever is wisest for business interests will be done, and that means co-operation." Harriman was quoted saying, "everything will be all right...I don't think there will be any more trouble." But that same day they went public with another attack on Hill. The *New York Times* ran a story headlined "Stock War Forced on Union Pacific Men," attributing it to a source "thoroughly reliable." The story, with Harriman–Schiff's fingerprints all over it, accused Hill in so many words of lying when he said he wasn't trying to buy the Burlington, that his refusal to allow the Union Pacific to protect its territory was the cause of the "furious and frantic" buying of Northern Pacific stock, and that it was Kuhn, Loeb that first announced measures "to protect both legitimate and speculative dealers against the terrible position in which these market interests had been placed. But these efforts were only tardily, unwillingly, and partially seconded by those without whose unreasonable action the situation could have been avoided."

Both sides then declared a cease-fire on name calling, perhaps on orders from Morgan, agreeing "the less said the sooner will the old friendly relations be restored." If the attack had any effect on Hill he didn't show it. He remained in New York for the week and took the train to New London, Connecticut, to visit his Great Northern Steamship Company, which was building four of the world's largest freight steamers to gain more trade on the Great Lakes to Europe and to Asia from Puget Sound. The next year he would be able to claim transporting about three-fourths of all U.S. cotton exports to Asia. He was looking to Asia more than to the eastern United States. "It is too far from the Pacific Coast to the Eastern States to ship many of the products of the Northwest to the East," he had said. He could earn more selling iron, coal, and lumber to Japan and China than he could to the eastern United States.

Meanwhile, New York arbitrage houses counted the hours until the White Star steamer *Oceanic* arrived at her pier at New York harbor, as it did the morning of Wednesday, May 15. It carried stock certificates for 40,000 to 50,000 shares of Northern Pacific common that had departed Liverpool the day of the panic. Seldom had such a delivery been so anxiously awaited. The solvency of the arbitrage houses hung in the balance. The sacks were loaded quickly on horse-drawn carriages and brought to the houses that had sold the stock pending its physical delivery across the North Atlantic.

Word of the delivery spread through the financial district, releasing speculative pressure on Northern Pacific common, which dropped 11 points and closed at 139. The stock was still very scarce, with only 1,400 shares traded. That same day, Hill cabled his old friend and financier, Gaspard Farrer of Baring Brothers: "Everything clearing here... feejees [J. P. Morgan] strength increasing daily general feeling city and country runs high against Schiff's conduct all our friends firm enemy making overtures." The May 9 panic, however, did nothing to curb speculation. A number of railroads and U.S. Steel rose in the morning and then gave way to a sharp sell-off just before noon, with Union Pacific down 8½ and the St. Paul down 6. The declines were so great and extensive that rumors spread of an after-shock collapse. Then in the afternoon prices recovered and rose even faster than they had declined. Unfazed by May 9, the shorts joined in the buying and most of the railroads closed higher for the day. The market couldn't decide if Harriman had won or lost; his Union Pacific traded as low as 95½ and as high as 106½ , closing up 2½.

Now it was Schiff's turn to agonize. Morgan had denied him a meeting just before he departed for Europe April 3. Schiff knew it was a snub, punishment for aligning with Harriman. Schiff had not seen Morgan in person perhaps since the January meeting in Harriman's office in which they all agreed to peaceably settle any competitive differences within the law. He was well aware of Morgan's intense dislike for Harriman. He knew if he wasn't careful it would rub off on him. Schiff couldn't afford to be on the wrong side of the world's most powerful financier, and there was always that undercurrent of anti-Semitism that threatened his ability to attract gentile clients. The past several days he had been composing in his mind a posterity letter to Morgan summarizing his view of the causes of the current stalemate, explaining his and Harriman's motives and seeking to be absolved of any blame. He also needed to signal Morgan that he and Harriman were eager to come to a fair, equitable compromise on Northern Pacific.

Dated May 16, a week after the panic, and sent to Morgan in London, it is an astonishing letter. Twice Schiff tries to drive a wedge between Morgan and Hill by accusing Hill, his self-proclaimed "friend," in so many words, of lying—"willingly" misleading and deceiving him and Harriman into thinking he had no designs on the Burlington and that Hill had "repeatedly" assured Schiff the evening of May 3 at Schiff's home that there would be no difficulty in bringing about "harmony and community of interest." Then Schiff, at his obsequious best, poured on the syrup:

> I trust you will accept my assurance that nothing was further on the part of Union Pacific interests than to do aught meant to be antagonistic to you or your firm, and that, as far as my partners and I are concerned, we have at all times wished as we continue to do, to be permitted to aid in maintaining your personal prestige, so well deserved. You will find Union Pacific interests, and certainly my firm and myself, entirely ready to do anything in reason that you may ask or suggest, so that permanent conditions shall be created which shall be just to all interests and not bear within them the seed of future strife, discord, and possible disaster. Trusting, then, dear Mr. Morgan, that you will understand the spirit in which this letter is written, and hoping that the rest of your stay abroad may be pleasant and not interrupted by any unsatisfactory events, I am, with assurances of esteem,
> Yours most faithfully,
> Jacob H. Schiff

There is no record of Morgan responding. He must have shaken his head at Schiff's line that he needed help from Kuhn, Loeb in "maintaining" his "personal prestige." But there is no doubt he agreed something had to be done quickly to avoid "future strife." But what?

Morgan returned to Paris to join family and friends for the rest of May, where he created a stir at 7, Rue St. Georges. With neither correspondence or papers exchanged, not even meeting the owner in person, he agreed on Friday, May 17, to buy the entire collection of 229 pieces of medieval art accumulated over twenty-three years by Charles Mannheim, the world's most famous living judge of fifteenth- and sixteenth-century European art. It included Sevres porcelain, Italian majolica, Limoges enamels, jewels, antique bronzes, Gothic ivory carvings, a diptych from the collection of Queen Christina of Spain, a Della Rocca ceramic bas-relief of the Madonna and Child, forty choice examples of Italian and Spanish mosques faience, a white marble clock by Falconnet, and a bas-relief on kehlheim stone by Hans Dollinger, dated 1522, representing the triumph of Charles V. The Rothschilds and many others had sought the collection but Mannheim declined their offers because they wouldn't agree to keep the collection intact. Morgan did. It was estimated he paid from $450,000 to $750,000 for it. No contract was signed. "Mr. Morgan's word," said Mannheim, sounding just like James J. Hill, "is good enough for me." The acquisition, said one critic, was "one of the greatest sensations the art world has ever known," and "scarcely rivaled by any museum purchase since the Imperial Art Gallery of St. Petersburg bought its collection of old masters." To avoid, temporarily at least, the 20 percent U.S. tariff on imported art, Morgan had it all shipped to the South Kensington Museum in London.

Back in New York, Morgan left it to Bacon, George Perkins, Steele, and Hill to thrash out details of a "memorandum of understanding" with Harriman and Schiff. Even if the document was purposely vague it was important to show a spirit of compromise to fill the vacuum of rumor and uncertainty that could roil the markets for months. Harriman agreed to let Morgan name a new board for the Northern Pacific if Harriman could have representatives on it. Hill agreed to help create and maintain "uniform methods of management and accounting of the transcontinental lines" and also for the "settlement of any grievances or differences which may now exist or hereafter arise between said companies." They would choose four representatives to form a plan. Vanderbilt of the New York Central would arbitrate, and if he couldn't serve then the Pennsylvania Railroad's Cassatt would. While the two sides debated, Hill boarded a train at Grand Central station on Sunday afternoon, May 19, to return to St. Paul. He fretted on the ride home and decided he needed to make absolutely sure he and Morgan had majority control of the Northern Pacific. Reaching St. Paul that Tuesday, he cabled his right-hand man, Edward Nichols, in New York to buy every share of Northern Pacific common available under $200 a share. The next Sunday he headed back to New York. On Friday, May 31, Harriman and Schiff, Hill, and Bacon sat around a table in a private dining room at the Metropolitan Club and signed the memorandum of understanding. No reporters or photographers were present. The *New York Daily Tribune* rosily called the agreement a "complete restoration of harmony."

Both sides knew better. Distrust ran deep. Long before the Northern Pacific panic, before his serious pursuit of the Burlington, as far back as 1893, Hill had envisioned a separate corporation as a strongbox for his railroad securities, and those of some of his longtime associates, to protect the Great Northern system from market manipulators and from raiders such as Harriman proved to be. He and the three others who turned a bankrupt railroad into a fortune for themselves and their investors twenty years earlier were getting on in years. Hill was sixty-three, John S. Kennedy and Mount Stephen were both seventy-one, Lord Strathcona was eighty-two.

This new holding company had a second purpose: to store earnings from Hill's railroad system that the State of Minnesota wouldn't allow him to distribute as dividends. In February 1899 he asked his lawyers to prepare a plan for something he would call Northern Securities Company, Ltd. Now, in the wake of the May 9 panic, someone suggested (perhaps Kennedy), "Why not put in the Northern Pacific?" And so it had a third purpose: to force Harriman to lock up all his Northern Pacific shares in such a holding company, and forever check his ability to raid any of the Hill–Morgan roads. This third purpose now became the most urgent of all. Morgan concurred, he wanted the two northern roads legally entwined as soon as possible to neutralize Harriman, and "delay might lead to serious consequences." Hill admitted he was spending all his time trying to unite his three railroads to make them more efficient and protect them from raiders and speculators. "This will give us within five years," wrote Hill, "the best railway property in America with larger annual income for dividends than the Pennsylvania or the New York Central combined."

Since it was illegal in some of the states through which his roads passed for any railroad company to own the stock of a competing or parallel road, then why not simply create a holding company in which to deposit the stock of both competing railroads, a holding company that would keep each of the roads separate from, and competitive with, each other? Harriman still owned a bare majority of Northern Pacific common and preferred combined. Something had to be done to disarm him. Morgan had a more personal reason: he didn't want his vacations interrupted. Northern Securities was created, he later testified, "so that I could go to Europe and not hear the next day that somebody had bought it [the Northern Pacific] for the Boston and Maine." It also could be the full, legal enshrinement of "community of interest," New York thumbing its nose at Washington, D.C.

Harriman pursued his own agenda. Flowing from their agreement at the Metropolitan Club, in early June he proposed putting in the hands of two men based in Chicago—one chosen by him, the other by Hill—the task of coordinating the traffic of all their roads within the law for more efficiency and profit. Running them, in effect, as if they were one. Harriman chose John C. Stubbs, who had managed traffic for Collis Huntington's Southern Pacific for thirty years. Hill chose Darius Miller of the Great Northern. It was a harmonious choice; the two knew their business and were old friends, but as an extension of "community of interest" it tiptoed defiantly near the appearance of collusion.

Morgan spent June in England being treated like the financial king of the world he was. In black frock coat and top hat he and his colleagues had lunch at Windsor Castle with the new King, Edward VII, and then met with King Leopold II of Belgium on his yacht. On Friday, June 28, Morgan and a group of other wealthy Americans gathered on one of the platforms at the aging Waterloo Station near the Thames bound for Southampton and their voyage home to New York on the *Deutschland*. They boarded a private express train for breakfast en route with one of the London & South Western Road's finest engines pulling a saloon carriage, a second-class car for servants, and a baggage car. There were so many millionaires on the platform, said one observer, there were rumors they had just bought London or Paris.

The Hamburg–American steamer that departed Southampton was called the "ship of millionaires," carrying not only Morgan but assorted Waterburys, Bakers, Laniers, Elkins, Wideners, Griscoms, Dawkins, Whitneys, Lorillards, Saltonstalls, Vanderbilts, and Cassatts. The evening of July 3 on the north Atlantic, the captain turned off the lights on the saloon deck before dinner, and when he turned them on all the tables were decorated in red, white, and blue. The morning of the Fourth, the *Deutschland* steamed up the bay to her pier at Hoboken in "breezy, delightful" weather. Reporters found Morgan in spirited conversation with friends. When they approached him he made a feint as if to run away, but then, laughing, he joined them to "face the music." Soon he was on his yacht the *Corsair*; with pennants flapping it steamed up the Hudson to Cragston to his gabled, country farmhouse of clapboard at Highland Falls on the Hudson, where fireworks were a staple on Fourth of July evenings. The next morning, President McKinley and his wife Ida left Washington, D.C., on a special western express for their home in Canton, Ohio, where they were to stay for eight weeks before heading north to Buffalo for the Pan-American Exposition.

The millionaires on Morgan's voyage home had an unwritten rule: no business talk when they were with family and friends. Morgan, however, surely had on his mind the next steps in his war with Harriman. Thirteen days later in a letter he sent to Harriman, Schiff, and Hill he announced his choices to fill vacancies on the Northern Pacific board, as the Metropolitan Club agreement authorized. It was, again, a Morgan-dictated interlocking "community of interest." Just after the market closed at 3 p.m. he revealed the names: Hill, Harriman, William A. Rockefeller (representing Standard Oil's interest in the

St. Paul railroad), Hamilton McKown Twombley (representing the Vanderbilts and their Chicago & North Western), and Samuel Rea of the Pennsylvania Railroad. The market responded by sending railroad stocks higher. Someone sold 200 shares of Northern Pacific common for 118. It was the first time anyone had let go of Northern Pacific shares since June 12, when it closed at 165.

Schiff now felt it safe to depart for a two-month hiatus with his family in Europe. He kept maneuvering for every advantage until departure. Two days after Morgan announced the names of the new Northern Pacific board, Schiff spent ten minutes with him at "the corner." He apparently failed to persuade him to allow Bacon to be nominated for a soon-to-be vacant board seat on the Union Pacific, perhaps as a goodwill bargaining chip for Harriman. Before he and Therese departed, he penned a note to Harriman reminding him to keep an eye on what Morgan's new Northern Pacific board did with the preferred stock, which remained a key to control of the company. Schiff still thought of Hill as a client. The day before he departed he took the elevator to the ninth floor in the Kuhn, Loeb building to try to convince him to combine the Great Northern and Burlington into one company and issue new stock to take advantage of both companies' surplus earnings. Hill later recalled Schiff told him he had it on sound legal authority that the Northern Pacific board did not have authority to retire the preferred shares. "I told him not to waste his breath," said Hill, "as our counsel had advised us that it could be done."

In early August, to encourage smaller shareholders to follow suit, Hill began rounding up Great Northern stock to exchange for shares in the new Northern Securities holding company. Hill pledged 80,049 shares, Kennedy 75,000, Lord Strathcona 54,000, and Mount Stephen 50,000 in various trusts. This alone represented almost 30 percent of Great Northern's stock. With McKinley launched on his second term, having just completed his victory lap tour of the South and West, there was little doubt his probusiness administration would bless the combining of two parallel, competing railroads in the same holding company.

Morgan brought Harriman and Hill together several times that August to try to reconcile their differences and smooth the way toward the holding company. One or more of their meetings was on Morgan's *Corsair*, gliding off Bar Harbor, Maine, summer colony for aristocrats and their yachts and a retreat for many of Morgan's men and their families. On one of these excursions, Morgan explained to Harriman through the smoke of his Cuban cigars why the Northern Pacific preferred should be retired. The offer terms weren't favorable to Harriman but surprisingly he agreed, perhaps to gain other concessions.

Through the summer Hill and Morgan did concede him points in exchange for locking him into a holding company that could hold Harriman captive as a minority stockholder. They compromised in the Pacific Northwest, agreeing to exchange rights to use each other's tracks. They allayed Harriman's fears that the Burlington might invade his Union Pacific territory. Quietly, Hill even agreed to create a new company called the Chicago, Burlington & Quincy Railway, which would lease the Burlington for 999 years. The Great Northern and the Burlington would have half the stock in the new company and the Union Pacific the other half, giving Harriman a voice in protecting his territory.

Morgan could mediate concessions all he wanted, but he couldn't make Harriman and Hill trust each other. Their temperaments and values just did not match: Harriman impatient, Hill deliberate. Both left the *Corsair* looking over their shoulders. The clock was ticking toward the early October meeting of the Northern Pacific board, reconstituted by Morgan, to decide when to retire the preferred shares by January 1, 1902, and solidify control for Hill and Morgan. The vote could not come, however, until Harriman surrendered to Morgan his large chunk of proxies for the preferred to be converted into common.

The uncertainty was driving Hill nuts. What if Harriman challenged the language of the Northern Pacific charter and bylaws in the courts? It boiled down to how one word was interpreted. He had read the most important line many times: "The *company* [emphasis added] shall have the right at its option, and in such manner as it shall determine, to retire the preferred stock in whole or in part at par, from time to time, upon any first day of January prior to 1917." Harriman's counsel had advised him "the company" meant all the *stockholders*. Morgan's counsel believed that in that context the *directors* were "the company." Who came first, directors or stockholders? It would make fascinating new law if the courts got hold of it and Harriman was just stubborn enough to sue. Hill and Morgan had to make sure that didn't happen.

Hill had refused Harriman's invitation in mid-May to visit him at Arden Farms, his country estate fifty miles north of the city in the Ramapo Valley. Harriman invited him again, and Hill couldn't say no. Hill and Morgan needed his proxies for his Northern Pacific shares, essential for their holding company, and now Hill and Harriman could meet face to face and resolve the uncertainty. Hill had tired of hotel life in New York and was staying in an apartment suite he had just acquired at the elegant new boutique hotel, the Bolkenhayn, on Central Park Plaza, seven stories of marble, white brick, and terra cotta rose designed by immigrant Alfred Zucker with a central hallway of onyx and bronze and a marble floor with the coats of arms of all the provinces of his Prussian homeland.

Hill rose early Sunday morning, September 1, and headed for Harriman's estate, by ferry across the North River and then on Morgan's Erie Railroad to Harriman's depot, accompanied by its new president and his former protégé, Frederick D. Underwood. Arden was more a principality than a country estate; their carriage wound through only a small part of its 15,000 acres of forest and mountains, orchard and meadow, lakes and streams, iron mines and dairy farms. They spent several hours with Harriman at his home, with its roof beams of railway steel, on the crest of a ridge of forest overlooking Lake Echo. They returned to New York that evening with Harriman having convinced Hill that he would provide the proxies on time. With that assurance, Hill headed home west on the Erie the next day, Labor Day, leaving on the ferry for Jersey City at 2 p.m.

Just as Hill's train was leaving the station, words were spoken in Minnesota that became the first volley of a campaign aimed squarely at the holding company Hill and Morgan were creating. A crowd of thousands had packed the grandstand at the Minnesota State Fair to hear Vice President Theodore Roosevelt, an appearance he had committed to four months earlier. Clad in a black frock coat, he removed his silk top hat and faced his audience square into the sun, squinting from the glare. His speech that day is remembered mostly for his first public use of "Speak softly and carry a big stick" about the Monroe Doctrine. What Hill and Morgan may not have noticed, however, was his threat of a big stick against big business. A third of the way into his speech on American enterprise, purposely chosen for an audience of farmers and cattlemen, anti–big business and anti-railroad, he pounded out the words:

> The vast individual and corporate fortunes, the vast combinations of capital, which have marked the development of our industrial system, create new conditions and necessitate a change from the old attitude of the state and nation toward property. It is probably true that the large majority of fortunes that now exist in this country have been amassed, not by injuring people, but as an incident to the conferring of great benefits upon the community; and this, no matter what may have been the conscious purpose of those amassing them. There is but the scantiest justification for most of the outcry against the men of wealth as such; and it ought to be unnecessary to state that any appeal which directly or indirectly leads to suspicion

and hatred among ourselves, which tends to limit opportunity and, therefore, to shut the door of success against poor men of talent, and finally which entails the possibility of lawlessness and violence, is an attack upon the fundamental properties of American citizenship. Our interests are at bottom common; in the long run we go up or down together. Yet more and more it is evident that the state, and if necessary, the nation, has got to possess the right of supervision and control as regards the great corporations which are its creatures; particularly as regards the great business combinations which derive a portion of their importance from the existence of some monopolistic tendency. The right should be exercised with caution and self-restraint, but it should exist, so that it may be invoked if the need arises.

The Northern Pacific corner had come home to roost. It was not mere "grandstanding." Roosevelt was testing a populist message on the western prairie. The wild response from the state fair audience told him he had struck a nerve. He would have a chance to translate words into action much earlier than he or anyone expected.

Two days later, intersecting Hill's path west to Minnesota, a train carrying President McKinley and his wife Ida headed north from Canton, Ohio, onto the plateau along the southern shore of Lake Erie. It passed ports receiving coal and ore at Cleveland and Erie, sand bars, ravines, and break waters, arriving at Terrace Station in Buffalo for the Pan-American Exposition.

Hill–Morgan and Harriman–Schiff disagreed on many things when it came to railroads, but they were unanimous for McKinley. It was on his watch that the economy had boomed, with every sign it would continue through at least 1904. It was because of McKinley that Hill had switched parties. He had been a lifelong low-tariff Democrat but he had had enough of Bryan's populist free-silver demagoguery. In 1896 in the roasting heat of August he led his friend, the rheumatic Senator Marcus Alonzo "Mark" Hanna, around Manhattan raising money for McKinley from Morgan, Schiff, and Cassatt at the Pennsylvania Railroad. They all agreed that McKinley and what he stood for (free enterprise, free trade, economic growth, stable markets, soft on anti-trust, open lines between Washington and New York) was the best thing that had happened to America in years. How appropriate to have McKinley in Buffalo to celebrate American technology, industrial power, and economic might—the most energetic, productive nation in the world. "The good work will go on," he said on

Teddy Roosevelt on the stump: "If you want to wake up a hundred million people, you've got to make a big and resounding noise." LIBRARY OF CONGRESS, PRINTS AND PHOTOGRAPHS DIVISION [LC-USZ62–5138].

arrival in Buffalo, "it cannot be stopped...Who can tell the new thoughts that have been awakened, the ambitions fired...through this Exposition?"

On Friday, September 6, a courier strode into Morgan's headquarters at 23 Wall Street with a secured satchel containing Harriman's proxies for his shares of Northern Pacific preferred and common. The Hill–Morgan plan for a holding company for the Great Northern and Northern Pacific could proceed. "Very confidential," Hill cabled a colleague, "Harriman has turned over their proxy to Morgan for October election. That settles it." But, it didn't.

It was warm and humid in Manhattan that afternoon just as it was in Buffalo where an organist was playing Schumann's *Traumerei* at the Pan-American Exposition's Temple of Music. Flanked by potted plants and security guards, McKinley stood ready to face a receiving line as the doors were thrown open for visitors to shake the hand of the president of the United States. Ten minutes of his schedule had been allotted, and time was almost up. His secretary left his side to close the doors. At 4:07 p.m. as the end of the receiving line approached, twenty-eight-year-old Leon Czolgosz, an anarchist and former steelworker from Cleveland, came to within a foot of the president. He raised his right hand swathed in a white handkerchief. McKinley thought it a bandage. He fired two Smith & Wesson cartridges from his .32-caliber silver-plated Iver Johnson pistol into McKinley's chest and abdomen. The second bullet passed through his stomach, cut through his kidney and pancreas, and lodged in his back. McKinley staggered between the potted plants but stayed standing while Czolgosz was punched and wrestled to the floor. An eternity passed before an ambulance arrived at 4:18 and rushed the president to a hospital, where doctors were unable to find the bullet but cleansed the wounds and sewed them up. Roosevelt was alerted and rushed to Buffalo.

Schiff was abroad, visiting relatives in Germany and taking the waters at Marienbad, west of Prague. Hill was in St. Paul. Harriman apparently was at his office in New York. Morgan was in his office at "the corner." It was about 5 p.m. The Stock Exchange was closed. Morgan had his hat on and his cane in his hand, ready to leave his office for a cruise on the *Corsair* to Great Neck on Long Island Sound with his son-in-law. He had glanced over a ledger on a clerk's desk and was walking to the door when a reporter ran in with the news of the shooting. Morgan dropped his cane, went back to his desk, and sat for several minutes in his office staring at the carpet. Another reporter came in with the first extra edition of a newspaper.

Morgan cruised to Great Neck mostly in silence, holding his one-month-old granddaughter, and spent the night on the anchored *Corsair* protected by security guards. Wall Street jammed the Waldorf that evening. One could trace the news, as reporter Edwin Lefevre did, "from face to face...like an autumn gust passing over a wheat field." When Morgan arrived at his office on Saturday morning he found the building cordoned by a dozen city police detectives. He left his office shortly after 9 a.m. and strode quickly two blocks up Nassau Street with Bacon for a meeting at the New York Clearing House.

To one reporter he looked flustered and nervous, in such a hurry he forgot to take off his office coat and his hat appeared to be on backward.

When trading opened on the Stock Exchange at 10 a.m. there was a "strange calmness" on traders' faces, "almost amounting to indifference." Perhaps it was because there were reports that Morgan ("powerful beyond description," wrote Lefevre) had agents on the floor with orders to buy everything offered, "no matter what the price." From 10 to 11 a.m. it was estimated Morgan's brokers acquired at least 350,000 of the 495,000 shares traded. Brokers also were said to be buying, to support prices, for Standard Oil and for the Gould, Vanderbilt, and Harriman interests. There were some brief price declines during the two-hour session but no panic, and some selling near the end when some bears spread a rumor that the president had died. Morgan, however, had helped the market find its bearings. "The financial situation is absolutely good," he said in a statement, "There is nothing to derange it. The banks will take care of that. You need not worry about that."

In Buffalo the president's condition was described as stable, his fever appeared to be receding. By Monday, September 9, there was talk he might be out of danger. "Society entertainments" even resumed at Newport with "the probability of his ultimate recovery." On Tuesday, Roosevelt, reassured by the president's condition, left Buffalo "with a light heart." The bullet wounds, however, had poisoned the walls of McKinley's stomach, and gangrene spread. By Wednesday he was drifting in and out of consciousness. He died at 2:15 a.m. Saturday, September 14. A Pennsylvania Railroad train carried his body in a glass observation parlor car from Buffalo to Washington, D.C., where his remains lay in state under a huge chandelier in the East Room of the White House, followed by the funeral in the Capitol rotunda. Then he made his last journey home for burial in Westlawn Cemetery in Canton, Ohio. The Stock Exchange closed Thursday for the burial. At 3:30 p.m., as the casket was carried to the cemetery, virtually every carriage, auto, trolley, and riverboat in New York, Washington, and other cities across the country stood still for five minutes of silence.

"Don't any of you realize," Senator Mark Hanna of Ohio had stormed after he lost control of the Republican convention a year earlier and watched stunned as the delegates nominated Roosevelt for vice president with McKinley, "that there's only one life between that madman and the Presidency? . . . What harm can he do as Governor of New York compared to the damage he will do as President if McKinley should die?"

Morgan, Hill, Harriman, and Schiff were about to find out.

11

THE "BIG STICK"

It was the afternoon of Wednesday, October 2, 1901 and J. P. Morgan settled in his seat at Trinity Church at the corner of Bush and Gough in San Francisco. He thumbed through his hymnal and prepared to worship God. Every three years over the past two decades he had dutifully set aside his business affairs, no matter how weighty and urgent, and traveled around the country to attend, as a lay delegate, the convention of the Protestant Episcopal Church of America. He believed his material wealth was not incompatible with his spiritual life. There was a juncture where his faith and finance met, where the world's most famous capitalist could do God's work by creating jobs, building companies, and saving scarce resources that were, after all, a gift from God. He often described his work not in terms of money or power but of "moral influence." His faith was so bedrock, so integral to his character, that he still sang hymns at home Sunday evenings and had personally penned for his last will and testament these astounding opening lines: "I commit my soul into the hands of my Saviour, in full confidence that having redeemed it and washed it in His most precious blood He will present it faultless before my Heavenly Father."

Morgan probably was not afraid to reflect on Mark 10:25–26, the same passage that had bothered Commodore Vanderbilt. Christ did say it is easier for a camel to go through the eye of a needle than for someone who is rich to enter the kingdom of God, but he also said for God all things are possible, and so they were for J. P. Morgan, too. He was a senior warden and a member of the vestry of his parish, supported it with an open, often anonymous, checkbook, and sometimes could be seen at the Sunday service passing the plate for offerings from his fellow congregants. At this convention, however, one local newspaper called him just a "simple lay delegate from St. George's Parish" on

Stuyvesant Square in New York City, seated in the fifth row from the front with his New York colleagues under the balcony in the right transept.

Morgan rose with the five hundred clergy and laity packed into the church to welcome the procession up the aisle of sixty-eight American bishops and two Lord Bishops of the Church of England in their white surplices and red academic hoods, then sang hymn 490, "Glorious Things of Thee Are Spoken." He listened intently as Bishop Benjamin Wistar Morris of Oregon pleaded for more donations to help Episcopal missionaries build churches to evangelize the immigrants settling the American West: "What folly it is for us to be wasting time and effort over 'copes and mitres,' candlesticks and incense, postures, and attitudes while we are omitting the weightier matters of judgment, mercy, and faith."

Morgan had just traveled across the frontier's great expanse, much of it west of Omaha and into the Bay Area on Harriman's tracks. It was his first journey by rail to California since the summer of 1869 when, half a lifetime earlier, his train had rolled along newly laid Union Pacific tracks past bands of Pawnee in Nebraska. When it came to settling the West, he and Jim Hill sang from the same hymnal as the Episcopal bishops. "Land without population is a wilderness," wrote Hill, "and population without land is a mob."

As always when he traveled, Morgan didn't mind trying to be a camel through the eye of a needle. He and his party, including Francis Lynde Stetson, known as his "attorney general" and also a lay delegate to the convention, and the Episcopal Bishop of New York, Henry Codman Potter, had boarded a special express train at Grand Central station a week ago. Signalmen from New York to California had routed trains to the side so Morgan's express need stop only for coal and water. The restaurateur Louis Sherry came along to cater the one-month trip, at a rumored daily cost of $300 for food and wine. When they arrived in San Francisco they proceeded on cable cars up Nob Hill where they rented Charles Crocker's seventy-room brownstone mansion, surrounded by an expansive lawn and an iron fence, occupying a full block.

The America Morgan journeyed across was still at half-staff in mourning. The shock of McKinley's death was one thing for Morgan; getting used to Teddy Roosevelt in the White House was quite another. The youngest president of the United States, Roosevelt was not yet forty-three, young enough to be Morgan's son. But the path of "His Accidency" to the White House was paved with solid experience at all levels of government. Few if any presidents were as broadly proficient, beyond public service, at such a young age; he was an explorer, hunter, soldier, conservationist, author, and bilingual, as well as a voracious reader, horseman, boxer, mountain climber, and ornithologist. Morgan, however, was troubled by Roosevelt's unpredictable populist streak, his impulsiveness, vanity, theatrics, and manic energy. He probably agreed with Mark Twain who called Roosevelt "the Tom Sawyer of the political world of the twentieth century; always showing off; always hunting for a chance to show off; in his frenzied imagination the Great Republic is a vast Barnum circus with him for a clown and the whole world for audience; he would go to Halifax for half a chance to show off and he would go to hell for a whole one." Most embarrassing was the way he showboated through the corridors of the Republican National Convention in Philadelphia the year before, preening in his Rough Rider hat, pretending not to want the vice presidential nomination but doing his best to pose for it. Inappropriate was too kind a word. When he did get the nomination, hardly anyone noticed his comment on the trusts, buried in his letter of acceptance: the states should regulate them but if they didn't "the National Government must step in."

When it came to fund-raising Roosevelt was a hypocrite, playing both sides of the street to his advantage. He privately loathed the extravagant rich but had no qualms patronizing them for contributions. Morgan had known and admired Roosevelt's father, and had been a founder with him of the American Museum of Natural History. He had supported "Teddy" for the New York Assembly in the early 1880s, and had reportedly contributed to his campaign for governor in 1898. As governor of New York, however, Roosevelt had criticized the trusts, and with the legislature had slapped a franchise tax on corporations. That convinced the New York Republican bosses they had to get him out of Albany; the open spot on the McKinley ticket looked like just the place to warehouse him. As vice president he refused to exempt two of Morgan's railroads from certain taxes and then tried to make up for it by staging a testimonial dinner for Morgan at the Union League Club in late December 1900. Roosevelt addressed him as "My dear Mr. Morgan" in the invite. It felt fawning and patronizing. Morgan kept his distance.

Then there was Hill, rugged individualist from the West, who should have been Teddy's kind of man. Their common ground was North Dakota, on the path of both the Northern Pacific and Great Northern, where Roosevelt had hunted and played at cattle ranching when it was a territory in the mid-1880s. It turned out to be their only common ground. The more Hill studied

Roosevelt's words and actions (or his "act" as Hill might have put it) the more he disliked him. He especially disliked Roosevelt's gun slinging approach to the Monroe Doctrine; he believed the key to global power was not grabbing land through war but success in commerce, and the key to that was railroads and steamships. Schiff was a conservative Democrat but a Roosevelt supporter. Harriman knew of Roosevelt from a distance going back to the 1880s when they lived a few short blocks from each other near Fifth Avenue. He gave regularly to Republican causes but had gotten deep into state politics only in the last three years or so. Shortly after Roosevelt was elected governor in 1898, Harriman hosted a dinner at the Metropolitan Club for Benjamin B. Odell, the head of the state's Republican executive committee who had promoted Roosevelt for governor. All the New York Republican kingmakers were there, and Harriman was at a center table with Roosevelt on one side and Odell on the other, with Schiff among the attendees. From that night on Roosevelt considered Harriman, for better or worse (later, the worst) an important influence in New York state politics. Morgan, Hill, Harriman, and Schiff were forever separated from Roosevelt by the chasm between commerce and government.

Morgan had departed for the West with the Northern Pacific situation in good hands. All seemed on plan. On October 1, the day of the regularly scheduled Northern Pacific annual stockholders meeting, his six board nominees would be elected: Harriman, Hill, Twombley (Vanderbilt), Stillman, Rea, and Rockefeller. It was still Morgan's board; the Harriman interests owned 23 percent of the stock and represented 20 percent of the board. Stetson had stage-managed it by remote control; before leaving New York with Morgan he gave an associate not just the meeting's agenda but the minutes.

And what about Roosevelt? Morgan talked with Bacon and Perkins before he left for San Francisco. They needed to go down to Washington together as soon as diplomatically possible after the McKinley funeral. They knew Roosevelt was personally drafting his first Annual Message to Congress; it would be public in only eight weeks and it would have a strongly worded section on regulating trusts and big business, which could jeopardize every large corporation connected with the House of Morgan, including the soon-to-be announced holding company for the Hill–Morgan western railroads.

Morgan could not have had two better ambassadors for the mission. Perkins had lobbied Governor Roosevelt against legislation limiting the premium volume of insurance companies. Roosevelt had willingly accepted campaign contributions from New York Life through Perkins. In fact, Perkins had worked behind the scenes in a cameo role to help Roosevelt get the Republican nomination for vice president the previous summer in Philadelphia. Sometime in 1901 Roosevelt even began sending drafts of his speeches and statements on the subject of trusts to Perkins for his review and comment. Ten years hence, Perkins managed Roosevelt's Bull Moose Progressive party campaign. And, of course, Roosevelt and Bacon went back to Harvard where they were both members of the class of '80 when Roosevelt was in awe of Bacon as scholar and athlete. The nearsighted Roosevelt had pestered Bacon into putting on the gloves, and Bacon did his best not to break Roosevelt's glasses. Roosevelt said he would have landed more punches if his arms had been longer and Bacon's shorter. As president, he addressed his letters to Bacon as "Dear Bob." Eight years hence, Bacon briefly would be his secretary of state.

Roosevelt considered both men to be "of the highest character... genuine forces for good as well as men of strength and weight," but he thought they were like two attorneys arguing a bad case, merely Morgan's minions. Roosevelt wanted more detailed reports from large corporations. Perkins told him all corporations financed by Morgan were now voluntarily disclosing their earnings and losses. That, said Roosevelt, wasn't good enough. He may have been arguing for what the New York Times offered in an editorial on October 7, a few days after Perkins and Bacon visited with Roosevelt and after U.S. Steel had issued a public financial report on its first six months of operation. A holding company such as U.S. Steel, the Times said, was nothing but the individual performance of its constituent companies. So give us, it said, detail on its constituent companies: their gross earnings, operating expenses, charges of all kinds, net earnings, dividend payments, capital stock, bonded debt, surplus reserves. The best railroad corporations had surplus reserves of 15 to 29 percent of total capital, but U.S. Steel, one economist guessed, had only 7 percent. "Perkins may just as well make up his mind," Roosevelt confided, "that I will not make my Message one hair's breadth milder."

Bacon and Perkins came away worried about the direction Roosevelt was headed. They had every right to be. Rumors roiled the market throughout October. Word began to leak that "a plan had been practically decided upon for the formation of a corporation which should control the securities" of the Great Northern and the Northern Pacific. The Morgan men denied the rumors, but said there was nothing to report "yet." At 11 a.m. on Monday, October 28, a carriage pulled up at 23 Wall Street and out stepped Morgan back from the West Coast after a month's absence.

Reporters staked out the corner and concluded that Morgan's whole schedule for the day appeared to be the Northern Pacific. Hill was waiting for Morgan, and they were said to have met for a half hour. In the afternoon, Harriman strode in and remained with Morgan for a longer audience, apparently, than Hill had. Then came Schiff, meeting twice with Morgan. Quietly, by mutual agreement with Hill, Schiff had agreed not to stand for reelection to the Great Northern board. (It was testimony to the naive principle of "community of interest" and to Schiff's opportunism that he conspired with Harriman to try to seize the Northern Pacific while still on Hill's Great Northern board.)

Tempers had flared while Morgan was gone. Someone in the Harriman group had told the New York Sun, Morgan's mouthpiece, that they had allowed Morgan to name the Northern Pacific board and had turned over to him their proxies for Northern Pacific shares, but that Hill "had assumed an unsatisfactory attitude and wanted to retire the preferred stock . . . so that the Harriman interests would be left out in the cold." We expect, they said, "an honorable and just decision from Mr. Morgan . . . everything depends on [him]. It is for him to stop little petty objections."

With Roosevelt's message to Congress a month away, Hill realized he had to meet with the president in person to get his oar in the water on several subjects and take his measure. On Friday evening, November 2, he dined at the White House with Roosevelt and Secretary of State John Hay, an advocate for open-door trading with China and Japan. Hay's presence may have meant Hill was lobbying, out of character for someone who never relied on public largesse, for a new bill in the House to subsidize the building of ocean freight steamers. Perhaps he also was advocating for Morgan's American syndicate, formed a year earlier, seeking control of the French concession to build the Panama Canal. Hill would not have let the evening pass without haranguing Roosevelt, twenty-one years his junior, that efficiency and order were the key to transport and transport was the key to commerce and commerce was the key to American economic might. The dinner lasted five hours. They adjourned at 11 p.m.

Morgan returned to find internal strife. The stress and overwork had gotten to the exhausted Bob Bacon. Morgan had left him in charge and Harriman and Schiff had caught Bacon napping (no matter they had caught Morgan napping, too). Bacon also was a victim of his workaholic sense of duty. The father who would choose work over watching his three sons row crew at Harvard had done himself in with fourteen-hour days, sleepless nights, with little time left for his wife and family. He became the first casualty of the battle; while Morgan was out West, Bacon suffered what was then called a nervous breakdown.

There also were rumors of a personality clash between the self-effacing Bacon and the ambitious George Perkins. In early November, Bacon's doctor advised him to take a leave of absence. Buried at the bottom of a story on the Northern Pacific in the *New York Times* on November 7: "Robert Bacon of J. P. Morgan & Co. sailed for Europe yesterday on the *Majestic* [for Liverpool], but it was stated by Mr. Morgan that his partner had no financial mission to fulfill, and that he had sailed simply for recuperation." Bacon and his wife remained in France through the following autumn; he was on the U.S. Steel board but absent from meetings. He retired from the House of Morgan at the end of 1902 and later embarked on a remarkable career in public service.

George Perkins had been with the firm only eight months. Now, with Bacon gone, he became the visible head in Morgan's absence. As de facto head of New York Life's business operations and a brilliant shaper of its culture, he had come to Morgan less a banker and more an industrial engineer. He had streamlined and centralized New York Life's operations by eliminating regional supervisors and having the company's 350 agents report directly to headquarters, and he pioneered profit sharing. Like young Otto Kahn at Kuhn, Loeb, Perkins was a new breed of "corporate communicator." Perkins had declined Morgan's first offer to join the firm, saying he said he didn't want to leave New York Life. Morgan wanted him so badly he ignored concerns over conflict of interest and allowed Perkins to maintain dual employment plus a guarantee, it was said, of $250,000 a year in addition to profit sharing. Perkins "now does all the talking" for the Morgan firm, said the *New York World* five months later, "He takes the reporters into his confidence, explains the entire situation to them frankly, and tells them just how much they may and may not print."

Five days after Bacon sailed for Europe, the bells of Trinity Church tolled midnight in the financial district. The lights were still on at "the corner" of Wall and Broad. Under the glow of street lamps a group of horse-drawn carriages were parked outside the House of Morgan. Hill, Harriman, and Perkins conferred on the final details of what would be the new corporate repository for the stock and profit of the Hill–Morgan railroads. The Northern Pacific board had resolved to retire the preferred stock on January 1, exchanging it for bonds convertible to common stock. Sometime around 2 a.m. Harriman, Hill, and Perkins agreed to file immediately for incorporation. Harriman declared he was "perfectly satisfied" with Hill's offer. He had held Hill and Morgan hostage with his majority of the Northern Pacific common and preferred. He had gotten all he wanted and, as was his wont, a bit more. Nine months earlier all he asked for was a third interest in the Burlington. He had not voiced any desire to own part of the Northern Pacific or the Great Northern. But now, in exchange for surrendering his ability to raid the Northern Pacific, he received a full half interest, but no management control, in the Burlington, he and Schiff both sat on the Burlington board, and he also owned 23 percent of the holding company that held the stock of the Great Northern and Northern Pacific.

Later that Tuesday, November 12, the Northern Securities Company was incorporated in the favorable charter state of New Jersey, which had been welcoming holding companies for the past decade with a law allowing one corporation to hold the stock of other corporations. Northern Securities had $400 million in capital (considerably more than the combined market value of the stock of the Northern Pacific and its land grants, and the Great Northern plus all its coal land, forests, iron mines, and steamships), the second largest company in the world behind U.S. Steel, and was the largest railroad combine of its time. Hill and his associates sold to Northern Securities thirty million shares of Great Northern at 180 a share and about thirty-five million shares of Northern Pacific at 115. J. P. Morgan and Company sold about seven million shares of Northern Pacific common. Harriman sold all his Northern Pacific stock, $37 million of common and $41 million of preferred, to Northern Securities for $82.5 million of shares in the holding company and $9 million in cash. There was a rumor the Hill–Morgan group paid Harriman a ransom of $15 million to pry away his Northern Pacific shares (it actually was $9 million, Hill called it a "cash bonus.")

Worried about spooking the market, the new board met in secret for forty-five minutes early that Tuesday afternoon at the office of board member John Stewart Kennedy at 31 Nassau. Hill was elected chairman of the fifteen-member Northern Securities board; Harriman, Schiff, and Stillman were named to the board but not as officers. Bacon initially was to be on the board but "resigned," replaced by Samuel Spencer, president of the Morgan-controlled Southern Railway. To maintain secrecy, the board members left the room one by one after the meeting and rushed into an elevator across the hallway. To mark the birth of Northern Securities the board presented Hill with a twenty dollar gold piece, which he proudly gave to his wife Mary that evening in their suite at the Bolkenhayn.

After the meeting, Morgan still had to referee. Baker and Hill hurried the two blocks down Nassau to consult with him at "the corner"; Schiff and Harriman followed later. Their Union Pacific interests were a decided minority in Northern Securities, but Schiff felt he and Harriman got what they wanted: "potent influence" on Hill, protection from his invasion into Union Pacific territory, and "extensive use of important lines on the northern Pacific Coast." Schiff felt it was worth their fight the past spring. Harriman still looked for every small advantage: he tried and failed to have Northern Securities headquartered in the Equitable, where he had his offices.

Morgan and Perkins delayed the announcement until after the market closed on Wednesday, November 13. Late that day and into Thursday morning the "Northern Securities" headlines, datelined Trenton, New Jersey, raced around the globe. Railroad stocks had been climbing steadily for two weeks on rumors some sort of holding company was in the works. When trading opened Thursday morning many speculators took their gains and began building cash for what they sensed could be more consolidation. If the Great Northern, the Northern Pacific, and the Burlington could be combined into one holding company what did that mean for the remaining independents in the West? Wealthy Europeans put their bets on Hill–Morgan: about a dozen members of French nobility and thirty titled English men and women, among them the head of the British Foreign Office, had significant holdings in Northern Securities.

Morgan and Hill knew that Northern Securities by its size and geography (its roads passed through nineteen states and territories) would be a lightning rod for regulators. They warned the Great Northern's 1,800 shareholders there was the threat of a lawsuit. Hill's lawyers presented it as an investment company: nowhere in the charter of Northern Securities do "railroad" or "railway" appear. They decided a holding company was the surest way to protect their properties, that it was legal and that there was nothing in the 1890 Sherman Anti-Trust Act or Supreme Court rulings that specifically forbade it. Owning stock in companies wasn't interstate commerce. Northern Securities was, Morgan's attorney Stetson argued later, like professional baseball. The owners didn't play baseball, they just owned the clubs.

Public opinion, however, doesn't care for legalities. Hill and Morgan may have been surprised that one of the first opposing voices came not from a regulator but from a crusty financier. "A combination of this sort throttles competition and the people don't like it," said Russell Sage. What really annoyed

Sage was a sentence in the charter of Northern Securities that seemed contrary to the best interests of its own stockholders, that its board "from time to time shall determine whether and to what extent and at what time and place and under what conditions and regulations the accounts and books of the corporation or any of them shall be open to the inspection of the stockholders." As red flags go, this was crimson. Roosevelt took notice.

On the same day the Northern Securities board held its secret first meeting Roosevelt finished the first draft of his Annual Message to Congress. He had been in office only fifty-nine days. Over lunch the next day at the White House he discussed it with Attorney General Philander Knox, who he had asked for ideas for the section on trusts. Knox was a wealthy attorney from Pittsburgh with impeccable "trust" credentials as former personal and corporate counsel to Andrew Carnegie and Henry Clay Frick and defender of the private fishing and hunting club whose dam burst in heavy rainfall in 1889 above Johnstown, killing more than two thousand people. Knox argued it was an act of God. He had earned about $350,000 a year in private practice and was paid about $600,000 to help form U.S. Steel as counsel for Carnegie Steel Company. He had known McKinley since college, and had been McKinley's second attorney general only five months at the time of the assassination.

At five feet five Roosevelt called him his little "sawed-off cherub." He was pale with a balding pate of thinning black hair, wore pearl cufflinks and a pearl in his tie, and his crossed eyes gave the impression that "Sleepy Phil," as he was known, was looking past you. It was a misleading nickname. Critics expected him to be a shill for Morgan, Rockefeller, and the trusts but Knox turned out to be a political opportunist who could argue just about any case for just about any client. He leapt smoothly from conservative McKinley to activist Roosevelt. There had been a warning sign even when he joined McKinley: he told him he felt he would have to test the Sherman act in the courts because he believed it was being violated. Roosevelt and Knox may have heard rumors of Northern Securities, but when the announcement came it gave even more import to the trust section of the draft, which Roosevelt shared with his cabinet eight days later.

The entire draft was pure Roosevelt: he dictated or wrote by hand all 25,000 words of it himself. Throughout November the powers of the Senate from his own party—Hanna of Ohio, Platt of Connecticut, Allison of Iowa, Spooner of Wisconsin, and Aldrich of Rhode Island (Morgan man through and through)—asked him to soften or gut passages in the trust section.

Sentence by sentence he gave some ground; deleting, for example, a section condemning price fixing and preferential rebates, but he protected the core and tone of his message. Mark Hanna urged him not to make the trust section so prominent. Roosevelt ignored him. He presented his message to Congress and the American people on December 3.

Unlike Harriman and Hill, who came from poor families and had little formal education, the Theodore Roosevelt who wrote the message came from privileged wealth. He was privately tutored and went to Harvard. He had never run a business and had inherited a small fortune ($187,500) from his parents, squandering almost half of it on North Dakota cattle ranching. He was nearly incompetent in managing his own money, had little interest in balance sheets, and had spent thirteen of his twenty-one years after college as a government employee and the other eight years writing and traveling.

At age twenty-four as a first-term member of the New York Assembly in 1882, where many of his colleagues seemed to be on the take, his first exposure to a capitalist of note was Jay Gould, whom he considered a member of the "wealthy criminal class." Roosevelt also, however, was a realist. He paid homage to private capital deserving the opportunity to earn a "return sufficiently liberal to cover all risks." The phrase "wealthy criminal class," however, became his banner and he used variations of it the rest of his political career. Twenty-five years later it became "malefactors of great wealth." Thirty-one years later it became "tyranny of plutocracy." Life for Roosevelt was all a morality play; he was unable to look past the messy flaws of Wall Street to see that buy and sell orders were an essential part of the machinery of capitalism, efficiently directing capital to its most productive use. To him, Harriman was just another Jay Gould.

Roosevelt could patronize the ultrawealthy such as Morgan and Hill but he nursed a personal grudge. Despite their philanthropy and sincere desire for the common good (they could say "we go up or down together" and mean it just as well as he could) he stereotyped them as leading "luxurious, grossly material" lives. He couldn't resist making it his business to judge how they spent their money. Morgan had encouraged him with his conspicuous buying of some of Europe's finest art. Deep down, Roosevelt felt Morgan, Hill, Harriman, Schiff, and their ilk had enriched themselves at the expense of laborers. An instinctive redistributor, he wouldn't mind if there was some legal way to confiscate the money Morgan spent on art and put it into the pockets of railroad brakemen.

"I am simply unable to understand," Roosevelt wrote seven years later to British diplomat Cecil Spring-Rice, "the value placed by so many people upon great wealth. I very thoroughly understand the need of sufficient means to enable the man or woman to be comfortable; I also entirely understand the pleasure of having enough more than this so as to add certain luxuries . . . but when the last limit has been reached, then increase in wealth means but little." In his first Annual Message to Congress he was careful to say, "We draw the line against misconduct, not against wealth." Ultrawealth was something else. It always seemed to him to be ill-gotten. Hill saw just the opposite. "The consolidation of wealth . . . does not mean the hoarding of money," he wrote, "it means rather the effective organization of effort."

Roosevelt came of political age during the birth of the trusts. On the day before he took office as a New York assemblyman on January 3, 1882, John D. Rockefeller's attorney, Samuel Calvin Tate Dodd of Pennsylvania, created the first trust agreement in American business. It was an ingenious union of stockholders of forty Standard Oil companies with one name, one headquarters, one executive committee, and one stock, thus preventing each state in which the trust did business from taxing the company's property outside the state. The vague Sherman Anti-Trust Act of 1890 left it to the courts to decide what was restraint of trade. The Supreme Court handed down three rulings in the 1890s, none definitive. It ruled in 1895 that the American Sugar Refining Company, known as the "sugar trust," had not violated the Sherman act because its monopoly of manufacture in any one state was not monopoly of interstate commerce. Therefore, a trust wasn't necessarily a monopoly. It ruled that six independent pipe companies had conspired in secret to fix prices. It ruled that several railroads had contracted to maintain freight rates and thus had violated the Sherman act. None of these decisions dealt with a situation in which a holding company was created as a repository for the stock of two competing railroads that had not merged or conspired to fix prices.

During the twenty-six months Roosevelt governed the State of New York, America was awash in consolidations and combinations. There were 20 multimillion dollar industrial trusts in 1898; three years later there were 185. Then, just as Roosevelt prepared to take office as vice president under McKinley, along came Morgan's gigantic U.S. Steel. The trusts, their advocates said, were not a perversion of the word but a natural tendency of free markets to seek the greatest efficiency. Hadn't they helped ensure steady production and supply and an even level of prices? Hill and his peers often used a down-home metaphor. This tendency to combine was like the pioneers who "united to help build one another's houses, when they had a 'barn raising,' it was a combination. When the owner of land or implements of capital in any other form first entered into partnership with labour to create more wealth, it was a combination," and thus it also was with the union of many "disconnected and weak" railroads in "one orderly and efficient system." What could be more thoroughly American and "progressive," asked Stuyvesant Fish of the Illinois Central, than a combination? Didn't the thirteen colonies come together for protection and mutual benefit to form the United States as a combination of all interests? "It is not, as a rule, exorbitant rates of which the shipper complains, but discrimination," said Fish. "The small shipper believes the big shipper gets a lower rate than himself, and the big shipper is constantly trying to induce the railroads to break the law, because he believes some other big shipper has been getting an inside rate. With territorial combination it will be possible to maintain rates and treat all alike."

It was, however, not so much the amassing of great fortunes that annoyed Roosevelt and many Americans but the flaunting of it, the showy excess, the wasteful extravagance. Pulitzer's *New York Evening World* and the magazines of the left were filled with it. The stock market gambling. The enormous mansions and country estates. The extravagant balls. The yachts and horse farms. The economist Thorstein Veblen, who grew up on a farm in Hill's Minnesota before the railroad came, had caught it perfectly two years earlier with his "conspicuous consumption." Since the depression of the 1890s and growth of the trusts, a new genre of socialist propaganda had mushroomed: panic novels about Wall Street. A month after the Northern Pacific corner, for example, there appeared Frederick Upham Adams's *The Kidnapped Millionaires*, about a newspaper reporter who causes a financial panic by kidnapping three financial titans, one based on Morgan, then lecturing them about the inequities of capitalism. It was just the past April, while Harriman and Schiff were secretly buying shares of Northern Pacific, that Doubleday, Page was shipping to bookstores across the country young Frank Norris's *Octopus: A Story of California*, in which a character says, "If it is not a railroad trust, it is a sugar trust, or an oil trust, or an industrial trust, that exploits the People, *because the People allow it.*" To his credit, Roosevelt read it and privately found it so filled with overstatement that he associated it with those reformers who are "half charlatan and half fanatic."

Class warfare against wealthy railroad owners even infected the rulings of U.S. Supreme Court justices. Six years earlier, Justice Henry Billings Brown wrote the majority opinion denying Hill's Great Northern the right to take the first step in buying the reorganized Northern Pacific, which had just emerged from bankruptcy. "There are thought to be other dangers," wrote Justice Brown, "to the moral sense of the community incident to such great aggregations of wealth which, though indirect, are even more insidious in their influence, and have awakened feelings of hostility which have not failed to find expression in legislative acts."

The activist left also was gaining momentum in politics. It wasn't just Bryan in Nebraska. "Fighting Bob" La Follette, anti-railroad and anti–big business, had been elected governor of Wisconsin: "The railroad is a natural monopoly." Albert Cummins, a former railroad attorney campaigning for rigid rate controls, had been elected governor of Iowa: "I regard the consequences of monopoly or a substantial monopoly . . . as infinitely more disastrous than the consequences of foreign importation." Socialist Eugene Debs, whose union won a strike against Hill six years earlier, had attracted notice as a presidential candidate: "For as long as the working class is divided, the capitalists will be secure in their domination of the earth and the seas." The Congregational pastor Washington Gladden was preaching what he called the Social Gospel, advocating state control of railroads, telegraphs, street railways, gas companies, electric light companies, or any industry that was a virtual monopoly. South Dakota and Utah had gone radical, experimenting with initiative and referendum.

Just four days before Roosevelt's message to Congress, thirty-one-year-old Ray Stannard Baker, a young activist journalist, attacked Northern Securities in Collier's magazine. It will, he wrote, "regulate, if not control, most of the traffic, by land or sea, in the hemisphere between Chicago and China," and is "absolute dictator in its own territory, with monarchial powers in all matters relating to transportation." Wasn't it also part of a vast oligarchic conspiracy of Morgan, the Rockefellers, Vanderbilt, Harriman, Hill, Stillman, Baker, and the rest? Didn't they control all the railroads, steel, oil, and coal commodities, and the banks and insurance? Weren't they all mansion- and yacht-owning buddies frequenting country clubs and ocean liners, all with offices "a stone's throw of Wall Street"? Didn't they all "get together any pleasant afternoon and dictate the policies and rule the destinies of a full half or more of the banking, industrial, commercial, and transportation interests of this half of the world"? Perhaps they had even conspired to orchestrate the panic on May 9. When everyone was dumping stocks at low prices there had to be, said the

Chicago Daily News, "somebody with limitless resources" to buy them. Certainly it must be the "warring giants." Shouldn't they be prosecuted?

Roosevelt, with his fundamentalist view of good and evil, could distill and channel this fear of virtual monopolies, corporate bigness, and showy wealth. It was just like old times. Teddy was police commissioner of New York City again. Didn't the corporate world have its own version of brothels, corrupt cops, and gambling parlors? He was going to roam the streets during the night again with Jacob Riis or Richard Harding Davis and root them out. But, careful, this wasn't New York. He couldn't afford to drift too far left or he'd be with the socialists, lose the confidence of investors, and send the market into a tailspin for which he, not Morgan, would be blamed. As R. W. Apple Jr. so aptly put it years later, it was like trying to steer through the French Revolution between Robespierre and Louis XVI.

Roosevelt began the section on the trusts by blaming the speculators and the shorts for causing the Northern Pacific corner, precipitating a stock market panic in which the business world, he said, had lost its head, caused by "men who seek gains not by genuine work with head or hand but by gambling in any form . . . a source of menace not only to themselves but to others." He spoke of a "startling increase" in the "number of very large individual, and especially of very large corporate, fortunes." Some antagonism against this wealth, he said, had warrant.

He needed the financial support of large corporations if he wanted to be elected president in his own right in three years, so he noted the "captains of industry" who built the railroads and "have on the whole done great good to our people" and enabled the United States to begin assuming a "commanding position" in international trade. The last thing anyone should do is interfere with this progress in "rashness or ignorance" to cause "hatred and fear." What we need is "calm inquiry" and "sober self-restraint" not "crude or ill-considered legislation." And yet, there are "real and grave evils" that are in their "tendencies hurtful to the general welfare." One is "over-capitalization." By that he meant corporations that overestimate their fair market value, water their stock, pay out of dividends from the proceeds, incent speculation, and deceive investors. These were "crimes of cunning." There should be a law to empower government to supervise "combination and concentration" in industry, and if Congress won't pass a law then the Constitution should be amended to give the federal government that power.

Perkins and Bacon had asked him to delete a certain paragraph but, rightly, he refused:

> The first essential in determining how to deal with the great indus-
> trial combination is knowledge of the facts—publicity. In corpora-
> tions engaged in interstate business, the Government should have
> the right to inspect and examine the workings of the great corpo-
> rations engaged in interstate business . . . the Nation should . . . also
> assume power of supervision and regulation over all corporations
> doing an interstate business.

Hill and Morgan and all the sculptors of Northern Securities didn't fully realize it yet, but this was Roosevelt's Fort Sumter in his war against the trusts. It
echoed Roosevelt at the Minnesota State Fair the past September when he
had arrived at the St. Paul train station "alone and unattended." An assassin's
bullet had put an activist in the White House. He needed a perceived evil to
crusade against for election in 1904, and Hill and Morgan unwittingly had
handed it to him. Wall Street and Big Business had "doped" the people, as
Roosevelt put it to Otto Kahn years later, and "if you want to wake up a hundred million people, you've got to make a big and resounding noise."

⤐ 12 ⬳

A THUNDERBOLT OUT OF THE BLUE

It was the afternoon of Wednesday, February 19, 1902, and Hill was coughing and sneezing and ached all over. He had always been vulnerable to deep bronchial chest colds. Now he was in bed with a bad one and felt lousy. From his bedroom on the second floor of his 36,000-square-foot Richardson Romanesque hulk of red sandstone on Summit Avenue, he could look out over the snow-drifted Mississippi River Valley in St. Paul. He could imagine himself the seventeen-year-old boy leaning over the steamboat railing for his first view around the bend of the settlement of St. Paul when there was not a single railroad track in the Minnesota Territory.

The temperature dropped to three degrees overnight, and the two huge boilers in the basement, which could store fifty tons of coal, were coursing hot water through clanking cast-iron radiators throughout all four stories of his mansion. Crackling warmth came from the fireplace in Hill's bedroom, one of twenty-two in the mansion. It was like a "feudal fortress," with a skeleton of huge beams of steel that could withstand fire and tornadoes and a roof that could support five locomotives. To make him even grumpier he was, except for his servants, home alone. He and his wife Mary had been married thirty-five years, and despite all his railroad travel and long absences he had never gotten used to being away from her. He was a faithful sender of letters and reassuring telegrams, and never was happier than when his horse-drawn carriage bore him up the bluff to Summit Avenue and his mansion, or out to his country retreat and experimental farm of 5,500 acres at North Oaks. For Mary's part, there were few days in her diary when she didn't mention "Papa," where he was, how he was feeling, when he was coming home. He called her "Mother"; she was the only one who could manage him. He had just telegrammed her in New York the day before, trying to hide his illness: "All well here. How are you?" She telegrammed back to reassure him, "Good night comfortable day promised."

Now it was the middle of winter and not only were they apart but Mary was sick, too. She had almost fainted a few days earlier from a chest cold and was in bed at their suite at the Bolkenhayn Hotel overlooking Central Park Plaza in New York, which was buried under a foot of fresh snow. She would have to stay a day or two more to regain her strength and make sure the storm passed for her return home.

As he lay in bed Hill's mind probably roamed over railroad matters. While he was in New York most of November and December, Samuel Van Sant had been stirring up trouble for his own political benefit. He had been elected governor of Minnesota two years earlier by a margin of less than 1 percent of all votes, was up for reelection the next year, and had latched on to Northern Securities to demagogue against the "trusts." Four days after the holding company was formed Van Sant said it was "clearly in open violation of the plain interest and purpose of the law." Then he went around the state accusing Hill of robbery. A lot of good Hill's free pass to Van Sant on the Great Northern for 1900 had done. Hill could not sit there and let Van Sant spread what Hill saw as lies. He wrote his son, Louis, and told him to "spend Forty or Fifty or Seventy-five thousand, if necessary, to good advantage" to get his side of the story out to editors and reporters. The *Saint Paul Globe,* which Hill owned and controlled, displayed on its front page a long piece with Hill's byline giving his view of the previous year's saga and why he had formed Northern Securities. Did Harriman want control of the Northern Pacific and Burlington because he wanted to benefit the economy of our Northwest and our trade with Asia? Of course not. What if we had sold out to Harriman and given him control of all the railroads from Canada to Mexico, would there have been some law against that? "Could we not legally," he wrote," put the money in our pockets and let the country learn what it was to be dominated by a parallel and competing railroad?"

Why, Hill asked,

did Governor Van Sant sit still from May to November, while a majority of the stock of the Northern Pacific was controlled by a parallel and competing railroad company, to which the law is clearly opposed, and wait until myself and friends have by our efforts and with our own money relieved the Northwest, not as a rival parallel or competing railroad, but doing what we clearly have the right to do as individuals working together for greater permanency and security as a financial corporation?

The State had sued on Tuesday, January 7, to dissolve Northern Securities, and a court decision on the lawsuit was expected that coming Monday, February 24. Hill searched for another venue to reach his constituents and chose a populist hotbed. Two days later he was in his private Great Northern car steaming 250 miles northwest across the snow-swept prairie to Fargo. It had been thirty-two years since he first saw the Red River Valley as a young steamboat man, when there was not a single house on the west side of the Red River for 200 miles to the Canadian border. He entered the three-story brick box called the Warner Opera House, its windows fogged from the breath and wooly sweat of four thousand farmers, businessmen, and politicians who watched him stride up the aisle at the Tri-State Grain and Stock Growers' convention. Sandwiched into an agenda including lectures on "Sheep on the Farm," "Farm Telephones," and "Shredded Corn," Hill took the podium in the afternoon.

In his low rasp and reading from a script he launched into an hour lecture on the economics of his business centered on his claim that, of the two great competing forces in American economic life, it was not competition but combination that had lowered railroad freight rates. This was laughable to many in his audience; "combination" to them was just another word for monopoly. He sounded like a Morgan puppet. But he persisted. There were far fewer railroads today than ten years ago, he said, because destructive rate wars and overbuilding had led inevitably to foreclosures, bankruptcies, and mergers. What had happened to rates during that time? Between 1890 and 1900 the number of tons carried one mile by railroads in the United States rose 120 percent. During that same time only 18 percent more track was built, railroad earnings rose less than 40 percent, and rates declined 80 percent. Today, he said, farmers can ship their grain from the Red River Valley to the Twin Cities or Duluth at rates 15 to 20 percent lower than farmers in the Des Moines Valley, and western Iowa can ship the same distance to Chicago, an area with many more railroad lines.

"Courts are open for the purpose of determining whether railway companies as carriers observe their obligations to the public, " he said. "The question of reasonableness of rates and service does not depend upon whether one man owns the capital stock of a railway or another, whether the capital stock is owned by ten men or one thousand, by persons or corporations." As for the Burlington, what if it didn't exist? What if the Great Northern and Northern Pacific got together and raised the money to build it? Would the states through which those rails ran be against it? Of course not! They would hail it!

A resolution had been passed in the morning at the Fargo convention to endorse Northern Securities, then a motion to reconsider it was adopted and a motion to expunge the endorsement was tabled. There was grumbling in the halls among Hill's opponents. Had he crafted the resolution in St. Paul and sent it to Fargo to try to rig an endorsement? He had sidestepped the most important question. What were the limits of combination? He left his audience as divided as he he'd found it.

Well, he had done what he could. He had no doubt the state lawsuit would be thrown out because the state lacked jurisdiction. The governors of Montana, Oregon, Idaho, Washington, and North Dakota were making noise, too, but not filing lawsuits on their own. And then there was a frivolous lawsuit, a time-consuming annoyance, against retiring the Northern Pacific preferred shares because it would require doubling the amount of common stock to use the proceeds of the sale of it to pay for retiring the preferred. He had just spent all of the day before and much of the day before that on the witness stand at the federal court building in St. Paul giving testimony in that case. It was a legal circus as far as he was concerned.

There also were those hearings the Interstate Commerce Commission held in a court room in the Monadnock Block in Chicago the previous month at which both he and Harriman testified. The ICC, prodded by Roosevelt, was probing for evidence of collusion in rates among the Hill and Harriman roads since they had appointed joint traffic managers, and even whether the principle of "community of interest" perhaps violated the Sherman Anti-Trust Act. Hill's lawyers had prepared him well and he did his best to dispel the allegations, but it was obvious the ICC was more aggressive under Roosevelt. When Harriman gave testimony he was a bit condescending, even reminding the commissioners he had a train to catch, an attitude that could get them all in trouble someday. The stock market had been quiet most of the day on February 19, as he lay in bed. Prices rose in the last hour of trading as call money rates stayed remarkably low despite rumors of higher outflows of gold abroad. Northern Securities was up a fraction on the so-called curb market. In New York, Morgan was preparing to welcome guests at a dinner party at his home at Madison and Thirty-Fourth.

The telephone rang in the Hill mansion. It was a message from his office downtown. Dateline, Washington.

> Within a very short time a bill will be filed by the United States to test the legality of the merger of the Northern Pacific and Great Northern Railway systems, through the instrumentality of the Northern Securities Company. In speaking of the matter to-day, Attorney General Knox said: "Some time ago the President requested an opinion as to the legality of this merger, and I have recently given him one to the effect that, in my judgment, it violates the provisions of the Sherman act of 1890, whereupon he directed that suitable action should be taken to have the question judicially determined. A bill in equity is now in course of preparation, which will ask that the merger effected through the exchange of shares of the Northern Securities Company for shares of the two railroad companies be dissolved, and such shares ordered re-exchanged to restore the stocks of the two railroad companies to their original holders. The two railroad companies, the Northern Securities Company, J. Pierpont Morgan, and James J. Hill, and their associates, stockholders in the two companies, will be the defendants in the bill. The district in which the proceedings will be instituted has not yet been determined. Most likely it will be in Minnesota.

Hill did not expect Northern Securities to go unchallenged, but this was a thunderbolt out of the blue. He had not been this stunned since last May 3 in New York when Schiff told him he thought he and Harriman had majority control of the Northern Pacific. He had misjudged Roosevelt. The dinner with him and Secretary Hay at the White House in November seemed to have gone well. Now he knew that was an illusion. Roosevelt disliked him from the start. There was no advance warning, not even a courtesy call. His mind raced. Morgan and his partners must have been blindsided. Mark Hanna, too. He remembered Hanna's warning before the assassination that if they formed the holding company McKinley might have to act against it simply to clarify what the Sherman act meant. Hill doubted that. McKinley had made only one statement about the trusts and didn't seem to have his heart in it. One historian later described McKinley as having "circled unconvincingly around the subject, like a worried man thinking out loud." Indeed, the past five years the Sherman act practically had been comatose. Knox's predecessor under

McKinley, the respected John W. Griggs, had declined every opportunity except one to try to enforce it.

But now they had called Roosevelt's bluff and he had called theirs. Legally, of course, it was Roosevelt's duty, just as he thought it his duty to enforce the Sunday liquor laws in New York when he was police commissioner. He had solemnly sworn to preserve, protect, and defend the Constitution. The Sherman act, for better or worse, was the law. Once Congress passed such an act then, constitutionally, it was as binding as if stated in the Constitution itself. It was his job to make sure it was constitutional and that it was enforced, and it couldn't be enforced unless its legal boundaries were clear.

The problem was Roosevelt had gone back on his word. Hadn't he said in his December 3 message to Congress that he needed the facts first? "The Government should have the right to inspect and examine the workings of the great corporations engaged in interstate business." Hadn't he ordered the ICC to investigate those "workings" (alleged rate collusion) in its hearings the past month? Now, all of a sudden, he had leap-frogged both the ICC and the State of Minnesota, deciding not to wait even five more days for a Minnesota court to rule on the state's lawsuit against Northern Securities. He had pounced on Northern Securities for spectacle value and political advantage. This would be great political theater: the government's first anti-trust suit against companies run by celebrities, preeminent public symbols of "big business." Morgan, Hill, Harriman, and Schiff had become deliciously vulnerable public targets, easy to demonize.

Hill must have sensed immediately that this was going to send the market into a tailspin the next morning. Whenever the lawsuit was filed it also would stop the flow of dividend payments to Northern Securities shareholders until the U.S. Supreme Court ruled. There was no doubt it had to go all the way to the high court. Morgan and George Perkins and Steele wouldn't have the stomach to fight it. They would worry it could spill over and jeopardize U.S. Steel or Morgan's merger of British steamship companies. Likewise, Schiff would run for cover to avoid a public confrontation (bad for business) and Harriman had shown no ability whatsoever to persuade or influence any of his publics. Hill would have to fight this by himself to the last ditch, and other corporations might have to be drawn into the battle.

His thoughts may have went like this. What if this leads to the unwinding of all consolidations of competing lines? It could be chaos. Why are we being singled out? If Northern Securities violates the Sherman act then what about the New York Central's agreement with the Lake Shore and Michigan Central? What about the Pittsburgh, Fort Wayne, and the "Panhandle"? The Southern Railway's control of the Mobile & Ohio, the Jersey Central of the Reading? How about the Pennsy, which owns 40 percent of the Baltimore & Ohio, parallels it in many markets, and virtually operates it? Scores of others! If you want to go after an industry go after the anthracite coal monopoly in the East. They collude to fix prices *and* control the output. They've already raised coal prices so high that they certainly have enough surplus funds to raise the wages of their workers without raising the price of fuel for their customers one penny. Imagine the howl there would be if the Great Northern and Northern Pacific colluded to raise rates to oppress wheat farmers and then raised the price of bread!

How would we like to go back to the days when we thought the best way to get cheap gas was to have competing gas companies lay their mains in the same streets? What if we had alternate parallel lines for streetcars? Well, there were bound to be holes in the government case. The Great Northern and Northern Pacific had not merged. They were still two separate companies. They had been charging mostly identical rates for twenty years. Was that "restraint of trade?" Northern Securities had no operational control over them. The goal is to encourage both systems to compete against each other for business, learn from each other, and make the most efficient use of their capacity. Perhaps the Sherman act wasn't "anti-trust" at all but simply government's misguided way of protecting the incompetent from the efficient. If a "trust" was simply another word for a "corporation" then was the phrase "anti-trust" simply a way to smear all corporations?

Of course, Hill may have thought, Roosevelt and Knox didn't care for the facts, didn't care that the Northern Pacific and the Great Northern controlled rates on only about 3 percent of the total interstate traffic. The telegraph lines that paralleled the railroads all across the country were on the very same land as the railroads and nearly all the telegraph lines in the United States were controlled by two companies! They could pass all the laws they wanted, to prevent the merger of parallel or competing railroads. That wouldn't change the immutable laws of railroad economics. Parallel railroads were a waste of capital, mergers inevitable. Roosevelt's "big stick" would snap someday like a toothpick. England had showed the way, allowing the market to work its will. In 1847 it had 5,000 miles of tracks and several hundred independent, competing lines. Thirty years later it had 15,000 miles of track and six noncompeting lines. Even

George Stephenson, father of the English railways, had said when railways were infants, "Where combination is possible, competition is impossible."

Maybe Northern Securities could be dissolved as a New Jersey–based company and chartered in Canada or England. In their zeal to neutralize Harriman perhaps they had overstepped by housing a super majority of the stock of the Great Northern and Northern Pacific in Northern Securities. Maybe they should return half that stock to the original holders but give themselves a strong enough minority influence, in "community of interest" fashion, to check Harriman, and still keep control of the railroads' mineral rights. No, that would simply turn the clock back to early April and leave them vulnerable to another Harriman raid.

While Hill tossed and turned in bed, Morgan and his partners and lawyers met late into the night at Morgan's home. A banker close to Morgan (perhaps Baker) told one reporter, "The business of the country appears to be conducted in Washington now."

As Hill discovered the next day, Roosevelt and Knox indeed had kept a tight lid on the announcement. No one in his cabinet knew, certainly not Secretary of War Elihu Root, the former corporate attorney and only cabinet member with the courage to disagree openly with Roosevelt. One investor on Wall Street later asked Knox why he hadn't warned him. "There is," Knox replied, "no stock ticker in the Department of Justice."

The day before the announcement the sixty-three-year-old Hanna, leaning on his cane, and Postmaster General Henry W. Paine (named receiver of the bankrupt Northern Pacific in 1893) had met with Roosevelt on a variety of matters. As they were about to leave after breakfast and Hanna was heading back to New York, Roosevelt casually asked, "Mr. Hanna, what do you think about the Northern Securities Company?" Hanna, who owned shares of Northern Securities and privately had asked Hill if he could buy more, told Roosevelt he thought it was the best thing possible for the economy of the whole Northwest. An alarm should have rung in Hanna's politically wired brain as to why Roosevelt would ask that question, but it did not. The day after the announcement, Hanna was on a train from New York back to Washington. John W. Griggs, Knox's predecessor who already was representing Northern Securities for Hill, was sitting in the parlor car chatting with Hanna and soon realized Hanna had not seen the newspapers. "The government," he told Hanna, "has brought suit against the Northern Securities Company." For perhaps the only time in his life, Marcus Alonzo Hanna was speechless.

Roosevelt and Knox had struck at Morgan, Hill, Harriman, and Schiff with devastating legal precision and political purpose. They had chosen Northern Securities because, unlike U.S. Steel or Standard Oil, it was new and happened on Roosevelt's watch. Unlike sugar refining it was clearly interstate commerce. There was a compelling legal need to clarify the Sherman act: it was to be the first challenge of a railroad "merger" for restraining trade. The "whole question of control of the transportation industry," said the *Wall Street Journal*, "is up for decision not merely in the United States law courts, but in the great forum of public opinion."

Roosevelt wrote later, with his penchant for hyperbole, that he feared Northern Securities could be "the first step toward controlling the entire railway system of the country," and called Morgan and Hill the "representatives of privilege" who were trying "to profit from governmental impotence." Politically, Morgan and Hill inadvertently had given Roosevelt a gift from heaven: Northern Securities could be seen as affecting farmers and cattle ranchers across a large slice of the western United States, a most important swing vote in the 1904 presidential election.

Roosevelt long felt the pendulum had swung too far, that big business had become more powerful than the federal government. The colonies had revolted against the king, but now a new era of tyrants appeared to be seizing commerce. They could become, as Senator Sherman feared twelve years earlier, autocrats of trade. Some balance had to be restored. "The total absence of governmental control had led to a portentous growth of corporations," Roosevelt wrote in his autobiography twelve years later. "In no other country...was such power held by the men who had gained these fortunes...The power of the mighty industrial overlords of the country had increased by giant strides," and the government was practically impotent. "Of all forms of tyranny the least attractive and the most vulgar is the tyranny of mere wealth, the tyranny of plutocracy."

Knox later called events such as those of May 1901 "storm centers of financial disturbances of far-reaching consequences." The market panic was caused by gambling and overcapitalization, which Knox called "a fraud upon those who contribute the real capital." The irony was that Northern Securities and the government's lawsuit against it were both motivated by fear. Morgan and Hill created the holding company because they feared Harriman might raid the Northern Pacific again. Roosevelt and Knox sued to break it up because they feared a railroad oligarchy accountable to no one. Hearst's *Eve-*

ning Journal had even quoted Carnegie back in May blithely predicting that one day all "American railways will be of one interest . . . and one man can fix rates."

Hill was fighting mad. He was the only principal who went on record. "I am not aware that the Northern Securities Company exists in violation of the law," he said, "and I am sure nothing could be further from the minds of its officers . . . If they [the plaintiffs] do fight they will have their hands full, and will wish they had never been born before they get through." He had always been annoyed by Roosevelt's vanity but now he was getting to despise him. Roosevelt seemed to want to turn everything over to Congress and let it run the economy. Pretty soon Congress would be doing the business of the country instead of business. Let the people be responsible for their actions not Congress. If someone does something wrong, punish him. If he does something right, protect him.

Privately, a few weeks later in a letter to his longtime colleague Willis D. James, Hill said Roosevelt was "undoubtedly honest and desires to serve his country, but he is so vain and self-willed that he has no judgment," and was of those "political adventurers who have never done anything but pose and draw a salary." Roosevelt privately returned the favor: "He detests me, but I admire him," he said of Hill. "He will detest me much more before I have done with him." Roosevelt had a nasty habit of publicly slurring adversaries. A friend of Hill's departed the White House in a fury after Roosevelt told him he thought Hill was a "fat spider."

Hill, Morgan, Harriman, and Schiff, however, had missed the most important point. They misread the temper of the American people. Roosevelt, unlike McKinley who spent too much time the last campaign on his front porch watching the world go by, had been out on the hustings. He had seen how his message against the trusts had played at western venues such as the Minnesota State Fair, had heard the spontaneous roar that rose from the throats of farmers and ranchers. He sensed what most Americans feared and the railroad men didn't seem to get, the fear of an uncontrolled railroad oligarchy. Roosevelt felt his legal case was sound, but even if he lost he could win with the voters. Knox promised him they would win—stripped to its essence Northern Securities to him was merely a joint creation of two competing, parallel railroads. The harmony of "community of interest" now could be seen as "collusion of interest."

The news had knocked Morgan on his heels. During the dinner he was hosting at his mansion at 219 Madison Avenue that evening of February 19 he was called to the telephone and a reporter gave him the news. He returned to the dinner table with an expression of "appalled dismay." Roosevelt, he told his guests, hadn't done the honorable thing, hadn't given Morgan a chance to dissolve Northern Securities. Gentlemen, Morgan thought, don't act that way, especially those who profess to be Christian gentlemen. If they have a complaint they make it directly.

Morgan attorney Charles Steele was so shocked by the news he thought it a hoax, but the resilient George Perkins and the other Morgan partners sprang into action. To avoid a panic in the stock market, Morgan's brokers bought shares steadily throughout the morning after Knox's announcement. Prices rallied near the close with Northern Securities dropping only 4 percent. Huge wet flakes of snow began falling on New York, filling the streets with slush, prelude to a violent snowstorm moving across the entire Northeast. Morgan and Perkins decided they had to get to Washington as soon as possible to clear the air with Roosevelt. Why didn't Roosevelt and Knox just go ahead and sue rather than announce they were going to sue? Were two separate announcements crafted to get two headlines? Did they want to use the announcement as a public cudgel to force concessions from Morgan and Hill? Perkins departed on Thursday and met with Roosevelt the following day at the White House, searching for any signal that Roosevelt might change his mind. He found none. Roosevelt was not about to "go back" on what he proudly called his "Minneapolis speech." Perkins seemed to want him to mouth platitudes.

By nightfall Friday seven members of the House of Morgan, including Morgan himself, had arrived in Washington in a private railroad car. Their train pulled into the station in an ice storm that had risen out of the south from Cape Hatteras, severing all telephone and telegraph wires out of the city in all directions. Sleet and slush had turned the streets into running rivers, as ice clogged sewer openings. Also in town were members of a tight circle of Morgan's friends known as the Corsair Club, colleagues he entertained on his yacht in the summer and hosted gatherings for in the winter. They convened for a morose dinner with Morgan Friday evening in the large oak-paneled dining room of the Corcoran House, the Italianate landmark rented by New York Senator Chauncey Depew, on Lafayette Square three blocks north of the White House. The group included Hanna, William Rockefeller, A. J. Cassatt (head of the Pennsylvania Railroad), and Secretary of War Root who had the audacity that evening to encamp with Roosevelt's adversaries.

As they finished dinner the telephone rang. Roosevelt had invited them to the White House for a late-night courtesy call. In auto coaches and carriages they were driven past lamp-lit Lafayette Square through streams that had been streets, toward the glow of the White House. In they trooped from the snow slush, Morgan and Perkins and the rest of them. Not a word was mentioned with Roosevelt about Northern Securities, Depew told a reporter afterward, it was just a social call. Depew and everyone there knew better: they were being used. Roosevelt had staged the meeting to give the impression of dialogue. Morgan later spent the night fuming in his suite of rooms, decorated to his taste, which he owned at the Arlington Hotel on the Square, two doors from the Corcoran House. Perhaps he played two-deck, Miss Milligan solitaire, his "constant solace," which he liked to do when he needed to calm his nerves and bring order from chaos. Morgan penned an angry letter to Roosevelt that night but never sent it. One of his attorneys persuaded him it would just make things worse.

Perkins and Hanna were staying at the Arlington, too. They returned there from the White House and walked across the lobby of Turkish carpet, Aubusson tapestry, and oak chairs of olive mohair. Perkins turned to Hanna and asked why he hadn't warned him earlier in the week that the announcement of the lawsuit was coming. Hanna said he was just as surprised as anyone. How could that be, said Perkins, the president told me at the White House today he "consulted" you the day before the announcement. Now Hanna knew what Roosevelt meant by consulting.

The next morning Morgan returned secretly and alone to the White House. It was not to be a one on one. At Roosevelt's side for legal cover was Knox. Morgan asked why hadn't they just called him to work out their problems with the Northern Securities charter? The only account of this conversation is Roosevelt's:

ROOSEVELT: That is just what we did not want to do.

MORGAN. If we have done anything wrong, send your man [Knox] to my man [Stetson] and they can fix it up.

ROOSEVELT: That can't be done.

KNOX: We don't want to fix it up, we want to stop it. [crossed eyes looking past Morgan]

MORGAN: Are you going to attack my other interests, the Steel Trust and others?

ROOSEVELT: Certainly not—unless we find out that in any case they have done something that we regard as wrong.

Baker tried to reassure Hill with a telegram. "Our friends on the corner have been over there and had personal conference have entire matter well in hand." Not exactly. Morgan and Perkins returned to snowbound New York empty handed. Roosevelt and Knox had not given an inch. They didn't have to. Why should they? They held all the cards.

It had taken ten years to build the new Federal Building in St. Paul. Workers dug the square block hole in 1892 just as Hill's Great Northern issued bonds on Wall Street to reach Puget Sound. Then came the four-year depression. By the late 1890s the economy and the railroads had revived, and now with the boom this elegant symbol of federal authority had taken shape, a five-story French castle of gray granite. Seven weeks before its formal opening, at 5 p.m. Monday, March 10, 1902, the thirty-five-year-old U.S. district attorney for Minnesota, Milton Dwight Purdy, strode through the building's Syrian front arches carrying a sheaf of government documents, a public maneuver orchestrated by Knox for maximum publicity. He climbed four flights of marble stairs to room 408, and under a barrel-vaulted ceiling of stained glass he presented the papers to Walter H. Sanborn, chief judge of the Eighth Circuit Court of Appeals. "At the same time that you are instructed by wire to file the bill," Knox had coached Purdy, "instructions together with the bill itself will be made public in this city." Hill's city. Just blocks up river from his office.

The document read "The United States of America, complainant vs. the Northern Securities Company, the Great Northern Railway Company, the Northern Pacific Railway Company," and it listed Hill, Morgan, Bacon, Baker, and Lamont among the major defendants. Roosevelt had waffled a bit behind the scenes. He asked Knox if it was necessary to list Morgan as a defendant. He could leave Morgan out, said Knox, but then he wouldn't sign his name to the bill. He knew if he left Morgan out he'd be the laughingstock of the American legal community. Harriman was granted technical anonymity as an "associate stockholder," but the government later called him one of the "great triumvirate" that sought to create a monopoly "infinite in scope, perpetual in character." It accused the defendants of "contriving and intending unlawfully to monopolize or attempt to monopolize such trade or commerce, and contriving and intending unlawfully to restrain and prevent competition" so that the holding company promotes the interests of both the Northern Pacific and the Great Northern "at the expense of the public," creating "a monopoly of the interstate and foreign commerce."

Hill in New York said the suit was filled with "false allegations and maliciousness...When we get through with the charge against us its own father won't know it...We shall force the fighting, depend upon it; and the outcome will be in our favor." Early the following month Schiff met with Roosevelt at the White House to advocate for Northern Securities, but like Morgan and his partners he was granted a polite audience and nothing more. His argument was wholly unconvincing; Roosevelt could barely have kept a straight face. Schiff claimed if the courts struck down Northern Securities it could bring "distress and suffering upon the country." A month after meeting with Schiff, Roosevelt bragged in a letter to the writer Hamlin Garland that he had "taken down the fences of a very great and very arrogant corporation."

Perhaps the idea came from Attorney General Knox, perhaps from an impatient, accidental president two years away from the next election. The federal government's anti-trust lawsuit against Northern Securities could be tied up, entangled in legal maneuvering, for years in the courts. The longer it languished the more uncertainty there was about potential restraint of trade in America's largest industry, about the legality of railroad mergers and joint ownership of competing or parallel lines. Virtually the entire industry was soldered together through interlocking ownership and "community of interest." It was estimated some 80 percent of the nation's railroad miles were consolidated or leased or jointly owned by competing railroads. The largest investors in railroad securities were railroads themselves. If Northern Securities was against the law then what was legal? What was the boundary of anti-trust? The whole thing reminded Hill of the English nursery rhyme:

Oh, The grand old Duke of York,
He had ten thousand men;
He marched them up to the top of the hill,

And he marched them down again.
And when they were up, they were up,
And when they were down, they were down,
And when they were only half way up,
They were neither up nor down.

Half way up, neither up nor down, would not do for the railroads. Even the defendants in the lawsuit wanted clarity. "Capital all over the country is anxious to know its rights in the matter of railroad construction and operation," Morgan was quoted. "Railroad men want to know where they stand." So Knox and the president proposed that there be a special act of Congress to authorize an unprecedented fast-track process. Any cases of "general public importance" pending on the calendars of federal courts could be given precedence over other cases, bypass appeals, and be advanced on approval of the attorney general directly to the U.S. Supreme Court. It came to be called the "hurry-up" bill. For the railroads, it would clear the legal clouds. For Knox it would clarify the general principles of the Sherman act. For Roosevelt it would bring, he hoped, a victory in the courts just in time for the 1904 presidential election. It became law, with no debate in the House or Senate, on February 11, 1903.

On Tuesday evening, March 17, 1903, a train from Washington, D.C., carrying a contingent from the Justice Department—lawyers, private secretaries, stenographers with suitcases and satchels—eased into the blocks-long canopy of Union Station in St. Louis, converging point on the national compass for twenty-three railroads. It did more than just route trains, freight, and passengers, however; it was a symbol of America's unified, self-governing system of railroads, legalized by Congress since the Civil War. Shaped by market forces, it was uniform in the gauge of track, in classifying freight, in publishing competitive rates, in equipment, and in the "union" of depots.

Among the group whose steps echoed on the marble floors of the grand concourse was forty-one-year-old James Montgomery Beck, the brilliant, self-effacing assistant attorney general whom Philander Knox had chosen to present the government's case the next morning. Beck was the son of a music publisher who had wanted him to be a minister. He had no Ivy League credentials, had attended public schools, and was graduated from Moravian College in Bethlehem, Pennsylvania. During college he worked briefly as a clerk for the Philadelphia & Reading Railroad, studied law at night, and was admitted to the bar in 1884. He practiced in Philadelphia, became assistant U.S. attorney for eastern Pennsylvania, and joined the Justice Department in 1888. President McKinley appointed him assistant to the U.S. attorney general in 1900. This was his last government case; he had delayed his departure from the government to argue against Northern Securities. After the case, however, he was going over to the other side. He had accepted an offer, essentially, to defend the trusts by joining the law firm of Stillman's counsel, John William Sterling, who had helped hatch the Harriman–Schiff plot to seize the Northern Pacific.

The Justice Department's lawsuit had been filed in St. Paul, but now would be tried on the circuit in St. Louis. Heads turned in the crowded oval courtroom when Beck and his entourage strode in Wednesday morning. He had the look of a church mouse, with a high forehead and wry smile, almost cartoonish with his thick pince-nez and its gold chain.

Beck stood facing four federal circuit court judges empowered to hear the case and send their decision directly to the U.S. Supreme Court, bypassing appeals. All four had roots in the country of the Harriman and Hill railroads. Seventy-year-old Henry Clay Caldwell, who was raised on an Iowa farm, served in the Iowa House, and fought with the Third Iowa that took Little Rock in the Civil War, had been thirty-nine years as a judge. Fifty-eight-year-old Walter Henry Sanborn, raised on his ancestors' farm in New Hampshire, came to St. Paul in 1870 and became an alderman. He had been involved in more than four thousand cases in private practice, and had been on the circuit court eleven years. Fifty-one-year-old Amos Madden Thayer from upstate New York, a Union Army veteran, had practiced law in St. Louis and was appointed a circuit court judge in 1876. Forty-three-year-old William Van Devanter, native of Marion, Indiana, was chief justice of the Wyoming Territorial Court at age thirty and then an assistant attorney general in the Interior Department. He had hunted grizzlies in the Bighorn Mountains with Buffalo Bill Cody, and had joined the Eighth Circuit Court two months earlier as a Roosevelt appointee.

Beck, seated at the government's table, began his opening argument at 10:30 a.m. He enunciated every word and statistic so everyone in the crowded courtroom could hear him. He leaned forward, sometimes reading from his prepared argument, sometimes quoting figures and references from memory. There was a change when he rose to address the court; "the voice did not quaver, or grow husky." The government had a strong case but Beck brought it to life with his gift for rhythmic phrasing. "The safety of the people lies in

free competition." "Great aggregations of capital will be prevented from stifling competition." The law cannot afford to "sacrifice the substance for the
shadow." Statutes to prevent monopoly "will have become waste paper." It
was Beck who characterized Harriman as being one of "the great triumvirate"
seeking to impose, through a holding company chartered in New Jersey, a
monopoly whose powers are "Infinite in scope. Perpetual in character. Vested
in the hands of a few. By methods secret even to shareholders."

The words were instantly memorable and repeatable. They had cadence
and emotive force, forward movement, a classical ring.

> To suggest that competition is possible where competition is useless
> is an absurdity. And if this be not a restriction of trade, then no com-
> bination whereby competition is limited ever was. Transportation
> is commerce, and its vehicles are instrumentalities of commerce,
> and as such when engaged in inter-State trade are so fully within
> the scope of the Federal power that Congress may even regulate the
> form of brakes used in railway transportation and the States may not
> forbid the entrance into their borders. These inter-State railway sys-
> tems, therefore, are Federal instrumentalities, and their business is
> essentially inter-State commerce...The American people are both
> conservative and practical, and when they recognize that monopoly
> is beneficent and competition is an evil, they will repeal existing laws,
> and by positive legislation facilitate and legalize railroad monopoly.
> Until that time, which is likely to be the Greek kalends, the law should
> be fairly, fully, and impartially enforced, for it is everlastingly true
> that the imperative need of this country, both at the hands of capital
> and of labor, is not more law, but more obedience to law.

The judges concluded testimony Friday afternoon, March 20. They were not
expected to rule for six or seven weeks.

Only three weeks later, on Thursday, April 9, 1903, the *Teutonic* eased into the
White Star Line pier at West Tenth Street at 8:45 a.m. after a stomach-churn-
ing voyage from Liverpool. Hill and the fourth of his ten children, twenty-
nine-year-old Clara, were only too happy to stride down the gangplank after a
five-week vacation in London and Paris, including a private audience with the

Queen and the Princess of Wales, and a lunch with Prince Albert of Belgium. They went directly to their apartment at the Savoy, then to lunch. Morgan had booked passage to England for a week earlier but had decided to postpone his trip, perhaps because he felt a court decision was imminent, and was in his office at "the corner."

Roosevelt was incommunicado, hiking deep into Yellowstone Park with the wildlife writer John Burroughs and Major Biltcher a week into his fourteen-thousand mile tour of twenty-five states. The president was to visit 150 towns and cities and give two hundred speeches. He had given three of them six days earlier on a swing through Hill's backyard, back in the state where he gave his "big stick" speech two years before. Among those who welcomed him were two protagonists in the legal challenges of Hill's Northern Securities: Minnesota Governor Van Sant and Federal Judge Sanborn. Tumultuous crowds greeted Roosevelt in St. Paul and Minneapolis where he told an audience at the University Armory that "we are now in a condition of prosperity unparalleled not merely in our own history but in the history of any other nation. That prosperity is deep-rooted and stands on a firm basis." When he departed at 10:30 that night from Minneapolis for Sioux Falls he rode west as a guest on Hill's Great Northern. Now, deep in Yellowstone, it would take a detail of soldiers and scouts to track him down in an emergency.

The phone rang at the restaurant where Hill, his wife, and their daughter Clara were dining. It was a message for Hill from the Northern Securities office at 32 Liberty Street. A month earlier than expected Judges Thayer, Caldwell, Sanborn, and Devanter had announced their decision in *United States v. Northern Securities Company* and filed it at the Federal Building in St. Paul. They upheld the federal government on every claim and denied every claim of the defense. Northern Securities was an illegal combination in restraint of trade. It stifled competition between parallel and competing railroads by placing the management of the two systems under one control. Northern Securities "destroyed every motive for competition between the two roads engaged in interstate traffic which were natural competitors for business, by pooling the earnings of the two roads for the common benefit of the stockholders of both companies." The holding company amounted to an agreement between competing railroads "that confers the power to establish unreasonable rates and directly restrains commerce by placing obstacles in the way of free and unrestricted competition." The Great Northern and Northern Pacific had two separate, independent boards, "but so long as directors are chosen by stockholders the latter will necessarily dominate the former, and in a real sense determine all important corporate acts."

The judges declared that the words "'in restraint of trade or commerce' do not mean an unreasonable or partial restraint of trade or commerce, but ANY direct restraint thereof." In other words, one did not have to restrain trade to violate the Sherman act. All one had to do was gain the power to do so. Intent was enough. "While most disappointing to papa," wrote his wife Mary in her diary, "he takes it well." The reason perhaps was his ultimate faith in the earnings power of his systems, regardless of what the courts or markets did. Even if he had to unravel Northern Securities, he said, "control would still be in the same hands and values would not be affected one iota. The value is not in the form but in the property." To underscore this, a week later in the cold and high wind on a wharf in New London, Connecticut, he watched his wife Mary smash a bottle of wine (every drop, she said, fell over the ship "like a veil") against the bow of the *Minnesota* of the Great Northern steamship line. Made from iron ore mined on Hill's land in northeastern Minnesota, it was the largest ocean-going vessel in the world. It was six stories high with the capacity of a train seven miles long or 125 trains of twenty cars each; sixty-five feet longer and two and a half times heavier than the *Teutonic*.

A unanimous opinion against Northern Securities, however, was something few expected. It would be difficult to overturn. It surprised Hill, Morgan, and their lawyers, one of whom, Morgan's Charles Steele, always insisted on having every argument "copper-fastened." It may even have surprised Beck. He was quoted two days after the decision saying he agreed with Knox that the Sherman act should be amended to forbid only *unreasonable* restraint of trade. Hill couldn't hide his anger. "Mr. Hill's voice was tremulous with suppressed energy," wrote a reporter, "when, in the writer's presence a few days after the decision . . . he declared he would do as he would with his own, even though it made a criminal of him." No matter, said the judges, that the combination "might prove to be of inestimable value to the communities which these roads serve," it was still restraint of interstate trade.

The ruling puzzled Jeffersonians such as Harriman and Hill, raised to believe that commerce thrives best when "left most free to individual enterprise." Did this mean there were limits to the property an individual could own, never mind the use to which the property was put? "Stripped to its logical essence, this decision says that it is unlawful to attain any position of influence or power in interstate commerce," said the *American Monthly*, "because the position might at some time be harmfully exercised." Should one not own a razor because one might use it to murder? One of those who professed no surprise was Jacob Schiff, who said he thought it might be a blessing in disguise. "The American people have a particular faculty for adapting themselves to conditions as they exist," he said, "and in due time the effects and results of even the situation now created will wear off, and as a consequence of the inactivity and further liquidation which we are certain to have, money will, after a time, become plentiful."

News of the court's decision hit the floor of the New York Stock Exchange at 1:12 p.m., but the initial effect was muted. Shares of Northern Securities were sold only on the free-for-all "curb" market outside on Broad Street at Exchange Place in front of the Mills Building where small lots of a hundred shares or less were traded. It dropped quickly from 106⅛ to 102⅜ but rallied to close at 103½ ask to 104 bid. Some observers were suspicious of the pattern of trading. Great Northern preferred dropped ten for the day but Northern Securities, which had bounced up and down the past few days, opened strong that morning with high volume. Had there been a leak of the court's decision that prompted some shorts to bid it up in the morning and profit on the quick drop in the afternoon?

The market closed for Good Friday and Holy Saturday and opened Monday morning with panic selling. Hill and Harriman met separately several times during the day with Morgan, who, according to Hill, at first was of a mind not to appeal the ruling, fearing the fight might jeopardize U.S. Steel. The market recovered in the afternoon but railroad stocks were punished enough. Had you bought a certain basket of them at their highs in 1902 the market this Monday, April 13, 1903, would have humbled you: Reading -34 percent, Louisville & Nashville -29, Illinois Central -26, New York Central -24, Pennsylvania -22, Chicago, Milwaukee & St. Paul -20. It was the start of a long slide, including the failures of banks and businesses and the cut-back by railroads in orders of steel and iron. U.S. Steel common plunged to $10 a share and eliminated its dividend. The bottom didn't come until August 1904.

The Hill–Morgan attorneys worked nights and weekends, and a week later Northern Securities appealed to the U.S. Supreme Court alleging thirty-four points of error in the circuit court decision. They may have discovered at least two weaknesses in the circuit court ruling. First, the Great Northern and the Northern Pacific were parallel lines but were they competitors? Hill–Morgan had admitted to have working control of the Northern Pacific since

1896 in a "community of interest" fashion, and the two lines had brokered peace for at least a decade before that. How could the two lines suddenly be competitors within Northern Securities? Second, the circuit court hadn't proved that merely pooling the earnings of the two lines in a holding company automatically destroyed "every motive" for the two to compete against each other. The more Hill thought about it the more he was convinced he had a case. Stillman's attorney, John W. Sterling, with whom Hill had remained friends, encouraged him to appeal. His friend Tuck in Paris reassured him that those four judges out on the prairie who had ruled against him simply represented "the unreasoning clamour of the masses against capital." It will be a different story in Washington, said Tuck, where the justices will be "surrounded by a class of people—the U.S. Senators for instance—who will realize what peril the decision of the Lower Court, if carried further, may bring to their private fortunes." While the Hill–Morgan lawyers worked on the appeal, Morgan's Perkins was floating a plan to spend $25,000 to influence public opinion through the newspapers for some way to amend the Sherman act to allow for "reasonable" restraint of trade. The *Wall Street Journal* and its railroad specialist Thomas Woodlock, for one, seemed to have fallen under Roosevelt's spell, predicting the president would prevail in the Supreme Court.

In May both Harriman and Hill traveled west to inspect their lines. Hill went to Seattle with Bob Bacon, who was back from recuperating in France and spending his last few months with the Morgan firm. Harriman took the Union Pacific to California accompanied by his twenty-two-year-old daughter Mary. Near Evanston, Wyoming, on the return trip he suffered a severe attack of appendicitis and was rushed back to New York for an operation. After he came out of the ether on May 28 he sent a telegram to Hill assuring him he was in "fine shape." Harriman's health had begun a slow decline. Hill tried compassion, sending telegrams to Harriman: "take good care of yourself," "sincere hopes that everything will be well," and "most hearty congratulations for you and yours." It all dissolved, however, when Harriman went to Europe in August and, perhaps at Schiff's insistence, tried a charm offensive in separate meetings with Hill's backers Mount Stephen and Farrer. If the Supreme Court ordered Northern Securities dissolved Harriman knew Hill would persuade the board to pay out as everyone had paid in, pro rata, in both shares of Great Northern and Northern Pacific. Harriman wanted the distribution "in kind"; since he paid in only with Northern Pacific he thought he should receive back only Northern Pacific. It would not only be a larger pay out for him in market value but it also would wind the clock back to May 4, 1901, when he claimed a majority of the shares of all Northern Pacific stock.

Mount Stephen and Farrer each wrote Hill in late August telling him how impressed they were with Harriman, which annoyed Hill no end. Hill couldn't help himself and shot back to Mount Stephen: "Privately speaking, he has a reputation of being able to turn a very sharp corner where he thinks it to his interest to do so." Never mind that Hill was just as capable of the same. Schiff's junior partner, Otto Kahn, later claimed they "came to respect and admire each other." There is no evidence of it.

While Harriman was in Europe a court ruling, for what it was worth, finally went in Hill–Morgan's favor. Federal Judge William Lochren in St. Paul ruled Northern Securities did not violate the State of Minnesota's law against owning a competing, parallel line because it was an investment company not a railroad company, holding stock of the two railroads as an investment, with no control of their operations. Further, said Lochren in so many words, how can one be guilty of committing, or about to commit, "a highly penal offense" merely because it can be shown that one could make a lot of money by doing so or that one could make others do so?

Perhaps, thought Hill and Morgan, there was hope at the U.S. Supreme Court, after all.

⫸ **13** ⫷

GREAT CASES AND BAD LAW

The previous quarter century the railroad empire of James J. Hill had grown from 656 miles of track in central and western Minnesota in 1880 to 19,263 miles across sixteen states and territories, and included one of the world's largest fleets of ocean steamships on the Great Lakes and the Pacific. Its earnings had grown from just over a half million dollars in 1880 to $33.5 million in 1904. With every leap in scope, however, came more complexity, and with every new state a tangle of separate laws, with the advance through Indian nations in Montana, with the push to Puget Sound, with the increasing control of the Northern Pacific, with the purchase of the Burlington, with the tense negotiations with Harriman for his Northern Pacific stock, and now with the creation and defense of Northern Securities, the world's second largest company in market capital. Hill was forced to spend less time in the Northwest on the ground ("where the money was spent") with his engineers and brakemen and more time in New York where the money was spent on fees for a growing legion of lawyers to write and file briefs and petitions, argue cases, and deal with the Interstate Commerce Commission.

Then came the Justice Department's lawsuit against Northern Securities, and the lawyers—for Northern Securities, the Great Northern, the Northern Pacific, the Burlington, and J. P. Morgan—seemed to multiply exponentially. With judicial momentum against them, Hill and Morgan had to find a preeminent lawyer to argue their case before the highest court in the nation. Not since Dred Scott in 1857, perhaps, had Americans been so fascinated with a case before their highest court. Seven weeks after he lost at circuit court, Hill received a letter from Stillman's lawyer John Sterling who suggested Hill retain John Graver Johnson. Hill did not need much persuading. Many respected judges regarded Johnson "the greatest lawyer in the English-speaking world."

There was hardly a major case on property rights before the U.S. Supreme Court he had not argued. He had been counsel for Standard Oil, Amalgamated Copper, the Pennsylvania Railroad, the New York Central, the National Hardware Association, and U.S. Steel. For many years Morgan had not taken a single significant step in business without consulting him. He once told Morgan he had mastered one of Morgan's cases in fifteen minutes. Before deciding whether to proceed with a merger, a group of railroad men cabled him for counsel while he was on vacation in Norway. The response came immediately, "Merger possible. Conviction sure."

The son of a blacksmith, educated in Philadelphia public schools, Johnson memorized Shakespeare as a boy, and as a lawyer could recite legal citations by heart. Throughout his illustrious career of a half century he kept "the freshness of an amateur." He often undercharged clients, accepted small cases simply for the principles involved, and sometimes turned down compensation he considered excessive. He deliberately sought obscurity, never attended public dinners, gave speeches, or answered requests for his biography. His Who's Who simply read, "Johnson, John G., corporation lawyer. Address, Land Title Bldg., Philadelphia." He also, like Morgan, had a passion for art; his collection, which he apparently never bothered to have appraised, was considered one of the finest in private hands in the United States, brimming with works by Pesellino, Correggio, Botticelli, Crivelli, Carpaccio, Bellini, Signorelli, and Breughel. It was displayed throughout his home in Philadelphia in his quirky style, on the backs of doors, at the foot of his bed, even a few on the ceiling. Johnson had no appetite for public office, refusing offers from Garfield in 1881 and Cleveland a few years later to be nominated for the U.S. Supreme Court. He would have looked the part, though: bushy white eyebrows, white walrus mustache, thick white hair, noble chiseled features, slender of frame. There were reports he was McKinley's first choice to be U.S. attorney general before Knox accepted. He did, however, accept Hill's offer to argue for Northern Securities before the U.S. Supreme Court.

At 12:30 p.m. on Monday, December 14, 1903, John Graver Johnson strode into the chambers of the U.S. Supreme Court on the second floor of the north wing of the U.S. Capitol. This had been the chamber of the U.S. Senate for a half century, where Calhoun, Webster, and Clay debated, where the Missouri Compromise was shaped, where Congressman Brooks of South Carolina caned Senator Sumner unconscious in a feud over abolition. Every upholstered seat of red velvet was occupied; it was standing room only behind the area reserved for members of the bar. In the semicircle chamber beneath an elaborate coffered white ceiling with gold leaf, Johnson faced the justices seated in their black robes behind a mahogany rail. He began by challenging the circuit court's decision that simply having the power to restrain trade, as opposed to using that power, violated the Sherman act.

Pacing the chamber, swinging his glasses on the end of their string, raising hands above his head to make a point, he framed his argument with six propositions. First, there was no agreement, contract, combination, or conspiracy in Northern Securities to restrain competition. Second, the Great Northern and the Northern Pacific competed against each other only somewhat. About three-fourths of the business of each was noncompetitive "because it originates or is consigned to a point or points on the line of one, not reached by the other. About twenty-two percent, nominally competitive, can be transported by other systems." If there was concerted action between the Great Northern and Northern Pacific then that would merely persuade customers to give their business to their competitors. They had combined to protect themselves to compete more effectively for the public advantage against a rival of a greater scale. Third, if Northern Securities violated the Sherman act then any agreement among any number of persons also would violate the act. Fourth, it was not illegal under the Sherman act for an entity to acquire two competing companies. Fifth, the act did not forbid the acquiring and holding of such shares. Sixth, if the Sherman act forbade such ownership then the act itself was unconstitutional. "You therefore are confronted," said Johnson,

> not with a proposition where persons conducting trade agree with one another for restraint of trade, but by a case where persons sell their property to another. And where has that ever been decided in a Federal court? Where is there a case in which it was ever held that bona fide acquisition or ownership of a property is a contract, combination, or conspiracy in restraint of trade?

Their acquisition of the Burlington enabled the Great Northern and the Northern Pacific to lower rates on westbound trains to ensure growing trade with China and Japan, and thus was "one of those bold enterprises by which at the beginning of the present century and the close of the last Americans carried American trade to the furthest corners of the World." The three railroads, working in concert, now could ship flour from the Mississippi Valley to China, 2,000 miles by rail and 5,700 by water, for eighty cents a barrel and fifty-five cents a barrel eastbound. After the Northern Pacific raid, he argued, "What was to be done? Remain quiet and allow these people who were waiting like the fox under the tree for something to drop, and let them have the prize, or to protect their alliance?"

The problem with the Sherman act was its lack of clarity; it did not distinguish between reasonable and unreasonable restraint of trade. "We have been taught to believe that it was the greatest injustice towards the common people of old Rome when the laws they were commanded to obey, under Caligula, were written in small characters, and hung upon high pillars, thus more effectually to ensnare the people," said Johnson.

> How much advantage may we justly claim over the old Roman, if our criminal laws are so obscurely written that one cannot tell when he is violating them?...If this court is embarrassed as to the true meaning of the Act, it will not legislate...It was the duty of Congress to put its intent in unequivocal language, and if its intent was to itself unknown...there can be no conviction...You may strike down this corporation, and undoubtedly you will strike it down if you find that its existence is in violation of the law, even though in so doing you destroy a commerce of magnitude and almost beyond our powers of imagination in the future.

Several critics called John Graver Johnson's defense of Northern Securities that day the finest argument they had ever heard before the U.S. Supreme Court. His fee for the case was said to be the largest ever paid up to that time for one man for legal services in the United States: $500,000. Even at that steep price James J. Hill and J. P. Morgan may have gotten their money's worth.

At 10 a.m., Monday, March 14, 1904, shares of Northern Securities opened on the curb market on Broad Street in at 84⅞ and by noon rose to 86. At that hour, the chambers of the U.S. Supreme Court were filled again. Northern Securities was on the calendar. Attorney General Knox, who seldom attended sessions, and Secretary of War Taft were in the first row with Solicitor General Henry

Hoyt. Nearby were the influential Republican senators John Coit Spooner and Henry Cabot Lodge and many other members of the Senate and House.

Some two dozen reporters stood in the back, notepads ready. "Oyez, oyez!" A rustle of black robes: Chief Justice Melville Fuller and Associate Justices John M. Harlan, David J. Brewer, Henry R. Brown, Edward D. White, Rufus W. Peckham, Joseph McKenna, Oliver Wendell Holmes Jr., and William R. Day. Justice Harlan shuffled a tall stack of papers in front of him and then announced "Case Number 277." *Northern Securities Company v. United States*, 193 U.S. 197. It took him about an hour to read the majority opinion from his printed copy of thirty pages. After some fifteen minutes reciting the Sherman act and stating the facts of the case he read the words that sent the reporters running for the telephones and telegraph, "In our judgment, the evidence fully sustains the material allegations of the bill, and shows a violation of the act of Congress."

The Associated Press moved the first bulletin: "NORTHERN SECURITIES DECISION AFFIRMED." Tickers spooled out the news at around 12:30 p.m. in brokerage and banking offices, at "the corner" at 23 Wall Street, at Harriman's office in the Equitable Life Building, in Schiff's office at 27 Pine, at Hill's offices of Northern Securities at 26 Liberty Street, and at dusk in London, Paris, Berlin, Frankfurt, and Amsterdam. The stock market lost a half a point, but ten minutes later, in spite of Harlan's words, it rallied sharply, perhaps because the shorts were covering their positions. Northern Securities began rising; maybe because a decision against the company already was "baked in" to the opening price. It rose to 97¼ and then with each decisive remark by Harlan against the merger it began dropping close to 85 by the end of trading.

"The mere existence of such a combination," said Harlan in his "strong, measured" voice, "and the power acquired by the holding company as trustee for the combination, constitute a menace to, and a restraint upon, that freedom of commerce which Congress intended to recognize and protect, and which the public is entitled to have protected." Just as the lower court had ruled, Northern Securities hadn't done anything wrong, but it might and that was enough. "Many persons, we may judicially know, of wisdom, experience and learning, believe that such a rule is more necessary in these days of enormous wealth than it ever was in any former period of our history; indeed, that the time has come when the public needs to be protected against the exactions for corporations wielding the power which attends the possession of unlimited capital." What prevented Northern Securities from obtaining "the absolute control throughout the entire country of rates for passengers and freight beyond the power of Congress to protect the public against their exactions?...A condition of utter helplessness, so far as the protection of the public against such combinations is concerned. The purpose of the combination was concealed under very general words that gave no clue to the real purpose of those who brought about the organization of the Securities Company...The freedom of interstate and international commerce shall not be obstructed or disturbed by any combination, conspiracy or monopoly which will restrain such commerce, by preventing the free operation of competition among interstate carriers engaged in the transportation of freight and passengers." The view that Northern Securities acquired the stock of the companies simply as an investment "is wholly fallacious...all the stock it held or acquired in the constituent companies was acquired and held to be used in suppressing competition between the companies." Northern Securities could not hide behind a state charter, especially a New Jersey one, to avoid the control of Congress.

Justices McKenna, Brown, Day, and Brewer joined Harlan in the majority. The swing vote in the majority came from the moderate conservative whom both Roosevelt and Hill assumed would vote against the government: David Josiah Brewer, son of Christian missionaries and educated at Yale, with fourteen years on the Kansas Supreme Court, six on the Federal Circuit Court, and fourteen on the Supreme Court. He filed a concurring opinion with a dissent tucked inside, saying the majority "went too far." He feared "the broad and sweeping language" of the majority opinion "might tend to unsettle legitimate business enterprises, stifle or retard wholesome business activities." He was "unable to assent to much that is said in the opinion just announced" because the "ruling should have been that the contracts presented were in themselves unreasonable restraints of interstate trade, and therefore within the scope of the act. Congress did not intend by the act to reach and destroy those minor contracts in partial restraint of trade which the long course of decisions at common law had affirmed were reasonable and ought to be upheld."

Assuming that freedom of action is "among the inalienable rights of every citizen" then Hill "could not by any act of Congress be deprived of the right of investing his surplus means in the purchase of stock of the Northern Pacific Railway Company...But no such investment by a single individual of his means is presented" in this suit. However, said Brewer, Northern Securities still was for him "an unreasonable combination in restraint of interstate commerce."

The full dissents were just as vigorous. The amicable, portly Justice Edward Douglass White, the Jesuit-educated son of a Louisiana governor, was a conservative Democrat and a former U.S. senator. Ten years on the court, he was a known "defender of the conservative faith," an advocate for clear boundaries between the authority of the federal and state governments. His robust, detailed dissent ran almost as many pages as Harlan's majority opinion. The principles laid down in the majority opinion, he said, were "destructive of government, destructive of human liberty, and destructive of every principle upon which organized society depends." The ownership of "stock in a State corporation cannot be said to be in any sense traffic between the States or intercourse between them." It is one thing for Congress to regulate the "exercise of interstate commerce," but quite another for it to "regulate the ownership and possession of property." What of the "farmer sowing his crops"? Could he be "limited to a certain production because overproduction would give power to affect commerce"? What of the individual who wanted to acquire a large amount of property? Could Congress regulate that because it might affect interstate commerce? What of the "wage-earner organized to better his condition"? What if Congress was to forbid labor unions because they affected interstate commerce"? We then could have a government "endowed with the arbitrary power to disregard the great guaranty of life, liberty and property and every other safeguard upon which organized civil society depends." The government has no authority to "limit the character and quantity of property which may be acquired or owned." The mere buying and owning of property was not interstate commerce.

It was the courageous, eloquent dissent of Justice Oliver Wendell Holmes Jr., however, that defined the moment, deprived Roosevelt and Knox of a decisive victory, and narrowed the application of the verdict. Harvard educated and a Civil War veteran, he had served on the Massachusetts Supreme Court for twenty years, including the last three as chief justice before Roosevelt nominated him to the U.S. Supreme Court in December 1902. His white handlebar mustache had a wingspan almost ear to ear. He was known as a forceful, super-literate, courageous jurist, just the kind Roosevelt thought would stand up to the big railroads. Roosevelt had called him "one of the most interesting men I have ever met," and "our kind right through." He even had been an overnight guest at Roosevelt's Sagamore Hill home before his appointment, and throughout 1903 was a frequent informal visitor at the White House. This day, however, their paths diverged. It was Holmes's first dissent as a Supreme Court justice and has been called one of his masterpieces, opening with his eloquent preamble, "Great cases like hard cases make bad law." Thus began his reputation as "The Great Dissenter" and, ultimately, the most famous U.S. Supreme Court justice of the century.

Northern Securities immediately became the most-discussed legal case of its time, not just because of Holmes's elegant dissent but because it addressed the moral right of owning property and the question of whether great concentrations of power are evil in and of themselves. That fear of great concentrations of power, as Hill's biographer Albro Martin wrote, "triumphed over evidence that great power had been greatly used." Roosevelt always insisted he wanted to use the power of government to punish corporations for their conduct not their size. Northern Securities, however, didn't have any conduct to punish. It merely existed. Holmes believed Roosevelt was perverting the judicial process for political advantage. That was why, in his dissent, he referred cynically to Roosevelt's lawsuit as an "accident of overwhelming interest." Reading between the lines of his dissent, he seemed to be telling his colleagues on the bench that Roosevelt had tricked them into letting their disdain for Morgan and Hill cloud their judicial fairness. In a private letter after Roosevelt's death he called him "a shrewd and I think pretty unscrupulous politician."

With four dissenters and with Brewer concurring with the majority but "unable to assent to much that is said in the opinion," the verdict, as someone quipped, was not really 5 to 4 against Northern Securities. It was more like $4\frac{5}{8}$ to $4\frac{3}{8}$. Roosevelt fumed over Holmes's dissent. "I could," he said, "carve out of a banana a judge with more backbone than that." Holmes dined at the White House two weeks later with frosty courtesy.

What counted for Roosevelt, however, was the value of the headlines for the election just eight months away, not so much the legal victory but a symbolic "moral" victory over his malevolent adversaries who made up "the wealthy criminal class." He wanted to show Washington was sovereign over New York, even if the ruling didn't change the landscape of ownership one iota. One Republican said the Supreme Court "has practically re-nominated Roosevelt . . . and all but insured his re-election."

It was now 2:45 p.m. and the court had dispensed with Northern Securities. Rumors swept the floor of the Exchange just before closing that the verdict could mean the dissolving of other railroad mergers. There was heavy selling of Union Pacific, the Pennsy, and the B&O, but not enough to dent prices. Hill wouldn't see the full text of the opinions for at least a day. He spent all afternoon at the company's offices in the Mutual Life Insurance building on Liberty Street with his lawyers, financier Kennedy, and Northern Pacific's

Lamont, and the next day he met with John Graver Johnson, Morgan's lawyer Stetson, and Harriman's lawyer Robert S. Lovett.

Hill tried to downplay the ruling. People were making a mountain out of a molehill, he said, when there wasn't even a molehill. The properties are still there, he said, in as good a shape as ever. "What are you going to do now, Mr. Hill?" a reporter asked. "Well," he replied, "I've still got the roads haven't I?" The decision would do nothing to change the Hill–Morgan control of the roads, nothing to change the "community of interest" between them, nothing to change the level of competition between them that John Graver Johnson had described in his argument to the court in December. Two certificates of stock will be issued instead of one, said Hill, "they are printed in different colors and that is the main difference."

Beneath the surface, however, the stress was taking its toll, and it didn't take much to light the fuse of his temper. A reporter from the *New York Evening World* ignored the warning of Hill's secretary and waltzed into Hill's office to ask him some questions. He described Hill pacing, screaming, and shaking his fist: "I am tired of this thing. I do not want to talk about it. I have not read the decision yet. Two-thirds of the reports are incorrect. I will hire a room. I will hire a man. He can tell you what he pleases. He can take all of you reporters and keep you all day. You can have a machine made to write all the stories you want. You can use the solar system. You can get your news from the moon. I say from the moon by the solar system."

In Minnesota, Governor Van Sant was jubilant. The decision, he said, "means more to the people of our country than any event since the great civil war." Roosevelt knew he had to tack right to avoid alienating business capital. "On wan hand I wud stamp thim [the trusts] underher fut," as Finley Peter Dunne imagined him thinking, "on th' other hand not so fast." There was no ticker in the Justice Department, as Knox had said, but he still kept a close watch on the market and on the flow of gold, because it still backed the currency. "Government does not intend to run amuck," said Knox, in the wholesale prosecution of combinations. He quoted someone he called "one of the best-known railroad presidents in the United States" who had said the court's decision "is sound law, good sense, and for the advantage of all legitimate interests and for the country's welfare; and it voices the judgment of probably nine-tenths of the most conservative businesses of the country . . . the danger of uncontrolled personal power in railway management has been averted."

The source of the quote was not a disinterested party but rather the Morgan adversary John Skelton Williams, forced to resign the previous December as head of the Seaboard Air Line Railroad. The company had fallen behind on bank loans after expanding too quickly trying to compete against Morgan's Southern Railway System and Henry Walters's Atlantic Coast Line Railroad, financed by Morgan. With his "will not run amuck" comment Knox tried to quell the witch hunt of corporate America, but it was too late. It was open season on big railroads for editors, politicians, and regulators. The newspapers wanted blood, none more so than the *New York Times*. "Nothing but the most contemptible hypocrisy and cowardice can now restrain the Administration from letting loose all the dogs of war upon the guilty restrainers of trade," said the *Times*. "Only by planting his feet upon the wreck of fifty great railroad corporations will [Roosevelt's] reputation as an honest, disinterested, and fearless Executive be secure."

Roosevelt seemed unperturbed. He had become enamored, like Harriman, with jiu-jitsu. He was taking lessons twice a week for an hour and a half in the evening at the White House to learn the martial art from Japan, using the energy of the attacker against him through holds, take-downs, and joint locks. No weapons allowed. Not even a big stick. Jiu-jitsu, Roosevelt wrote his son Kermit, is "really meant for practice in killing or disabling our adversary." He learned of the ancient rite through an American businessman who had brought Japanese jiu-jitsu experts to the United States. The businessman happened to be the son-in-law of James J. Hill.

There were only two ways to unscramble the omelet of Northern Securities. Hill and Morgan, as expected, chose the one that would protect their control of all their properties, giving all those who paid in a pro-rata distribution of shares of both Great Northern and Northern Pacific. Schiff, who could not resist playing mediator, tried one last time and failed to help Harriman and Hill reconcile their differences and head off another court fight. One could not blame Harriman; Northern Pacific had risen relatively higher in market value than Great Northern since November 13, 1901, and he would have, as a result, received far more dollar value for the exchange if he received only Northern Pacific. Schiff and Stillman, as always, were there to help him make money. Harriman had deposited his Northern Securities stock in a trust company, issued and sold bonds against them as collateral, and reaped the interest that the Northern Securities stock would have paid in dividends.

Eight days after the Supreme Court ruling, the Northern Securities board, with Harriman as lone dissenter, approved a pro-rata distribution, offering $39.27 in Northern Pacific stock and $30.17 in Great Northern stock for each share of Northern Securities they surrendered. Back they went to court. Harriman sued in early April to stop it. Northern Securities hadn't been allowed to pay a dividend in ten months, the stockholders were getting antsy, and now Harriman's lawsuit would keep the faucet off even longer. Hill was enraged. He somehow got the impression from Harriman that he could live with a pro-rata distribution, but then went back on his word. "As a piece of conscious lying it is a rare effort," Hill wrote to Mount Stephen. "I would not, under any circumstances, be associated with them in any business. All they want to make them crooked is an opportunity to cheat someone." By "them" he also meant Stillman and William A. Rockefeller, whom he suspected were behind the curtain. In July, Stillman accompanied Harriman to London for return meetings with Hill's allies Gaspard Farrer and Mount Stephen, who told Hill he saw in Harriman a "tired worn look" but also tenacity. "We do not believe he is raising this trouble from vanity or greed but he is determined to safeguard what he has, and he will miss no opportunity to fight you on the present issue, and oppose you in all your future moves until that object is obtained."

On the populist crest of his Northern Securities victory, which he later called "one of the greatest achievements of my administration," Roosevelt was elected president on November 8, 1904, in a landslide over the Democratic candidate, the lackluster Judge Alton B. Parker, carrying thirty-three of forty-five states. Roosevelt had kept his pipeline open to the "malefactors of wealth." Harriman, Morgan (and his partners), Stillman, Gould, Henry Clay Frick, and H. H. Rogers of Standard Oil were among his largest campaign contributors. Hill, and Morgan's banking ally, George F. Baker, squandered generously on Parker's lost cause. The following January, a federal circuit court in Philadelphia ruled in favor of Northern Securities, defended by former Roosevelt cabinet member Elihu Root, and against Harriman. On March 6, 1905, the Supreme Court upheld the decision unanimously. Schiff sent Hill a note of congratulations. Hill was in no mood to celebrate. "I do not agree with you that the fight had been a fair one," he replied. "I think it was the foulest and most unnecessary fight that I have ever known."

EPILOGUE: THE LAST CORNER

After the U.S. Supreme Court broke up Northern Securities James J. Hill said, "I've still got the railroads, haven't I?" It was true, he did, and they were as profitable as ever, for the time being at least. The court's decision, in a way, changed nothing; it had about as much effect, said one writer to Hill, as a straw of wheat in front of a train. For at least six years before it overturned Northern Securities, Hill–Morgan had been managing the Northern Pacific in concert with the Great Northern as if they were one. Nothing in the court's ruling changed that.

Now, however, there were other forces gathering to threaten, weaken, and marginalize the railroad industry that Hill and Harriman had mobilized so much private capital to help build. Energized by Roosevelt's narrow Supreme Court victory, "progressive" politicians, who really were bureaucratic central planners and distorters of markets in disguise, embarked on what turned out to be a half-century stranglehold on the railroads, which, after all, were "federal instrumentalities," state-chartered, and deemed to be common carriers, in effect, public highways. They showered subsidies of public money on railroads' competitors and deprived the railroads of their ability to decide how much they could charge for their service.

Two years after the Northern Securities decision, Congress through the Hepburn Act, with Roosevelt's vigorous support, gave the Interstate Commerce Commission the power to set maximum rates for railroads, thus amounting to government-authorized price fixing. Four years later, through the Mann-Elkins Act, Congress forbade any discrimination in pricing between long and short hauls and required railroads to prove a rate was reasonable, the first time the government targeted one industry for price controls in peacetime, and it did so as prices were rising in virtually every other industry. Ten years later, the Panama Canal Act forbade any ship owned by a railroad from using the canal. World War I gave the government an excuse to federalize the railroads. After the war ended it briefly considered nationalizing them, but instead chose even more restrictive federal controls.

The Transportation Act of 1920 essentially overturned the Supreme Court's Northern Securities decision by pretending to encourage combinations. There was one catch: one railroad could buy another but they couldn't merge. What is the economic value, one might ask, of a merger if 1 plus 1 equals only 2? The act also allowed the federal government to further distort market forces and prop up weak competitors by socializing earnings. The government could compute the "excess" profits of the most efficient railroads over their statutory maximum rate of return, confiscate some of that profit and give it to weaker, poorly managed railroads. Six months after the act became law, the Interstate Commerce Commission hired a railroad economist and anthropologist from Harvard, William Zebina Ripley, to recommend a restructuring of the industry into a central planner's Xanadu that would keep rates uniform and revenues about equal.

Ripley, who had never worked for a railroad, proposed grouping all the nation's major railroads into twenty-one systems. He wanted to break up the Hill roads, making the Burlington and the Northern Pacific one system and grouping the Great Northern with one of Ginx's babies, the Rockefellers's sickly Chicago, Milwaukee, St. Paul & Pacific. The Great Northern and the Northern Pacific argued that their "community of interest" had worked very well the past three decades, that uniting their management and operations would save $10 million a year, and that 98 percent of their freight traffic did not involve competition between the two lines, anyway. That made too much economic sense and the ICC commissioners ignored it. It was best that Hill did not live to see this. The sight of a Harvard professor and eleven bureaucrats in Washington trying to restructure the industry would have killed him. Fortunately, the Ripley plan went nowhere.

Five years later, in 1925, the Great Northern's Ralph Budd forced the matter. An Iowa farm boy who studied civil engineering, he had worked for three railroads, joined the Great Northern in 1901, was groomed by Hill to be president, and was a pall bearer at Hill's funeral. He wanted to merge the Great Northern and the Northern Pacific into a new entity to be incorporated in Delaware called the Great Northern Pacific Railway Company, leaving the Burlington as its separately owned and operated subsidiary. The Chicago, Milwaukee & St. Paul, by now bankrupt, opposed the merger by saying it violated the 1920 act. The ICC spent five months taking testimony from 147 witnesses and gathered four thousand pages of testimony. It said the Great Northern and the Northern Pacific could merge but they would have to sell the Burlington. The Great Northern and the Northern Pacific rightly found that to be nonsense. The Great Depression deepened and they withdrew their merger plan in 1931. The ICC, created in 1887 to try to ensure fairness in railroad rates, had morphed into a government monster that essentially created cartels in regulated industries by raising prices, limiting consumer choice, and reducing efficiency.

The Depression needed scapegoats. Railroad builders were easy targets. Typical of the tracts of that period that criticized free enterprise was one by thirty-five-year-old Matthew Josephson, who lived among expatriates of the literary left and surrealists in Paris in the 1920s and helped draft the manifesto for the Communist Party ticket in the United States in 1932. Morgan, Hill, Harriman, and Schiff all appear in his 1934 *The Robber Barons: The Great American Capitalists, 1861–1901*. The book is capably written and documented, but always assumes the worst of successful capitalists. The scurrilous phrase in the title tarred all capitalists with the same brush and perpetuated animosity against the railroads, and "robber baron" thus infested the American lexicon. That Morgan, Hill, Harriman, and Schiff had not "robbed" but refinanced and rebuilt the world's most extraordinary railroad system didn't seem to fit the title.

Except for the original land grant western railroads chartered in the mid-nineteenth century, the great majority of subsequent U.S. rail miles were built without public subsidies, as were urban streetcars. In the end, however, Washington "cornered" the railroads, the nation outgrew and marginalized them, and they became a segment of the larger, faster-growing transportation industry. Hill estimated in 1906 that it would take another 110,000 miles of railroad to handle the projected growth in freight, about five times the combined miles of the Great Northern, the Northern Pacific, and the Burlington. Congress instead began subsidizing roads, commercial trucking, aviation, and water transport, all at the expense of railroads. Morgan, dealing "with things as they exist," couldn't see past railroads, couldn't see around the corner, and had little interest in automobiles or trucks. In 1913, the year Morgan died—the same year forty-two state legislatures passed 230 railroad laws—there already were some seven thousand Ford dealerships across America.

At the start of World War I in 1914, two years before Hill died, there were about 100,000 registered trucks in the United States. By the end of the war there were one million. Five weeks after Hill died in 1916, the Federal Highway

Act became law, authorizing state highway departments, matching state highway money with federal money, and financing roads for mail delivery in the countryside. Total U.S. railroad track miles peaked that year at 254,000. Forty-one years later it was 112,000. Another Congressional Act in 1921 offered states matching federal funds to build a national network of two-lane hard-surface roads; the federal gasoline tax came a decade later.

Trucks became faster, bigger, more efficient, with pneumatic tires, six-cylinder engines, power brakes, three axles, diesel engines, and semi-trailers loaded on flatbed railroad cars. Then came container shipping, the federal interstate highway system, and five-axle eighteen wheelers. The final indignity was that rack trucks, not railroads, ended up hauling most of the new cars. By the end of the twentieth century the subsidized trucking industry, mostly nonunion, had long surpassed railroads in tons and value of goods shipped; railroads were left largely with low-profit long hauls of coal and grain.

Washington saddled railroads with expensive, byzantine "value of service" freight pricing (some six thousand product categories and six rate levels). Truckers priced simply by "weight of product." The government also subsidized public urban transit. Railroads themselves were unwitting early promoters of what became the so-called highway-motor complex that employed one of six American workers by the mid-twentieth century. On April 20, 1901, the day Hill's train returned to St. Paul from Seattle, an eleven-car Illinois Central train called the "Good Roads Special" departed Chicago for New Orleans. Campaigning for better roads on which wagons could haul produce and materials to railroad depots, the train was sponsored by the National Good Roads Association, carrying graders, rock crushers, rollers, sprinklers, ditchers, plows, and wagon-loaders for laying down quarter-mile sample stretches of macadam.

At the same hour that attorney John Graver Johnson climbed the steps of the U.S. Capitol on Monday, December 14, 1903, to argue the case of Northern Securities before the U.S. Supreme Court, two brothers named Orville and Wilbur were on the windy dunes of Kitty Hawk crafting spruce, muslin, wire, and aluminum to launch the age of propelled flight. A year after Harriman died, the Wright Brothers gave birth to commercial air cargo in 1910 when they flew ten bales of silk from Dayton, Ohio, to Columbus.

On February 4, 1902, as Roosevelt and Knox were at the White House preparing the Justice Department's lawsuit against Northern Securities, Charles Augustus Lindbergh was born in Detroit, Michigan. In 1925, he became one of the first pilots to fly the mail for the U.S. Postal Service as it began shifting long-distance mail delivery away from the railroads. A year later, the government through the Air Commerce Act began subsidizing the building of airports; a decade later the federal government took over air traffic control.

Hill argued that the railroads could handle all the freight traffic above St. Louis, but in 1906 Congress authorized the Army Corps of Engineers to carve the Upper Mississippi into a six-foot deep channel (now nine feet), thus making it a government-controlled shipping canal of locks and dams to compete with rail. America's inland waterways and coasts today transport 20 percent of America's coal and 60 percent of America's grain, but the Harriman–Hill style of private enterprise is watching from the shore: U.S. taxpayers have been said to pay for 92 percent of maintaining the nation's inland water system.

The notoriously private George F. Baker never talked to reporters. Two days after Attorney General Knox announced in early 1902 that the federal government would sue to break up Northern Securities, a reporter from the *New York Times* asked Baker, the head of the First National Bank of New York, ally of Morgan and Hill, and an officer of Northern Securities, to comment. Baker, predictably, said he would have none. The *Times* then quoted someone whom it called "one of the important interests" at Baker's bank who probably was Baker speaking not for attribution: "No matter what is done," he said, "this consolidation [Northern Securities] is going to become an accomplished fact in one form or another. If the present merger is contrary to law, a merger which obeys the law will be effected. It is absolutely impossible to stop these combinations so long as they are formed for legitimate purposes."

The prediction came true but it took sixty-six years. Almost a quarter century after Great Northern President Ralph Budd gave up trying to merge all the Hill roads into one efficient unit, his son John ascended through the system to be president. John Budd was born in Des Moines in 1907, studied civil engineering and transportation at Yale, and joined the Great Northern as an electrical engineer in 1930. He was promoted through a number of staff and line positions and became president in 1951. Four years later he and his board began merger talks with the Northern Pacific. The two railroads formed a joint committee, hired consultants and investment bankers, agreed to merger principles and a share-for-share exchange, and filed with the ICC in 1961 to form a new company called the Great Northern Pacific & Burlington Lines, Inc. with 27,000 miles of track in nineteen states and two Canadian provinces.

Railroad rate controls and public subsidies for trucking, barge, and air freight had devastated railroad earnings. In 1916 Hill's Great Northern had a net profit of $27.6 million, in 1961, $18.6 million.

Stockholders of both railroads approved the merger by wide margins. The ICC spent eighty-two days hearing from 623 witnesses, gathering 15,000 pages of testimony. Competitor railroads opposed the merger. Attorney General Robert Kennedy opposed it. The U.S. Agriculture Department opposed it. Organized labor opposed it. Senate Majority Leader Mike Mansfield of Montana opposed it. In 1964 the ICC examiner, however, recommended approval, saying, self-evidently, "Efficiency and economy are essential to the survival of railroad common carriers as private enterprises in these years of increased competition from other modes of. . . transportation." A year and a half later, held hostage by labor unions and weak competitors, still hypnotized by the ghosts of anti-railroad "progressives" a half century dead, the full ICC voted 6 to 5 against the merger. After concessions to labor and to two of its competitors ("Ginx's babies": the Chicago, Milwaukee & St. Paul and the Chicago & North Western), the Great Northern and the Northern Pacific asked the ICC to reconsider. In late November 1967 it voted 8 to 2 to approve the merger. The same day Senator Mansfield and seven of his colleagues introduced a bill to strip the ICC of some of its merger authority. The following April the ICC voted 7 to 2 to reaffirm the merger. The Justice Department asked a judge to delay it. A panel of three judges upheld the merger but in December 1968 the Supreme Court blocked it and agreed to hear the case, and the next fall it heard oral arguments on the Justice Department's claim that the merger's public benefit did not outweigh less competition.

Charles Joseph Burger was one of the men who kept the railroads and their customers honest. In the early twentieth century he worked for the Northern Pacific in St. Paul. His job was to inspect the freight, verify how much each shipment weighed, ensure fair and accurate rates were being charged, and make sure the boxes and crates held what the customers said they held. The integrity of the system depended on his judgment and vigilance. If a customer tried to avoid paying a higher rate by claiming his boxes held pickles when they really held pepper sauce then he was cheating not only the railroad but everyone else. Burger also farmed twenty acres near St. Paul, sold his produce from the back of a truck, and traveled by railroad selling weighing scales.

He and his wife Katherine were Swiss-German, had seven children, and lived in a little house that still stands at 695 Conway Street in the Dayton's Bluff neighborhood overlooking downtown St. Paul, literally on the other side of the tracks from the Hill mansion on Summit.

Their fourth child, Warren, was born in 1907. The year James J. Hill died nine-year–old Warren was ill, missing an entire year of school, during which he spent much of his time at home reading biographies of great figures in American history. Young Burger attended night school at the University of Minnesota, sold insurance, was graduated from the St. Paul College of Law with honors in 1931, and practiced for twenty-two years with the state's oldest law firm. He became active in Republican politics, helped swing his party's nomination to Eisenhower at the 1952 convention, and spent four years at the Justice Department and thirteen years on the U.S. Court of Appeals for the District of Columbia. On May 21, 1969, President Richard Nixon nominated him to be chief justice of the United States. He was sworn in two months later.

On February 2, 1970, Warren Burger, the son of a Northern Pacific freight inspector, announced the court's decision in *United States v. Interstate Commerce Commission*, 396 U.S. 491. The vote was 7 to 0 to uphold the merger of the Great Northern, the Northern Pacific, and the Burlington.

There was no eloquence in the opinion, there were no reporters running for telephones, simply a straightforward statement that the Transportation Act of 1940 clearly expressed "the desire of Congress that the railroad industry proceed toward an integrated national transportation system through substantial corporate simplification." On March 3, 1970, the new Burlington Northern opened for business as the longest railroad system in the United States, including two smaller railroads in the Pacific Northwest. James J. Hill's Great Northern ceased to exist as a corporation. Ten years later, President Jimmy Carter signed into law the Staggers Rail Act, named after the retiring chair of the U.S. House committee on interstate and foreign commerce. It allowed railroads to lower and raise rates within wider, more reasonable limits and negotiate long-term contracts with shippers. The first transportation industry to be regulated was one of the last to be deregulated.

The hammer came down, the auction was over, the crowd dispersed in front of the railroad freight house at Ninth and Jones. It was time for Jacob Schiff to shake the prairie dust of Omaha from his black leather Fifth Avenue shoes and climb aboard the chartered train back to New York. It was Monday, November 1, 1897, the syndicate he controlled had just bought the bankrupt Union Pacific from the federal government, and he probably had filled the two ivory tablets in his small silver book with notes and reminders. If Schiff had walked five blocks west to South 14th Street then taken a right and walked four blocks north to Farnam Street, he would have come to a small storefront at 315 South 14th that said S. H. Buffett Grocery.

Had he walked inside past the shelves of canned vegetables and sacks of flour to the counter he would have been greeted by the owner, Sidney Buffett, or his twenty-year-old son Ernest. Sidney had come to Omaha thirty years earlier as a teenager, opened the first grocery store in town when all its streets were dirt, and took his father's advice: "Save your credit, for that is better than money... If you go into business, be content with moderate gains. Don't be too hasty to get rich."

One hundred and twelve years later, almost to the day, at the bottom of the nation's worst recession in eighty years, Ernest Buffett's grandson, Warren, announced that his company, Berkshire–Hathaway, had agreed to buy the Burlington Northern Santa Fe for $26 billion, or $100 a share in cash and stock, a premium of 32 percent over the previous day's closing price. His company had bought 15 percent of it two years earlier, then another 7 percent, and now the final 78 percent. The Burlington Northern Santa Fe remains one of just four dominant railroads in the United States, with the Union Pacific in the West and CSX Transportation and Norfolk Southern Corp in the East. It stretches 32,000 miles through twenty-eight states and two Canadian provinces. It hauls more low-sulfur coal than any other railroad in the United States, enough to generate 10 percent of the nation's electricity. It is a "rolling pipeline" for crude oil and hauls more grain than any other railroad, enough to provide nine hundred million people with a year's supply of bread. It hauls enough asphalt to lay a one-lane road four times around the equator. It carries more truck containers than any other railroad, loading one onto its freight cars an average of every six seconds.

Wall Street, with its appetite for earnings per share increase every quarter, increased dividends, and stock buybacks, never seemed to have the patience for a business that buys assets still in use twenty or thirty years later. Warren Buffett called the private takeover an "all-in bet" on the U.S. economy, but it was much more than that. It affirmed that railroads were the most energy-efficient way to move heavy freight long distances and that America needed more track than ever before. It was a bet that the federal government would not have the resources to fix and replace decaying bridges and patched freeways, that highways would be more congested than ever, which would mean higher user fees for trucks, which would mean trucks gradually would be consigned to do more of the short haul, pick-up, and final delivery of freight. That would leave more of the long hauls to container cars on . . . railroads.

Warren Buffett's purchase of the Burlington Northern Santa Fe also was an "all-in bet" on the world's premier freight rail system, the only one in the world today that private enterprise owns and runs entirely. It also was a bet on what drives the American economy: the capitalist, free enterprise vision of Edward H. Harriman, James J. Hill, J. P. Morgan, and Jacob H. Schiff, guided by thoughtful regulation, which remains the hope of the world, what Alexis de Tocqueville a century earlier called the "foremost cause of [America's] rapid progress, its strength and its greatness." Upon reading the words "all-in bet," one can almost hear Mr. Schiff whispering to Mr. Buffett, as he once did to Max Warburg: "Too short and not optimistic enough."

Years passed and, one by one, so did the four major principals of this story. In February 1908, Jacob and Therese Schiff were cruising down the Nile when Jacob took pen in hand and wrote to Edward Henry Harriman: "The imposing ruins on shore remind me how hollow everything earthly is; how we strive so often for naught; how short a time we live & how long we are then dead." Schiff knew Harriman was not well and urged him to retire. The following year, Harriman took the curative baths at Bad Gastein south of Salzburg, Austria, but returned home sicker than ever, suffering from a gastric ulcer, hemorrhoids, and rheumatism. Sometime in late August 1909 he invited J. P. Morgan to Arden to make peace. Morgan was happy to do so, fulfilling what he believed his Christian duty.

A pale, wasted Harriman greeted him wearing an overcoat, lying in a steamer chair on the veranda at Arden with a blanket over his legs, as if on some voyage. After a contrite discussion, with Morgan holding one of his big, black cigars, the reconcilement was complete. Morgan departed with a warm, gracious handshake. Harriman died a few days later on September 9 at age sixty-two. When a reporter told Hill of Harriman's death he said Hill "paused a moment, apparently deep in thought, and said slowly: 'After all, I believe he is happier now.'"

Three days later an express train carrying about one hundred distinguished mourners from New York City left Jersey City bound for Harriman's memorial service at the little country Episcopal church where he and his family had worshipped so many Sundays at Arden. Among those on the train were Schiff, James Stillman, and his attorney John W. Sterling, and Morgan and Company's George Perkins. James J. Hill was not present nor did he send a word of condolence to the family. Ditto, Theodore Roosevelt. Two years earlier, as part of what Otto Kahn called the Harriman Extermination League, Roosevelt had slandered Harriman by publicly calling him an "undesirable citizen." A most suitable epitaph for Harriman could be the words he spoke to the Economic Club of New York a year before he died: "There are two factors that work against prosperity. One is idle money and the other is idle labor.... We must create conditions where both can be used properly and fairly."

In late December 1912, after hours of partisan grilling from the Democrats' lawyer Samuel Untermyer, in hearings before a U.S. House committee about the alleged existence of a so-called Money Trust, a weight seemed to lift from the shoulders of seventy-three-year-old John Pierpont Morgan. He entered his library Christmas morning singing a full-throated, joyous "O Come, All Ye Faithful." Then he was off the next month for an extended trip abroad beginning with a cruise down the Nile in early February. During the cruise, however, his chronic depression returned. He sank into what his biographer Jean Strouse called "paranoid, suicidal delusions." Then, apparently in part from the stress of the hearings, came insomnia, nightmares, chest pains, and an irrational fear he would be subpoenaed or held in contempt of court.

He and his party escaped to Rome where he occupied the royal suite of eight bedrooms and two parlors at Cesar Ritz's elegant Grand Hotel. He wanted to visit Aix again but was too weak to travel, then somehow summoned the strength to receive Easter Communion. He became "irrational, incoherent," refusing even to play solitaire, but managed a drive up the Janiculum Hill to see the construction of the American Academy he had endowed. He died March 31, 1913, at the Grand Hotel. Two weeks later, James J. Hill, Harriman's widow Mary, and Kuhn, Loeb's Otto Kahn were among thousands present for his funeral at St. George's Episcopal Church at Second Avenue and Sixteenth Street in New York. Bob Bacon and George Baker were among the honorary pallbearers. As Morgan instructed, there were no eulogies.

In May 1916 James Jerome Hill received a letter at his St. Paul home from George Perkins. The Republican convention was weeks away in Chicago. The former Morgan partner was promoting Roosevelt for president one last time. Perkins asked Hill if he would come out in support for his old adversary. Hill laughed at the very thought of it. He needed the amusement. He was dying from a bacterial infection from hemorrhoids that became gangrenous in his left thigh. The Mayo brothers came from Rochester, Minnesota, to operate but it was hopeless. Hill died on May 29 at age seventy-seven in the home where fourteen years earlier he had received news of the federal government's lawsuit against Northern Securities.

At 2 p.m. May 31, during his funeral at his mansion at 240 Summit Avenue, all Great Northern and Northern Pacific trains from Chicago to the West Coast stopped for five minutes. One could hear train whistles echoing in his honor up and down the Mississippi River valley at St. Paul and Minneapolis. "How many things we were going to do in the future that might have been done in the past," his wife Mary wrote a few months before her death five years later, "The present is all that is ours."

In September 1920 Therese and Jacob Henry Schiff were spending the month as usual at their summer home in Sea Bright, New Jersey, when Jacob, frail and weak, insisted on observing the Yom Kippur fast. On the 23rd he told his family he wanted to return to their Fifth Avenue home. He died there on Sabbath evening, September 25, at age seventy-three. His funeral was held three days later at Temple Emanu-El, his synagogue for more than a half century, where he made his legendary decision nineteen years earlier in the battle for the Northern Pacific. Like Morgan, Schiff had instructed there be no eulogies.

The synagogue was packed beyond capacity and thousands were turned away; thousands more marched to Temple Emanu-El from the tenements of the Lower East Side to pay homage. Someone remembered it had been Schiff's custom to attend the funerals of obscure men and women who had died on the East Side. "No tenement house was too humble for him to enter," said the New York Times, "no stairs were too high for him to climb if it was to comfort a family in sorrow." In his final years he said he believed he had enjoyed the friendship of James J. Hill to the last, despite their fight over the Northern Pacific, which Schiff said was "solely the result of his and my desire to do what we thought was necessary to defend and protect interests confided to each of us, and which at the time were running apart."

ACKNOWLEDGMENTS

The author is grateful for the discerning editorial eye of Pieter Martin, and the guidance of Kristian Tvedten and Laura Westlund of the University of Minnesota Press; copy editor Jean Brady and proofreader Robert Frame; Margaret Bresnahan for help at the Morgan Library in New York; Paul Olson and Michael Haeg for valuable insights at an early draft stage; Marschall Smith for saving me from not a few embarrassing errors; Wendy Robson for compiling the index; and the staffs of the Wilson Library at the University of Minnesota, the Minnesota Historical Society, and the St. Paul Public Library. At Wells Fargo & Company, I am especially indebted to John Stumpf and Dick Kovacevich, for leading with integrity and framing every business decision based on what is best for the customer. Most important, here's to my wife, Mary, for her patient support and careful reading of the manuscript at several stages, and let's hear it for the next generation of young readers, including our grandchildren Adele, Atticus, Dexter, Evelyn, Fritz Nico, Theodore, and Penelope.

APPENDIXES

Supreme Court of the United States, No. 277, *Northern Securities Company*, &c, *vs. The United States*, Appeal from the Circuit Court of the United States for the District of Minnesota. March 14, 1904

Excerpts of Dissenting Opinion
by Associate Justice Oliver Wendell Holmes

Great cases like hard cases make bad law. For great cases are called great, not by reason of their real importance in shaping the law of the future, but because of some accident of immediate overwhelming interest which appeals to the feelings and distorts the judgment. These immediate interests exercise a kind of hydraulic pressure which makes what previously was clear seem doubtful, and before which even well settled principles of law will bend. What we have to do in this case is to find the meaning of some not very difficult words. We must try, I have tried, to do it with the same freedom of natural and spontaneous interpretation that one would be sure of if the same question arose upon an indictment for a similar act which excited no public attention, and was of importance only to a prisoner before the court. Furthermore, while at times judges need for their work the training of economists or statesmen, and must act in view of their foresight of consequences, yet when their task is to interpret and apply the words of a statute, their function is merely academic to begin with—to read English intelligently—and a consideration of consequences comes into play, if at all, only when the meaning of the words used is open to reasonable doubt . . . The statute of which we have to find the meaning is a criminal statute. The two sections on which the Government relies both make certain acts crimes. That is their immediate purpose and that is what they say. It is vain to insist that this is not a criminal proceeding. The words cannot be read one way in a suit which is to end in fine and imprisonment and another way in one which seeks an injunction. . . . So I say we must read the words before us as if the question were whether two small exporting grocers should go to jail. . . . the statute is of a very sweeping and general character. It hits "every" contract or combination of the prohibited sort, great or small, and "every" person who shall monopolize or attempt to monopolize, in the sense of the act, "any part" of the trade or commerce among the several States. There is a natural inclination to assume that it was directed against certain great combinations and to read it in that light. It does not say so. On the contrary, it says "every," and "any part." Still less was it directed specially against railroads. There even was a reasonable doubt whether it included railroads until the point was decided by this court . . . If the act before us is to be carried out according to what seems to me the logic of the argument for the Government, which I do not believe that it will be, I can see no part of the conduct of life with which on similar principles Congress might not interfere. This act is construed by the Government to affect the purchasers of shares in two railroad companies because of the effect it may have, or, if you like, is certain to have, upon the competition of these roads. If such a remote result of the exercise of an ordinary incident of property and personal freedom is enough to make that exercise unlawful, there is hardly any transaction concerning commerce between the States that may not be made a crime by the finding of a jury or a court. The personal ascendancy of one man may be such that it would give to his advice the effect of a command, if he owned but a single share in each road. The tendency of his presence in the stockholders' meetings might be certain to prevent competition, and thus his advice, if not his mere existence, become a crime . . . The act says nothing about competition. I stick to the exact words used. The words hit two classes of cases, and only two—Contracts in restraint of trade and combinations or conspiracies in restraint of trade . . . There is a natural feeling that somehow or other the statute meant to strike at combinations great enough to cause just anxiety on the part of those who love their country more than money, while it viewed such little ones as I have supposed with just indifference. This notion, it may be said, somehow breathes from the pores of the act, although it seems to be contradicted in every way by the words in detail . . . it might be that when a combination reached a certain size it might have attributed to it more of the character of a monopoly merely by virtue of its size than would be attributed to a smaller one. I am quite clear that it is only in connection with monopolies that size could play any part. But my answer has been indicated already. In the first place size in the case of railroads is an inevitable incident and if it were an objection under the act, the Great Northern and the Northern Pacific already were too great and encountered the law. In the next place in the case of railroads it is evident that the size of the combination is reached for other ends than those which would make them monopolies. The combinations are not formed for the purpose of excluding others from the field. Finally, even a small railroad will have the same tendency to exclude others from its narrow area that great ones have to exclude others from a greater one, and the statute attacks the small monopolies as well as the great. The very words of the act make such a distinction impossible in this case and it has not been attempted in express terms...I do not expect to hear it maintained that Mr. Morgan could be sent to prison for buying as many shares as he liked of the Great Northern and the Northern Pacific, even if he bought them both at the same time and got more than half the stock of each road...I should assume, and I do assume, that one purpose of the purchase was to suppress competition between the two roads. I appreciate the force of the argument that there are independent stockholders in each; that it cannot be presumed that the respective boards of directors will propose any illegal act; that if they should they could be restrained, and that all that has been done as yet is too remote from the illegal result to be classed even as an attempt. Not every act done in furtherance of an unlawful end is an attempt or contrary to the law. There must be a certain nearness to the result...The law, I repeat, says nothing about competition, and only prevents its suppression by contracts or combinations in restraint of trade, and such contracts or combinations derive their character as restraining trade from other features than the suppression of competition alone. To see whether I am wrong...then a partnership between two stage drivers who had been competitors in driving across a state line, or two merchants once engaged in rival commerce among the States whether made after or before the act, if now continued, is a crime...if the restraint on the freedom of the members of a combination caused by their entering into partnership is a restraint of trade, every such combination, as well the small as the great, is within the act.

North American Railroads, 1901

Ranked by miles (excluding side and double tracks). Source: S. A. Nelson, *The A B C of Wall Street*, 150.

1. Chicago & North Western 8,346
2. Chicago, Burlington & Quincy 7,859
3. Atchison, Topeka & Santa Fe 7,718
4. Canadian Pacific 7,684
5. Southern Pacific. 7,201
6. Pennsylvania 7,098
7. Chicago, Milwaukee & St. Paul 6,420
8. Southern Railway. 6,416
9. Missouri Pacific 5,326
10. Great Northern 5,203
11. Northern Pacific 4,746
12. Grand Trunk 4,183
13. Illinois Central. 3,996
14. Chicago, Rock Island & Pacific 3,771
15. Louisville & Nashville 3,235
16. Union Pacific . . . . , . . . 3,060
17. New York Central & Hudson River 2,924
18. Big Four 2,345
19. Missouri, Kansas & Texas 2,222
20. Baltimore & Ohio. 2,204
21. Plant System 2,140
22. Erie. 2,104
23. Mexican Central. 2,054
24. New York, New Haven & Hartford. 2,047

Wall Street Primer, 1901

Source: S. A. Nelson, *The A B C of Wall Street*, 126–64.

arbitrage: Trading in two markets, such as London and New York, to profit from the price difference.

bear: A speculator for profit in declining stock prices.

break: Decline in the price of a stock after the price has been kept artificially high.

broker: Trader who executes orders to buy or sell a property.

bucket shop: A gambling house for stocks.

bull: A speculator for profit in rising stock prices.

call loan: Money loaned, upon collateral, subject to the call by the lender, who can demand its return plus agreed-upon interest any day before the end of banking hours.

coalers: Northeastern railroads transporting primarily coal, such as the Baltimore & Ohio and the Norfolk & Western.

commission house: Trades for customers only, not speculating on its own account.

corner: The purchase by a party or parties of all outstanding shares of stock in a company, usually to increase its price at will.

covering short sales: Raising funds to "cover" one's loss in a short sale.

discretionary pool: A pool of stock purchased in a company, formed by influential, predatory speculators to lower or raise the price of the stock.

grangers: Railroads depending largely on farm products for freight.

margin: Money deposited by a customer with a broker to buy stock, usually 10 percent of a stock's par value.

market capital: Total market value of a company's stock (market price multiplied by total shares).

matched orders: Orders to buy and sell a stock at the same time to give the appearance of trading activity in the stock to influence its price.

"Nipper": Investor nickname for shares of Northern Pacific. "Little Nipper" is Northern Pacific common stock; "Big Nipper" is Northern Pacific preferred shares.

Pacifics: Railroads reaching the Pacific Ocean, sometimes with a transcontinental link: Missouri Pacific, Northern Pacific, Southern Pacific, Texas Pacific, and Union Pacific.

par: Face value of a stock, usually $100 a share.

plunger: Speculator who trades heavily and makes big bets.

point: In stocks one point equals $1 a share.

pool: A group of large investors that accumulates shares of a certain stock at low prices to stabilize the price at high levels for the pool's benefit, sometimes to seek a corner.

short-selling: A short-term bet that the price of a stock will go down: selling shares one doesn't own, paying interest to rent borrowed shares, then buying the shares at their (potentially) lower price and pocketing the difference.

specialist: A broker who trades in very few or only one stock.

transcontinental: A U.S. railroad with a "through" line connection ocean to ocean or border to border.

through rate: Guaranteed long-haul railroad freight rate.

trunk lines: "Through" railroad lines from the Atlantic to Chicago and other points west such as the New York Central and the Pennsylvania.

wire house: Commission brokerage houses in New York and Chicago that connect with offices in other cities through leased private telegraph wires.

watered stock: An increase in capital stock with no corresponding increase in assets.

NOTES

Preface

Page xii As the esteemed: Johnson to William D. Guthrie, December 17, 1903, quoted in Swaine, *The Cravath Firm and Its Predecessors*, 712–13.

Page xii To translate the: According to the consumer price index provided by www.measuringworth.com, $100 in 1901 was worth $2,650 in 2010.

Page xiii Several years ago: CNBC, December 1, 2007, interview with reporter Becky Quick.

Introduction

Page 1 The battle was: Carosso, *The Morgans*, 474.

Page 2 All the human: Spero, *"What the Bible Teaches about Capitalism,"* 15.

Page 3 You could do: Nelson, "The Machinery of Wall Street," 977.

Page 3 Like the "stags": Duguid, *The Story of the [London] Stock Exchange*, 149.

Page 3 "When a speculator": Lorimer, *Letters from a Self-Made Merchant*, 193.

Page 3 "Americans are great": Lefevre, "The American Gambling Spirit," 704.

Page 4 In 1901 there: The days of stock corners ended in 1934, prompted in part by the memory of the Northern Pacific corner, inadvertent though it may have been, and by two deliberate attempts in the 1920s (against the Stutz Bearcat Company in 1920 and the Piggly Wiggly stores in 1923). The Securities and Exchange Act of 1934 prohibited the manipulation of security prices in Section 9(a)2: "It shall be unlawful for any person, directly or indirectly, by the use of the mails or any means or instrumentality of interstate commerce, or of any facility of any national securities exchange, or of any member of a national securities exchange . . . to effect, alone or with one or more other persons, a series of transactions in any security registered on a national securities exchange . . . creating actual or apparent active trading in such security, or raising or depressing the price of such security, for the purpose of inducing the purchase or sale of such security by others." Also, beginning in 1968, Schedule 13(d) of the SEC, the so-called beneficial ownership report, required any party buying more than 5 percent of a voting class of a company's stock to publicly disclose it through the SEC within ten days after the purchase.

Page 4 The average construction: U.S. Bureau of Labor Statistics, bls.gov/opub/uscs/1901.pdf.

Page 4 Neither bank dirtied: Adams, *The Kidnapped Millionaires*, 278.

Page 4 Baker was renowned: "Not for Small Bank Accounts," *New York Evening Post*, May 4, 1901, 7.

Page 5 Morgan replied: "Record Day for Stock," *Wall Street Journal*, January 28, 1901, 1.

Page 5 "If the affairs": "Integrity in Business," *Harper's Weekly*, March 9, 1901, 244.

Page 5 Only six days: "'Community of Interest,' Again," *New York Evening Post*, May 15, 1901, 6; Eight years earlier, Marion Marsh Todd, an opponent of mega-railroads, asked in her *The Railways of Europe and America* "whether the Railways shall own the people or the people own the Railways," 3.

Page 5 "first necessity of": Trollope, *North America*, 178.

Page 6 Railroads represented the: Sterne, "Railways," 15–16.

Page 6 Their annual revenue: H. S. Haines, "Problems of Railway Regulation," *Sayings and Writings about the Railways*, 16.

Page 6 Deemed to be: White, *Railroaded*, 111, 333.

Page 6 A stockbroker's bible: Clews, *Fortuna*, 72–73.

Page 6 About one of: A. Maurice Low, "The Railways and the Public," *Sayings and Writings about the Railways*, 75.

Page 6 In the early: Chandler, *Visible Hand*, 204.

Page 6 Even then, however: Ibid., 455.

Page 6 One could travel: Ibid., 84–85.

Page 7 Some of those: Allen, *The Great Pierpont Morgan*, 49.

Page 7 In 1887 alone: "Railway Building Prospects for 1901," 193–94.

Page 7 It all turned: Moody quoted in Lyon, *To Hell in a Day Coach*, 88.

Page 7 They made a: Cronon, *Nature's Metropolis*, 125.

Page 8 Railroads created mail: Ibid., 336.

Page 8 They even were: Martin, *Railroads Triumphant*, 307.

Page 8 Railroads were the: Ibid., 343.

Page 9 It was no: DiLorenzo, *How Capitalism Saved America*, 119.

Page 9 "Mobility of population": Turner, 30.

Page 9 "the best regulated": Nimmo, *Commercial, Economic, and Political Questions Not Decided in the Northern Securities Case*, 15–16.

1. Mr. Morgan and Mr. Hill

Page 10 "magnetic pole of": Burton J. Hendrick, "The Financial Center of the World," *Metropolitan Magazine*, March 1905, 737.

Page 10 At the iron: "How Quotations Are Made on 'Change,'" *Bradstreet's Weekly*, February 21, 1891, 115.

Page 10 Rimming the floor: Nelson, "The Machinery of Wall Street," 981.

Page 11 The Exchange was: Ibid., 978.

Page 11 Some members had: "Life on 'Change,'" *New York Tribune*, December 31, 1902, 4.

Page 11 There was no: Earl D. Berry, "The Stock Exchange," *New York Times Weekly Magazine*, October 31, 1897, SM2.

Page 11 One man said: "Vignettes of the Slump," *Chicago Tribune*, May 10, 1901, 1.

Page 11 Their gain was: Short-selling dated back four centuries. The Dutch government banned it in 1610 after merchant Isaac Le Maire, former board member of the Dutch East India Company, and his associates feared British ships soon would destroy many of the company's ships on the Baltic Sea route. They were accused of trying to drive down the company's stock by selling large quantities of it, some of which they didn't own. In 1720 the South Sea Company was accused of inflating the price of the company's stock from £130 to £1,000 by spreading false rumors about the company's success. Three years later the British government banned naked short-selling, the practice of not even borrowing the stock before selling it. Napoleon in 1803 accused short-sellers of being enemies of the state because they shorted French government bonds. He wrote the financier Mollien, "I ask if the man who offers to deliver in one month five per cent rentes at thirty-eight francs which are selling to-day for forty francs, does not proclaim and prepare for their discredit—if he does not at least announce that, personally, he has no confidence in the Government." Shorts, however, can add to liquidity and pop bubbles simply by asking what the "longs" ask: Does a company's stock price accurately reflect the company's fundamental value? Financier Bernard Baruch argued in 1913 that home builders sell short when they sell a home before it's made, so do farmers when they sell a crop before it's harvested. "Short selling isn't one of the 'great commercial evils of the day,'" wrote James Surowiecki in *The Wisdom of Crowds*, "The lack of short-selling is" (228).

Page 12 When a stock: "James R. Keene, The Story of His Career with Its Record of Ups and Downs," *New York Times Magazine*, January 30, 1910, 2.

Page 12 It was, however: Nelson, "The Machinery of Wall Street," 979.

Page 12 Some brokers watching: "Rock Island's Advance," *New York Herald*, April 4, 1901, 6.

Page 12 When Hill–Morgan: Hill believed a true U.S. transcontinental, ocean to ocean, under one management or ownership, would not be practical because the east and the west were so radically different. "Under one ownership there would be a demand for uniformity in rates over the entire system," he was quoted saying in the *Railway Age* newspaper on May 10, 1901. "The Nebraska shipper who has to pay 105 per ton per mile on his business would be asking the courts why he should pay double the price charged shippers east of Chicago, who have only to pay 55 per ton per mile.... Railroad men understand the reason why rates should be higher in thinly populated parts of the country than in areas thickly populated, but their explanations might not be understood by courts, juries or shippers. So long as the country which would have to be traversed by a through line from ocean to ocean remains uneven in point of population and business, just so long will a transcontinental system under one management be difficult." Or, as one unnamed conservative railroad investor told the *New York Evening Post*, "The idea that it is necessary for a road to extend from the Atlantic to the Pacific is about as sensible as for a man flying a kite to want to hold the string in New York and have the tail drop in San Francisco" ("Stock Market Direction," May 4, 1901, 2).

Page 13 The Dow distributed: Nelson, "The Machinery of Wall Street," 982.

Page 14 Gusts up to: The account of Morgan's departure is based on "Morgan Sails for Europe," *New York Tribune*, April 4, 1901, 6; "J. P. Morgan Off for London," *New York Evening World*, April 3, 1901, 6; "Soaking Rain Swept City," *New York Evening World*, April 3, 1901, 12; "Pierpont Morgan Sails," *New York Times*, April 4, 1901; "Nor'easter Wrecks Umbrellas," *New York Tribune*, April 4, 1901, 7; *Ocean: Magazine of Travel*, September 1889, 41; John T. Maginnis, "Sailing Day," *New York Times—Illustrated Magazine*, June 20, 1897, 6; "Morgan's Plans Not Fixed," *Minneapolis Journal*, April 4, 1901, 4; "The Largest Passenger List of the Season Yesterday," *New York Tribune*, April 3, 1901, 5; "Mr. Morgan Goes Abroad," *Commercial Advertiser* (New York), late edition, Wall Street Extra, 1; and "Winds and Waves High at the Hook," *New York Evening Telegram*, April 3, 1901, 4.

Page 14 America was, as: "Wall Street and the Country," *Harper's Weekly*, May 18, 1901, 498.

Page 14 American capital now: "The Rise in Railway Stocks," *New York Evening Post*, April 3, 1901, 6.

Page 15 The United States: Morris, *Theodore Rex*, 20.

Page 15 From the cab: Chernow, *House of Morgan*, 28.

Page 15 Protected by a: "Mr. Morgan Goes Abroad," *Commercial Advertiser* (New York), April 3, 1901, 1.

Page 15 "With the right": Stead, "The Money Kings of the World," 320; Allen, "American Securities in Europe," 116.

Page 15 "When the cable": *Life*, May 2, 1901, 364, 965.

Page 16 He still had: Brands, *American Colossus*, 65; Johnson, *A History of the American People*, 565.

Page 16 Other close friends: Burrows, *Gotham*, 1087.

Page 16 To interest investors?: "J. Pierpont Morgan Sails," *New York Times*, April 4, 1901.

Page 16 Despite the grand: Moody and Turner, "The Masters of Capital" (November 1910), 20.

Page 16 He always said: Allen, *The Great Pierpont Morgan*, 193.

Page 18 Thirty-four firms: Chandler, *Visible Hand*, 332.

Page 18 He was born: Stead, "The Money Kings of the World," 319.

Page 20 It was an: Chernow, *House of Morgan*, 43–44.

Page 20 By April 1901: Moody and Turner, "The Masters of Capital" (May 1911), 80. Strouse, *Morgan*, 307; Lefevre, "Harriman," 121.

Page 21 "I want business": Allen, *The Great Pierpont Morgan*, 206.

Page 21 "He was not": Ibid., 77.

Page 21 Months before his: Ibid., 7.

Page 21 The center of: Martin, *Railroads Triumphant*, 236; Cronon, *Nature's Metropolis*, 42, 283.

Page 21 Chicago had become: Cronon, *Nature's Metropolis*, 63.

Page 21 It was the: *Railway Age*, January 4, 1901, 11.

Page 21 It had just: Cronon, *Nature's Metropolis*, 279.

Page 22 It was already: Martin, *Railroads Triumphant*, 30.

Page 22 Perhaps he even: "The New Catechism," *Life*, January 3, 1901, 66.

Page 22 Four hundred miles: "Heavy Rains; High Winds," *Times* (Richmond, Va.), April 4, 1901, 1.

Page 22 He had a: Waterloo and Hanson Jr., *Famous American Men and Women*, 294; "Daniel S. Lamont Dies after Drive," *New York Times*, July 24, 1905; Price, "Secretaries to the Presidents," 491; Medved, *The Shadow Presidents*, 85.

Page 22–23 as chief presence: "Wall Street's Buoyancy Contrasts with London," *New York Herald*, April 1, 1901, 13; "Daniel S. Lamont Dies after Drive," *New York Times*, July 24, 1905, 1; Price, "Secretaries to the Presidents," 491.

Page 23 But, as Mary: MTH Diary, 16 JJHP.

Page 23 The time had: Pyle, *The Life of James J. Hill*, 129.

Page 23 Only two railroads: Called the "Milwaukee Road" later in the twentieth century, at the time of this story investors and newspapers called it the "St. Paul," as in, "How's Paul?" It was incorporated May 5, 1863, as the Milwaukee & St. Paul, and eleven years later it became the Chicago, Milwaukee & St. Paul (*Selected Investments for Banks, Trustees, and Private Investors*, 30).

Page 23 If either fell: Cushing, "Hill Against Harriman," 420, 422.

Page 24 Only by controlling: Schonberger, "James J. Hill and the Trade with the Orient," 185.

Page 24 The Burlington could: Pyle, *The Life of James J. Hill*, 117.

Page 24 America had only: "Mr. J. J. Hill as a Seer," *New York Times*, August 22, 1902, 8.

Page 24 Hill's view was: "President Hill's Horizon," *New York Times*, October 22, 1902.

Page 24 It was simply: Hill–Charles Steele, January 16, 1903, JJHP, MHS.

Page 24 his "land bridge": Martin, *Railroads Triumphant*, 241.

Page 25 For all these: JJH–Mount Stephen, June 15, 1904, JJHP.

Page 25 Many of its: Carr, "A Great Railway Builder," 394. A 1 percent grade is a rise of about fifty feet a mile.

Page 25 Five or six: *Wall Street Journal*, April 12, 1901.

Page 25 the curving surface: Lyon, *To Hell in a Day Coach*, 8.

Page 25 "There is but": Martin, *James J. Hill*, 390.

Page 25 For a very: Robert Harris to C. Balance, August 29, 1868, quoted in Cronon, *Nature's Metropolis*, 84.

Page 25 When his St. Paul: Folsom, *Entrepreneurs vs. the State*, 34.

Page 26 The goal for: Martin, *James J. Hill*, 221.

Page 26 An empty car: Hill, *Highways of Progress*, 159.

Page 26 Railroading is a: Cronon, *Nature's Metropolis*, 85.

Page 26 Every railroad car: Martin, *Railroads Triumphant*, 129.

Page 26 One colleague said: George F. Baker quoted in Paine, *George Fisher Baker*, 199.

Page 26 dressing for business: Martin, *James J. Hill*, 264.

Page 26 When traveling alone: Ibid., 234.

Page 26 Even when Hill's: Malone, *James J. Hill*, 188.

Page 26 One newspaper called: *Seattle Post-Intelligencer* quoted in Kris, *The White Cascade*, 115.

Page 26 "Please have all": Martin, *James J. Hill*, 218.

Page 26 When his crews: Martin, *Railroads Triumphant*, 293.

Page 27 Alternate the thick: Blossom, "James J. Hill," 732.

Page 27 "I know you": Martin, *James J. Hill*, 163.

Page 28 "How many men": Latzke, "Romances of Success," 448.

Page 28 He liked to: Moody and Turner, "The Masters of Capital" (December 1910), 125.

Page 28 Middlemen were "economic": Hill, *Highways of Progress*, 119.

Page 28 Lawmakers were akin: Ibid., 127.

Page 28 So-called progressives: Martin, *Railroads Triumphant*, 350.

Page 28 "Trade will go": Hill, *Highways of Progress*, 92.

Page 28 "All progress is": Ibid., 114.

Page 28 He cut the: White, *Railroaded*, 425.

Page 28 erupted in episodes: Latzke, "Romances of Success," 448.

Page 28 At age sixty-nine: "J. J. Hill in Fight with His Assistant," *New York Times*, August 10, 1907, 2; "McGuigan Resigns," *New York Tribune*, August 10, 1907, 1; "James J. Hill Resigns," *New York Tribune*, April 3, 1907, 1.

Page 28 he never gave: Moody and Turner, "The Masters of Capital" (December 1910), 131; Knowles, *From Telegrapher to Titan*, 255; McDonald, *Lord Strathcona*, 379.

Page 29 As a young: Martin, *James J. Hill*, 71.

Page 29 "I have been": Ibid., 162.

Page 29 They were married: For an account of the legal battle among Hill's children over the estate of Hill and his wife, Mary, both of whom died without wills, see Young and McCormack, *The Dutiful Son.*

Page 29 He compensated with: One of the clearest physical descriptions of Hill is in Latzke, "Romances of Success," 436.

Page 29 Hill read widely: Carr, "A Great Railway Builder," 392.

Page 29–30 Over his desk: Hubbard, "The Study Habit," 719.

Page 30 His longtime banker: Paine, *George Fisher Baker,* 199.

Page 30 As a young: "Character Sketch of James J. Hill," *Saint Paul Globe,* October 15, 1899, 14.

Page 30 Hill began stalking: Morison, *The Oxford History of the American People,* 745.

Page 31 He and his: Martin, *James J. Hill,* 131.

Page 31 He planned his: Englehardt, *Gateway to the Northern Plains,* 52.

Page 31 In five years: Martin, *James J. Hill,* 144.

Page 31 By 1883 Hill: Ibid., 277.

Page 31 When an old: JJH–Lamont, December 6, 1904, JJHP.

Page 31 One friend swore: Paine, *George Fisher Baker,* 200; "Spokane Men Recall Anecdotes of Hill," *Saint Paul Pioneer Press,* May 30, 1916, 3.

Page 31 It didn't matter: "Railway World Leaders," *New York Evening Post,* May 4, 1901, 2.

Page 31 "No, you're wrong": "The Man in the Street," *New York Times Magazine,* August 18, 1901, 1.

Page 31 The next summer: Martin, *James J. Hill,* 346.

Page 32 By early 1889: Ibid., 411.

Page 32 "This country," he: Martin, *Railroads Triumphant,* 145.

Page 32 A third of: Daggett, *Railroad Reorganization,* v.

Page 32 From his perch: Blossom, "James J. Hill," 723.

Page 32 Hill considered its: Pyle, *The Life of James J. Hill,* 456–57.

Page 33 It was conceived: DiLorenzo, *How Capitalism Saved America,* 111.

Page 33 Its early weakness: Smalley, *History of the Northern Pacific Railroad,* 146.

Page 33 "You can't build": Lubetkin, *Jay Cooke's Gamble,* xv.

Page 33 Its federally granted: Wilgus, "The Northwestern Railway Situation," 255.

Page 33 He persevered, inspired: Ibid., 79.

Page 33 In just two: Smalley, *History of the Northern Pacific Railroad,* 223.

Page 34 The early Northern: *Northern Pacific Railroad Company,* 28.

Page 34 In 1879, representing: Daggett, *Railroad Reorganization,* 273.

Page 34 He also built: Martin, *Railroads Triumphant,* 293.

Page 35 Its fixed charges: Daggett, *Railroad Reorganization,* 270.

Page 35 so, some 300,000: Lyon, *To Hell in a Day Coach,* 105.

Page 36 In 1896 the: "No railroad corporation, or the lessees, purchasers or managers of any railroad corporation, shall consolidate the stock, property of franchises of such corporations with, or lease or purchase the works or franchises of, or in any way control any other railroad corporation owning or having under its control a parallel or competing line; nor shall any officer of such railroad corporation act as an officer of any other railroad corporation owning or having the control of a parallel or competing line" (*The General Statutes of the State of Minnesota,* prepared by George B. Young, fourth edition, 1883, 381.)

Page 36 He installed three: Allen, *The Great Pierpont Morgan,* 104.

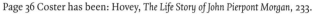

Page 36 Coster has been: Hovey, *The Life Story of John Pierpont Morgan*, 233.

Page 36 Three days after: Malone, *James J. Hill*, 181.

Page 36 from this day: Schonberger, "James J. Hill and the Trade," 184.

Page 37 The following Saturday: "Funeral of C. H. Coster," *New York Times*, March 17, 1900.

Page 37 Weeks before Coster's: Twining, *George S. Long*, 4.

Page 37 Hill and Morgan: Paine, *George Fisher Baker*, 196–208.

Page 37 Cash would require: "Burlington Deal Closed," *New York Evening Post*, April 8, 1901, 2.

Page 38 There to greet: Christopher Gray, "History by the Numbers," *New York Times* Nov. 7, 2008; Stapleton, *Where Liberty Dwells*, 21.

Page 38 Morgan found him: Scott, *Robert Bacon*, 70.

Page 38 Some wondered if: Chernow, *House of Morgan*, x.

Page 40 Despite all his: John Woodbury, "Robert Bacon," *Harvard Graduates Magazine*, September 1919, 76.

2. Mr. Harriman and Mr. Schiff

Page 41 Passing under its: Landau and Condit, *Rise of the New York Skyscraper*, 68–70, 75.

Page 41 Entering one of: Harriman's physical appearance makes him forever the target of caricaturists, this one based partly on John Kobler's, excerpted from Ellis and Vertin, *Wall Street People*, 91.

Page 41 until, that is: Garrett

Page 42 The Southern Pacific: Orsi, *Sunset Limited*, 33.

Page 42 The board would: "Harriman Syndicate Gives Demonstration of Its Control of Southern Pacific System," *San Francisco Call*, April 4, 1901, 1.

Page 42 "a little better": Klein, *The Life and Legend of E. H. Harriman*, 94.

Page 42 Surely because he: Klein, *The Life and Legend of E. H. Harriman*, 97; Figliomeni, *E. H. Harriman at Arden Farms*, 3.

Page 43 Morgan had his: Martin, *Railroads Triumphant*, 188.

Page 43 One admirer, Otto: Kahn, "Edward Henry Harriman,"17; Kennan, *E. H. Harriman*, 142.

Page 43 Christian gentleman though: Keys, "The Builders," 9789.

Page 43 Harriman never dined: Johnson, *A History of the American People*, 563.

Page 43 He was one: Kennan, *E. H. Harriman*, 13–14.

Page 43 A contemporary described: Ibid., 107.

Page 43 He developed an: Ibid., 244.

Page 44 When his bile: Lefevre, "Harriman," 129.

Page 44 He abhorred dictating: Klein, *Union Pacific*, 54; Keys, "A 'Corner' in Pacific Railroads," 5819.

Page 45 One of the: Klein, *The Life and Legend of E. H. Harriman*, 46.

Page 45 The death in: Ibid., 71.

Page 45 "stiff-necked to": Kahn, *Of Many Things*, 114.

Page 45 He became known: Ibid., 106.

Page 45 No surprise he: Moody and Turner, "The Masters of Capital in America" (January 1911), 335.

Page 45 He became a: *New York Sun,* September 10, 1909.

Page 45 Her father, William: Moody and Turner, "The Masters of Capital in America" (January 1911), 336.

Page 46 "If you buy": Ibid., 338.

Page 46 In a few: Ibid.

Page 47 During all these: Lefevre, "Harriman," 115.

Page 47 "He noticed everything": Klein, *The Life and Legend of E. H. Harriman,* 125.

Page 47 He asked the: Ibid., 123.

Page 47 In his first: Ibid., 132.

Page 47 "The train makes": "The Railroads and the People," *Independent,* March 28, 1907, 702.

Page 48 "It's a great": Klein, *The Life and Legend of E. H. Harriman,* 174.

Page 48 He regretted having: Ibid., 699–700.

Page 49 "What the brush": Casson, *The History of the Telephone,* 205.

Page 50 His was not: The first time he gained national attention was not for his railroad work but for a family cruise to Alaska in 1899 that he turned into a major scientific expedition. He had refitted one of his commercial steamers into a cruiser and recruited twenty-three scientists, including John Muir, to join him and his family on what became a two-month summer expedition. When he visited the U.S. Department of Agriculture in March 1899 for help from its biologists to recruit scientists for the trip, the head biologist had never heard of him. He thought Harriman was a crank (Klein, *The Life and Legend of E. H. Harriman,* 183).

Page 50 Or as one: Meyer, *History of the Northern Securities Case,* 523.

Page 51 It should not: Allen, *The Great Pierpont Morgan,* 90.

Page 51 The era's most: Lefevre, "The American Newspaper," 145.

Page 51 He was only: Jacob H. Schiff, 1847–1920. Memorialized by the Jacob H. Schiff Memorial in the New York Community Trust, 909 Third Avenue, New York (nycommunitytrust.org).

Page 52 "Behind the gray": Phillips-Matz, *The Many Lives of Otto Kahn,* 45. Kuhn, Loeb was acquired by Lehman Brothers (1977), then subsumed into American Express (1984), which spun Lehman Brothers Kuhn Loeb off ten years later as Lehman Brothers Holdings, Inc., which went bankrupt in 2008.

Page 52 In his more: Birmingham, *"Our Crowd,"* 155.

Page 52 As a boy: Ibid., 154–55.

Page 52 The Germans called: Ibid., 256–57.

Page 52 At Kuhn, Loeb: Ibid., 54.

Page 52 Abraham Kuhn and: Ibid., 9.

Page 53 "he knew English": Lefevre, *The Golden Flood,* 160.

Page 53 Schiff never had: B. C. Forbes, 328.

Page 53 "Whenever anything occurred": Adler, *Jacob H. Schiff,* 2: 344.

Page 53 Paul D. Cravath, senior: Ibid., 353.

Page 54 Two years before: Frederic, *The Market-Place,* 205. "I used to watch those Jews' hands, a year ago, when I was dining and wining them. They're all thin and wiry and full of veins. Their fingers are never still; they twist round and keep stirring like a lobster's feelers. But there aint any real strength in 'em. They get hold of most of the things that are going, because they're eternally on the move. It's their hellish industry and activity that gives them such a pull, and makes most people afraid of them."

Page 55 "To form a more": Adler, *Jacob H. Schiff,* 1: 70.

Page 55 "On the mountain": Ibid., 1: vi.

Page 56 He read every: Birmingham, *"Our Crowd,"* 178.

Page 56 Family, strictly bound: Ibid., 386.

Page 56 "I have made": Adler, *Jacob H. Schiff*, 2: 322.

Page 56 So, every Friday: "Jacob H. Schiff, 1847–1920," Memorialized by the Jacob H. Schiff Memorial in the New York Community Trust.

Page 56 Jacob blessed the: Birmingham, *"Our Crowd,"* 182.

Page 57 That is why: It was called the "Sub-Treasury" but there was nothing "sub" about it. It was the most important government building in the country for the economy because almost every bank in the nation had an account in a New York bank and sent its surplus funds there. At the time of this story, it transacted two-thirds of the U.S. government's gross money business and three-fourths of its interest and bond business. New York was the economic heart of the nation: almost two-thirds of the nation's imports and half its exports passed through the Port of New York (King, *King's Views of the New York Stock Exchange,* 2, 3, 23).

Page 57 When Warburg sat: Adler, *Jacob H. Schiff*, 1: 25.

Page 57 "Be Americans above": "Rabbis Hear Schiff put America First," *New York Times,* November 10, 1915.

Page 57 Morgan, who had: Winkler, *Morgan the Magnificent,* 10.

Page 57 Schiff tried to: Hill–Schiff, August 20, 1891, quoted in Martin, *James J. Hill and the Opening of the Northwest,* 439.

Page 58 He was oriented: Moody and Turner, "The Masters of Capital in America" (January 1911), 339.

Page 58 When it went: Daggett, *Railroad Reorganization,* 249.

Page 58 "Markets are better": A. Lamb, "The Game in Wall Street," *Life,* May 9, 1901, 401.

Page 58 He was called: Ibid., 408.

Page 58 Common stockholders, in: Daggett, *Railroad Reorganization,* 249.

Page 59 "It's that little": Klein, *Union Pacific,* 24.

Page 59 Ten years later: Adler, *Jacob H. Schiff*, 1: 121.

Page 59 It was perhaps: Kennan, *E. H. Harriman,* 123–25; Klein, *The Life and Legend of E. H. Harriman,* 112.

Page 60 Then sometime later: Moody and Turner, "The Masters of Capital in America" (January 1911), 340–41: Klein, *The Life and Legend of E. H. Harriman,* 113.

Page 60 Its reorganization committee: Klein, *Union Pacific,* 50.

Page 60 Off stepped Schiff: "Great Auction Sale, Union Pacific Will Be put Under the Hammer Today," *Omaha Daily Bee,* November 1, 1897, 1.

Page 60 Schiff's committee was: Klein, *The Life and Legend of E. H. Harriman,* 114.

Page 60 The government auctioneer: "Great Public Sale, Government Closes Out Its Lien on Pioneer Western Railroad," *Omaha Daily Bee,* November 2, 1897, 1.

Page 61 The only bid: The $81.5 million (minus the Union Pacific's $18.2 fund for paying bonded debt) included another $27.6 million of first mortgage bonds and $13.6 million in other securities (Klein, *Union Pacific,* 28.) Regardless, the purchase proved a bargain. Union Pacific common closed with a bid price of just under $23 a share that November 1, 1897. By the end of 1901 it was just over $103.

Page 61 "Now, who the": Klein, *The Life and Legend of E. H. Harriman,* 117.

Page 61 "Let me be": Birmingham, *Our Crowd,* 204:

Page 61 With his certainty: Robeson, *The Portrait of a Banker,* 204.

Page 61 During that time: Kennan, *E. H. Harriman,* 160.

Page 61 The Union Pacific: Ibid., 159.

Page 61 It spent sixty-two: Ibid., 170–71.

Page 61 In 1899 it: Ibid., 164.

Page 61 It not only: Martin, *James J. Hill and The Opening of the Northwest,* 482.

Page 62 Hill always wanted: Moody and Turner, "The Masters of Capital in America" (December 1910), 134.

Page 62 Hill was a: Birmingham, *Our Crowd,* 162.

Page 62 Even during the: "Bulge in Northern Pacific," *Commercial Advertiser* (New York), May 8, 1901, 1.

Page 63 Hill's loyal lieutenant: Nichols–Hill, October 24,1894, JJHP, 20.B.2.7.

Page 63 Morgan's office—where: Chernow, *House of Morgan,* 39; Allen, *The Great Pierpont Morgan,* 127.

Page 63 Among those granted: "Mr. Morgan to Sail To-Day," *New York Tribune,* April 3, 1901, 6.

Page 63 It was perhaps: "Mr. Gates May Wage War on J. P. Morgan," *New York Herald,* May 16, 1901, 3.

Page 64 He repeated a: Adler, *Jacob H. Schiff,* 1: 105.

3. The End of the "Days of Small Things"

Page 65 Ten of its eleven: Charles J. Paine, William Endicott, Francis W. Hunnewell, Richard Olney, Edward W. Hooper, J. Malcolm Forbes, George P. Gardner, and Nathaniel Thayer were all from Boston; T. Jefferson Coolidge was from Manchester, Mass.; and Charles E. Perkins kept his office at and lived in Burlington but was a Boston agent. The sole outsider was Smith of New York City (*Forty-Sixth Annual Report of the Board of Directors of the Chicago, Burlington & Quincy,* 1900, 3).

Page 65 "Ship only if": Larson, *Bonds of Enterprise,* 20.

Page 66 "Imagine a deep": Ibid., 45.

Page 66 He was a: Overton, *Burlington Route,* 179.

Page 66 He was portly: Larson, *Bonds of Enterprise,*173.

Page 66 Perkins succeeded Forbes: Ibid., 168, 173.

Page 67 By 1883 it: Overton, *Burlington Route,* 215.

Page 67 From 1875 to: Ibid., 175, 197.

Page 67 "The railroad is": Cather, *The Song of the Lark,* 366; Wenzl, *Mytholgia Americana,* 6; "Chicago, Burlington & Quincy," 6.

Page 67 Forbes and Perkins: Martin, *Railroads Triumphant,* 276.

Page 67 Perkins later called: Martin, *James J. Hill,* 324.

Page 68 The Burlington's big: Bacon, *Boston Illustrated,* 84.

Page 68 Thus the incessant: Martin, *James J. Hill,* 487.

Page 68 "Hill is in": Ibid., 491.

Page 69 "Our business will": Ibid., 345.

Page 69 Perkins had seen: Martin, *Railroads Triumphant,* 270.

Page 69 It had more: "Value of the Burlington," *New York Evening Post*, April 6, 1901, 11.

Page 69 Side tracks along: "Prosperity in the West," *New York Evening Post*, April 12, 1901, 10.

Page 69 "cut rates almost": "Community of Interest," *New York Times*, letter to editor from "Facts," February 18, 1901, 6.

Page 70 The Sherman Anti-Trust: Letwin, *Law and Economic Policy in America*, 143.

Page 70 It forbade restraint: It prohibited "every contract, combination in the form of a trust or otherwise, or conspiracy, in restraint of trade or commerce among the several States or with foreign nations" Harvey, *A Manual of the Federal Trade Comisssion*, 279).

Page 70 "drive a coach": "Community of Interest," *New York Times*, letter to editor from "Veteran," May 9, 1901.

Page 70 if railroad capital: Earl D. Berry, "The First Railway Merger," *Everybody's Magazine*, April 1903, 305.

Page 70 Sometime in late: Ibid.

Page 70 If they invested: "Nine Railroad Kings," *Washington Post*, May 2, 1901, 3:1.

Page 70 It was one: *American Architect and Building News* 44: 957, April 28, 1894, comments on the Association for the Promotion of Profit-Sharing to promote "a greater community of interest, and more friendly relationship, between employers and employed" (37).

Page 71 Broker Henry Clews: Clews, "Publick Occurences: The Northern Securities Deal," *Saturday Evening Post*, January 4, 1902, 15.

Page 71 Morgan denied it: Testimony in Peter Power vs. Northern Pacific Railway Company, March 26, 1902, reprinted in Northern Securities Company et al. vs. The United States, October 1903 term, 342.

Page 71 Morgan himself defined: Ibid., 343.

Page 71 A handful of: E. J. Edwards, "The Men Who Control the Nation's Railways," *New York Times*, June 27, 1909.

Page 71 "It is human": "Jacob H. Schiff Says Legislation Has Forced Railroads into 'Community of Interest' Plan," *New York Herald*, May 23, 1901, 5.

Page 71 Almost overnight with: "The Pennsylvania Railroad," *Railway Times*, April 18, 1903, 389.

Page 71 It bought 16: "The Railway Situation, 'Community of Interest' Still Effective in Fact if Not in Form," *New York Times*, Weekly Financial Review, August 16, 1903, 25.

Page 71 The New York: Holdsworth, "Transportation," 168.

Page 72 Almost every board: New York Central President Chauncey Depew was an officer or director of fifty-six transportation companies; William K. Vanderbilt, fifty-one; Missouri Pacific President George Gould, thirty-five; E. V. Rossiter, treasurer of the New York Central & Hudson River Railroad, thirty-one; Harriman, twenty-eight; Michigan Southern President Charles F. Cox, twenty-seven; Northern Pacific Vice President Daniel Lamont, twenty-eight; Morgan, twenty-three (Meyer, "History of the Northern Securities Case," 240).

Page 72 Practical pooling—through: Noyes, *A Treatise on the Law of Intercorporate Relations*, 544.

Page 72 Into this froth: Noyes, *Forty Years of American Finance*, 290.

Page 72 The "days of small": Perkins to John N. Griswold, January 2, 1901, quoted in Overton, *Burlington Route*, 251.

Page 72 "The railroads had": Bellamy, *Looking Backward*, 74.

Page 72 Perkins confided to: Overton, *Burlington Route*, 253.

Page 73 It set a: Martin, *James J. Hill*, 488.

Page 74 "I believe Schiff": Ibid.

Page 74 He personally invested: blog.citigroup.com/2012/04.

Page 74 Groomed to be: Moody and Turner, "The Masters of Capital in America" (May 1911), 76.

Page 75 It was chief: Lander, *World's Work*, 1313.

Page 75 A decade later: Moody and Turner, "The Masters of Capital in America" (May 1911), 84.

Page 75 He had met: Robeson, *The Portrait of a Banker*, 124.

Page 75 By 1899 he: Winkler, *The First Billion*, 101; Kennan, "The Chicago & Alton Case," xx.

Page 75 Secretive like Harriman: In March, 1902, attorney William A. Lancaster of Minneapolis took testimony in New York, in a lawsuit against the Northern Securities Corporation, from Hill's close associate and financier, John Stewart Kennedy. Lancaster read Kennedy the names of the Northern Securities directors and asked, "The next name is that of James Stillman. Who is he?" Kennedy replied, "He is President of the City Bank. I thought everybody knew who he was." "I never heard of him," replied Mr. Lancaster ("Northern Securities Plan and Scope," *New York Times*, March 20, 1902, 3).

Page 75 His blank, melancholy: Robeson, *The Portrait of a Banker*, 180.

Page 75 Stillman asked what: Kennan, *E. H. Harriman*, 356–57.

Page 76 Like Harriman, Stillman: Winkler, *The First Billion*, 79.

Page 76 He cut her: Ibid., 86.

Page 76 He would send: Ibid., 124.

Page 76 Stenographers froze in: Ibid., 70.

Page 76 Hill's longtime financial: Farrer–Hill, August 25, 1905, JJHP, MHS.

Page 76 One New York: Clipping with letter from J. A. Wheelock, editor-in-chief, *Saint Paul Pioneer Press*, to Hill, February 7, 1901, President's Records, Great Northern Railway Company, Minnesota Historical Society.

Page 76 Hill said the: Pyle, *The Life of James J. Hill*, 126.

Page 77 It carried a: "Huntington's Body Here," *New York Times*, August 16, 1900, 3.

Page 78 Huntington confessed little: White, *Railroaded*, 254.

Page 78 The train carrying: "Collis P. Huntington's Body Brought Here," *New York Times*, August 16, 1900, 12.

Page 78 He had warred: Bancroft, *Chronicles of the Builders of the Commonwealth*, 37.

Page 78 About a month: Klein, *The Life and Legend of E. H. Harriman*, 216.

Page 78 Harriman, who six: White, *Railroaded*, 409.

Page 79 "The more I": Pyle, *The Life of James J. Hill*, 451.

Page 79 Hill initially had: Hill–Messrs. J. P. Morgan & Company, November 8, 1898, JJHP. Hill testified in Peter Power vs. Northern Pacific Railway Company in February 1902 that he and his associates had acquired about $26 million par value of Northern Pacific stock shortly after the 1896 reorganization at an average cost of about $16 a share (J. P. Morgan testimony, Peter Power vs. Northern Pacific Railway Company, March 26, 1902, 314, from Supreme Court of the United States, October term, 1903, No. 277, 18,294, Northern Securities Company et al. vs. The United States; Paine, *George Fisher Baker*, 197).

Page 80 "I will send": Paine, *George Fisher Baker*, 182.

Page 80 At a word: *Time*, April 14, 1924.

Page 80 When he built: Beard, *After the Ball*, 64.

Page 80 "Yes," replied Morgan": Paine, *George Fisher Baker*, 197.

Page 80 As Morgan later: Testimony, Peter Power vs. Northern Pacific Railway Company, March 26, 1902, reprinted in Northern Securities Company et al. vs. The United States, October 1903 term, 335.

Page 82 "I was thinking": Paine, *George Fisher Baker*, 199.

Page 82 The next morning: "Great Rise in Prices on the Stock Exchange," *New York Times*, November 8, 1900.

Page 82 "This country is": Ibid.

Page 82 Whispered to be: "New Blood in Wall Street," *New York Times Magazine*, November 6, 1904, 3:3.

Page 82 As Hill's private: "Henry Villard Is Dead," *New York Times*, November 13, 1900; Villard, *Memoirs of Henry Villard*, 2:365.

Page 82 He and his: De Borchgrave, *Villard*, 378.

Page 82 Morgan cabled Hill: November 12, 1900, JJHP.

Page 83 The two railroads: Wallace, *From Harrison to Harding*, xx.

Page 83 Some hundred thousand: "Welcome Twentieth Century," *New York Times*, January 1, 1901, 1.

Page 83 The White House: Leech, *In the Days of McKinley*, 566.

Page 83 Banks and investment: "Stocks as a Rule Higher," *New York Times*, January 3, 1901, 12.

Page 83 "Every man who": Lefevre, "The American Newspaper," 146.

Page 84 At Grand Island: Martin, *James J. Hill*, 487–88.

Page 84 "It seems safe": Lorimer, *Letters from a Self-Made Merchant to His Son*, 192.

Page 84 The following Sunday: Millett, *Lost Twin Cities*, 152–53.

Page 84 "I am just": Wade, *Chicago's Pride*, 221.

Page 84 Hill called rumors: "Hill Says It's Rubbish," *Saint Paul Globe*, January 5, 1901, 8.

Page 84 Union Pacific interests: *Wall Street Journal*, January 8, 1901.

Page 85 The animosity ran: Hill testimony, Peter Power vs. Northern Pacific Railway Company, February 17, 1902, 71.

Page 85 Hill felt an: Hill–Harriman, January 29, 1901, JJHP.

Page 85 It may have: Hill–Kennedy, May 16, 1901, JJHP.

Page 85 "So as to": Martin, *James J. Hill*, 496.

Page 86 So much for: The *Wall Street Journal* had Hill in mind when it published the following statement on April 24, 1901 ("Community of Ownership on Trial"): "It really became clear that perhaps a dozen men were able to dominate the policy of more than half the railway mileage in the country. Were these men willing habitually to subordinate personal preferences to the genial wish, also to accept a disadvantage in the property in which they were primarily interested, in order to obtain an advantage on the property in which their interest is only secondary, there could be little chance for friction. Should, however, any one of this small number of railway magnates seek to obtain undue advantage for his particular property, or for himself personally, it was equally clear that community of ownership might not prevent hostilities along new lines of cleavage" (1).

Page 86 "The Street is": "A Short Look and a Long Look," *Wall Street Journal*, January 24, 1901, 1.

Page 86 Miller admitted weeks: "Deal with J. J. Hill Is Off," *New York Times*, April 16, 1901.

Page 86 Further, he must: Klein, *Union Pacific*, 103.

Page 86 Behind the scenes: Stedman, *The New York Stock Exchange*, 395.

Page 86 As inheritor two: "The Social Career of 'Silent' James Henry Smith," *New York Times*, September 16, 1906; Craven, *Stanford White*, 113.
Page 86 He knew Schiff: Hill–Mount Stephen, June 4, 1901, JJHP.

4. The Battle for the Burlington

Page 87 Patrician, a bit: Korom, *The American Skyscraper*, xx.
Page 87 Drifts banked several: "Second Storm Fetters Chicago," *Chicago Tribune*, February 9, 1901, 1.
Page 87 Amid palm trees: *Illinois Central Railroad Company Fiftieth Anniversary*, n.p.
Page 87 The distinguished audience: "Half Century for a Railroad," *Chicago Tribune*, February 10, 1901, 8.
Page 88 Gentlemen: I know: *Chicago Tribune*, February 10, 1901.
Page 88 "When Mr. Hill": Peter Power vs. Northern Pacific Railway Company, March 26, 1902, reprinted in Northern Securities Company vs. The United States, October term 1903, 332.
Page 89 He cabled Morgan: Martin, *James J. Hill*, 489.
Page 89 "He believed more": Strouse, *Morgan*, 220.
Page 89 Morgan cabled back: Martin, *James J. Hill*, 490.
Page 89 That same day: *Wall Street Journal*, February 14, 1901.
Page 89 Hill worried: were: Hill–Charles E. Perkins, February 18, 1901, JJHP.
Page 90 Yes, the Burlington's: CEP-JJH, Burlington, Iowa, February 19, 1901, JJHP.
Page 90 Then another rumor: "J. J. Hill Going on a Cruise," *New York Times*, February 10, 1901, 1.
Page 90 Veteran Exchange member: *Wall Street Journal*, February 19, 1901, 2; "New Blood in Wall Street," *New York Times Magazine*, November 6, 1904, 3:3.
Page 90 It was said: Grant, *Bernard M. Baruch*, 21.
Page 90 Several of its: *Wall Street Journal*, February 21, 1901, 2.
Page 90 "If Hill means": Overton, *Burlington Route*, 257.
Page 91 If the Burlington: Ibid.
Page 91 If the Burlington didn't: *Wall Street Journal*, March 6, 1901.
Page 91 "If I had $100,000,000": "Mr. Hill and Northern Pacific," *New York Evening Post*, May 11, 1901, 1.
Page 91 "He did not": Boren, *Legacies of the Turf*, 11.
Page 91 His office off: "Vignettes of the Slump," *Chicago Tribune*, May 10, 1901, 1.
Page 92 For his services: Strouse, 407; Simon, "The Man Who Loved Racing," 26–27.
Page 92 Keene never met: Geisst, *Wall Street*, 116.
Page 92 The morning after: Leech, *In the Days of McKinley*, 574.
Page 93 Hill left for: JJH–CEP, March 2, 1901, JJHP.
Page 94 "I don't own": *Wall Street Journal*, March 13, 1901, 5.
Page 94 Morgan and Bacon: *Wall Street Journal*, March 25, 1901, 1.
Page 95 There were rumors: Ibid.
Page 95 There was talk: *Wall Street Journal*, March 26, 1901, April 1, 1901; Paine, *George Fisher Baker*, 191.
Page 95 Schiff later wrote: Adler, *Jacob H. Schiff*, 1: 103.

Page 95 Schiff and Harriman: *Wall Street Journal*, April 2, 1901.

Page 95 Hill denied it: James J. Hill testimony, Peter Power v. Northern Pacific Railway Company, February 17, 1902, 26. Hill also said under oath: "It was expressly understood by Mr. Morgan and myself that no one should buy, either of his people or any of my associates should buy, any stock of the Burlington Railroad Company for themselves, and certainly not for the Company; not even for themselves to operate in it. That understanding was clear and explicit, and I believe it was carried out" (44).

Page 95 Trading opened volatile: *New York Sun*, March 27, 1901, 10.

Page 95 On March 11: "Another Feast for Great Northern Stockholders," *Railway Age*, March 22, 1901, 362.

Page 96 He had ended: "Plans Completed," *Saint Paul Pioneer Press*, March 30, 1901, 3.

Page 96 U.S. Steel common: Smith, *Toward Rational Exuberance*, 33.

Page 96 Perkins watched the: Perkins–Hill, March 1901, JJHP.

5. "Peacemakers" Arming for Combat

Page 97 He was Stillman's: Robeson, *The Portrait of a Banker*, 51.

Page 97 His law firm: Winkler, *The First Billion*, 92.

Page 97 The ideal client: quoted in Payne, "Lawyers and the Laws of Economics," 366.

Page 97 To pay the: Ibid., 202.

Page 97 Sterling and Stillman: Ibid., 94.

Page 97 Sterling lived at: Robeson, *The Portrait of a Banker*, 182.

Page 97 He had a: Winkler, *The First Billion*, 93.

Page 97 Despite his family's: Robeson, *The Portrait of a Banker*, 188; Garver, *John William Sterling*, 3.

Page 97 Sterling was a: Winkler, *The First Billion*, 10.

Page 97 He even locked: Garver, *John William Sterling*, 99.

Page 98 Sterling was known: Ibid., 97, 102.

Page 99 He had an: Chernow, *Titan*, 375; Lawson, "Outside Wall Street," 157.

Page 99 Unlike his older: Redmond, *Financial Giants of America*, 159; Chernow, *Titan*, 103.

Page 99 "I like William": Nevins, *Study in Power*, 285–86.

Page 100 Stillman was still: Poor, *Poor's Manual of the Railroads*, 584.

Page 100 When Morgan reorganized: Testimony of James J. Hill in Peter Power vs. Northern Pacific Railway Company, defendant, U.S. Circuit Court, District of Minnesota, Fourth Division, February 18, 1902.

Page 100 We believe the: Smith, *Toward Rational Exuberance*, 33.

Page 101 We believe many: "J. J. Hill before Commerce Commission," *New York Times*, January 25, 1902, 3.

Page 101 There are many: "Millions for Hill if He Sold Out Pierpont Morgan in 'N.P. Corner,'" *New York Evening World*, February 12, 1902, 2.

Page 101 We know a: "Northern Pacific Fight," *New York Evening Post*, May 7, 1901, 1.

Page 102 Many of them: "Stock Flies Skyward," *Chicago Daily News*, May 8, 1901, 1; "The Great Smash in Speculation Comes at Last," *New York Journal*, May 9, 1901, 1.

Page 103 They remembered John: Marcosson, "The Perilous Game of Cornering a Crop," 624.

Page 103 They remembered Cincinnati: Ibid., 625.

Page 104 On June 13: Ibid.; Wendt and Kogan, *Bet a Million!* 134. Leiter's escapades inspired Frank Norris's 1903 novel *The Pit.*

Page 105 On April 9: "Wall Street Gossip," *Commercial Advertiser* (New York), April 9, 1901, 10.

Page 105 And a week: "Wall Street Gossip," *Commercial Advertiser* (New York), April 17, 1901, 12.

Page 105 "buyers and sellers": "Wild Stock Seesaw," *New York Herald,* April 5, 1901, 3.

Page 105 When the bears: Ibid.

Page 105 "What constitutes the": "New York: Speculation Runs Riot in Wall Street," *New York Herald,* April 8, 1901, 13.

Page 105 The *Wall Street Journal* said: *Wall Street Journal,* April 4, 1901, 1.

Page 105 Hill negotiated all: MTH Diary, 1901, 16, JJHP.

Page 105 Pulitzer's *New York:* "What He Will Be There For," *New York Evening World,* March 30, 1901, 6.

Page 106 Hill was a: *Brooklyn Eagle,* April 8, 1901, 7; W. Thomas White, introduction to Martin, *James J. Hill,* xx.

Page 106 The bells had: "Thousands Crowd St. Patrick's," *New York Herald,* April 8, 1901, 5.

Page 106 "the blowing of": "Seeking Victory, Buy Burlington," *New York Herald,* May 13, 1901, 5.

Page 106 It was Harriman: Baker and Schiff give conflicting versions of how this Easter Sunday meeting was orchestrated and Hill's path to it, April 5–7, 1901. In her diary, Mary Hill has her husband going from the *Wacouta* to Boston early on Good Friday, April 5, spending all day in Boston, then arriving in New York early Saturday morning (and he "was very tired so went to bed and slept several hours"). She then has him busy in meetings in New York City all Easter Sunday afternoon and at Baker's for dinner that evening (presumably the meeting with Harriman and Schiff). Schiff in his letter to J. P. Morgan on May 16, 1901, says he had learned that Hill intended to leave Washington, D.C., and "go to Boston that night," then has his son Mortimer intercepting Hill at the ferry landing in New York and bringing him to Baker's home, but Schiff mentions no dates. (Adler, *Jacob H. Schiff,* 1: 105). Albro Martin repeats the Schiff version (*James J. Hill,* 497) and even names the ferry slip as Pennsylvania Station's at Desbrosses Street, although Schiff doesn't specify it in his letter to Morgan. Baker's version seems more logical and convincing; Schiff's seems designed to give Morgan the impression Schiff arranged the meeting.

Page 106 They were escorted: Description of interior from Paine, *George Fisher Baker,* 168–69.

Page 106 Hill had a: Birmingham, "*Our Crowd,*" 183.

Page 106 Schiff said he: Adler, *Jacob H. Schiff,* 1: 103.

Page 107 "violent combat among": *Life,* May 23, 1901, 430.

Page 108 A newspaper claimed: "News of the Railroads," *Commercial Advertiser* (New York), April 8, 1901, 2.

Page 108 "Dear Mr. Hill": Schiff–Hill, JJHP.

Page 109 "My dear Mr. Schiff": JJHP, general correspondence, April 9–10, 1901 file 20.C.4.3.

Page 111 That afternoon, April: "J. J. Hill's Burlington Deal," *New York Times,* April 11, 1901.

Page 111 Exhausted, he had: Strouse, *Morgan,* 412; Allen, *The Great Pierpont Morgan,* 113.

Page 111 A cordon of: *New York Evening World,* April 10, 1901, 10; *New York Times,* April 11, 1901.

Page 111 There was good: "Threats to Kill Morgan," *Saint Paul Pioneer Press,* March 27, 1901, 1.

Page 111 His son Jack: "J. P. Morgan at London," *New York Evening Post,* April 11, 1901, 2; Allen, *The Great Pierpont Morgan,* 188.

Page 111 Northern Pacific's acquisition: *Wall Street Journal*, April 12, 1901.

Page 112 Tuck retired from: Robert Davis, "The Unofficial Ambassador to France," *Dartmouth Alumni Magazine*, August 1928, 789.

Page 112 Hill and Tuck: "Negotiations Completed," *Saint Paul Pioneer Press*, April 16, 1901, 1.

Page 113 The rate on: "J. P. Morgan & Co's Loans," *New York Times*, April 13, 1901.

Page 113 After the long: MTH Diary, 18, JJHP.

Page 113 It had been: Robert S. McGonigal, "How a Steam Locomotive Works, ABC's of Railroading," trn.trains.com, May 1, 2006.

Page 113 The ten-wheel: I am indebted to Kenneth C. Middleton for helping identify (personal e-mail, November 6, 2012); Middleton and Pirebe, *Steam Locomotives of the Great Northern Railway*, 109, 480.

Page 113 Engine and tender : Details of the Rogers locomotive and the Great Northern purchase are from "The Year in Locomotive Construction," *Daily Railway Age*, June 14, 1899; "Manufactures–Supplies," *Railway Age*, January 6, 1899; "Personal Mention," *Railway Age*, May 17, 1901, June 16, 1899, 457; *American Engineer and Railroad Journal*, February 1899, 65; and C. B. Conger, "Plain Talks to the Boys: Breaking in New Engines," *Railway and Locomotive Engineering*, January 1900, 8. "President Hill's Wild Run from Seattle to St. Paul," *Saint Paul Dispatch*, April 20, 1901, 1, states that this Rogers passenger locomotive was not hooked to the Hill train until the return trip at Cut Bank, Montana.

Page 114 Their passage west: "Fast Run the Great Northern," *Railway Age*, April 26, 1901, 460; Potter, *101 Best Stories of Minnesota*, 24. The four mountain ranges include the Rockies, Cabinet, Kootenai, and Cascades; the nine Indian nations: Dakota, Ojibwe, Assiniboine, Gros Ventre, Blackfoot, Kutenai, Salish, Spokane, and Pend d'Oreille; and the ten rivers: Mississippi, Missouri, Red, Milk, Yellowstone, Marias, Flathead, Wenatchee, Tye, and Columbia.

Page 114 In New York: *Wall Street Journal*, April 15, 1901.

Page 114 They needed 375,000: Smith, *Toward Rational Exuberance*, 34.

Page 114 "A story circulated": "Wall Street Gossip," *Commercial Advertiser* (New York), April 15, 1901, 10.

Page 114 Also wrong, perhaps: "Wall Street Gossip," *Commercial Advertiser* (New York), April 10, 1901, 13.

Page 115 From Anoka north: *Appleton's General Guide to the United States and Canada*, 489; Jacobson, *An American Journey by Rail*, 106.

Page 115 They sped north: *Appleton's General Guide to the United States and Canada*, 491.

Page 115 He had bought: "Interview with Clare Strom," *Fedgazette*, the Federal Reserve Bank of Minneapolis, March 2007, 14; *Minnesota: A State Guide*, 335.

Page 115 but native-born Americans: "The Big Rush Continues," *Saint Paul Dispatch*, March 21, 1901, 3.

Page 115 "Enormous areas of": Hill, *Highways of Progress*, 153.

Page 115 Past shelter belts: Jacobson, *An American Journey by Rail*, 106.

Page 115 Great heaps of: *Appleton's General Guide to the United States and Canada*, 492.

Page 116 They set their: http://www.lewisandclarktrail.com.

Page 116 Brokerage firms secretly: Lord, *The Good Years*, 72.

Page 116 He was reported: *New York Times*, April 16, 1901, 1.

Page 116 His father wanted: Strouse, *Morgan*, 162, 412.

Page 116 Six days before: McIntyre, *The Napoleon of Crime*, 225.

Page 116 "Nobody will ever": "Morgan Won't Tell," *Minneapolis Journal*, April 19, 1901, 1: "An Invasion from Pittsburg," *Life*, May 14, 1901, 411.

Page 117 When Hill was: W. Thomas White, introduction to Martin, *James J. Hill*, xv.

Page 117 It was there: Martin, *James J. Hill*, 346–47; Malone, Roeder, and Lang, *Montana*, 180.

Page 117 It was the: Hidy and Hidy, "John Frank Stevens," 347–48; Malone, Roeder, and Lang, *Montana*, xx.

Page 118 This fall the: Smith, *The World's Food Resources*, 388; Washington State Horticultural Association, *Proceedings, Annual Meeting*, 1951, 61.

Page 118 He climbed and: Hidy and Hidy, "John Frank Stevens," 348–49.

Page 118 Then the switchbacks: Yenne, *Great Northern, Empire Builder*, 25; Clark, *Over the Hump*.

Page 119 It was a: "Wall Street Gossip," *Commercial Advertiser* (New York), April 17, 1901, 12.

Page 119 Hill wanted to: *Minneapolis Journal*, April 19, 1901.

Page 119 At 5:15 a.m. on: Sale, *Seattle*, 66.

Page 119 Work had begun: *Railway Age*, August 24, 1900, 157.

Page 119 They sweetened the: *Wall Street Journal*, April 19, 1901.

Page 119 Hill's train spent: Historians such as Ron Chernow (*The House of Morgan*) and Stephen Birmingham ("*Our Crowd*") have repeated the story, without citing a source, that during this trip while sleeping in his private car in Seattle Hill was visited in a dream by a "dark-complected angel" who supposedly warned him of trouble in New York. It is a self-perpetuating myth; Hill's definitive biographer, Albro Martin, ignored it.

Page 119 Hill wanted to: "Hill Hurries Home," *Minneapolis Journal*, April 19, 1901, 6; "President Hill Rushes East," *Seattle Star*, April 18, 1901, 1; "Seattle to St. Paul in Two Day Run," *New York Herald*, April 21, 1901, 5. It was a cramped sleeping car from Spokane to St. Paul, housing Hill, Tuck, French, and Hill's son James Norman.

Page 120 They arrived in: "The Great Northern Fast Fruit Train," *Railway Age*, April 12, 1901, 425: "President Hill's Wild Run from Seattle to St. Paul," *Saint Paul Dispatch*, April 20, 1901, 1.

Page 120 Hill's train stopped at: "Fast Run from Pacific Coast," *Saint Paul Pioneer Press*, April 21, 1901, 2.

Page 120 "This would be": Ibid.

Page 120 The engine vibrated: *Minneapolis Journal*, April 22, 1901.

Page 121 Buying erupted on: "New Record Day in Wall Street," *New York Herald*, April 20, 1901, 4.

Page 121 Every important stock: "Exciting Day on the Stock Exchange," *New York Times*, April 20, 1901, 1.

Page 121 Hill said he: "Seattle to St. Paul in Two Day Run," *New York Herald*, April 21, 1901, 5; "Ride of J. J. Hill," *Minneapolis Journal*, April 22, 1901, 6.

Page 121 Is it your: Lamont–Hill, April 20, 1901, JJHP.

Page 121 There were no: "Berlin Bourse Dull; Transactions Light," *New York Herald*, April 22, 1901, 13.

Page 121 Morgan agreed to: Paine, *George Fisher Baker*, xx.

Page 122 On the same: Stedman, *The New York Stock Exchange*, 395; Kennan, *E. H. Harriman*, 299.

Page 122 The lone dissenter: "Mr. Hill and Northern Pacific," *New York Evening Post*, May 11, 1901, 1.

Page 122 The St. Paul: Hill–Mount Stephen, June 15, 1905, JJHP.

Page 122 As the Hill: "A Record Day in Wall Street," *New York Sun*, April 20, 1901, 1.

Page 123 Chairman Kennedy, every: "Stocks at It Again," *Commercial Advertiser* (New York), April 20, 1901, 1.

Page 123 "Then the machine": Ibid.

Page 124 "Can come last": Hill–Lamont cable, April 21, 1901, JJHP.

Page 124 Lamont responded the: Lamont–Hill cable, April 22, 1901, JJHP.

Page 124 Bacon wanted him: Bacon–Hill cable, April 21, 1901, JJHP.

Page 124 Looking back months: Baker, "The Great 'Northern Pacific Deal,'" 542.

Page 124 A great backlog: "In Clutch of a Storm," *Saint Paul Globe*, April 21, 1901, 1.

Page 124 Stocks of some: "The Week's Operation in Stocks," *New York Tribune*, April 22, 1901, 10.

Page 124 Colorado Fuel and: "Records Yield to Western Gold in Wall Street," *New York Herald*, April 22, 1901, 3.

Page 124 One of Stillman's: "Percy A. Rockefeller Weds Miss Stillman," *New York Times*, April 24, 1901, 9.

Page 124 Union Pacific accounted: "Old Records Broken by Union Pacific," *New York Herald*, April 25, 1901, 4.

Page 125 The Journal wasn't: *Wall Street Journal*, April 24, 1901.

Page 125 More worrisome, even: "Talked about in Wall Street," *New York Herald*, April 26, 1901, 12.

Page 125 The rise in: *Wall Street Journal*, April 25, 1901.

Page 125 There he bought: Strouse, *Morgan*, 414.

Page 125 Twelve years later: "J. P. Morgan's Famous Picture," *New York Times*, March 30, 1902; "J. Pierpont Morgan's Wonderful Gathering of European Art Treasures," *St. Louis Republic*, September 7, 1902, 48.

Page 125 On Friday, April: "Sidelights That Bring Out Characteristics of Mr. Hill," *Saint Paul Pioneer Press*, May 30, 1916, 2; MTH Diary, JJHP.

Page 125 "We have been": Hill–Mount Stephen, April 26, 1901, JJHP.

Page 126 Volume had tripled: http://www.usequities.nyx.com/markets/new-york-stock-exchange-history.

Page 126 The floor was: "Passing of Old Stock Exchange," *New York Herald*, April 27, 1901, 3; "Moving Day in Wall Street," *New York Herald*, April 28, 1901, 8; "Last Day of Old Board," *New York Evening Post*, April 26, 1901, 2.

Page 126 "Got to take": "Stocks Recover," *Commercial Advertiser* (New York), May 4, 1901, 1.

Page 126 In St. Paul: Martin, *James J. Hill*, 499.

Page 127 One analyst had: Klein, *Union Pacific*, 102.

Page 127 "There has been": *Wall Street Journal*, April 27, 1901.

Page 127 White-bearded Archibald: MTH Diary, JJHP ; President's files, Great Northern Railway Company, A.W. Clark–L.W. Campbell telegram, April 26, 1901, MHS.

Page 127 "For Jacob message": Hill–Nichols, President's files, Great Northern Railway Company, April 27, 1901, MHS.

6. "The Weak Link in Your Chain"

Page 128 The hall was: Landau, *George B. Post*, xx.

Page 128 They were separated: "Brokers Swamped Again," *New York Sun*, May 2, 1901, 10;

"Market Wobbles a Bit," *New York Sun*, May 4, 1901, 10; "Stock Exchange Moving," *Commercial Advertiser* (New York), April 26, 1901, 8.

Page 128 Spectators crowding the: Public galleries were an entirely American custom; non-members were not allowed in any of the exchanges in London, Paris, Amsterdam, Berlin, Frankfurt, or Vienna.

Page 128 Their temporary space: "Great Day for Stocks," *New York Sun*, April 30, 1901, 3.

Page 129 Since the stock: A. Lamb, "The Game in Wall Street," *Life*, May 9, 1901, 401.

Page 129 It had taken: "Moving Day on Exchange," *New York Tribune*, April 28, 1901, 6.

Page 129 Over the weekend: Ibid.; "Trading in Stocks," *Commercial Advertiser* (New York), April 27, 1901, 1.

Page 129 The Exchange employed: "Many Novelties in the New Stock Exchange," *New York Times*, February 9, 1901.

Page 129 The building evoked: Landau, *George B. Post*, 192; Silver, *Lost New York*, 102.

Page 129 Chairman Kennedy stood: "More Records at Exchange," *New York Tribune*, April 30, 1901, 1.

Page 129 The small gallery: "2,500,000-Share Day," *Commercial Advertiser* (New York), April 29, 1901, 1.

Page 129 Among the observers: "Feverish Wall Street Smashes All Records," *New York Herald*, April 30, 1901, 4.

Page 129 One large brokerage: "New Stock Quarters Poor," *New York Evening Post*, April 29, 1901, 1.

Page 130 heard a block: "All Records Surpassed," *New York Times*, May 1, 1901, 1.

Page 130 At precisely 10:30: "Departure from Washington," *New York Tribune*, April 30, 1901, 1; Miller, *The President and the Assassin*, 290; "Beginning the Long Journey," *Washington Post*, May 1, 1901, 6.

Page 130 This day McKinley's: "Progress through Virginia," *New York Tribune*, April 30, 1901, 1.

Page 131 By noon, trading: "More Records at Exchange," *New York Tribune*, April 30, 1901, 1.

Page 131 Chicago investors were: *Wall Street Journal*, April 30, 1901.

Page 131 Some major Wall: *New York Sun*, April 30, 1901, 8.

Page 131 Many traders, drenched: "All Records Surpassed," *New York Times*, May 1, 1901, 1.

Page 131 Southern Pacific buying: Philip King, "The Financial Situation," *New York Sun*, April 29, 1901, 7.

Page 131 "Some of the": *Wall Street Journal*, April 30, 1901, 1.

Page 131 On this day: "Seat in Stock Exchange for $66,000," *New York Tribune*, April 30, 1901, 1.

Page 131 A sheriff walked: *New York Times*, May 3, 1901, 3.

Page 132 Hill arrived in: "Talked about in Wall Street," *New York Herald*, April 30, 1901, 14.

Page 132 Lamont and the: Ibid.

Page 133 One report called: Norman and Jonson, *The London Stock Exchange*, 187.

Page 133 One reporter described: "New Blood in Wall Street," *New York Times*, November 6, 1904.

Page 133 If one got: Lefevre, *Sampson Rock of Wall Street*, 130.

Page 133 More than a: *New York Times*, January 2, 1902, 12.

Page 133 It was so: "Bulls Toss Stock Records to Wind," *New York Herald*, May 1, 1901, 6.

Page 133 Buy orders poured: "Dealing Unprecedented," *New York Evening Post*, April 30, 1901, 1.

Page 134 Volume surpassed 3.2: "The Year's New York Stock Exchange Transactions," *New York Times*, Annual Financial Review, January 5, 1902, 45.

Page 134 After the wedding: Simon, *Fifth Avenue*, 113.

Page 134 With the market: "Steamer Delayed by Terrific Crush," *New York Herald*, May 1, 1901, 10; "Crush on Big Kaiser's Pier," *New York Tribune*, May 1, 1901, 16.

Page 134 He also commented: Perkins–Hill, April 30, 1901, JJHP.

Page 135 The letter never: There was one Northern Pacific official, President Charles S. Mellen, the Morgan appointee who had a reputation for talking too much, who may have suspected something was up. "I don't know what the Union Pacific people propose to do," he was quoted as having said sometime around April 18, 1901, by the *New York Evening Post* two days after the corner and panic, "but I suspect that Mr. Harriman will consider that the best way to protect the Union Pacific, if he considers it endangered, will be to buy into Northern Pacific, and to be in a position to demand a voice in its management." Whether he voiced his concerns to Hill or whether Hill took him seriously isn't known. More peculiar, Mellen telegraphed the *Post* and told it his quote was "unauthorized, misleading, false and embarrassing" ("Control of N.P. Stock," *New York Evening Post*, May 9, 1901; "President Mellen Denies Interview," *New York Evening Post*, May 10, 1901).

Page 135 By scanning the: Allen, *The Great Pierpont Morgan*, 294.

Page 135 In addition to: "J. P. Morgan & Co. to Buy the Leyland Line," *New York Times*, April 30, 1901, 2.

Page 135 On Wednesday, May: Pyle, *The Life of James J. Hill*, 2: 146.

Page 135 He saw Northern: John W. Sterling–JJH, May 6, 1901, JJHP.

Page 136 "I have word": Paine, *George Fisher Baker*, 206; Hill was ever grateful for his loyalty. Six years after Hill died, Lord Strathcona's grandson honeymooned in the United States. Hill's heirs "lavishly entertained" him and his bride, who recalled years later that Hill had told his heirs never to forget what Lord Strathcona had done for him in 1901 (Wilkins. *The History of Foreign Investment in the United States to 1914*, 741.).

Page 136 "I cannot tell": Ellis–Hill, May 9, 1901, JJHP.

Page 136 A large portion: "E. D. Adams Seller of 'Nipper' Stock," *New York Herald*, May 27, 1901, 3.

Page 136 Sometime between April: Martin, *James J. Hill*, 441; "One Loser in the Panic; A Northern Pacific Executive Committee Member Caught Short," *New York Times*, May 28, 1901, 6.

Page 136 Adams was living: "E. D. Adams Seller of 'Nipper' Stock," *New York Herald*, May 27, 1901, 3.

Page 136 Estimates were that: Robeson, *The Portrait of a Banker*, 172.

Page 136 Using Kuhn, Loeb's: Harriman–G.W. Batson quoted in Kennan, *E. H. Harriman*, 316.

Page 137 If he'd gained: "Inquiry Into Harriman Lines," *Amsterdam [N.Y.] Evening Record*, February 27, 1907, 1.

Page 137 He and his: A. Lamb, "The Game in Wall Street," *Life*, April 25, 1901, 964.

Page 137 Then it swung: *Cook's Handbook to the Health Resorts of the South of France*, 134.

Page 137 With two wings: www.patrimoine-aixlesbains.fr.

Page 138 "two half-naked": *Chicago Tribune*, November 8, 1891.

Page 138 Then back Morgan: Brachet, *Aix-les-Bains*, 13.

Page 138 He may have: "Baths Are Helping Morgan," *New York Times*, May 4, 1901.

7. The Consequences of a "Hostile Act"

Page 139 In one span: "Union Pacific Control Discussed," *New York Herald*, May 2, 1901, 12.

Page 139 Otto Loeb, a: "Wall Street Gossip," *Commercial Advertiser* (New York), May 1, 1901, 12.

Page 139 One customer ordered: "Talked about on Wall Street," *New York Herald*, May 2, 1901, 12.

Page 139 Brokers "howled and": *Wall Street Journal*, May 2, 1901.

Page 139 Some leading commission: "Exciting Scenes in the Stock Exchange," *New York Times*, May 2, 1901, 3.

Page 139 Brokers were so: "Wall Street Boom, Backed by the Entire World," *New York Journal*, May 1, 1901, 5.

Page 139 One broker wanted: "Great Rise in Atchison," *New York Evening Post*, May 2, 1901, 1.

Page 140 Red-eyed clerks worked: Ibid.; Plunz, *A History of Housing in New York City*, 68; Homberger, *Mrs. Astor's New York*, 71.

Page 140 The Exchange fined: "Brokers, Clerks Overworked," *New York Times*, May 2, 1901.

Page 140 The rush of: "Brokers Swamped Again," *New York Sun*, May 2, 1901, 10.

Page 140 There were reports: Nelson, "The Machinery of Wall Street," July 1901, 977.

Page 140 One commission broker: *New York Sun*, May 2, 1901.

Page 140 The federal government: "Stamps in the 'Bull' Movement," *New York Tribune Illustrated Supplement*, April 23, 1899, 5; "Boom Takes Atchison," *Chicago Tribune*, May 3, 1901, 11.

Page 140 Was Vanderbilt conferring: *Wall Street Journal*, May 2, 1901, 1.

Page 141 There had never: *Wall Street Journal*, May 1, 1901, 1.

Page 141 "Where is there": "Stock Market Quakes and Prices Tumble," *New York Times*, May 4, 1901.

Page 141 As early as: Adler, *Jacob H. Schiff*, 1: 33.

Page 141 On the ferry: Stedman, *The New York Stock Exchange*, 397.

Page 142 Mobs gathered from: Lefevre, "The American Newspaper," 148.

Page 142 Hearst's *New York Journal*: "Wall Street Boom, Backed by the Entire World, Again Sends Records to Smash," *New York Journal*, May 1, 1901, 5.

Page 142 Speculators scoured the: Brokerage house color from "Unprecedented Craze for Speculation in Stocks," *Chicago Tribune*, May 5, 1901, 5:1.

Page 142 "The air was": Lefevre, *Wall Street Stories*, 179.

Page 142 Someone heard of: "Millions Made by Master, Man and Maid in Money Mad Market," *New York Herald*, May 5, 1901, 4:2.

Page 142 One could buy: A. Lamb, "The Game in Wall Street," *Life*, April 25, 1901, 964.

Page 142 "Are there tickers": Charles Henry Webb, "The Late Addison Cammack," *New York Times*, February 10, 1901.

Page 142 One conservative banker: "Records Yield to Western Gold in Wall Street," *New York Herald*, April 22, 1901, 3.

Page 143 For the first: Josephson, "Profiles: Fifty Years of Wall Street," 22.

Page 143 "There's U.P.": Women Join the Gamble," *New York Sun*, May 2, 1901, 7; Peterson, *The Greenwood Encyclopedia of Clothing*, xx.

Page 143 There always seemed: Lefevre, *Wall Street Stories*, 87.

Page 143 There were even: Clews, *The Wall Street Point of View*, 61.

Page 143 It was all: Duguid, *The Story of the [London] Stock Exchange*, 148.

Page 143 The market had: Lefevre, "Gambling in Bucket Shops," xx; Thomas Patton, "The Bucket Shop in Speculation," *Munsey's*, October 1900, 68.

Page 143 These were the: Fabian, *Card Sharps and Bucket Shops*, 156; "What Is a Bucket-Shop?" *Chamber's Journal*, July 22, 1893, 457; Thomas Patton, "The Bucket Shop in Speculation," *Munsey's*, October 1900, 117.

Page 143 If the stock: Smitten, *Jesse Livermore*, 45–47.

Page 143 They advertised in: Clews, *The Wall Street Point of View*, 62.

Page 143 The afternoon of: "Police Raid a Bucket Shop," *New York Times*, May 3, 1901, 7.

Page 143 Some New York: Nelson, "The Machinery of Wall Street," 983–84.

Page 144 Many relied on: Thomas Patton, "The Bucket Shop in Speculation," *Munsey's*, October 1900, 70.

Page 144 Clerks and secretaries: "Small Stock Plungers," *New York Tribune*, May 10, 1901, 3.

Page 144 In Chicago it: "Clerks Risk All in Speculation," *Chicago Tribune*, May 5, 1901, 1.

Page 144 An official of: "Bulls Charge Back into Wall Street Ring, Flushed and Eager to Renew the Fray," *New York Herald*, May 6, 1901, 4.

Page 144 In the countryside: "Wall Street's Unparalleled Speculation," *New York Herald*, May 2, 1901, 8.

Page 144 One New York: "Every Man His Own Gambler," *New York Evening Post*, April 20, 1901, 2.

Page 144 Even McKinley called: Leech, *In the Days of McKinley*, 587.

Page 144 "A man goes": "Flush Times Here Indeed," *New York Sun*, May 1, 1901, 7.

Page 144 The city's premier: "What Stock Goes Up Next?" *New York Sun*, May 7, 1901, 4.

Page 145 Women of means: "Money Enough: Want Rest," *New York Sun*, May 3, 1901, 2.

Page 145 *Life* magazine called: "An Invasion from Pittsburg[h]," *Life*, May 14, 1901, 411.

Page 145 One "old operator": "Stocks Recover," *Commercial Advertiser* (New York), May 4, 1901, 1.

Page 145 "I often think": "Money Enough: Want Rest," *New York Sun*, May 3, 1901, 2.

Page 145 In one of: "Women Join the Gamble," *New York Sun*, May 2, 1901, 7.

Page 145 The manager of: Homberger, *Cities of the Imagination*, 208; "Barroom Nymphs Emerge from Past," *New York Times Book Review*, January 10, 1943, 50; Corrine Robins, "The Great American Nude," *New York Times*, February 16, 1975, 6–7.

Page 145 Carriages, "hacks," and: "Another Huge Day in Wall Street," *New York Herald*, May 2, 1901, 5.

Page 146 They poured into: "'Diamond Jim' Brady Dies while Asleep," *New York Times*, April 14, 1917; Jeffers, *Diamond Jim Brady*, 137–38.

Page 146 It was a "green": Bloom, *Broadway*, 427.

Page 146 It converged on: Hughes, *The Real New York*, 53.

Page 146 Guests streamed into: Lloyd Morris, "Meet Me at the Waldorf," in Klein, *The Empire City*, 223.

Page 147 The hotel's jewel: Hughes, *The Real New York*, 54.

Page 148 Pages in tuxedoes: Ibid., 52.

Page 148 James R. Keene: Ibid, 54; "James R. Keene," 2–3.

Page 148 So did the: William Bryk, "Bet a Million Gates," *New York Press*, October 20, 1998.

Page 149 The wire services: Ibid.

Page 149 He was known: Paine, *George Fisher Baker*, 311.

Page 149 Bernard Baruch said: "Baruch, My Own Story," excerpt from *Deseret News* (Salt Lake City), February 5, 1958, 3; Wendt and Kogan, *Bet a Million!* 230.

Page 149 It enabled him: McCarthy, *Peacock Alley*, 141.

Page 149 Boldt would not: McCarthy, *Peacock Alley*, 15.

Page 150 He was never: Ibid., 43.

Page 150 The arbitrage houses: "Feverish Excitement at the Waldorf," *New York Times*, September 14, 1901.

Page 150 "What is Mr.": "The Man in the Street," *New York Times Magazine*, November 24, 1901.

Page 150 "It's not that": "Bulls Charge Back into Wall Street Ring, Flushed and Eager to Renew the Fray," *New York Herald*, May 6, 1901, 4.

Page 151 Traders for these: Nelson, *The A B C of Stock Speculation*, 93.

Page 151 As John Durand: Durand, "Business of Trading Stocks," 20–21.

Page 151 For Wall Street: Lefevre, "The American Newspaper," 142.

Page 151 The Union Pacific: "Features of the Market," *Wall Street Journal*, May 3, 1901, 8.

Page 151 There were reports: "Great Rise in Atchison," *New York Evening Post*, May 2, 1901, 1.

Page 151 "If they had": "An Invasion from Pittsburgh," *Life*, May 14, 1901, 967.

Page 151 Some brokers circulated: "Money Enough: Want Rest," *New York Sun*, May 3, 1901, 2.

Page 152 "My dear boy": "Millions Made by Master, Man and Maid in Money Mad Market," *New York Herald*, May 5, 1901, 4: 2.

Page 152 "I have not": *Wall Street Journal*, May 4, 1901.

Page 152 A treasurer for: James J. Hill testimony, Peter Power vs. Northern Pacific Railway Company, February 17, 1902, 63.

Page 152 Now it was: "Won in Wall Street Game," *New York Sun*, May 5, 1901, 3.

Page 152 He had bought: "A Chicago Capitalist's Gains," *New York Times*, May 3, 1901, 1.

Page 152 Like Orr, he: "Tales of Riches Made in Stocks," *Chicago Tribune*, May 3, 1901, 3.

Page 153 "I have wealth": Homberger, *Mrs. Astor's New York*, xiv.

Page 153 While he was: Beard, *After the Ball*, 97.

Page 153 Furthermore, on that: Ibid., 107.

Page 153 A cord was: *New York Times*, May 3, 1901; Beard, *After the Ball*, 108.

Page 154 He took the: MTH Diary, JJHP.

Page 154 The market opened: "Ahead on the Market," *Washington Post*, May 7, 1901, 2.

Page 154 Then, as a: "Stock Market Quakes and Prices Tumble," *New York Times*, May 4, 1901, 3.

Page 154 Three-fourths of: "Down Go Stocks, Death in Train," *New York Herald*, May 4, 1901, 3.

Page 154 The volatile ups: "Expired in Broker's Office," *New York Times*, May 4, 1901, 3.

Page 154 Either way, sometime: Klein, *Union Pacific*, 569; Paine in *George Fisher Baker* (203) has this Schiff–Hill meeting at Hill's residence uptown with Hill then going to Baker's office to tell him the news, then to Morgan's.

Page 155 Just this morning: Sobel, *The Big Board*, 165.

Page 155 We also offer: Paine, *George Fisher Baker*, 203.

Page 155 Harriman said something: Hill–Mount Stephen, July 22, 1904, JJHP.

Page 156 "During the time": Hill–Mount Stephen, June 4, 1901, JJHP.

Page 156 In his testimony: Pyle, *The Life of James J. Hill*, 147.

Page 156 Throughout the meeting: Hill–Mount Stephen, July 22, 1904, JJHP.

Page 156 "glided along the": "Sidelights That Bring Out Characteristics of Mr. Hill," *Saint Paul Pioneer Press*, May 30, 1916, 2.

Page 156 have leapt up: Description of J. P. Morgan and Company's offices is from Turner, "Morgan's Partners," 34.

Page 157 So was George: Paine, *George Fisher Baker*, 205.

Page 158 Morgan's own firm: White, *Railroaded*, 383.

Page 158 After dinner with: Birmingham, *"Our Crowd,"* 180, 340; Nissenson, *The Lady Upstairs,* 10.

Page 159 As he had: Birmingham, *"Our Crowd,"* 183.

Page 159 An exasperated Schiff: Klein, *The Life and Legend of E. H. Harriman,* 231.

8. Decision at Temple Emanu-El

Page 160 Historian Frederick Lewis: Allen, *The Lords of Creation,* 109.

Page 160 Windows were open: "Spring, Gentle Spring," *Commercial Advertiser* (New York), April 6, 1901, 1.

Page 161 The columns and: "Dedication of the New Hebrew Temple," *Frank Leslie's Illustrated Newspaper,* October 3, 1868.

Page 161 Jacob and Therese: E-mail to author, Elka Deitsch, senior curator, Bernard Museum of Judaica, Congregation Emanu-El of the City of New York, May 5, 2011.

Page 162 Hill urged Bacon: Carosso, *The Morgans,* 476.

Page 162 He kept asking: Paine, *George Fisher Baker,* 205. Inexplicably, Hill waited four days before cabling Mount Stephen, Farrer, Tuck, and Kennedy on May 7 to "hold fast" and not sell their Northern Pacific shares. He did not receive all their assurances until May 8. (Hill–Tuck, May 7; Hill–Mount Stephen, May 7; Hill–Kennedy, May 8; Mount Stephen–Hill, May 8; Tuck–Hill, May 8; Farrer–Hill, May 8, all JJHP.)

Page 162 Schiff and all: Kennan, *E. H. Harriman,* 309.

Page 162 They also surely: The 1896 reorganization charter for the Northern Pacific said "the *company* [emphasis added] may retire the preferred stock, in whole or in part, at par, from time to time, on any first of January up to and including January 1, 1917." Thus, the question, what is the company? Kuhn, Loeb's lawyers claimed it was all holders of the stock, common and preferred. Morgan's counsel claimed the provision for retiring the preferred meant the common shares were superior ("War May Be Over Soon," *New York Daily Tribune,* May 15, 1901, 1). Further, the pre-1896 charter of the Northern Pacific said two-thirds of the company's shares were needed to vote approval of a purchase such as the Burlington; the 1896 reorganization charter vested that power in the Board (*St. Louis Republic,* May 10, 1901, 1).

Page 162 As he recalled: Harriman to G. W. Batson, quoted in Kennan, *E. H. Harriman,* 1: 305–6.

Page 163 He had a: Phillips-Matz, *The Many Lives of Otto Kahn,* 44.

Page 163 "Never have I": Schiff–Ernest Cassell, January 7, 1909, from Adler, *Jacob H. Schiff,* 1: 20.

Page 163 "All right," said: Wheeler, *Pierpont Morgan and Friends,* 249.

Page 163 "A man does": Letwin, *Law and Economic Policy in America,* 191.

Page 164 Did Schiff not: Schiff's strict observance of the Sabbath was widely known. As Hill's Great Northern assistant Edward Nichols wrote him (October 15, 1892) while trying to do some banking business for the firm on a Saturday, "This morning Mr. Schiff was away (as usual with him Saturdays) so could not do anything here." Schiff likely took a broader view of the Sabbath as did his rabbi Dr. Joseph Silverman, who believed it should be not a puritanical day of enforced religious devotion but a day of rest and relaxation so that one did not become "narrow and brutal in mind and weak in body" ("Rabbi Silverman's Views," *New York Tribune,* December 16, 1901, 9).

Page 164 Railroads which for: "Mr. Keene's Confidence," *New York Times*, May 5, 1901, 24.

Page 165 Bacon had sent: Allen, *The Great Pierpont Morgan*, 294. (Allen says the Bacon–Morgan cable of May 4, 1901 does not appear in the books of the J. P. Morgan archives, perhaps because Bacon sent it from his home.)

Page 165 Morgan was standing: Morgan's attire is from Allen, *The Great Pierpont Morgan*, 268.

Page 165 Morgan strode immediately: Klein, *The Life and Legend of E. H. Harriman*, 231.

Page 165 He later described: Testimony in Peter Power vs. Northern Pacific Railway Company, quoted in Moody and Turner, "The Masters of Capital in America" (January 1911), 344.

Page 165 Financier John Stewart: Hovey, *The Life Story of John Pierpont Morgan*, 248.

Page 165 Bacon and Hill: Carosso, *The Morgans*, 476.

Page 166 It was left: Keenan, *E. H. Harriman*, 1:307.

Page 166 Harriman tended to: Beard, *After the Ball*, 101.

Page 166 As Harriman claimed: "Harriman on Northern Pacific," *Minneapolis Journal*, January 25, 1902, 1.

Page 167 He worked on: Birmingham, *"Our Crowd,"* 311, 342.

Page 167 He knew reporters: Phillips-Matz, *The Many Lives of Otto Kahn*, 61; Birmingham, *"Our Crowd,"* 310.

Page 167 He later criticized: Kahn, *Of Many Things*, 128.

Page 167 Perhaps he learned: Phillips-Matz, *The Many Lives of Otto Kahn*, 48; Kahn's "mellow" voice from "Business Men Who Make Speeches and Write Books," *New York Times*, April 30, 1911.

Page 167 Kahn simply referred: Kahn, *Of Many Things*, 135; Klein, *The Life and Legend of E. H. Harriman*, 234.

Page 168 Sunday, May 5: "Like Picnic Ground in Central Park," *New York Herald*, May 6, 1901, 11.

Page 168 Maître d' Oscar Tschirky: "Bulls Charge Back into Wall Street Ring, Flushed and Eager to Renew the Fray," *New York Herald*, May 6, 1901, 4.

Page 168 They would have: *Wall Street Journal*, May 7, 1901.

Page 168 It had been: "Millions Made by Master, Man and Maid in Money Mad Market," *New York Herald*, May 5, 1901, 4: 2.

Page 168 "Railroad stocks of": "The Financial Situation," *New York Sun*, May 6, 1901, 8.

Page 169 On Saturday night: "Jamieson & Co. of Chicago Fail," *New York Sun*, May 7, 1901, 4.

Page 169 Another Chicago firm: "Another Chicago Firm Has to Suspend," *New York Times*, May 9, 1901.

Page 169 "Three or four: "Won in Wall Street Game," *New York Sun*, May 5, 1901, 3.

Page 169 Someone was rumored: Ibid.

Page 169 A quiet investor: "Bulls Charge Back into Wall Street Ring, Flushed and Eager to Renew the Fray," *New York Herald*, May 6, 1901, 4.

Page 169 Then there was: Sarnoff, *Russell Sage*, 23.

Page 169 London commission houses: "Won in Wall Street Game," *New York Sun*, May 5, 1901, 3.

Page 170 He once bought: "Russell Sage in His Office," *Bankers' Magazine*, August 1909, 222.

Page 170 Part of the: "Northern Pacific Fight," *New York Evening Post*, May 7, 1901, 1.

Page 170 On the newsstands: "Madness of the Stock Pit as a Famous Poet Saw It," *New York Journal*, May 6, 1901, 2.

Page 170 After what would: "James R. Keene, The Story of His Career With Its Record of Ups and Downs," *New York Times Magazine*, January 30, 1910, 2.

Page 170 Since he was: Description of Keene's voice from "James R. Keene, A Glimpse of the Famous Operator at His Ticker," *Ticker*, December 1907, 2.

Page 170 Known as the: Sobel, *Panic on Wall Street*, 290.

Page 171 His infamous colleague: Josephson, "Profiles: Fifty Years of Wall Street," 22–25.

Page 171 Content's phone operator: "Leonard Hockstader, 82, Dies; Partner in Investment Concern," *New York Times*, May 12, 1962, 23; Leonard, *Who's Who in Finance*, 599–600.

Page 171 In other words: "Wall Street Was Taken by Assault," *New York Times*, May 12, 1901; Sobel, *Panic on Wall Street*, 290.

Page 171 The thirty-eight-year: *American Ancestry*, 88; Norton's engagement to Louise Seggermann from *New York Times*, November 11, 1886.

Page 171 Eddie and his: "Wall Street Houses Go Down," *New York Times*, May 5, 1893, 5.

Page 172 When the stock: Winkelman, *Ten Years of Wall Street*, 66.

Page 172 Seven years later: "Confidence in Values," *New York Times*, September 2, 1900.

Page 172 Norton was the: *New York Times*, May 7, 1901.

Page 172 On the morning: Strouse, *Morgan*, 423.

Page 172 The Keene–Content: Josephson, "Profiles: Fifty Years of Wall Street," 24.

Page 172 Chairman Kennedy gaveled: "NP Stock Skyrockets," *New York Sun*, May 7, 1901, 10.

Page 172 "There was," said: "Northern Pacific Jumps 23 Points," *New York Herald*, May 7, 1901, 6.

Page 173 The gallery was: "Big Upward Movement in the Stock Market," *New York Times*, May 7, 1901, 3.

Page 173 One trader bought: Ibid.

Page 173 Norton started buying: "Wall Street Was Taken by Assault," *New York Times*, May 12, 1901, 3.

Page 173 Minutes later, an: "More Stock Sensations," *New York Evening Post*, May 6, 1901, 1.

Page 173 A week later: "Wall Street Was Taken by Assault," *New York Times*, May 12, 1901.

Page 174 Nipper common "began": "Northern Pacific Jumps 23 Points," *New York Herald*, May 7, 1901, 6.

Page 174 "We received an": Allen, *The Great Pierpont Morgan*, 213, 294; according to J. P. Morgan and Company's books, brokers buying on Morgan's behalf acquired not less than 127,000 this day.

Page 174 In a diversion: Paine, *George Fisher Baker*, 204.

Page 174 That was what: Hill–Mount Stephen, May 8, 1901, JJHP.

Page 174 Farrer told Hill: Farrer–Hill, May 8, 1901, JJHP. S. A. Nelson in his 1903 *The A B C of Stock Speculation* quoted the New York Stock Exchange's Daniel F. Kellogg likely referring to Schiff: "It is trustworthily stated that a great man in one of the banking houses having much to do with the great Northern Pacific fight for control, admitted that not until he had so far engaged in the battle for the possession of the Northern Pacific shares that he could not retreat from it, had he read the certificate of the preferred stock, upon whose disputed construction the question of defeat or victory in the struggle depended. A very much surprised man he was when he found that there were clauses in the certificate of which he was not aware" (227).

Page 174 There was one: "New Price Records," *New York Tribune*, May 7, 1901.

Page 174 Street and Norton: "Wall Street Was Taken by Assault," *New York Times*, May 12, 1901, 3.

Page 174 The *New York*: "Mr. Vanderbilt and the N.P.," *New York Tribune*, May 7, 1901; "Comment and Conjecture," May 7, 1901.

Page 174 Whoever Street and: "Big Upward Movement in the Stock Market," *New York Times*, May 7, 1901, 3.

Page 174 One report said: "The Day's Operations in Stocks," *New York Tribune*, May 7, 1901, 10.

Page 175 Hill told one: "NP Stock Skyrockets," *New York Sun*, May 7, 1901, 10.

Page 175 "Mr. Hill has": *Wall Street Journal*, May 7, 1901.

Page 175 Someone recalled seeing: "Wild Panic in Wall Street Checked by Banks' Timely Cash," *New York Herald*, May 10, 1901, 3.

Page 175 Norton was overheard: "Swirling Malestrom of Speculation," *New York Herald*, May 10, 1901, 3

Page 176 He stood six-feet: "Bernard M. Baruch," *Munsey's*, September 1917, 595.

Page 176 Thirty-year-old: Grant, *Bernard M. Baruch*, 2.

Page 176 Early this morning: Ibid., 60.

Page 176 Standing next to: "Talbot J. Taylor," *Successful American*, April 1900, 17.

Page 176 Like Keene, he: "Members of the Taylor Firm," *New York Times*, July 25, 1903, 2.

Page 177 So Baruch would: Grant, *Bernard M. Baruch*, 60–62.

Page 177 Houses such as: "Wall Street Taken by Assault," *New York Times*, May 12, 1901, 3.

Page 177 It was rumored: "What Stock Goes Up Next?" *New York Sun*, May 7, 1901, 4.

Page 177 The crowd around: "So Long as Stocks Go," *New York Sun*, May 8, 1901, 2.

Page 177 That put even: Sobel, *Panic on Wall Street*, 291.

Page 177 Some commission houses: "Control of the NP," *New York Times*, May 8, 1901, 3.

Page 178 That panicked some: Klein, *Union Pacific*, 106.

Page 178 One brokerage firm: "Big Stock Corner," *Commercial Advertiser* (New York), May 7, 1901, 1.

Page 178 "fresh vigor from": "Standard Oil Interests Clash with Those of J. P. Morgan," *New York Herald*, May 8, 1901, 3; "The Control of the N.P.," *New York Tribune*, May 8, 1901, 3.

Page 178 Those who still: Lord, *The Good Years*, 76.

Page 178 Under the Exchange's: Peter Low, "The Northern Pacific Panic of 1901," *Financial History*, Winter 2010, xx.

Page 179 The brokerage firm: "Standard Oil Forces Hold Northern Pacific," *New York Herald*, May 9, 1901, 3.

Page 179 "I haven't got": "Standard Oil Interests Clash with Those of J. P. Morgan," *New York Herald*, May 8, 1901, 4.

Page 179 The shorts who: Ibid., 3.

Page 179 One broker ran: Ibid.

Page 179 He was among: Lamont–Hill, July 31, 1900, JJHP.

Page 180 "I have not": Lord, *The Good Years*, 76.

Page 180 And to another: "Smash Came with Corner," *New York Sun*, May 9, 1901.

Page 180 My dear sir: Lord, *The Good Years*, 77.

Page 180 A year later: James J. Hill testimony, Peter Power v. Northern Pacific Railway Company, February 17, 1902, 46. Hill's white lies were adding up: "On several occasions Mr. Hill seems to have alleviated the harshness of truth in such a way as to mislead persons who supposed that they had a right to trust his assurances," said *Life* magazine. "What Mr. Morgan says still goes. What Mr. Hill says goes, nowadays, under the microscope. There is a good deal of speculation as to whether the respective standards of conduct of

Mr. Morgan and Mr. Hill are near enough alike to permit those gentlemen to continue to be intimately associated in business dealings. Mr. Hill is superlatively able, and has been wonderfully successful, so that he has long been held up as a model for aspiring youth. It is not a little disconcerting to have him suspected of ethical defects" (May 30, 1901, 462).

Page 180 Morgan and Company: "R. H. Thomas Caught in Northern Pacific," *New York Times,* September 2, 1904, 14.

Page 180 Hill cabled Mount: Hill–Mount Stephen, May 8, 1901, JJHP.

9. *"Hell Is Empty and All the Devils Are Here"*

Page 181 The five hundred: "The Great Smash in Speculation Comes at Last," *New York Journal,* May 9, 1901, 1.

Page 181 One broker, Cornelius: "Standard Oil Forces," *New York Herald,* May 9, 1901, 3.

Page 181 Another broker, John: "Bulge in Northern Pacific," *Commercial Advertiser* (New York), May 8, 1901, 1. The *New York Journal* claimed Manning made $60,000 by selling 2,000 Nipper common at 180 and covering at 150 seven minutes later ("Wild Scenes on Consolidated Board," May 8, 1901, 3).

Page 181 Down it went: "Smash Came with Corner," *New York Sun,* May 9, 1901, 1.

Page 181 Robert Bacon authorized: Sobel, *Panic on Wall Street,* 291.

Page 181 A bulletin from: "Wild Scenes at the Opening of Trading," *New York Journal,* May 8, 1901, 3.

Page 181 At 120 Broadway: Klein, *Union Pacific,* 106.

Page 182 One trader loaned: Lord, *The Good Years,* 76.

Page 182 The mob pinned: Baruch, *My Own Story,* 143–44; "Hill Loses in Stock Duel," *New York Sun,* May 8, 1901, 1.

Page 182 Another broker was: "Standard Oil Interests Clash with Those of J. P. Morgan," *New York Herald,* May 8, 1901, 3.

Page 182 He was offering: "Prices Fall: Stock Market Demoralized," *New York Evening Telegram,* May 8, 1901, 1.

Page 182 Bernard Baruch watched: Baruch, *My Own Story,* 144.

Page 183 It was rumored: "Wall Street Was Taken by Assault," *New York Times,* May 12, 1901.

Page 183 "At first sight": "An Emotional Market," *New York Times,* May 9, 1901, 10.

Page 183 "If legitimate holders": "Agony Pervaded the Loan Crowd," *New York Herald,* May 9, 1901, 3.

Page 183 He replied, "We": "Smash Came with Corner," *New York Sun,* May 9, 1901.

Page 184 It was adamant: Schiff and Harriman: "Smash Came with Corner," *New York Sun,* May 9, 1901.

Page 184 "It is all": "Calls It Ghost Dancing; Mr. Hill's Opinion of the Cause of the Flurry," *Saint Paul Globe,* May 9, 1901, 1.

Page 184 "Hell is empty": "Wall Street Settlement," *New York Sun,* May 9, 1901, 1.

Page 184 It was easy: "The Great Smash in Speculation Comes at Last," *New York Journal,* May 9, 1901.

Page 184 A rumor swept: *New York Sun,* May 9, 1901.

Page 185 At 7:30 p.m.: "Features of the Market," *Wall Street Journal*, May 9, 1901, 1.

Page 185 A few minutes: "Night Session at the Waldorf–Astoria," *New York Herald*, May 9, 1901, 3.

Page 185 The head bartender: "Bankers Crowd Waldorf," *New York Times*, May 9, 1901, 1.

Page 185 An Austrian immigrant: *National Cyclopaedia of American Biography*, 394–95.

Page 185 Gates was watching: "Bankers Crowd Waldorf," *New York Times*, May 9, 1901, 1.

Page 185 It was whispered: "Mr. Gates May Wage War on J. P. Morgan," *New York Herald*, May 16, 1901, 3.

Page 185 Gates denied rumors: "Fortunes Vanish while Panic Reigns," *St. Louis Republic*, May 10, 1901, 1; "Panic Sweeps Stock Exchange," *Chicago Tribune*, May 9, 1901, 1.

Page 185 "I tell you": "Incidents of the Panic," *New York Times*, May 11, 1901, 2.

Page 186 A rumor swept: "Bankers Crowd Waldorf," *New York Times*, May 9, 1901, 1.

Page 186 At the White: "Panic and Cornered," *New York Sun*, May 10, 1901, 1.

Page 186 They had borrowed: "Smash Came with Corner," *New York Sun*, May 9, 1901, 1.

Page 186 Another steamer, the: "Northern Pacific Corner Now Broken," *New York Times*, May 10, 1901, 1.

Page 186 Then came the: Lefevre, *Wall Street Stories*, 7, 9.

Page 186 "The letters and": Pratt, *The Work of Wall Street*, 133–39.

Page 186 London opened with: "Disaster and Ruin in Falling Market," *New York Times*, May 10, 1901; "London Feels the Shock," *New York Sun*, May 10, 1901, 2.

Page 186 The American flag: Lord, *The Good Years*, 77.

Page 188 Kuhn, Loeb offered: "Panic and Cornered," *New York Sun*, May 10, 1901, 1.

Page 188 The floor held: "The Panic of 1901: At the Stock Exchange," *New York Times*, May 10, 1901.

Page 188 Traders climbed over: *New York Times*, May 9, 1901.

Page 188 Just off the: "Disaster and Ruin," *New York Times*, May 10, 1901, 1.

Page 188 Exchange members who: "Vignettes of the Slump," *Chicago Tribune*, May 10, 1901, 3.

Page 188 Under New York: Hughes, *The Vital Few*, 384.

Page 188 Broker H. P. Frothingham: "Wall Street Gossip," *Commercial Advertiser* (New York), May 9, 1901, 10.

Page 188 The 60 percent: "Wall Street Was Taken by Assault," *New York Times*, May 12, 1901; Henry Harrison Lewis, "A Day with Thomas F. Ryan," *Success Magazine*, October 1905, 137.

Page 189 To prove he: *New York Times*, May 10, 1901.

Page 189 A sale that: "Millions for Hill If He Sold Out Pierpont Morgan in 'N.P.' Corner," *New York Evening World*, February 12, 1902, 2.

Page 189 Now came what: Quoted in Macleod, *Manitoba History*, 26.

Page 189 It meant the: Stedman, *The New York Stock Exchange*, 399.

Page 189 Two or three: "Money Kings in Earnest Conference Planning to Break Corner," *New York Journal*, May 19, 1901, 1.

Page 189 A record number: "Corner in Messenger Boys," *Chicago Tribune*, May 10, 1901, 4.

Page 189 Some were given: Nelson, "Machinery of Wall Street," 984.

Page 189 About two weeks: "Fighting Mob on Broad Street," *New York Evening Post*, April 23, 1901, 2; "'Riot' in Wall Street," *Commercial Advertiser* (New York), April 23, 1901, 1.

Page 190 At 11:15 a.m. in: "Shock to Values," *Washington Post*, May 10, 1901, 3. From 10 a.m. through noon the May 9 trading in Northern Pacific common was: 10 a.m.: 500 at 170, 200 at 175, 300 at 180, 200 at 170, 300 at 190 cash, 500 at 165, 200 at 160, 300 at 170, 300 at 200 cash, 200 at 205 cash, 100 at 210 cash, 300 at 170, 100 at 159, 200 at 225 cash, 400 at 205, 100 at 225, 300 at 230, 500 at 280 cash, 500 at 300 cash, 100 at 230, 200 at 300 cash, 100 at 400 cash, 300 at 320, 100 at 650 cash, 100 at 530; 11 a.m: 300 at 700, 300 at 1,000 cash, 200 at 600 cash, 100 at 600, 400 at 500 cash, 300 at 500 cash, 100 at 450 cash, 700 at 500 cash, 500 at 700 cash; Noon: 100 at 700 cash, 100 at 700 cash, 100 at 700.

Page 190 The buyer first: "Wall Street Was Taken by Assault: Leaders in Finance Blind to Opportunity or Danger," *New York Times*, May 12, 1901, 3; "R. H. Thomas Caught in Northern Pacific," *New York Times*, September 2, 1904.

Page 190 The 100-share: "The Northern Pacific Corner Now Broken," *New York Times*, May 10, 1901.

Page 190 "All strangers out": "Swirling Maelstrom of Speculation," *New York Herald*, May 10, 1901, 3.

Page 191 A rumor spread: "Fortunes Vanish while Panic Reigns, Forced by Northern Pacific Corner," *St. Louis Republic*, May 10, 1901, 1.

Page 191 The elevators became: "Incidents of the Panic," *New York Times*, May 11, 1901, 2.

Page 191 The crowd of: "Swirling Maelstrom of Speculation," *New York Herald*, May 10, 1901, 3.

Page 191 Between 11 a.m.: "The Eight Most Striking Features of Yesterday's Remarkable Wall Street Day," *New York Journal*, May 10, 1901, 3.

Page 191 The bucket shops: "$30,000,000 Won by Bucket Shops in Stock Panic," *New York Journal*, May 10, 1901, 2.

Page 191 At about noon: "J. W. Gates Calls in a Hurry on Morgan & Co.," *New York Journal*, May 9, 1901, 3; Wendt and Kogan, *Bet a Million!* 35.

Page 191 Gates, after all: Apple, "The Case of the Monopolistic Railroadmen," 177.

Page 191 At the same: "Dies in Vat of Hot Beer," *New York Times*, May 10, 1901.

Page 191 At 2:15 Al: Coit, *Mr. Baruch*, 92.

Page 191 Minutes later came: Strouse, *Morgan*, xi.

Page 191 In Street and Norton's: "Ruin in the Great Smash," *New York Sun*, May 10, 1901, 2.

Page 192 As darkness came: "London in the Throes of the New York Panic," *New York Journal*, May 10, 1901, 1.

Page 192 For that reason: "London Feels the Shock," *New York Sun*, May 10, 1901. 2; "Panic on Curb in London," *New York Evening World*, May 10, 1901, 2.

Page 192 The New York Central: "Stock by Special Engine," *New York Sun*, May 10, 1901; "Race to Make Big Profits," *New York Times*, May 10, 1901.

Page 192 Today it is: John Cassidy, "The Minsky Moment," *New Yorker*, February 4, 2008, 18–19.

Page 192 A broker rushed: "Millionaires Meet for Peace at Night," *New York Journal*, May 10, 1901, 3.

Page 192 Delaware & Hudson: "Disaster and Ruin in Falling Market," *New York Times*, May 10, 1901.

Page 192 "They were throwing": "Incidents of the Panic," *New York Times*, May 11, 1901, 2.

Page 193 "They have plenty": "Swirling Maelstrom of Speculation," *New York Herald*, May 10, 1901, 3.

Page 193 It so happened: "G. B. Schmidt, Not Yet Twenty-One, Pays $70,000 for Seat on 'Change,'" *New York Herald*, May 9, 1901, 5; King, *King's Views of the New York Stock Exchange*, 4; "Talked about on Wall Street," *New York Herald*, April 9, 1901, 14.

Page 193 He offered the: "Queer Breaks by the Brokers and Patrons," *St. Louis Republic,* May 10, 1901, 2.

Page 193 A wealthy speculator: H. T. White, "Side Lights on the Stock Market," *Chicago Tribune,* May 11, 1901, 4.

Page 193 Another top-tier: "Vignettes of the Slump," *Chicago Tribune,* May 10, 1901, 3.

Page 193 She was told: "Women Watch Fortunes Melt," *Chicago Tribune,* May 10, 1901, 3; Sobel, *Panic on Wall Street,* 294.

Page 193 Theodore S. Baron: "Loses One Million by Thinking Twice," *New York Herald,* May 15, 1901, 5; "Caught in Northern Pacific," *New York Evening Post,* May 14, 1901, 1.

Page 194 He had learned: "Gossip of Wall Street," *New York Sun,* March 16, 1904.

Page 194 This was nothing: "Lost $7,100 in Sugar Stocks," *New York Times,* September 2, 1894, 2.

Page 194 Delaware & Hudson: "Panicked and Cornered," *New York Sun,* May 10, 1901, 1; Nelson, *The A B C of Stock Speculation,* 75.

Page 194 The best stocks: "Disaster and Ruin in Falling Market," *New York Times,* May 10, 1901, 1.

Page 194 All stocks fell: Nelson, *The A B C of Stock Speculation,* 75.

Page 194 While Morgan was: U.S. Steel declined in that half hour, as follows: 1,000 at 40; 600 at 39½; 1,500 at 39; 2,000 at 38½; 500 at 38; 30 at 37; 500 at 36; 200 at 34½; 100 at 34; 400 at 32; 1,000 at 34½; 100 at 34; 200 at 32; 500 at 31; 800 at 32; 200 at 30⅞; 100 at 29¾; 1,000 at 29; 4,000 at 28; 500 at 27; 100 at 26; 600 at 27; 500 at 27½; 2,500 at 29; 1,000 at 28½; 300 at 29; 1,000 at 28½; 100 at 26; 600 at 25½.

Page 194 He fancied himself: Durand, "Business of Trading Stocks," 52–53.

Page 195 "We were going": Lefevre, *Reminiscences of a Stock Operator,* 45.

Page 195 He thought he: Smitten, *Jesse Livermore,* 45–47.

Page 195 "I was accustomed": Lefevre, *Reminiscences of a Stock Operator,* 47.

Page 195 Livermore had unknowingly: Durand, "Business of Trading Stocks," 22.

Page 195 Some men will: Lefevre, "Panic Days in Wall Street," 520.

Page 196 "Steel, 24," said: Ibid.

Page 196 He had bought: "Corbett Loses $15,000," *New York Sun,* May 10, 1901, 2.

Page 196 "Oh well," he: Standard Oil Forces Hold Northern Pacific," *New York Herald,* May 9, 1901, 3.

Page 196 He was thought: "Louisville Man Loses $100,000," *New York Sun,* May 10, 1901, 2.

Page 196 "Billy, this damn": "Ruin in the Great Smash," *New York Sun,* May 10, 1901, 2.

Page 197 Someone else overheard: "Incidents of the Day," *New York Tribune,* May 10, 1901, 3.

Page 197 A broker, whose: "Swirling Maelstrom of Speculation," *New York Herald,* May 10, 1901, 3.

Page 197 Harry Content, who: Josephson, "Profiles: Fifty Years of Wall Street," 22, 24.

Page 197 During the market: "William K. Vanderbilt Home," *New York Tribune,* May 10, 1901, 2; *New York Sun,* May 10, 1901.

Page 197 When he reached: "Incidents of the Day," *New York Tribune,* May 10, 1901, 3.

Page 197 He had spent: "President at Carnival," *New York Tribune,* May 10, 1901, 4.

Page 197 The stock had: "$300,000 for His 350 Shares," *New York Sun,* May 10, 1901, 1.

Page 198 His broker filled: "Excitement in St. Paul," *New York Times,* May 10, 1901, 3.

Page 198 He had tried: Marcosson, "The Perilous Game of Cornering a Crop," 70; Taylor, *Board of Trade,* 254–56.

Page 198 This day it: "Chicago Brokers Hit Hard," *St. Louis Republic,* May 10, 1901; "Stocks on Up Grade," *Chicago Daily News,* May 10, 1901, 2.

Page 198 All along the: Descriptive color from Will Payne's 1898 novel *The Money Captain*, 5.
Page 198 One young Chicago: Ibid.; "Great Crash in Stocks," *Chicago Daily News*, May 9, 1901, 1; "Stocks on Up Grade," *Chicago Daily News*, May 10, 1901, 2.
Page 198 One trader compared: "Vignettes of the Slump," *Chicago Tribune*, May 10, 1901, 3.
Page 198 In Cincinnati, local: "Fortunes Made in Cincinnati," *New York Sun*, May 10, 1901, 2.
Page 198 A young man: "Bought N.P. at 25, Sold at 400," *New York Tribune*, May 10, 1901, 2.
Page 198 At the brokerage : "Incidents of the Day," *New York Tribune*, May 10, 1901, 3.
Page 198 McQueen, recovering in: "Lucky Owner of N.P. Stock," *New York Sun*, May 14, 1901, 10; "Millions Made; Fortunes Lost," *Chicago Tribune*, May 10, 1901.
Page 199 If the shares: "Incidents of the Panic," *New York Tribune*, May 11, 1901, 2.
Page 199 He sold it: "Waldorf Corridors Jammed with Brokers," *New York Times*, May 10, 1901, 3.
Page 199 "It was a": "Disaster and Ruin," *New York Times*, May 10, 1901, 1.
Page 199 If you had: "Panicked and Cornered," *New York Sun*, May 10, 1901, 1.
Page 199 Someone bought U.S.: "Bargain Day," *New York Sun*, May 10, 1901, 2.
Page 199 "I'm not interested": "Chicago Not Hurt by the Slump," *New York Sun*, May 10, 1901, 2.
Page 200 He was making: "Details of the Crash: Panic Stricken Operators Make the Exchange a Veritable Bedlam," *New York Tribune*, May 10, 1901, 1; Sarnoff, *Russell Sage*, 4, 117; *Bankers' Magazine*, August 1909, 2.
Page 200 "It seems outrageous": "Will Cool Off, Says Sage," *New York Tribune*, May 10, 1901, 2.
Page 200 "This difficulty," said: "Panic and Cornered," *New York Sun*, May 10, 1901, 1.
Page 200 This signaled that Kuhn: "The N.P. Settlement," *New York Tribune*, May 10, 1901, 1.
Page 201 They rushed the: "How the 'Corner' Came to an End," *New York Times*, May 11, 1901, 1.
Page 201 "It is the": "Victims of Panic Threaten Brokers with Lawsuits," *New York Herald*, May 14, 1901, 3.
Page 201 Some lawsuits stemming: Nelson, *The A B C of Stock Speculation*, 85.
Page 201 "All right," said: "Brokers Were Hit Hard by Welchers," *New York Herald*, May 19, 1901, 3.
Page 201 Many firms and: "Stockbrokers to Be Sued," *New York Evening Post*, May 14, 1901, 3.
Page 202 "Crazy come," and: "Mr. Dooley: On Recent Events in Speculative Circles," *Harper's Weekly*, June 1, 1901, 569.
Page 202 Stillman's National City: Perhaps the *Commercial Advertiser* (New York) was referring to Stillman: "A little touch of cynicism came from the lips of the president of one of the large lending banks, a bank which was not in the syndicate. Said he: 'I did not join the syndicate yesterday, for the reason that I did not see that it was absolutely necessary. Banks could have done individually what the syndicate did concertedly" (May 10, 1901, 1).
Page 202 The entire fifty-five: "Brokers Transfer Accounts," *New York Times*, May 28, 1901, 6.
Page 202 If the banks: "Panicked and Cornered," *New York Sun*, May 10, 1901, 1.
Page 202 The total was: "Chicago Loans to New York," *New York Tribune*, May 10, 1901, 3.
Page 202 When the big: "The Crash in Wall Street," *Commercial and Financial Chronicle*, May 11, 1901, 900.
Page 203 Had he delayed: "Incidents in the Street," *New York Times*, May 11, 1901.
Page 203 An individual identified: "Millions for Hill If He Sold Out Pierpont Morgan in 'N.P. Corner," *New York Evening World*, February 12, 1902, 2.
Page 203 Keene, Taylor, Norton: "Waldorf Corridors Jammed with Brokers," *New York Times*, May 10, 1901.

Page 204 To which Hannihan: "The Passing Throng: Why New York Is Wealthy," *New York Tribune*, May 11, 1901, 7.

Page 204 He was surrounded: Morgan's suite from Allen, *The Great Pierpont Morgan*, 71–72.

Page 204 He paused a: "Morgan to Be Here May 24," *New York Sun*, May 12, 1901, 1.

Page 204 He rushed immediately: *New York Sun*, May 11, 1901, 1.

Page 204 He cabled Bacon: "Millionaires Meet for Peace at Night," *New York Journal*, May 10, 1901, 3.

Page 204 He was reported: "Morgan to Sail Next Wednesday; Leaves on Teutonic for This City, He Says in Paris—In Angry Mood," *New York Evening World*, 3; "Mr. Morgan Is Silent," *New York Times*, May 12, 1901, 3. Jean Strouse in *Morgan: American Financier* capably picks apart the myth that Morgan ever said "I owe the public nothing" when a reporter supposedly asked him in Paris that weekend if he owed the public an explanation since he was being blamed for the panic (xi–xii). All signs point to a reporter-manufactured quote.

Page 204 He had reserved: "Paris: A Budget That Causes Apprehension," *New York Tribune*, May 12, 1901, 2.

Page 205 She had chosen: Adler, *Jacob H. Schiff*, 1: 389.

Page 205 The discussion ended: Ibid.

Page 205 He changed into: "There Has Been Some Wicked Work; Men Have Disgraced Themselves," *St. Louis Republic*, May 10, 1901, 2.

Page 205 Looking "pale and": "Hill Denies He Was in the Deal," *New York Evening World*, May 10, 1901, 2.

Page 205 The newspapers and: "Railway World Leaders," *New York Evening Post*, May 4, 1901, 2.

Page 206 "I am a farmer": "Hill Says He's a Farmer: Not Concerned with What Men are Doing on Wall Street, He Declares," *New York Tribune*, May 10, 1901, 1.

Page 206 "The struggle was": "The N.P. Settlement," *New York Tribune*, May 10, 1901, 1. In a 1923 biography of Bacon, author James Brown Scott includes a footnote from Harriman biographer George Kennan claiming Dr. Henry S. Pritchett, president of MIT, was in Harriman's office the day of the panic and said he saw Hill there "chatting amiably about other things" with Harriman as if the two were close friends. It may have been wishful thinking on Pritchett's part (*Robert Bacon*, 95).

Page 206 It was reported: "Truce in Stock War and Combatants Rest on Their Arms," *New York Herald*, May 11, 1901, 4.

Page 207 "So many persons": "Ruin in the Great Smash," *New York Sun*, May 10, 1901, 2.

Page 207 By one estimate: "The Northern Pacific Settlements Effected," *New York Times*, May 11, 1901, 2.

Page 208 Few bears profited: "Leaders in Finance Blind to Opportunity or Danger," *New York Times*, May 12, 1901, 3.

Page 208 About 4,000 shares: "Wall Street Was Taken by Assault," *New York Times*, May 12, 1901.

Page 208 Those who cabled: "A 'Corner' in Wall Street," *New York Herald*, May 8, 1901, 19.

Page 208 The *New York*: *New York Times*, May 10, 1901, 3.

Page 208 The people who: Lefevre, *The Golden Flood*; Lefevre, *Wall Street Stories*, 82.

Page 208 Maybe, someone suggested: "Stock Market Panics," *New York Times*, May 11, 1901.

Page 208 The *Herald* said: "Wild Panic in Wall Street Checked by Banks' Timely Cash," *New York Herald*, May 10, 1901, 3.

Page 208 In Niles, Michigan: "Speculation's Lure Is Wrecking Banks," *New York Herald*, May 14, 1901, 4.

Page 209 In Vancouver, Washington: "Bankers End Their Lives," *Saint Paul Pioneer Press*, April 28, 1901, 3.

Page 209 The cashier and: "Speculation's Lure Is Wrecking Banks," *New York Herald*, May 14, 1901, 4.

Page 209 The shorts and: The exception was *Life* magazine (May 14, 1901, 423): "Old Mother Wall Street / Went to the cupboard / To get her poor shorts some N.P. / When she got there / The cupboard was bare /And so the poor shorts got it in the neck."

Page 209 "If the gentlemen": "The Struggle for Control," *New York Times*, May 10, 1901, 8.

Page 209 William Jennings Bryan: "Criminal Speculation," *Commoner*, 21:17, May 17, 1901, 1.

Page 209 The *Kansas City*: "McKinleyism and Panic," *Marshall (Missouri) Republican*, May 17, 1901, 3.

Page 210 The *New York*: "The 'Community of Interest,'" *New York Evening Post*, editorial, May 10, 1901, 6.

Page 210 "The 'community of interest'": *New York Evening Post*, editorial, May 10, 1901, 6.

Page 210 Only a day: Ibid.

Page 211 "to destroy the": B. O. Flowers, "The Eternal Vanguard of Progress," *Arena* 25:1, July, 1901, 91.

Page 211 Episcopal Bishop William: "Bishop Sees Perils Ahead," *Chicago Daily Tribune*, May 9, 1901, 2.

Page 211 The pastor of: "James R. Keene in a Pulpit Pillory," *New York Herald*, May 20, 1901, 7.

Page 211 Pastors of some: "Gambling in Society," *Saint Paul Dispatch*, April 13, 1901, 1.

Page 211 Word of the: "Stops Church Convention," *Chicago Daily Tribune*, May 10, 1901, 4; *San Francisco Call*, May 16, 1901, 6; "Stock Panic Breaks Up Church Convention," *New York Journal*, May 10, 1901, 3.

Page 211 Among those rescued: "Millionaires Meet for Peace at Night," *New York Journal*, May 10, 1901, 3.

Page 212 Depending on which: "Western Senator Saved from Ruin in Crash by Eastern Colleague," *New York Herald*, May 11, 1901, 4; "Reputed Winners in Denver," *New York Herald*, May 11, 1901, 4; "Lambs Sheared in Wall Street," *Times* (Richmond, Virginia), May 15, 1901, 5.

Page 212 His brother-in-law: "Unlucky Washington Speculators," *New York Evening Post*, May 10, 1901, 2.

Page 212 There was talk: "Panic Sweeps Stock Exchange," *Chicago Tribune*, May 9, 1901, 1.

Page 212 A few other: "Buffalo Reports Speculative Winnings," *New York Evening Post*, May 10, 1901, 2.

Page 212 Former U.S. senator: "How Pettigrew Did It," *Minneapolis Journal*, April 26, 1901, 1.

Page 212 Sometime before Saturday: Livingston–Hill, May 6, 1901, JJHP.

Page 212 Stock pools were: "Western Senator Saved from Ruin in Crash by Eastern Colleague," *New York Herald*, May 11, 1901, 4.

Page 212 A number of: "Ahead on the Market," *Washington Post*, May 7, 1901, 2.

Page 213 He was a tall: "Personal," *Harper's Weekly*, April 6, 1901, 355.

Page 213 He had a taste: Wendt and Kogan, *Bet a Million!* 225; Erickson, "Six of the Greatest," 27.

Page 213 He had bought: Erickson, "Six of the Greatest," 27; "Wolhurst," *Western Garden* 2:12, October 1893, 12.

Page 213 He was said: "Reputed Winners in Denver," *New York Herald*, May 11, 1901, 4.

Page 213 New York State: "Senator McCarren a Winner," *Commercial Advertiser* (New York), May 4, 1901, 1; George, *The Menace Of Privilege*, 250.

Page 214 The early wagers: "Rapid Recovery Emphasizes Crash," *New York Herald*, May 11, 1901, 4.

Page 214 At one point: Keys, "A 'Corner' in Pacific Railroads," 5820; Hill testimony, February 17, 1902, Peter Power v. Northern Pacific Railway Company, U.S. Circuit Court, District of Minnesota, Fourth Division, St. Paul.

Page 214 The Burlington's Perkins: Perkins–Hill, May 11, 1901, JJHP.

Page 214 Look at the: "Wall Street at Rest," *Commercial Advertiser* (New York), May 11, 1901, 1.

Page 214 This morning I: Perhaps it was a letter dated May 7, 1901, from a woman who signed her name Mrs. Susan B. King of Chicago: "Dear Sir: My husband left me an insurance of seven thousand dollars which is invested and brings 4 per cent. It is not enough for me to live on so have taken the liberty to write to ask you if you would tell me how to invest it while those big deals are on in railways to make some money, or if you would not care to tell me, would you let me send you my money to you to invest in for me. My husband was a railroad man[,] he was with the I.C.R.R. [Illinois Central] 24 years[;] he died suddenly last Oct. I have a boy at school I am very anxious to educate and to do so must make some money but do not know how unless you will be kind enough to take a deal with my money in stocks for me. I have care of an insane sister, and have tried to rent out some of my rooms but cannot. Please forgive me for troubling you over my small amount of money but if you would help me by investing it (out of the kindness of your heart), I should indeed be very grateful to you. Hoping to hear from you soon. Yours truly. . ." JJHP, MHS.

Page 214 Hill spent Saturday: Perkins–Hill, May 11, 1901, JJHP.

Page 214 It showed Hill–Morgan: Carosso, *The Morgans*, 477; Hill and friends now held more than half (223,800); Morgan's New York office claimed 146,450.

Page 215 "We appreciate very": Ibid.

Page 215 Choked with emotion: Macleod, "Two Railway Titans Meet at Winnipeg, 1909," 26.

Page 215 In the *New York Herald*: "Truce in Stock War," *New York Herald*, May 11, 1901, 4.

Page 215 They told the *New*: "The Northern Pacific Settlements Effected," *New York Times*, May 11, 1901, 2.

Page 216 The Union Pacific: "His Own Treatment for Mr. Hill," *New York Herald*, May 13, 1901, 5.

Page 216 "None of us": "Wall St. Smiles Again," *New York Sun*, May 11, 1901, 1.

Page 216 He was quoted: "Hill Confident as Ever," *New York Tribune*, May 12, 1901, 1.

Page 217 "The true value": "Jacob H. Schiff Says Legislation Has Forced Railroads into 'Community of Interest' Plan," *New York Herald*, May 23, 1901, 5.

Page 217 "He takes these": Adler, *Jacob H. Schiff*, 1: 107.

10. Northern Insecurities

Page 218 *Harper's Weekly* compared: E. S. Martin, "This Busy World," *Harper's Weekly*, May 25, 1901, 539.

Page 218 The British called: The delivery date rule had its roots in the aftermath of England's railway mania of 1845 when one could buy scrip in new railways with no money down and no delivery date required for the shares when sold. The Special Settlements rule enforced payment on a fixed date for shares purchased and delivery of shares sold (Duguid, *The Story of the [London] Stock Exchange*, 155).

Page 219 A survey showed: "Let London Worry Now," *New York Sun*, May 12, 1901, 1.

Page 219 If Morgan and: Carosso, *The Morgans*, 477.

Page 219 There also were: "Anxious about Stocks," *New York Tribune*, May 13, 1901, 1.

Page 219 "I've got nothing": "Fight for Control in Union Pacific," *New York Times*, May 14, 1901, 3.

Page 219 Thus Harriman obediently: "Harriman at J. P. Morgan's," *New York Sun*, May 14, 1901, 10.

Page 219 Harriman emerged "smiling": "Morgan and Harriman Getting Together," *Commercial Advertiser* (New York), May 14, 1901, 1.

Page 219 At about this: Martin, *James J. Hill*, 505.

Page 220 He was more: U.S. vs. Northern Securities Co., Record, I, 241, cited in Martin, *James J. Hill*, 505.

Page 220 "It stands to": "Fight for Control in Union Pacific," *New York Times*, May 14, 1901, 3.

Page 220 The Associated Press: "Quit Buying 'Nipper' and Saved London," *New York Herald*, May 16, 1901, 3.

Page 220 "We will recommend": Carosso, *The Morgans*, 477.

Page 220 Both sides announced: "The Situation Saved in London," *New York Tribune*, May 14, 1901, 1.

Page 221 In the New: "War May Be Over Soon," *New York Tribune*, May 15, 1901, 1.

Page 221 "Whatever is wisest": "N.P. Fight Is Over," *Minneapolis Journal*, May 15, 1901, 5.

Page 221 The story, with: "Stock War Forced on Union Pacific Men," *New York Times*, May 13, 1901.

Page 221 He remained in: *Harper's Weekly*, May 25, 1901, 5427; Pyle, *The Life of James J. Hill*, 2: 171; Carr, "A Great Railway Builder," 397.

Page 221 "It is too": "Ships without Subsidy," *New York Times*, January 24, 1900, 6.

Page 221 Meanwhile, New York: "Oceanic Brings in Many," *New York Evening World*, May 15, 1901, 6; "Oceanic Brings a Lot of N.P.," *New York Sun*, May 16, 1901; "Harmony to Rule Northwest Roads," *New York Herald*, May 16, 1901, 16.

Page 222 The sacks were: "Arbitrage Houses Relieved," *New York Times*, May 16, 1901, 3.

Page 222 The stock was: "The Market Recovers after Serious Break," *New York Times*, May 16, 1901; "Market Strong Again," *New York Tribune*, May 16, 1901, 1.

Page 222 That same day: Strouse, *Morgan*, 424.

Page 222 The market couldn't: "The Market Recovers after Serious Break," *New York Times*, May 16, 1901.

Page 222 Dated May 16: Adler, *Jacob H. Schiff*, 1: 102–7.

Page 223 With neither correspondence: "Mr. Morgan Buys Rare Curiosities," *New York Herald*, May 21, 1901, 3. Purchase price listed in the *Chicago Daily News Almanac and Year Book for 1903*, James Langland, compiler, 1902, 182.

Page 224 The acquisition, said: "J. Pierpont Morgan's Wonderful Gathering of European Art Treasures," Gustav Kobbe, *St. Louis Republic*, September 2, 1902, 48; "Morgan's Great Art Collection," *Saint Paul Globe*, July 14, 1901, 18.

Page 224 To avoid, temporarily: "Mr. Morgan's Object Lesson," *New York Evening Post*, May 31, 1901, 8.

Page 224 Harriman agreed to: A story about Schiff in the April 1903 *Cosmopolitan* magazine (p. 699) gave him credit for "voluntarily" suggesting that Morgan name the board. If he did he was simply suggesting the only possible choice. Only Morgan had the global prestige to merit such responsibility. One could imagine no one else in that role.

Page 224 Hill agreed to: Martin, *James J. Hill*, 506.

Page 224 Reaching St. Paul: Ibid.; Hill–Nichols, telegram, May 21, 1901, JJHP.

Page 224 The *New York*: "Northern Pacific Peace," July 18, 1901, 1.

Page 224 Long before the: "Griggs Closes Case," *New York Times*, March 21, 1903, 7.

Page 225 This new holding: The General Statutes of the State of Minnesota, 1883, 437: "It shall not be lawful for such company to make, declare or pay in any form, any dividend upon its capital stock exceeding ten per cent, per annum thereupon, and upon the surplus funds to be formed hereunder, until after its guaranty surplus fund and its special reserve fund shall have together accumulated to an amount equal to its said capital stock; and the entire surplus profits of such company, above such annual dividend of ten per cent, shall be equally divided between, and be set apart to constitute, the said guarantee surplus fund and the said special reserve fund, which funds shall be held and used as hereinafter provided, and not otherwise; and any company doing business under this act, which shall declare or pay any dividend contrary to the provisions herein contained, shall be liable to be proceeded against by the attorney general for its dissolution."

Page 225 Morgan concurred, he: Strouse, *Morgan*, 427.

Page 225 "This will give": Hill–Stephen, May 18 and June 4, 1901, JJHP.

Page 225 Northern Securities was: U.S. vs. Northern Securities Co., Record, I, 241, cited in Martin, *James J. Hill*, 545.

Page 225 It was a harmonious: Klein, *Union Pacific*, 108; Klein, *The Life and Legend of E. H. Harriman*, 237.

Page 226 There were so: "Ship of Millionaires," *New York Sun*, July 5, 1901, 7; *New York Tribune*, June 29, 1901, 6; "Prominent Men Return," *New York Tribune*, July 5, 1901, 7.

Page 226 Soon he was: "Ship of Millionaires," *New York Sun*, July 5, 1901, 7; Allen, *The Great Pierpont Morgan*, 42, 71–72.

Page 227 It was the: "Northern Pacific Peace," *New York Sun*, July 18, 1901, 8; "Northern Pacific Peace," *New York Tribune*, July 18, 1901, 1.

Page 227 He apparently failed: "Union Pacific Situation," *New York Times*, July 20, 1901.

Page 227 Before he and: Klein, *Union Pacific*, 108–9.

Page 227 The day before: Hill–Gaspard Farrer, July 22, 1901, JJHP.

Page 227 "I told him": "No Agreement Made with Mr. Harriman," *Washington Times*, February 19, 1902, 1.

Page 227 Hill pledged 80,049: Martin, *James J. Hill*, 510.

Page 227 One or more: Strouse, *Morgan*, 372; Klein, *The Life and Legend of E. H. Harriman*, 238.

Page 228 They compromised in: Klein, *Union Pacific*, 109.

Page 228 The Great Northern: Ibid., 11, from *Wall Street Journal*, November 8–11, 14–15, 22–23, December 2, 1901; "Securities Company Officers Are Chosen," *New York Times*, November 16, 1901, 8; *Chicago Chronicle*, December 17, 1901.

Page 228 Their temperaments and: Klein, *Union Pacific*, 146.

Page 228 Hill had tired: Christopher Gray, "Streetscapes: The Bolkenhayn on Fifth Avenue," *New York Times*, September 1, 2002.

Page 229 Hill rose early: MTH Diary, JJHP.

Page 229 Arden was more: Figliomeni, *E. H. Harriman at Arden Farms*, 4.

Page 229 They spent several: "Harriman Vindicated in Great Biography," *Current Opinion* 73, July 1922, 74.

Page 229 an appearance he: "'Teddy' Will Surely Come," *Saint Paul Pioneer Press*, April 28, 1901, 3. Hardly anyone noticed that Roosevelt had come through the night from Chicago in a private sleeper, arriving in St. Paul at 7:40 that morning "alone and unattended," in a special car, attached to the "Pioneer Limited." It had been offered to him for his exclusive use, likely gratis, by the general traffic manager of the Chicago, Milwaukee & St. Paul Railroad (the "St. Paul"), controlled by the Rockefellers.

Page 229 Clad in a black: "Roosevelt Captured Them," *Saint Paul Globe*, September 3, 1901, 1.

Page 229 The vast individual: "Vice Pres. Roosevelt's Eloquent Address at the State Fair," *Saint Paul Globe*, September 3, 1901, 6.

Page 230 Two days later: Cook, *America*, 414–15.

Page 230 In 1896 in: Martin, *James J. Hill*, 427.

Page 230 "The good work": Bryan, *The World's Famous Orations*, 247.

Page 231 "Very confidential": Martin, *James J. Hill*, 506.

Page 232 An eternity passed: Rauchway, *Murdering McKinley*, 3.

Page 232 Morgan had his: Strouse, *Morgan*, 435.

Page 232 Another reporter came: "How News Was Received in New York," *New York Times*, September 7, 1901, 2; Pringle, *Theodore Roosevelt*, 237.

Page 232 Morgan cruised to: "Stocks Beaten Down," *New York Evening World* September 7, 1901, 8.

Page 232 Wall Street jammed: "The News in Wall Street," *Harper's Weekly*, 45: 2334, September 14, 1901, 913.

Page 233 Perhaps it was: "Stocks Beaten Down in Mad Rush by Excited Bears," *New York Evening World*, September 7, 1901, 8.

Page 233 "The financial situation": Strouse, *Morgan*, 435.

Page 233 "Society entertainments" even: "The News of Newport," *New York Times*, September 10, 1901.

Page 233 On Tuesday, Roosevelt: Brands, *T. R.*, 413.

Page 233 A Pennsylvania Railroad: Morris, *Theodore Rex*, 20.

Page 233 The Stock Exchange: "Simple and Brief but Impressive Funeral," *New York Evening World*, September 19, 1901, 2.

Page 233 "Don't any of": Dunn, *From Harrison to Harding*, 335.

11. The "Big Stick"

Page 234 He often described: Morgan testimony, Peter Power vs. Northern Pacific Railway Company, March 26, 1902, 337.

Page 234 His faith was: Allen, *The Great Pierpont Morgan*, 13, 69.

Page 234 Morgan probably was: Burton J. Hendrick, "The Most Powerful Man in America," *McClure's*, October 1909, 56.

Page 234 He was a: "Episcopal Prelates," *San Francisco Call*, October 3, 1901, 1.

Page 234 At this convention: "Episcopal Prelates, Clergy and Laymen Assemble," *San Francisco Call*, October 3, 1901, 1; "Dr. Lindsay Is Chairman," *San Francisco Call*, October 3, 1901, 5.

Page 235 Morgan rose with: "Episcopalian Church Convention," *San Francisco Call*, October 3, 1901, 1.

Page 235 He listened intently: "Triennial Convention," *New York Tribune*, October 3, 1901, 5.

Page 235 It was his: Strouse, *Morgan*, 132.

Page 235 "Land without population": Hill, *Highways of Progress*, 45.

Page 235 Signalmen from New: Strouse, *Morgan*, 429.

Page 235 The restaurateur: "J. P. Morgan Criticized," *New York Times*, November 6, 1901, 6.

Page 236 He probably agreed: DeVoto, *Mark Twain in Eruption*, 49.

Page 236 When he did: Roosevelt, *The Letters of Theodore Roosevelt*, 140.

Page 236 Morgan had known: Chernow, *House of Morgan*, 106.

Page 236 He had supported: Strouse, *Morgan*, 436.

Page 236 As vice president: Morris, *Theodore Rex*, 29; Strouse, *Morgan*, 436.

Page 237 He especially disliked: Schonberger, "James J. Hill and the Trade with the Orient," 181.

Page 237 From that night: Klein, *The Life and Legend of E. H. Harriman*, 361–62.

Page 237 Stetson had stage-managed: Strouse, *Morgan*, 429.

Page 237 Perkins had lobbied: Garraty, *Right-Hand Man*, 74.

Page 238 Sometime in 1901: Ibid., 223.

Page 238 Roosevelt said he: Scott, *Robert Bacon*, 29.

Page 238 Roosevelt considered both: Strouse, *Morgan*, 439.

Page 238 A holding company: "The Protection of Investors," *New York Times*, October 7, 1901, 6.

Page 238 "Perkins may just": Morris, *Theodore Rex*, 64.

Page 238 Word began to: "J. J. Hill's Plan," *New York Tribune*, October 11, 1901, 5.

Page 239 Hill was waiting: "Morgan Busy with N.P. War," *New York Evening World*, October 28, 1901, 10.

Page 239 Someone in the: "Street Boils with Rumors," *New York Sun*, October 29, 1901, 10.

Page 239 Hill would not: "Message Nearly Drafted," *Washington Times*, November 2, 1901, 7.

Page 240 In early November: Strouse, *Morgan*, 443.

Page 240 Buried at the: "Northern Pacific Settlement Plan," *New York Times*, November 7, 1901.

Page 240 He retired from: "Society at Home and Abroad," *New York Times*, January 19, 1902, 9. Mr. and Mrs. Robert Bacon are listed as seen at the performance of *Beyond Human Power*.

Page 240 Morgan wanted him: Garraty, *Right-Hand Man*, 89.

Page 240 Perkins "now does": *New York Evening World*, March 9, 1902.

Page 240 Hill, Harriman, and Perkins: "N.P. Settlement Agreed On," *New York Sun*, November 13, 1901, 10.

Page 240 Sometime around 2 a.m.: Morris, *Theodore Rex*, 59.

Page 241 Harriman sold all: Stevens, *History of the Bench and Bar of Minnesota*, 2: 206.

Page 241 There was a: *Economist*, November 16, 1901, 1697; Hill–Gaspard Farrer, July 22, 1904, JJHP.

Page 241 Worried about spooking: "Giant Deal Is Consummated," *Times* (Richmond, Virginia), November 14, 1901, 1; "Topping It Off," *Saint Paul Globe*, November 15, 1901, 1.

Page 241 To mark the: MTH Diary, JJHP.

Page 242 Baker and Hill: "The N.P. Contest Settled," *New York Tribune*, November 14, 1901, 1.

Page 242 Their Union Pacific: Adler, *Jacob H. Schiff*, 1: 110.

Page 242 Harriman still looked: Martin, *James J. Hill*, 520.

Page 242 When trading opened: "Big Railroad Deal's Scope Far Reaching," *New York Times*, November 15, 1901, 1.

Page 242 Wealthy Europeans put: "The Northern Securities Case," *Railway News*, 2162: 83, June 10, 1905, 930.

Page 242 They warned the: Stevens, *History of the Bench and Bar of Minnesota*, 2: 207.

Page 242 Hill's lawyers presented: Ibid., 206.

Page 242 They decided a: Martin, *James J. Hill*, 511.

Page 242 Northern Securities was: encyclopedia.com/doc/1G2–3468300153.html.

Page 242 "A combination of": "Danger Warning by Russell Sage," *New York Evening World*, November 14, 1901, 1.

Page 243 Knox was a: McCullough, *The Johnstown Flood*, 58, 260.

Page 243 He had earned: Villard, *Memoirs of Henry Villard*, 248–49.

Page 243 At five feet: Ibid., 248.

Page 243 The entire draft: Morris, *Theodore Rex*, 68. The final version is 19,619 words.

Page 244 Sentence by sentence: Ibid., 65.

Page 244 Mark Hanna urged: Bishop, *Theodore Roosevelt and His Time*, 159.

Page 244 He had never: Zacks, *Island of Vice*, 128.

Page 244 At age twenty-four: Morris, *The Rise of Theodore Roosevelt*, 177.

Page 244 He paid homage: "Regulating Railways by Law," *The Roosevelt Policy*, 2: 513.

Page 244 Thirty-one years later: Roosevelt, *Theodore Roosevelt*, 425.

Page 245 "I am simply": Auchincloss, *Theodore Roosevelt*, 568.

Page 245 In his first: Roosevelt, *The Roosevelt Policy*, 1: 181

Page 245 "The consolidation of": Hill, *Highways of Progress*, 115.

Page 245 There were 20: Morris, *Theodore Rex*, 28. A sampler: United States Leather Co. American Ice Company. Continental Tobacco. Writing Paper Trust. American Sugar Refining Co. United States Flour Milling Co. American Bicycle Co. American Hide and Leather Co. American Tobacco. Anaconda Copper Mining Co. American Woolen Co. Window Glass Combine. National Biscuit Company. American Spirits Manufacturing. National Wall Paper Co. Rubber Goods Manufacturers. National Carpet Company. International Cement Co. Glucose Sugar Refining Company. American Alkali Co. National Enamel and Stamping Co. United Fruit Company. Cotton Yarn Company. United States Glue Co. Kentucky Distilleries. General Electric. American Sugar Beet Company. National Lead Co. American Malting Co. Union Typewriter. Diamond Match Co. Westinghouse.

Page 246 This tendency to: Hill, *Highways of Progress*, 114–15.

Page 246 "It is not": "Combinations Not Evil, Says Mr. Fish," *New York Herald*, April 25, 1901, 14.

Page 246 "If it is": Norris, *Octopus*, 20.

Page 246 To his credit: TR–Owen Wister, July 20, 1901, *Theodore Roosevelt, Letters and Speeches*, 234.

Page 247 "There are thought": Stevens, *History of the Bench and Bar of Minnesota*, 2: 204.

Page 247 "The railroad is": Speech delivered at the annual banquet of the Periodical Publishers Association, Philadelphia, February 2, 1912, La Follette, *La Follette's Autobiography*, 772.

Page 247 "I regard the": from *The Campaign Textbook of the Democratic Party of the United States*, Democratic National Committee, 1908, 42.

Page 247 "For as long": "Craft Unionism," Chicago, November 24, 1905, in Debs, *Debs: His Life, Writings, and Speeches,* 404.

Page 247 The Congregational pastor: Gladden, *Tools and the Man,* 299.

Page 247 It will, he: Ray Stannard Baker, "The Great Northern Pacific Deal," *Collier's,* November 30, 1901, 542.

Page 247 When everyone was: "The Week in Money," *Chicago Daily News,* May 11, 1901, 9.

Page 248 As R. W. Apple Jr.: Garraty, *Quarrels That Have Shaped the Consitution,* 177.

Page 248 Roosevelt began the: Roosevelt, *State of the Union Addresses,* 7.

Page 249 Wall Street and: Kahn, *Of Many Things,* 184.

12. A Thunderbolt Out of the Blue

Page 250 It was like: Carr, "A Great Railway Builder," 398.

Page 250 He called her: Paine, *George Fisher Baker,* 200.

Page 250 He had just: February 18, 1902, JJH–MTH, JJHP.

Page 251 She telegrammed back: February 19, 1902, MTH–JJH, JJHP.

Page 251 She had almost: MTH Diary, JJHP.

Page 251 Four days after: *Minneapolis Journal,* November 18, 1901, 7.

Page 251 A lot of: Van Sant–Hill, Great Northern Railway, Law Dept. records, MHS.

Page 251 He wrote his: Strouse, *Morgan,* 432. Much to Hill's dismay, Morgan had installed his arrogant yes-man, Charles S. Mellen, as president of the Northern Pacific during the years when the Morgan voting trust controlled the railroad. Mellen was still president of the Northern Pacific in early 1901 when, with Morgan's assent, he proposed to offer bribes of $5,000 (a pittance as bribes went in those days) probably to influence Van Sant staff members on legislation affecting railroad rates (Strouse, *Morgan,* 433).

Page 251 The *Saint Paul Globe*: "The Truth about the Formation of the Northern Securities Company," December 22, 1901, 1.

Page 252 "Courts are open": "President Hill's Address," *Minneapolis Journal,* January 10, 1902, 2.

Page 253 When Harriman gave: Klein, *The Life and Legend of E. H. Harriman,* 309.

Page 253 Northern Securities was: Pringle, *Theodore Roosevelt,* 255.

Page 253 In New York: Ibid., 254.

Page 254 Within a very: "Government to Test Big Railway Merger," *New York Times,* February 20, 1902, 3.

Page 254 One historian later: Leech, *In the Days of McKinley,* 547.

Page 254 Knox's predecessor under: Letwin, *Law and Economic Policy in America,* 138, 141.

Page 255 This would be: Ibid., 182.

Page 255 They would worry: Martin, *James J. Hill,* 516.

Page 256 If you want: "The Progress of the World," *American Monthly,* May 1903, 522.

Page 256 Of course, Hill: Meyer, *History of the Northern Securities Case,* 247.

Page 256 The telegraph lines: Argument of W. C. Bunn in *United States v. Northern Securities,* December 14, 1903; *New York Times,* December 15, 1903.

Page 256 In 1847 it: Moody, *The Truth about Trusts,* 446.

Page 256 Even George Stephenson: Ibid., 445.

Page 257 Maybe Northern Securities: "Stock Market Rallies," *New York Tribune*, February 22, 1902, 4.

Page 257 Maybe they should: Tuck–Hill, April 30, 1903, JJHP.

Page 257 While Hill tossed": "President's Action Startles Wall Street," *New York Times*, February 21, 1902.

Page 257 "There is," Knox: Morris, *Theodore Rex*, 90.

Page 257 As they were: Martin, *James J. Hill*, 514; Morris, *Theodore Rex*, 89.

Page 257 "The government," he: Martin, *James J. Hill*, 514; Morris, *Theodore Rex*, 60.

Page 258 There was a: Klein, *The Life and Legend of E. H. Harriman*, 310.

Page 258 The "whole question: *Wall Street Journal*, March 21, 1902; quoted in ibid.

Page 258 Roosevelt wrote later: *Autobiography*, 1913, 428.

Page 258 Politically, Morgan and: Brand, T.R., 436.

Page 258 Roosevelt long felt: Pringle, *Theodore Roosevelt*, 254.

Page 258 They could become: Letwin, *Law and Economic Policy in America*, 92.

Page 258 The total absence: Ibid., 255.

Page 258 Knox later called: "The Commerce Clause of the Constitution and the Trusts," Philander C. Knox, Chamber of Commerce, Pittsburgh, Pa., October 14, 1902.

Page 258 Hearst's *Evening Journal*: "Carnegie as Prophet," *New York Evening Journal*, May 7, 1901.

Page 259 "I am not": "Hill Talks Fight," *Minneapolis Journal*, February 21, 1902, 2; "J. J. Hill Surprised," *New York Sun*, February 21, 1902, 1.

Page 259 Let the people: "James J. Hill Talks on Industrial Enterprises," *New York Times*, September 28, 1902.

Page 259 Privately, a few: Hill–James, March 8, 1902, JJHP.

Page 259 "He detests me": Morris, *Theodore Rex*, 251.

Page 259 A friend of: Beer, *Hanna*, 242.

Page 259 Knox promised him: Morris, *Theodore Rex*, 89.

Page 259 During the dinner: Allen, *The Great Pierpont Morgan*, 219

Page 260 He returned to: Ibid., 220.

Page 260 Perkins departed on: "Merger Case Discussed with President," *Washington Times*, February 22, 1902, 1.

Page 260 Roosevelt was not: Roosevelt, *The Letters of Theodore Roosevelt*, 159.

Page 260 Their train pulled: "City Isolated by Ravages of Storm," *Washington Times*, February 22, 1902, 1.

Page 260 Also in town: Strouse, *Morgan*, 207.

Page 261 Not a word: "Morgan at White House," *New York Tribune*, February 24, 1902, 7.

Page 261 Perhaps he played: Allen, *The Great Pierpont Morgan*, 70.

Page 261 One of his: Bishop, *Theodore Roosevelt and His Time*, 185.

Page 261 How could that: Martin, *James J. Hill*, 515.

Page 261 The only account: Bishop, *Theodore Roosevelt and His Time*, 184–85.

Page 262 "Our friends on": Baker–Hill, February 22, 1902, JJHP.

Page 262 "At the same": Knox–Purdy, March 8, 1902, Department of Justice, Instruction Book No. 156, 358–59, quoted in Letwin, *Law and Economic Policy in America*, 213.

Page 262 He could leave: Morris, *Theodore Rex*, 92.

Page 262 He knew if: Villard, *Prophets True and False*, 248–49.

Page 262 Harriman was granted: Morris, *Theodore Rex*, 92.

Page 263 It accused the: "Merger Papers Filed," *Saint Paul Globe*, March 11, 1902, 1.

Page 263 Hill in New York: "Hill Will Force the Fighting," *Minneapolis Journal*, March 12, 1902, 1.

Page 263 Schiff claimed if: Adler, *Jacob H. Schiff*, 1: 112.

Page 263 A month after: Klein, *The Life and Legend of E. H. Harriman*, 308.

Page 263 It was estimated: Hendrick, "The Most Powerful Man in America," 647.

Page 263 The whole thing: "Wall Street on the Decision," *New York Times*, April 19, 1903.

Page 264 "Capital all over": "Against the Merger," *New York Sun*, April 10, 1903, 1.

Page 264 it was a symbol: See Nimmo, *Commercial, Economic, and Political Questions Not Decided in the Northern Securities Case*, 1903, for a brilliant argument for the broad economic benefits of railroad mergers.

Page 264 He had no Ivy: "James M. Beck, 74, New Deal Foe, Dies," *New York Times*, April 13, 1936, 1; *Biographical Directory of the United States Congress, 1774–2005*, 630.

Page 265 He had accepted: "Trust 'Buster' Won by Trusts," *New York Evening World*, April 4, 1903, 3.

Page 265 There was a: "Headway Made in Argument on Railway Merger Suit," *St. Louis Republic*, March 19, 1903, 1.

Page 265 "The safety of": "Argument Is Begun on Railway Merger," *New York Times*, March 19, 1903.

Page 266 Until that time: The "kalends" were the first day of the ancient Roman month but not part of the Greek calendar, thus a time that never arrives.

Page 266 Hill and the fourth: MTH Diary, JJHP.

Page 267 Morgan had booked: "Against the Merger," *New York Sun*, April 10, 1903, 1.

Page 267 Among those who: "The President's Minneapolis Address," *Minneapolis Journal*, April 6, 1903.

Page 267 Northern Securities was: "Against the Merger," *New York Sun*, April 10, 1903, 1.

Page 267 Northern Securities "destroyed": "N.P. Merger Declared Void," *New York Tribune*, April 10, 1903, 1.

Page 268 "While most disappointing: MTH Diary, JJHP.

Page 268 Even if he: "Heavy Break in Stocks," *New York Tribune*, April 14, 1903, 3.

Page 268 It was six: MTH Diary, April 16, 1903, JJHP; "The 'Minnesota' Launched Today," *Minneapolis Journal*, April 16, 1903, 1; White, "Review of Past Progress in Steam Navigation," 201.

Page 268 He was quoted: *Washington Post*, April 11, 1903, quoted in Nimmo, *Commercial, Economic, and Political Questions Not Decided in the Northern Securities Case*, 27.

Page 268 Mr. Hill's voice: *Week's Progress*, March 26, 1902, 302.

Page 268 The ruling puzzled: Jefferson's First Message to Congress, December 8, 1801.

Page 268 "Stripped to its": "The Progress of the World," *American Monthly*, May 1903, 525.

Page 269 Should one not: Hill–Morgan attorney John Graver Johnson, quoted in Apple, "The Case of the Monopolistic Railroadmen," 187.

Page 269 "The American people": "Say It May Be a Blessing," *New York Tribune*, April 14, 1903, 2.

Page 269 Shares of Northern: "Affects Stocks Little," *New York Tribune*, April 10, 1903, 1.

Page 269 who, according to: Hill–Farrer, April 27, 1903, JJHP, MHS.

Page 269 The bottom didn't: Strouse, *Morgan*, 477.

Page 270 Second, the circuit: Letwin, *Law and Economic Policy in America*, 221–24.

Page 270 His friend Tuck: Tuck–Hill, April 30, 1903, JJHP, MHS.

Page 270 While the Hill–Morgan: Lamont–Hill, May 8, 1903, JJHP, MHS.

Page 270 Near Evanston, Wyoming: Klein, *The Life and Legend of E. H. Harriman*, 297.

Page 270 "take good care": May 15, 18, and 19, 1903, JJHP, MHS.

Page 271 Hill couldn't help: September 10, 1903, JJHP, MHS.

Page 271 Schiff's junior partner: "The Fight for the West," *Boston Evening Transcript*, March 7, 1910, 3.

Page 271 Federal Judge William: "Lochren Holds Merger Is Legal," *Minneapolis Journal*, August 1, 1903, 1.

13. Great Cases and Bad Law

Page 272 Its earnings had: Moody and Turner, "The Masters of Capital in America" (December 1910), 139.

Page 272 Not since Dred: Apple, "The Case of the Monopolistic Railroadmen," 187.

Page 272 Seven weeks after: Martin, *James J. Hill*, 518.

Page 272 Many respected judges: "John G. Johnson, Noted Lawyer, Dies," *New York Times*, April 15, 1917.

Page 274 Pacing the chamber: Apple, "The Case of Monopolistic Railroadmen," 187; Martin, *James J. Hill*, 518.

Page 275 The three railroads: "Merger Case Argued," *New York Times*, December 15, 1903, 1.

Page 275 After the Northern: "Attorneys Dissect the Northern Securities Case," *Saint Paul Globe*, December 15, 1902, 7.

Page 275 "We have been": Johnson's reference to Caligula is from *United States v. Comerford*, District Court, W.D. Texas, November 1885, p. 902, *The Federal Reporter*, St. Paul: West Publishing Company, Vol. 25–26.

Page 275 His fee for: "John G. Johnson, Noted Lawyer, Dies," *New York Times*, April 15, 1917.

Page 276 "The mere existence": Harlan, J., Judgment of the Court, Supreme Court of the United States, 193 U.S. 197, *Northern Securities Co. v. United States*, Appeal from the Circuit Court of the United States for the District of Minnesota, No. 277, Argued: December 14–15, 1903, Decided, March 14, 1904.

Page 276 Just as the: Klein, *Union Pacific*, 148; Martin, *James J. Hill*, 520.

Page 277 He feared "the": Harlan, J., Judgment of the Court, Supreme Court of the United States, 193 U.S. 197, *Northern Securities v. United States*.

Page 277 The amicable, portly: Highsaw, *Edward Douglass White*, 5.

Page 278 The principles laid: Harlan, J., Judgment of the Court, Supreme Court of the United States, 193 U.S. 197, *Northern Securities v. United States*.

Page 278 Roosevelt had called: Morris, *Theodore Rex*, 130, 291.

Page 279 That fear of: Martin, *James J. Hill*, 520.

Page 279 Roosevelt always insisted: Strouse, *Morgan*, 665.

Page 279 In a private: Holmes–Sir Frederick Pollock, February 9, 1921, quoted in Letwin, *Law and Economic Policy in America*, 236.

Page 279 "I could," he: John Hay diary, March 15, 1905, quoted in Morris, *Theodore Rex*, 316.

Page 279 Holmes dined at: Strouse, *Morgan*, 534.

Page 279 There was heavy: "Wall Street Shaken," *New York Tribune*, March 15, 1904, 3.

Page 279 He spent all: "Return of Merger Stocks," *New York Sun*, March 16, 1904, 9; "Another Plan Ready," *New York Times*, March 15, 1904, 1; "Lawyers Confer with Mr. Hill," *Saint Paul Globe*, March 17, 1904, 1.

Page 280 "What are you": "Believe Hill Is Equal to Crisis," *Minneapolis Journal*, March 17, 1904, 1.

Page 280 A reporter from: "J. J. Hill Stunned," *Minneapolis Journal*, March 16, 1904, 1.

Page 280 In Minnesota, Governor: "Greatest Event since Civil War, says Van Sant," *Washington Times*, March 15, 1904, 2.

Page 280 "On wan hand": Dunne, *Observations by Mr. Dooley*, 223.

Page 280 He quoted someone: "He Will Obey the Law, Says Merger King," *New York World*, March 15, 1904, 1.

Page 281 The source of: Prince, *Seaboard Air Line Railway*, 86. Long before commercial aviation, some railroads used "air line" in their names to suggest that their routes were the shortest distance between two points and thus more convenient than competitors.

Page 281 "Nothing but the": "As to Running Amuck," *New York Times*, March 16, 1904, 8.

Page 281 Jiu-jitsu, Roosevelt: *Theodore Roosevelt's Letters to His Children*, White House, February 24, 1905.

Page 281 He learned of: "President Jiu-Jitsu Enthusiast," *Washington Times*, March 14, 1904, 3.

Page 281 Schiff, who could: Klein, *The Life and Legend of E. H. Harriman*, 311.

Page 281 Harriman had deposited: "Believe Hill Is Equal to Crisis," *Minneapolis Journal*, March 17, 1904, 1.

Page 282 "As a piece": June 15, 1904, JJHP.

Page 282 By "them" he: Klein, *The Life and Legend of E. H. Harriman*, 414.

Page 282 "We do not": Mount Stephen–Hill, July 15, 1904, JJHP.

Page 282 On the populist: Bishop, *Theodore Roosevelt and His Time*, 325.

Page 282 Harriman, Morgan (and: Josephson, *The Robber Barons*, 450.

Page 282 Hill, and Morgan's: Morris, *Theodore Rex*, 360.

Page 282 "I do not": Schiff–Hill, March 10, 1904, JJHP.

Epilogue: The Last Corner

Page 283 The court's decision: Dean Gordon–Hill, March 16, 1901, JJHP, MHS.

Page 283 They showered subsidies: Martin, *Railroads Triumphant*, 381.

Page 283 Four years later: Ibid., 299, 354; Larson, *Bonds of Enterprise*, 205.

Page 283 Ten years later: Rose, *The Best Transportation System in the World*, 3.

Page 284 An Iowa farm: Hidy et al., *The Great Northern Railway*, 155; "J. J. Hill Dead in St. Paul Home at the Age of 77," *New York Times*, May 30, 1916.

Page 284 The ICC spent: Hidy and Hidy, "John Frank Stevens," 193.

Page 285 The ICC, created: Adam Thierer, "How to Keep the Promise to Reinvent Government: Abolish the ICC," Heritage Foundation, June 14, 1994.

Page 285 Typical of the: "Matthew Josephson, Biographer and Muckraker, Dies," *New York Times*, March 14, 1978.

Page 285 Except for the: O'Toole *Gridlock*, 134.

Page 285 Hill estimated in: "National Rivers and Harbors Congress: Proceedings of the Convention," Washington, D.C., December 6–7, 1906, 99.

Page 285 Morgan, dealing "with": Strouse, *Morgan*, 667, 671.

Page 285 In 1913, the: Goddard, *Getting There*, 39, 54.

Page 285 Five weeks after: Ibid., 63.

Page 286 Total U.S. railroad: Ibid., 64.

Page 286 Forty-one years: Ibid., 175.

Page 286 Washington saddled railroads: Ibid., 36.

Page 286 Railroads themselves were: Ibid., ix.

Page 286 On April 20, 1901: "An Undertaking Unique in History: The Good Roads Train Awakens the Sunny South," *Good Roads Magazine*, June 1901, 5.

Page 287 America's inland waterways: "Fact Sheet: Historic Subsidy of Inland Waterways Navigation System," from "Big Price—Little Benefit," prepared by Nicollet Island Coalition, available through Taxpayers for Common Sense, taxpayer.net.

Page 287 The *Times* then: "President's Action Startles Wall Street," *New York Times*, February 21, 1902.

Page 288 In 1916, Hill's: Hidy and Hidy, "John Frank Stevens," 133, 291.

Page 288 Stockholders of both: Ibid., 297.

Page 288 A year and: Ibid., 299.

Page 288 The same day: Ibid., 301.

Page 288 In the early: http://www.politicalfamilytree.com.

Page 289 He and his: "Tour St. Paul: Dayton's Bluff," historicsaintpaul.org.

Page 289 The year James: notablebiographies.com.

Page 289 There was no: Hidy and Hidy, "John Frank Stevens," 304.

Page 289 Ten years later: Rose, *The Best Transportation System in the World*, 208.

Page 290 If Schiff had: *Omaha Bee*, July 11, 1895, 2; a one-sentence ad, "Texas freestone peaches and fancy tomatoes. S. H. Buffett, 315 So. 14th St."

Page 290 Sidney had come: Schroeder, *The Snowball*, 36.

Page 290 It hauls more: Zack O'Malley Greenburg, "Burlington Santa Fe: Warren Buffett's Favorite Railroad," *Forbes*, December 20, 2007, forbes.com.

Page 290 Wall Street, with: "Why Is Buffett Betting on the Railroads?" *Railway Age*, December 2009, 16–20.

Page 291 Warren Buffett's purchase: "Buffett's Bet on Trains, *New York Times*, November 3, 2009.

Page 291 "foremost cause of": Tocqueville, *Democracy in America*, 2: 282.

Page 291 Edward Henry Harriman: Martin, *James J. Hill*, 522; Klein, *The Life and Legend of E. H. Harriman*, 421, 434, 440; Kennan, *E. H. Harriman*, 2: 346; "Harriman Funeral a Simple Service," *New York Times*, September 13, 1909; "Harriman Dead, Long Fight Over," *New York Sun*, September 10, 1909, 1; Kahn, *Of Many Things*, 41; "I'll Talk When Free, Says E. H. Harriman," *New York Times*, December 1, 1908, 1.

Page 292 John Pierpont Morgan: Strouse, *Morgan*, 663, 671–72, 674–78, 682–83; Johnson, *A History of the American People*, 563.

Page 292 James J. Hill: Martin, *James J. Hill*, 582, 595, 797–98, 600, 605, 611, 613–14; "James J. Hill Is Buried," *New York Times*, June 1, 1916.

Page 293 Jacob Henry Schiff: "City Will Pay Honor to Mr. Schiff Today," *New York Times*, September 28, 1920, 3; Adler, *Jacob H. Schiff*, 1: 109.

BIBLIOGRAPHY

Adams, Frederick Upham. *The Kidnapped Millionaires: A Tale of Wall Street*. Boston: Lothrop Publishing Company, 1901.

Adler, Cyrus. *Jacob H. Schiff: His Life and Letters*. 2 vols. New York: Doubleday, Doran and Company, 1929.

Allen, Frederick Lewis. *The Great Pierpont Morgan*. New York: Dorset Press, 1948 [1989].

———. *The Lords of Creation*. New York: Harper and Brothers, 1939.

Allen, W. H. "American Securities in Europe," letter to the editor, *Bankers' Magazine* 73: 1, July 1906.

American Ancestry: Giving the Name and Descent, in the Male Line, of Americans Whose Ancestors Settled in the United States previous to the Declaration of Independence, A.D. 1776. Vol. 10: *Embracing Lineages from the Whole of the United States*. Albany, New York: Joel Munsell's Sons, 1895.

Apple, R. W. Jr. "The Case of the Monopolistic Railroadmen." In *Quarrels That Have Shaped the Constitution*, ed. John A. Garraty. New York: Harper and Row, 1964.

Appleton's General Guide to the United States and Canada. New York: D. Appleton and Company, 1893.

Auchincloss, Louis, ed. *Theodore Roosevelt: Letters and Speeches*. New York: Library of America, 2004.

Bacon, Edwin M., ed. *Boston Illustrated*. Boston: Houghton Mifflin, 1886.

Balthazar, Henry Meyer. "A History of the Northern Securities Case." In *Railway Problems*, ed. William Z. Ripley. Boston: Ginn and Company, 1907.

Bancroft, Hubert Howe. *Chronicles of the Builders of the Commonwealth*. San Francisco: History Company, 1891.

Baruch, Bernard. *My Own Story*. New York: Henry Holt, 1957.

Beard, Patricia. *After the Ball*. New York: HarperCollins Publishers, 2003.

Beck, James Montgomery. *May It Please the Court*. Atlanta: Harrison Company, 1930.

Beer, Thomas. *Hanna*. New York: Alfred A. Knopf, 1929.

Bellamy, Edward. *Looking Backward*. Boston: Ticknor and Company, 1888.

Biographical Dictionary of the United States Congress, 1774–2005. Washington, D.C.: U.S. Government Printing Office, 2005.

Birmingham, Stephen. *"Our Crowd": The Great Jewish Families of New York*. New York: Harper and Row, 1967.

Bishop, Joseph Bucklin. *Theodore Roosevelt and His Time*. New York: Charles Scribner's Sons, 1920.

Bloom, Ken. *Broadway: An Encyclopedia*. New York: Routledge, 2004.

Blossom, Mary C. "James J. Hill." *World's Work* 2:1, May 1901.

Boren, Edward L. *Legacies of the Turf: A Century of Great Thoroughbred Breeders*. Lexington, Kentucky: Blood-Horse Publications, 2005.

Brachet, Leon. *Aix-les-Bains (in Savoy): The Medical Treatment and General Indications*. 2d ed. London: Henry Renshaw, 1891.

Brands, H. R. *American Colossus: The Triumph of Capitalism, 1865–1900*. New York: Doubleday, 2010.

———. *T. R.: The Last Romantic*. New York: Basic Books, 1998.

Brown, Charles H. *The Correspondent's War*. New York: Charles Scribner's Sons, 1967.

Bryan, William Jennings, ed. *The World's Famous Orations*. Vol. 10. New York: Funk and Wagnalls Company, 1906.

Burrows, Edwin G., and Mike Wallace. *Gotham: A History of the City to 1898*. New York: Oxford University Press, 1999.

Carosso, Vincent. *The Morgans: Private International Bankers, 1854–1913*. Cambridge, Mass.: Harvard University Press, 1987.

Carr, John Foster. "A Great Railway Builder." *Outlook* 87: 8, October 26, 1907.

Casson, Herbert Newton. *The History of the Telephone*. Chicago: A. C. McClurg, 1910.

Cather, Willa. *The Song of the Lark*. New York: Library of America, 1987 [1915].

Chandler, Alfred, Jr. *Visible Hand: The Managerial Revolution in American Business*. Cambridge, Mass.: Harvard University Press, 1977.

Chernow, Ron. *House of Morgan: An American Banking Dynasty and the Rise of Modern Finance*. New York: Atlantic Monthly Press, 1990.

———. *Titan: The Life of John D. Rockefeller*. New York: Random House, 1998.

Churchill, Allen. *Park Row*. New York: Rinehart and Company, 1958.

Clark, Gordon. *Over the Hump: A Photographic Folio of Great Northern Railway's Cascade Division, 1898–1906*. Weaverville, N.C.: Gordon Clark, 2011.

Clews, Henry. *The Wall Street Point of View.* New York: Silver, Burdett and Company, 1900.

Clews, James B. *Fortuna: A Story of Wall Street.* New York: J. S. Ogilvie Publishing Company, 1898.

Coit, Margaret L. *Mr. Baruch.* Boston: Houghton Mifflin, 1957.

Collins, Theresa M. *Otto Kahn: Art, Money, and Modern Time.* Chapel Hill: University of North Carolina Press, 2002.

Cook, Joel. *America: Picturesque and Descriptive.* Vol. 1. New York: P. F. Collier and Son, 1900.

Cook's Handbook to the Health Resorts of the South of France, Rivieras, and Pyrennes. London: Thomas Cook and Son, 1905.

Corey, Lewis. *The House of Morgan: A Social Biography of the Masters of Money.* New York: G. Howard Watt, 1930.

Craven, Wayne. *Stanford White: Decorator in Opulence and Dealer in Antiques.* New York: Columbia University Press, 2005.

Cronon, William. *Nature's Metropolis: Chicago and the Great West.* New York: W. W. Norton and Company, 1991.

Cushing, George H. "Hill against Harriman: The Story of the Ten-Years' Struggle for the Railroad Supremacy of the West." *American Magazine* 63: 5, September 1909.

Daggett, Stuart. *Railroad Reorganization.* Boston: Houghton, Mifflin and Company, 1908.

De Borchgrave, Alexandra Villard, and John Cullen. *Villard: The Life and Times of an American Titan.* New York: Doubleday, 2001.

Debs, Eugene Victor. *Debs: His Life, Writings, and Speeches.* Chicago: Charles H. Kerr and Co., 1908.

DeVoto, Bernard, ed. *Mark Twain in Eruption: Hitherto Unpublished Pages about Men and Events.* New York: Harper Brothers, 1940.

DiLorenzo, Thomas J. *How Capitalism Saved America.* New York: Three Rivers Press, 2004.

Duguid, Charles. *The Story of the [London] Stock Exchange: Its History and Position.* London: Grant Richards, 1901.

Dunn, Arthur Wallace. *From Harrison to Harding.* New York: G. P. Putnam, 1922.

Dunne, Peter Finley. *Observations by Mr. Dooley.* New York: Harper and Brothers Publishers, 1902.

Durand, John. "Business of Trading Stocks." *Magazine of Wall Street,* 1927.

Ellis, Charles D., with James R. Vertin. *Wall Street People: True Stories of the Great Barons of Finance*. New York: John Wiley and Sons, 2003.

Englehardt, Carroll. *Gateway to the Northern Plains: Railroads and the Birth of Fargo and Moorhead*. Minneapolis: University of Minnesota Press, 2007

Erickson, David L. "Six of the Greatest: Edward O. Wolcott." *Colorado Lawyer* 32: 7, July 2003.

Fabian, Ann. *Card Sharps and Bucket Shops: Gambling in Nineteenth Century America*. New York: Routledge, 1999.

Figliomeni, Michelle P. *E. H. Harriman at Arden Farms*. New York: Orange County Historical Society, 1997.

Folsom, Burton W. *Entrepreneurs vs. the State: A New Look at the Rise of Big Business in America, 1840–1920*. Herndon, Va.: Young America's Foundation, 1987.

Forbes, B. C. *Men Who Are Making America*. New York: B. C. Forbes Publishing, 1917.

Forty-Sixth Annual Report of the Board of Directors of the Chicago, Burlington & Quincy Railroad Company, to the Stockholders, for the year ending June 30, 1900. Cambridge, Mass.: University Press, John Wilson and Son, 1900.

Frederic, Harold. *The Market-Place*. New York: Frederick A. Stokes Company, 1899.

Garraty, John. *Right-Hand Man: The Life of George W. Perkins*. New York: Harper and Brothers, 1960.

———, ed. *Quarrels That Have Shaped the Constitution*. New York: Harper and Row, 1964.

Garrett, "Interesting People," *American Magazine*, 69: 3, January 1910, 331–34.

Garver, John A. *John William Sterling*. New Haven, Conn.: Yale University Press, 1929.

Geisst, Charles R. *Wall Street: A History*. New York: Oxford University Press, 1997.

George, Henry, Jr. *The Menace of Privilege: A Study of the Dangers to the Republic from the Existence of a Favored Class*. New York: Grossett and Dunlap Publishers, 1905.

Gladden, Washington. *Tools and the Man: Property and Industry under the Christian*. London: James Clarke, 1893.

Goddard, Stephen B. *Getting There: The Epic Struggle between Road and Rail in the American Century*. New York: Basic Books, 1994.

Grant, James. *Bernard M. Baruch: The Adventures of a Wall Street Legend*. New York: John Wiley and Sons, 1997.

Harvey, Richard Seldon. *A Manual of the Federal Trade Commission*. Washington, D.C.: John Byrne and Company, 1916.

Hidy, Ralph W., and Muriel E. Hidy. "John Frank Stevens: Great Northern Engineer." *Minnesota History*, Winter 1969.

Hidy, Ralph W., Muriel E. Hidy, Roy V. Scott, and Don L. Hofsommer. *The Great Northern Railway: A History*. Minneapolis: University of Minnesota Press, 2004.

Highsaw, Robert Baker. *Edward Douglass White: Defender of the Conservative Faith*. Baton Rouge: University of Louisiana Press, 1981.

Hill, James J. *Highways of Progress*. New York: Doubleday Page and Company, 1910.

Holdsworth, J. T. "Transportation. Part V: The Merger Period." *Journal of Geography* 6: 1, April 1905.

Homberger, Eric. *Cities of the Imagination: New York City*. New York: Signal Books Limited, 2002.

———. *Mrs. Astor's New York: Money and Social Power in a Gilded Age*. New Haven, Conn.: Yale University Press, 2002.

Hovey, Carl. *The Life Story of John Pierpont Morgan*. New York: Sturgis and Walton, 1911.

Hubbard, Elbert. "The Study Habit," *Popular Mechanics*, June 1907.

Hughes, Jonathan. *The Vital Few: The Entrepreneur and American Economic Progress*. New York: Oxford University Press, 1965.

Hughes, Rupert. *The Real New York*. New York: Smart Set Publishing Company, 1904.

Illinois Central Railroad Company Fiftieth Anniversary, 1851–1901. Chicago: Press of Rogers and Smith Company, 1901.

Jacobson, Timothy. *An American Journey by Rail*. New York: W. W. Norton and Company, 1988.

James J. Hill Papers [JJHP]. Minnesota Historical Society, St. Paul, Minnesota.

Jeffers, Harry Paul. *Diamond Jim Brady: Prince of the Gilded Age*. New York: John Wiley and Sons, 2001.

Johnson, Paul. *A History of the American People*. New York: Harper Perennial, 1999.

Josephson, Matthew. "Profiles: Fifty Years of Wall Street." *New Yorker*, October 1, 1932.

———. *The Robber Barons*. New York: Harcourt Brace and Company, 1934.

Kahn, Otto H. "Edward Henry Harriman." Address delivered before the Finance Forum, New York, January 25, 1911.

———. *Of Many Things*. New York: Boni and Liveright, 1926.

Kennan, George. *The Chicago and Alton Case: A Misunderstood Transaction*. Garden City, New York: Country Life Press, 1916.

———. *E. H. Harriman: A Biography*. 2 vols. Boston, New York: Houghton Mifflin Company, 1922.

Keys, C. M. "The Builders: I. The House of Morgan," *World's Work* 15: 3, January 1908.

———. "A 'Corner' in Pacific Railroads." *World's Work* 9: 4, February 1905.

King, Moses. *King's Views of the New York Stock Exchange, 1897–1898*. New York: Moses King, Publisher, 1897.

Klein, Alexander, ed. *The Empire City: A Treasury of New York*. New York: Rinehart, 1955.

Klein, Maury. *The Life and Legend of E. H. Harriman*. Chapel Hill: University of North Carolina Press, 2000.

———. *Union Pacific: The Rebirth*. Vol. 2, 1894–1969. Minneapolis: University of Minnesota Press, 2006.

Knowles, Valerie. *From Telegrapher to Titan: The Life of William C. Van Horne*. Toronto: Dundurn Press, 2004.

Korom, Joseph J., Jr. *The American Skyscraper, 1850–1940: A Celebration of Height*. Boston: Brandon Books, 2008.

Kris, Gary. *The White Cascade: The Great Northern Railway Disaster and America's Deadliest Avalanche*. New York: Henry Holt and Company, 2007.

La Follette, Robert Marion. *La Follette's Autobiography: A Personal Narrative of Political Experiences*. 3d ed. Madison: Robert La Follette Company, 1919.

Landau, Sarah Bradford. *George B. Post: Architect, Picturesque Designer, and Determined Realist*. New York: Monacelli Press, 1998.

Landau, Sarah Bradford, and Carol W. Condit. *Rise of the New York Skyscraper: 1865–1913*. New Haven, Conn.: Yale University Press, 1996.

Lander, John B. "James Stillman, Banker." *World's Work* 2: 1, October 1901.

Larson, John Lauritz. *Bonds of Enterprise: John Murray Forbes and Western Development in America's Railway Age*. Iowa City: University of Iowa Press, 2001.

Latzke, Paul. "Romances of Success: James J. Hill, Builder of the Northwest Empire." *Everybody's Magazine*, April 1907.

Lawson, Thomas W. "Frenzied Finance: The Story of Amalgamated." *Everybody's Magazine*, August 1904.

———. "Outside Wall Street." *Everybody's Magazine*, November 1905.

Leech, Margaret. *In the Days of McKinley*. New York: Harper and Brothers, 1959.

Lefevre, Edwin. "The American Gambling Spirit." *Harper's Weekly*, May 3, 1903.

———."The American Newspaper: The Newspaper and Wall Street." *Bookman* 19: 2, April 1904.

———. "Gambling in Bucket Shops." *Harper's Weekly*, May 11, 1901.

———. *The Golden Flood*. New York: McClure, Phillips and Company, 1905.

———. "Harriman." *American Magazine* 64: 2, June 1907.

———. "Panic Days in Wall Street." *Harper's Weekly*, May 18, 1901.

———. "The News in Wall Street." *Harper's Weekly*, September 14, 1901.

———. *Reminiscences of a Stock Operator*. Hoboken, N.J.: John Wiley & Sons, 2010 [1923].

———. *Sampson Rock of Wall Street*. New York: Harper and Brothers, 1907.

———. "The Tipster." *McClure's*, November 1901.

———. *Wall Street Stories*. New York: McClure, Phillips and Company, 1901.

Leonard, John William, ed. *Who's Who in Finance*. New York: Joseph and Sefton, 1911.

Letwin, William. *Law and Economic Policy in America: The Evolution of the Sherman Antitrust Act*. Chicago: University of Chicago Press, 1965.

Lord, Walter. *The Good Years: From 1900 to the First World War*. New York: Harper Brothers, 1960.

Lorimer, George Horace. *Letters from a Self-Made Merchant to His Son*. Boston: Small, Maynard and Company, 1902.

Lubetkin, M. John. *Jay Cooke's Gamble: The Northern Pacific Railroad, the Sioux, and the Panic of 1873*. Norman: University of Oklahoma Press, 2006.

Lyon, Peter. *To Hell in a Day Coach*. New York: J. B. Lippincott Company, 1968.

Macleod, Margaret Arnett. "Two Railway Titans Meet at Winnipeg, 1909." *Manitoba History* 53, October 2006, 24–26.

Malone, Michael P. *James J. Hill: Empire Builder of the Great Northwest*. Norman: University of Oklahoma Press, 1996.

Malone, Michael P., Richard B. Roeder, and William L. Lang. *Montana: A History of Two Centuries*. Seattle: University of Washington Press, 2003 [1976].

Marcosson, Isaac F. "The Perilous Game of Cornering a Crop." *Munsey's* 41: 6, August–November 1909.

Martin, Albro. *James J. Hill and the Opening of the Northwest*. St. Paul: Minnesota Historical Society Press 1991 [1976].

———. *Railroads Triumphant: The Growth, Rejection, and Rebirth of a Vital American Force*. New York: Oxford Press, 1992.

McCarthy, James Remington. *Peacock Alley: The Romance of the Waldorf–Astoria.* New York: Harper and Brothers, 1931.

McCullough, David G. *The Johnstown Flood.* New York: Simon and Schuster, 1968.

McDonald, Donna. *Lord Strathcona: A Biography of Donald Alexander Smith.* Toronto: Dundurn Press, 2002.

McIntyre, Ben. *The Napoleon of Crime: The Life and Times of Adam Worth, Master Thief.* New York: Random House, 1997.

Medved, Michael. *The Shadow Presidents: The Secret History of the Chief Executives and Their Top Aides.* New York: Times Books, 1979.

Meyer, Balthasar H. "History of the Northern Securities Case." *University of Wisconsin Bulletin,* no. 142, 1906.

Middleton, Kenneth C., and Norman F. Pirebe. *Steam Locomotives of the Great Northern Railway.* St. Paul: Great Northern Historical Society, 2010.

Miller, Scott. *The President and the Assassin: McKinley, Terror, and the Empire at the Dawn of the American Century.* Old Saybrook, Conn.: Tantor Media, 2011.

Millett, Larry. *Lost Twin Cities.* St. Paul: Minnesota Historical Society Press, 1992.

Minnesota: A State Guide. American Guide Series. New York: Viking, 1938.

Moody, John. *The Art of Wall Street Investing.* New York: Moody Corporation, 1906.

————. *The Truth about Trusts.* New York: Moody Publishing Company, 1904.

Moody, John, and George Kibbe Turner. "The Masters of Capital in America: The Inevitable Railroad Monopoly." *McClure's,* January 1911.

————. "The Masters of Capital in America: The Multimillionaires of the Great Northern System." *McClure's,* December 1910.

————. "The Masters of Capital in America: Wall Street: The City Bank—The Federation of the Great Merchants." *McClure's,* May 1911.

————. "The Masters of Capital in America: Morgan, The Great Trustee." *McClure's,* November 1910.

Morison, Samuel Eliot. *The Oxford History of the American People.* New York: Oxford University Press, 1965.

Morris, Edmund. *The Rise of Theodore Roosevelt.* New York: Coward, McGann, and Geoghegan, 1979.

————. *Theodore Rex.* New York: Random House, 2001.

National Cyclopaedia of American Biography, Supplement I. New York: James T. White Company, 1910.

Nelson, Samuel Armstrong. *The A B C of Stock Speculation*. New York: S. A. Nelson, 1903.

———. *The A B C of Wall Street*. New York: Doubleday, Page and Company, 1909 [1900].

———. "The Machinery of Wall Street." *World's Work* 2: 3, July 1901.

Nevins, Allen. *Study in Power. John D. Rockefeller: Industrialist and Philanthropist*. 2 vols. New York: Charles Scribner's Sons, 1953.

Nimmo, Joseph Jr. *Commercial, Economic, and Political Questions Not Decided in the Northern Securities Case*. Washington, D.C.: Darby Printing Company, 1903.

Nissenson, Marilyn. *The Lady Upstairs: Dorothy Schiff and the New York Post*. New York: St. Martin's Press, 2007.

Norman, Henry, and G. C. Ashton Jonson. *The London Stock Exchange*. 1903.

Norris, Frank. *Octopus: A Story of California*. New York: Doubleday and Company, Inc., 1920.

Northern Pacific Railroad Company. *The Northern Pacific Railroad: Its Land Grant, Resources, Traffic and Tributary Country, Valley Route to the Pacific*. Philadelphia: Jay Cooke and Company, 1873.

Northern Pacific Railroad Company: Charter, Organization, and Proceedings. Boston: Alfred Mudge and Son, 1865.

Noyes, Alexander D. *Fifty Years of American Finance*. New York: G. P. Putnam's Sons, 1909.

Noyes, Walter Chadwick. *A Treatise on the Law of Intercorporate Relations*. 2d ed. Boston: Little, Brown, and Company, 1909.

Orsi, Richard J. *Sunset Limited*. Berkeley: University of California Press, 2005.

O'Toole, Randal. *Gridlock: Why We're Stuck in Traffic and What to Do about It*. Washington, D.C.: Cato Institute, 2009.

Overton, Richard C. *Burlington Route: A History of the Burlington Lines*. New York: Alfred A. Knopf, 1965.

Paine, Albert Bigelow. *George Fisher Baker: A Biography*. New York: Knickerbocker Press (G. P. Putnam's Sons), 1938.

Payne, John C. "Lawyers and the Laws of Economics." *American Bar Association Journal* 365, April 1960.

Payne, Will. *The Money Captain*. Chicago: Herbert S. Stone and Company, 1898.

Peterson, Amy T., and Ann T. Kellogg, eds. *The Greenwood Encyclopedia of Clothing through American History, 1900 to the Present*. Westport, Conn.: Greenwood Publishing Group, 2008.

Phillips-Matz, Mary Jane. *The Many Lives of Otto Kahn*. New York: Pendragon Press, 1984 [1963].

Plunz, Richard. *A History of Housing in New York City*. New York: Columbia University Press, 1990.

Poor, Henry Varnum. *Poor's Manual of the Railroads of the United States*. New York, 1900.

Potter, Merle. *101 Best Stories of Minnesota*. Minneapolis: Harrison and Smith, 1931.

Pratt, Sereno S. *The Work of Wall Street*. New York: D. Appleton, 1903.

Price, W. W. "Secretaries to the Presidents." *Cosmopolitan*, March 1901.

Prince, Richard E. *Seaboard Air Line Railway: Steamboats, Locomotives, and History*. Green River, Wyo.: Richard E. Prince, 1966.

Pringle, Henry Fowles. *Theodore Roosevelt: A Biography*. New York: Harcourt, Brace and Co., 1931.

Pyle, Joseph Gilpin. *The Life of James J. Hill*. 2 vols. New York: Doubleday, Doran and Company, 1916 [1936].

Railway Age Gazette. *Sayings and Writings about Railways, by Those Who Have Managed Them and Those Who Have Studied Their Problems*. New York: Railway Age Gazette, 1909.

Rauchway, Eric. *Murdering McKinley: The Making of Theodore Roosevelt's America*. New York: Hill and Wang, 2003.

Redmond, George F., II. *Financial Giants of America*. Boston: Stratford Company, 1922.

Ripley, William Z., ed. *Railway Problems*. Boston: Ginn and Company, 1907.

Robeson, Anna Burr. *The Portrait of a Banker: James Stillman, 1850–1918*. New York: Duffield and Company, 1927.

Roosevelt, Theodore. *The Letters of Theodore Roosevelt: The Square Deal, 1901–1903*. Cambridge, Mass.: Harvard University Press, 1951.

———. *The Roosevelt Policy: Speeches, Letters, and State Papers, Relating to Corporate Wealth and Closely Allied Topics*. 2 vols. New York: Current Literature Publishing Company, 1908.

———. *State of the Union Addresses of Theodore Roosevelt*. Middlesex, U.K.: Echo Library, 2013.

———. *Theodore Roosevelt: An Autobiography*. New York: Charles Scribner's Sons, 1922.

———. *Theodore Roosevelt's Letters to His Children*, ed. Joseph Bucklin Bishop. New York: Charles Scribner's Sons, 1919.

Rose, Mark H. *The Best Transportation System in the World: Railroads, Trucks, Airlines,* and American Public Policy in the Twentieth Century. Columbus: Ohio State University Press, 2006.

Russell, Charles Edward. Stories of the Great Railroads. Chicago: Charles H. Kerr and Company, 1912.

Sale, Roger. Seattle: Past to Present. Seattle: University of Washington Press, 1978.

Sarnoff, Paul. Russell Sage: The Money King. New York: Ivan Obolensky, 1965.

Schonberger, Howard. "James J. Hill and the Trade with the Orient." Minnesota History, Winter 1968.

Schroeder, Alice. The Snowball: Warren Buffett and the Business of Life. New York: Bantam, 2008.

Scott, James Brown. Robert Bacon: Life and Letters. New York: Doubleday, Page and Company, 1923.

Selected Investments for Banks, Trustees, and Private Investors. Vol. 2. Wellesley Hills, Mass.: Babson's Statistical Organization, 1912.

Silver, Nathan. Lost New York. New York: Houghton Mifflin Company, 1967.

Simon, Kate. Fifth Avenue: A Very Social History. New York: Harcourt Brace Jovanovich, 1978.

Simon, Mary. "The Man Who Loved Racing." Thoroughbred Times, August 18, 2001.

Smalley, Eugene, V. History of the Northern Pacific Railroad. New York: G. P. Putnam's Sons, 1883.

Smith, B. Mark. Toward Rational Exuberance: The Evolution of the Modern Stock Market. New York: Farrar, Straus and Giroux, 2002.

Smith, J. Russell. The World's Food Resources. New York: Henry Holt and Company, 1919.

Smitten, Richard. Jesse Livermore: World's Greatest Stock Trader. New York: John Wiley and Sons, 2001.

Sobel, Robert. The Big Board. New York: Free Press, 1965.

———. Panic on Wall Street. New York: Truman Talley Books (E. P. Dutton), 1988.

Spero, Rabbi Aryeh. "What the Bible Teaches about Capitalism." Wall Street Journal, January 30, 2012.

Stapleton, Craig Roberts. Where Liberty Dwells, There Is My Country. Lanham, Md.: Hamilton Books, 2010.

Stead, W. T. "The Money Kings of the World." Windsor Magazine, June 1903.

Stedman, Edmund Clarence, ed. The New York Stock Exchange. New York: Stock Exchange Historical Society, 1905.

Stevens, Hiram F. History of the Bench and Bar of Minnesota. 2 vols. Minneapolis: Legal Publishing and Engraving Company, 1904.

Strouse, Jean. *Morgan: American Financier*. New York: Random House, 1999.

Surowiecki, James. *The Wisdom of Crowds*. New York: Doubleday, 2004.

Swaine, Robert T. *The Cravath Firm and Its Predecessors, 1819–1947*. Clark, N.J.: Lawbook Exchange, Ltd., 1948.

Taylor, Charles H., ed. *History of the Board of Trade of the City of Chicago*. Chicago: Robert O. Law Company, 1917.

Tocqueville, Alexis. *Democracy in America*. 2 vols. New York: Schocken Books, 1961.

Todd, Marion Marsh. *The Railways of Europe and America*. Boston: Arena Publishing Company, 1893.

Trollope, Anthony. *North America*. New York: Harper Brothers, 1862.

Turner, Frederick Jackson. *The Frontier in American History*. New York: Henry Holt and Company, 1921.

Turner, George Kibbe. "Morgan's Partners." *McClure's*, April 6, 1913.

Twining, Charles E. *George S. Long: Timber Statesman*. Seattle: University of Washington Press, 1994.

Villard, Henry. *Memoirs of Henry Villard, Journalist and Financier, 1835-1900*. Westminster, U.K.: Archibald Constable and Co., 1904.

Villard, Oswald Garrison. *Prophets True and False*. New York: Alfred A. Knopf, 1928.

Wade, Louise Carol. *Chicago's Pride*. Champagne–Urbana: University of Illinois Press, 1987.

Wallace, Henry E., ed. *The Manual of Statistics: Stock Exchange Handbook, 1900*. New York: Charles H. Nicoll, 1900.

Waterloo, Stanley, and John Wesley Hanson Jr., eds. *Famous American Men and Women*. Chicago: P. A. Lindberg and Co., 1896.

Wendt, Lloyd, and Herman Kogan. *Bet a Million!* Indianapolis: Bobbs Merrill Company, 1948.

Wenzl, Bernhard. *Mytholgia Americana: Willa Cather's Nebraska Novels and the Myth of the Frontier*. Norderstedt, Germany: Grin, 2001.

Wheeler, George. *Pierpont Morgan and Friends: The History of a Myth*. New York: Prentice Hall, 1973.

White, Richard. *Railroaded: The Transcontinentals and the Making of Modern America*. New York: W. W. Norton and Company, 2011.

White, Sir William. "Review of Past Progress in Steam Navigation and Forecast of Future Development." *Marine Engineering* 4: 5, November 1899.

Wilgus, H. L. "The Northwestern Railway Situation." *Michigan Law Review*, 1:4, January 1903.

Wilkins, Mira. *The History of Foreign Investment in the United States to 1914*. Cambridge, Mass.: Harvard University Press, 1989.

Winkelman, Barnie F. *Ten Years of Wall Street*. New York: Cosimo, 2007 [1932].

Winkler, John. *The First Billion: The Stillmans and the National City Bank*. New York: Vanguard Press, 1934.

————. *Morgan the Magnificent: The Life of J. Pierpont Morgan, 1837–1913*. New York: Vanguard Press, 1930.

Yenne, Bill. *Great Northern, Empire Builder*. St. Paul: MBI Publishing, 2005.

Young, Biloine W., and Eileen R. McCormack. *The Dutiful Son: Louis W. Hill*. St. Paul, Minn.: Ramsey County Historical Society, 2010.

Zacks, Richard. *Island of Vice: Theodore Roosevelt's Doomed Quest to Clean Up Sin-Loving New York*. New York: Doubleday, 2012.

Zimmerman, David A. *Panic! Markets, Crises, and Crowds in American Fiction*. Chapel Hill: University of North Carolina Press, 2006.

Newspapers

Brooklyn Eagle

Chicago Daily News

Chicago Daily Tribune

Commercial Advertiser (New York)

Commercial and Financial Chronicle

Minneapolis Journal

New York Evening Post

New York Evening Telegram

New York Evening World

New York Herald

New York Journal

New York Sun

New York Times

New York Tribune

Omaha Bee

Omaha World-Herald

St. Louis Republic

Saint Paul Dispatch

Saint Paul Globe

Saint Paul Pioneer Press

San Francisco Call

Seattle Star

Times (Richmond, Virginia)

Wall Street Journal

Washington Post

Washington Times

INDEX

Potter, Henry Codman (bishop), 16, 235
Produce Exchange. *See* New York Produce Exchange
property rights, 57, 71, 207; U.S. Supreme Court on, 2, 273
prosperity, American, 3, 14–15, 209; McKinley and, 82, 130, 144; "moral hazard," 141; new money, 144–45; Roosevelt on, 267; "wealth without labor," 142
Provost, Cornelius W., 181
Purdy, Milton Dwight, 262

Q. *See* Chicago, Burlington & Quincy Railroad

railroads: activist left and, 247; Advisory Committee, 85; and American industry, 5, 6, 7–9, 21, 248, 290, 291; best-conceived merger, 21; collapse and foreclosures, 32; combination and, 32, 246, 284, 287; community of interest and, 71–72, 263; demise of Chicago-based lines, 122; efficiencies, 8, 26–27, 104, 285, 288; as federal instruments, 6, 33, 70, 74, 283–84; and "happiness of the people," 29; Harriman and Hill routes, 48–49; merger talks and stock increases, 21, 101, 124–25, 213; Northern Securities and, 225, 237, 242; owners as scapegoats, 209, 246–47, 281, 285; power structure, 88; regulations and, 2, 70, 283, 284, 285, 286; remaining dominant roads, 290; Ripley and, 284; Staggers Rail Act, 289; stranglehold on, 283; system, 24, 51, 69, 72, 155, 285, 289; western, 1, 33, 46, 69, 88, 156, 213, 285
Raphael: *Madonna and Child Enthroned in Saints*, 125
Rea, Samuel, 227, 237
Read, William, 203–4
Reading Railroad. *See* Philadelphia & Reading Railroad
Ream, Norman B., 140
"Reddy" (a bootblack), 129
Reuters, 13
Ripley, William Zebina, 284
risk: arbitrage and, 176; the Burlington's, 69; buying on margin, 11; of insider leaks, 103; reward and, 3, 4, 104, 141; syndicated loans and, 18; underwriting, 33, 55
RMS *Teutonic*, 14, 50, 268; Hill and, 266; Morgan and, 15–16, 20, 111
Robber Barons: The Great American Capitalists, 1861–1901, The (Josephson), 285
Rockefeller, John D., 99
Rockefeller, William "Will" A., 22; Harriman and, 1, 76; Hill on, 282; with Morgan in

Washington, 260–61; Northern Pacific board, 226, 237; Northern Pacific raid scheme, 99–100, 186; Stillman and, 75; the St. Paul and, 13, 83; United States Steel and, 94
Rock Island Railroad, 10, 12, 13, 83, 84, 300
Rogers, Elizabeth Putnam Peabody, 16
Rogers Locomotive Company: steam locomotive efficiency, 113
Rogers, William Allen: *Harper's Weekly* and, 210
Roosevelt, Theodore "Teddy," 5, 38, 48, 92, 248, 253; Annual Message to Congress, 243, 244, 248–49; "Big Stick" speech, 229–30, 260; description, 235–38; elected president, 282; Harriman and, 292; Hill and, 239, 258, 259; Holmes's dissenting opinion and, 279; Interstate Commerce Commission and, 75; jiu-jitsu and, 281; McKinley shooting and, 232, 233; "moral victory," 279; Morgan and, 258, 259, 260, 261; Northern Securities lawsuit and, 254, 255, 256, 257, 258, 259, 264, 277; private meeting with Morgan, 261–62; Schiff and, 263; "trustbuster," 2, 237, 243, 255, 258; U.S. tour, 267; wealthy class and, 245, 246
Root, Elihu, 257, 260; Harriman lawsuit, 282
R. Raphel and Sons, 220
Ruskin, John, 30
Russell, Lillian, 146
Ryan, Thomas Fortune: call loans and, 188

Sage, Russell, 169–70, 185, 199–200; on Northern Securities, 242–43
Saint Paul, the (railroad). *See* Chicago, Milwaukee & St. Paul Railway
Saint Paul Globe, 251–52
Sampson Rock of Wall Street (Lefevre), 133
Sanborn, Walter Henry, 262, 265, 267
Schiff, Clara (née Niederhofheim) (Schiff's mother), 52
Schiff, Frieda (Schiff's daughter), 56
Schiff, Jacob H., 1, 28; anti-Semitism and, 54; battle for Northern Pacific control, 167, 168; on circuit court ruling, 269; community of interest, 71, 106; death and funeral, 293; description, 51–54; dinner with Hill, 158–59; family, 56, 227; friendship with Hill, 62–63, 106; Harriman funeral, 292; and Harriman's buy order, 164, 166; Henry Street Settlement House and, 205; Kuhn, Loeb and, 51–52, 153, 208; letter to Hill, 108–9; letter to Morgan, 106, 137, 155, 222–23; mediator for Harriman, 281; meeting with Bacon, 64; meeting with Hill, 154–55; Northern Pacific raid scheme, 99–100, 174; Northern

Larry Haeg was for more than two decades head of corporate communications for Norwest Corporation and its successor, Wells Fargo and Company, as well as a member of the company's management committee. He is the author of *In Gatsby's Shadow*.